FOREWORD

The *African Development Report 2001* reviews Africa's current socio-economic performance and prospects, and examines in-depth issues relating to good governance on the Continent. Africa recorded a modest recovery in economic performance in 2000 propelled by higher international oil prices and export growth coupled with progress in economic policy reforms. Real GDP growth in 2000 was estimated at 3.2 percent, slightly higher than the 2.7 percent growth rate in 1999. A stronger growth prospect at 4.1 percent is forecast for 2001.

The present and projected growth rates, however, still fall short of those required to bring about a marked reduction in poverty. African countries would have to accelerate their economic growth rate to some 7 percent per annum in order to attain the international development goal of reducing poverty by half by 2015. This goal cannot be achieved in the absence of good political and economic governance, which establishes the foundation for sustainable socio-economic development.

In recent years, many African countries have made progress towards the desired norms of good political and economic governance. For instance, during the last decade, some 42 African countries held multiparty presidential or parliamentary elections. Although the results have been mixed, there are notable success stories. Furthermore, most of our countries have embarked on improving economic governance evidenced by the adoption of a new development path comprising a set of strategic choices that place poverty reduction at the centre of the development process and recognise the pivotal role of the private sector in promoting economic growth.

Notwithstanding these positive developments, much remains to be done in the spheres of political and economic governance. The number of African people struggling amidst instability and conflict is a clear testimony that participatory democracy and social cohesion are yet to take root on the entire Continent. Corrupt practices in both the public and private domains continue to exact heavy economic costs by distorting the operation of free markets, hampering economic development and impairing the ability of institutions to deliver services to the public. Also, the power of the State in terms of its regulatory, extractive, administrative and technical capacities remains inadequate in many African countries. Critical among these is the lack of expertise and institutional capacity to meet the challenges of globalisation and participate effectively in the global economy.

It is thus essential to enhance the conduct of political and economic governance with the aim of attaining a level of socio-economic development compatible with the potential of the Continent and the aspirations of its peoples. Good governance requires, first, that our citizens should be endowed with the means to elect their leaders and hold them accountable for their actions and conduct in government. Second, leaders would need to be responsive and responsible in terms of their attitudes as public trustees and their adherence to the rule of law. Third, there must be social reciprocities, in which the different groups in a country and their leaders are capable of transcending the boundaries of religion, kinship, ethnicity, and race. Fourth, there must be a clear development vision that stipulates the main strategic choices of the State and defines the economic paradigm that the government would fol-

ethnicity, and race. Fourth, there must be a clear development vision that stipulates the main strategic choices of the State and defines the economic paradigm that the government would follow. Fifth, the State must adopt the policies that foster accountable and transparent business environment. Sixth, the government apparatus must be endowed with the capacity to initiate, design and implement such policies with the aim of realising the shared development vision.

These tasks require an efficient civil service capable of meeting the challenges of development management in the 21st Century. This necessitates not only streamlining the public sector but also providing incentives to attract and retain highly qualified civil functionaries. An integral part of this process is the adoption of strategies aimed distinctly at fighting corruption through creating a legal, judicial and social environment that is unambiguously hostile to corrupt practices. Improving governance and fighting corruption should, however, go hand in hand with efforts to raise the image of Africa in the international arena so as to correct the negative perceptions about the Continent.

As Africa embarks on the process of reforming its political and economic apparatus, the support of its development partners would be needed not only to foster such reforms but also to address the challenges emanating from the increased globalisation of political, social, and economic problems. In today's globalised world, good governance cannot be implemented within a closed system. It is, rather, an open process in which all countries in the world are increasingly obliged to adhere to an emerging set of universal laws. Thus, efforts to overcome some of the challenges pertaining to the conduct of governance in Africa, such as corruption, excessive military expenditure, conflicts and wars, and transparency in international political and economic relations would need to be supported by actions at the global level. Likewise, international assistance is needed to support African countries in preparing for the new rules-based trading system of the WTO, and to ensure that the process of globalisation works for improving socio-economic conditions of African peoples.

On its part, the African Development Bank Group is fully aware that the adherence to the axioms of good governance is necessary both in countries striving for growth and development as well as in the agencies mandated to help African countries realise this goal. It is for this reason that the Bank has embarked, since 1995, on an evolving process of internal reform with the aim of optimising its development effectiveness. The reform aims at upgrading the quality of Bank operations, strengthening financial management, overhauling the organisational and management structure of the Bank and improving its institutional governance. The Bank has also developed comprehensive operational policy guidelines that acknowledge the multidimensional nature of issues pertaining to governance and recognise the need for a more differentiated approach between countries. In pursuing its operations in Regional Member Countries, the Bank believes that good governance is not only a worthy human goal in itself, but it is also essential for realising Africa's overarching objectives of fostering economic growth and reducing poverty.

Omar Kabbaj
President
African Development Bank

AFRICAN DEVELOPME~~NT~~ ~~ORT~~
2001

PUBLISHED FOR THE AFRICAN DEVELOPMENT BANK
OXFORD UNIVERSITY PRESS

Oxford University Press, Great Clarendon Street, Oxford OX2 6DP

Oxford New York
Athens Auckland Bangkok Bogota Buenos Aires
Calcutta Cape Town Chennai Dar-es-Salaam
Delhi Florence Hong Kong Istanbul Karachi
Kuala Lumpur Madrid Melbourne Mexico City
Mumbai Nairobi São Paolo Singapore
Taipei Tokyo Toronto Warsaw

and associated companies in
Berlin Ibadan

Oxford is a trade mark of Oxford University Press

Published in the United States
by Oxford University Press Inc., New York

British Library Cataloguing in Publication Data
data available

Library of Congress Cataloging in Publication Data
data available

ISBN   0-19-829715-7

Typeset by African Development Bank
Printed in Great Britain
on acid-free paper by
Butler and Tanner Ltd., Frome, Somerset

IPEP	International Panel of Eminent Personalities
ISPs	Internet Service Providers
JSE	Johannesburg Stock Exchange
MFIs	Multilateral Financial Institutions
MVA	Manufacturing Value-Added
NGOs	Non Governmental Organizations
NGP	National Governance Programme
NIRP	National Institutional Renewal Programme
NISER	Nigerian Institute for Social and Economic Research
NPV	Net Present Value
OAU	Organization of African Unity
ODM	Operational Debt Management
OECD	Organization for Economic Co-operation and Development
OHADA	Organisation pour l'Harmonisation en Afrique du Droit des Affaires
OPEC	Organization of the Petroleum Exporting Countries
PAC	Public Appointments Committee
RMCs	Regional Member Countries
SACU	Southern African Customs Unions
SADC	Southern African Development Community
SARB	South African Reserve Bank
TAF	Technical Assistance Fund
TI	Transparency International
UA	Units of Account
UK	United Kingdom
UN	United Nations
UNCTAD	United Nations Conference on Trade and Development
UNECA	United Nations Economic Commission for Africa
UNESCO	United Nations Educational, Scientific and Cultural Organization
UNICEF	United Nations Children's Fund
UNICRI	United Nations Interregional Crime and Justice Research Institute
UNDP	United Nations Development Program
UNEP	United Nations Environmental Program
US	United States
USAID	U.S. Agency for International Development
VAT	Value Added Tax
VRA	Volta River Authority
WAEMU	West African Economic and Monetary Union
WB	World Bank
WTO	World Trade Organization
ZCCM	Zambia Consolidated Copper Mines
ZSE	Zimbabwe Stock Exchange

CONTENTS

BOXES

TEXT FIGURES

TEXT TABLES

PART ONE

AFRICA IN THE WORLD ECONOMY

Overview

The *African Development Report 2001* reviews Africa's current socio-economic performance and prospects, and examines in-depth the issues and elements of fostering good governance in the continent. Part I of the *Report* covers two chapters. The first chapter, on "The African Economy in 2000", presents and assesses the continent's economic performance as well as prospects for the medium-term. The second chapter analyses the regional economic profiles, including their recent economic trends, policy developments, emerging regional economic relations, and growth outlook.

Real GDP growth in 2000 was estimated at 3.2 percent, slightly above the population growth rate but higher than the 2.7 percent growth rate recorded in 1999. The factors responsible for this modest economic recovery in 2000 over the previous year include higher international oil prices and exports, progress in economic policy reforms, and continued recovery in some smaller economies in the continent. Sectorally, growth in the industrial and services sectors were the main contributors to output expansion in 2000. Unlike in 1999 when these two sectors recorded growth rate of 3.1 percent and 3.3 percent respectively, in 2000 they grew by 4.4 percent and 4.0 percent, respectively.

Africa's economic recovery in 2000 was led by the rebound in the economies of oil exporters whose growth was 4.1 percent against only 2.6 percent in net oil importers. Unfortunately, political instability and civil conflict impacted negatively on economic growth. Growth rates in countries in conflict averaged 2.8 percent, lagging behind the overall regional growth rate, although much higher than the average of 1 percent recorded in the previous three years. However, per capita income among this group of countries is two and half times below that of the continental average.

In 2000, Northern Africa at 4.1 percent recorded the highest economic growth rate among the five sub-regions of Africa, up from 3.8 percent in 1999. This was followed by Eastern Africa at 3.8 percent in 2000, down from 4.5 percent in 1999. Southern Africa had a growth rate of 2.6 percent in 2000, up slightly from 2.1 percent recorded in 1999. Western Africa grew at 3.1 percent in 2000 from 2.8 percent the previous year while Central Africa experienced no growth in 2000 though this represented a significant recovery from a contraction of 4 percent in 1999.

A number of African countries remain committed to the implementation of sound economic reforms to promote macroeconomic stability and make the private sector the engine of economic growth. Consequently, a stronger growth prospect at 4.1 percent is forecast for the region in 2001. Stronger expansion in South Africa, steady growth in the other larger economies, and the continued strength of some of the continent's smaller economies will underpin this growth. However, this expected recovery still falls short of what is required to improve the living conditions of millions of Africans and sustain the continent's structural transformation. This will require increased domestic investment; the promotion of broad-based growth through mobilizing domestic and foreign resources for development; and tackling issues related to human development, including HIV/AIDS.

CHAPTER 1

The African Economy in 2000

Highlights

The African economy made a modest recovery in 2000. Rebounds in the region's major economies, particularly the oil exporters, and the continued strength in some of the smaller economies led the recovery. Buoyant exports boosted by strong international oil prices and progress with macroeconomic stabilization, structural adjustment and governance were important factors driving economic recovery.

After slowing to 2.7 percent in 1999, real GDP growth in Africa recovered modestly to an estimated 3.2 percent in 2000 (Table 1.1 and Figure 1.1). Twenty countries achieved growth rates of between 3 and 5 percent compared to fourteen in the previous year (Tables 1.2a and 1.2b). Six countries— Democratic Republic of Congo (DRC), Côte d'Ivoire, Eritrea, Gabon, Kenya and Zimbabwe—experienced recession in 2000. Although the number of countries with negative growth declined to six from eleven, those with growth rates above 5 percent has been declining since the mid-1990s.

As a result, the growth trend for most countries appears to be firmly established at 3.2 per-

Table 1.1: Africa: Macroeconomic Indicators, 1996- 2001						
Indicators	**1996**	**1997**	**1998**	**1999**	**2000**[a/]	**2001**[b/]
1. Real GDP Growth Rate	5.3	3.2	3.2	2.7	3.2	4.1
2. Real Per Capita GDP Growth Rate	2.8	0.7	0.8	0.4	0.9	1.8
3. Inflation (%)	27.0	14.1	11.2	12.0	12.7	10.2
4. Investment Ratio (% of GDP)	18.1	18.2	20.2	20.4	19.9	20.3
5. Fiscal Balance (% of GDP)	-2.6	-2.7	-3.6	-3.4	-1.0	-1.3
6. Growth of Money Supply (%)	18.7	17.5	14.2	17.9	13.4	10.9
7. Export Growth, volume (%)	4.7	3.6	0.0	0.6	7.3	5.3
8. Import Growth, volume (%)	2.5	6.8	4.7	2.6	4.8	5.1
9. Terms of Trade (%)	4.8	0.6	-11.3	8.6	15.7	-5.8
10. Trade Balance ($ billion)	4.8	2.2	-17.5	-10.4	11.4	2.9
11. Current Account ($ billion)	-5.3	-6.4	-24.6	-18.5	-2.0	-8.6
12. Current Account (% of GDP)	-1.0	-1.2	-4.5	-3.4	-0.3	-1.4
13. Debt Service (% of Exports)	22.9	19.2	20.4	19.3	16.2	20.6

Notes: a/ Preliminary estimates.
       b/ Forecast.
Source: ADB Statistics Division and IMF.

Figure 1.1: Africa: Major Economic Indicators, 1996-2000

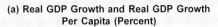

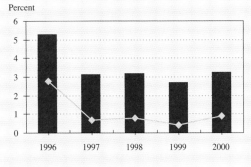

(a) Real GDP Growth and Real GDP Growth Per Capita (Percent)

■ Real GDP Growth Rate
◇ Real Per Capita GDP Growth Rate

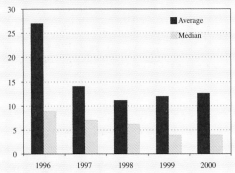

(b) Inflation
(Change in Consumer Price Index, Percent)

■ Average
Median

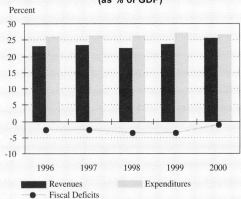

(c) Revenues - Expenditures and Fiscal Deficits
(as % of GDP)

■ Revenues   Expenditures
● Fiscal Deficits

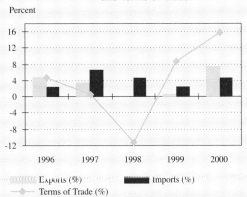

(d) Changes in Merchandise Trade (Percent) and Terms of Trade

Exports (%)   Imports (%)
◇ Terms of Trade (%)

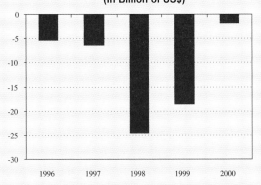

(e) Current Account Balance
(In Billion of US$)

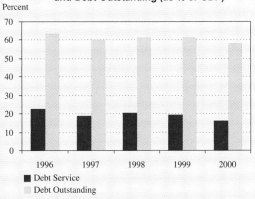

(f) Debt Service (as % of Exports)
and Debt Outstanding (as % of GDP)

■ Debt Service
Debt Outstanding

Table 1.2a: Africa: Frequency Distribution of Countries According to Real GDP Growth Rates, 1996-2000

Real GDP Growth Rate (%)	1996	1997	1998	1999	2000[a]
Negative	6	4	9	11	6
0 - 3	4	11	8	13	15
Above 3 to 5	17	18	20	14	20
Above 5	26	20	16	15	12
Total	53	53	53	53	53

Note:a/ Preliminary estimates
*Source:*ADB Statistics Division.

Table 1.2b: Africa: Frequency Distribution of Countries According to Real Per Capita GDP Growth Rates, 1996-2000

Real Per Capita GDP Growth Rate (%)	1996	1997	1998	1999	2000[a]
Negative	9	12	18	21	16
0 - 1.5	6	13	10	9	14
Above 1.5 to 5	26	25	18	19	20
Above 5	12	3	7	4	3
Total	53	53	53	53	53

Note:a/ Preliminary estimates
*Source:*ADB Statistics Division.

cent a year—barely above the rate of population growth. Faster long-term economic growth will require raising the productivity as well as the volume of investment while sustaining recent progress with macroeconomic, structural and governance reforms.

Africa remained the slowest growing region in the developing world. Output growth among developing economies reached 5.6 percent from an average of 3.7 percent in the previous two years (Table 1.3). Growth was spurred by a robust recovery of the emerging economies of Asia which grew by 6.7 percent due to strong exports and improvements in domestic policies. Economic growth in Latin America and the Caribbean rebounded sharply to 4.3 percent from a marginal 0.3 percent in 1999. Buoyant exports and a recovery in consumer confidence were major determinants of the economic rebounds. Recent economic developments in Central and Eastern Europe have also been positive, underpinning the economic expansion in countries in transition, which grew by 4.9 percent.

The overall fiscal position for African countries showed a marked improvement in 2000 with budget deficits of 1 percent of GDP compared to an average of 3.5 percent in the previous two years. This reflects the increase in oil export revenues as well as the improved fiscal discipline of countries undertaking stabilization and structural adjustment programs. These programs target fiscal stability and lower inflation as part of their core objectives. Overall inflation rates remained stable at about 13 percent in 2000. However, this average was influenced by the few countries that experienced hyper-inflation. The median inflation rate is less than 5 percent.

Higher oil revenues also contributed toward significant improvements in external balances with the value of exports reaching $150 billion for the

Table 1.3: Selected International Economic Indicators, 1996-2000
(Percentage changes from preceeding year, except otherwise specified)

	1996	1997	1998	1999	2000[a]
Changes in output					
World	4.1	4.1	2.6	3.4	4.7
Advanced economies[b]	3.2	3.4	2.4	3.2	4.2
Developing Countries	6.5	5.7	3.5	3.8	5.6
-Asia	8.3	6.5	4.1	5.9	6.7
-Latin American and Caribbean countries	3.6	5.4	2.2	0.3	4.3
-Africa[c]	5.3	3.2	3.2	2.7	3.2
Countries in transition	-0.5	1.6	-0.8	2.4	4.9
Changes in Consumer Price Index					
Advanced economies	2.4	2.1	1.5	1.4	2.3
Developing Countries	15.3	9.7	10.1	6.6	6.2
-Asia	8.3	4.7	7.5	2.4	2.4
-Latin American and Caribbean countries	21.6	13.4	10.2	9.3	8.9
-Africa[c]	27.0	14.1	11.2	12.0	12.7
Changes in Merchandise Trade (volume)					
World Trade	5.8	10.0	4.1	5.2	10.4
Advanced economies					
-Exports	5.4	10.9	3.9	4.3	10.2
-Imports	5.2	9.5	5.4	7.6	10.4
Developing Countries					
-Exports	8.7	10.9	3.5	5.3	10.3
-Imports	7.8	8.8	0.2	0.5	11.2
Africa[c]					
-Exports	4.7	3.6	0.0	0.6	7.3
-Imports	2.5	6.8	4.7	2.6	4.8

Notes: a/ Preliminary estimates.
          b/ Comprises the industrial market economies, Israel and four newly industrialized Asian economies.
          c/ ADB Regional Member Countries.
Sources: IMF, World Economic Outlook, October 2000 and ADB Statistics Division.

first time. Export volume increased by 7.3 percent—the highest in five years. With exports volume growing faster than that of imports and with improved terms of trade for major oil exporters, the continent's trade surplus strengthened to $11 billion. Reflecting this improvement and a smaller increase in net services receipts, the current account deficit is estimated to have declined from $18 billion or 3.4 percent of GDP in 1999 to $2 billion or 0.3 percent of GDP in 2000.

In sectoral terms, growth in the industrial and services sectors were the main contributors to output expansion in 2000. The two sectors recorded growth rates of 4.4 percent and 4 percent, respectively, from 3.1 and 3.3 percent attained in 1999. Growth in agriculture remained at less than 1 percent, a far cry from 10.6 percent attained in 1996. The main influences on agriculture have been developments in global commodity prices and the adverse weather conditions in countries such as Ethiopia and Morocco. Higher oil prices and constraints on production capacity were the main factors influencing the performance in the energy sector in key economies including Algeria and Nigeria. Sectoral policy developments including privatization of Zambia's state-owned copper company coupled with civil war and conflicts in the main production areas of Angola and the Democratic Republic of Congo impacted on mining output. With the exception of South Africa, weak domestic demand, rising costs of imported raw materials, energy shortages and lack of competitiveness continued to undermine performance of the manufacturing sector. The growing importance of tourism is a major factor enhancing the contribution of the services sector in several African economies.

The remaining part of this chapter is divided into five main sections. The next section describes the diversity of economic performance among African countries. The overall trends influencing aggregate economic performance are subsequently discussed under the sections on macroeconomic policy developments, the external sector, and sectoral performance. The chapter concludes with a section on medium-term prospects.

Economic Performance in Africa

Growth led by oil exporters

Africa's economic recovery was led by the rebound in the economies of major oil exporting countries as higher oil prices and volumes fuelled faster GDP growth, while strengthening fiscal and external balances (Table 1.4). Real GDP growth in the ten major oil exporting countries—Algeria, Angola, Cameroon, Congo Brazzaville, Egypt, Equatorial Guinea, Gabon, Libya, Nigeria and Tunisia— averaged 4.7 percent, well above the continental average of 3.4 percent (Figure 1.2).

In Nigeria, higher oil revenues helped to spur the revival of economic growth, which more than tripled from the anaemic rate of the previous two years. Economic performance is also being helped by efforts of the new civilian administration to restore investor confidence by tackling corruption, restoring macroeconomic stability and improving relations with external creditors. Growth potential, however, continues to be limited by the difficulty in implementing structural and governance reforms needed for economic diversification.

In Algeria, real GDP growth was boosted by buoyant earnings from the oil and hydrocarbons sector, while Libya's economy also benefitted from the oil price boom and the resumption of trade and investment ties with European countries. Sudan, which recently joined the ranks of Africa's oil-exporting countries, had its economic growth continued to grow at a rapid pace averaging more than 6 percent in the last five years. Higher oil export revenues also had a positive impact on the economies of Cameroon and the Congo. Recent exploration and exports of oil in Equatorial Guinea contributed significantly to the expansion of economic activity with the growth rate of GDP averaging more than 20 percent annually in the last three years.

Diverse performances among oil importers

African oil importers, however, faced a very different set of international economic pressures, with the result that their GDP growth averaged only 2.7 percent in 2000 (Figure 1.2). Oil importers were hit hard by higher energy costs, weak non-fuel commodity prices, droughts and adverse weather conditions. In some countries erratic macroeconomic policies and poor governance undermined economic performance.

The sharp drop in prices of robusta coffee slowed export growth in Kenya, Uganda, and Tanzania, while in Ghana and Côte d'Ivoire, exports were constrained by weak cocoa prices. Despite this, Tanzania and Uganda maintained their recent impressive growth performance benefitting from an improved policy environment and donor support. Côte d'Ivoire was pushed into recession by the combination of increased energy costs, weak beverage prices, poor domestic policies and political uncertainty.

Amongst the metal producers, Zambia benefitted from higher copper prices and the successful, if belated, privatization of the Zambia Consolidated Copper Mines (ZCCM). This is expected to boost investor confidence in the economy while improving productivity and output from 2001 onwards. Botswana maintained

its impressive growth with GDP increasing 7 percent in 2000 after a 9 percent rise in 1999. Strong international demand for diamonds increased foreign direct investment and a competitive currency offset the flood damage suffered by the farming sector early in the year. In the Democratic Republic of Congo, higher output of copper and cobalt were not enough to offset the damage to the other sectors of the economy caused by the civil war.

Growth in a number of agricultural countries slowed under the impact of adverse climatic conditions. Agricultural output was adversely affected by drought in Eastern and Northern Africa with Ethiopia, Eritrea, Morocco and Tunisia suffering some of the worst setbacks. In Morocco, although agricultural output contracted by more than 15 percent, growth in the other sectors of the economy, particularly manufacturing and the services sector, cushioned the impact on the economy. In the first quarter of 2000, Cyclone Eline caused widespread damage to agriculture and infrastructure, including roads and railways, in parts of Southern Africa, with Mozambique being the worst affected. South Africa, Swaziland, Madagascar, Botswana and Zimbabwe were all adversely affected in different degrees. In Mozambique, growth slowed from the 10 percent average for the three previous years to 7 percent, while inflation escalated sharply and the currency depreciated. Implementation of policy reforms and the comprehensive reconstruction plan supported by the donor community should help restore economic growth in 2001.

Governance

Growth rates in countries in conflict averaged 2.8 percent lagging behind the overall regional growth, although much higher than the average of 1 per-

Figure 1.2:

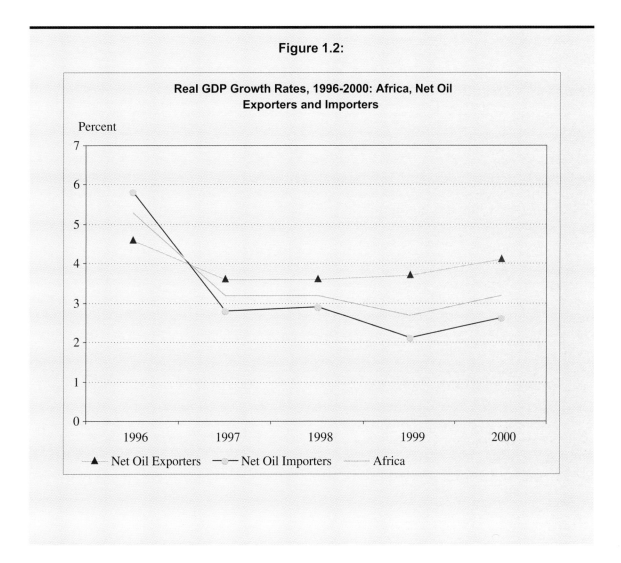

Real GDP Growth Rates, 1996-2000: Africa, Net Oil Exporters and Importers

Percent

▲ Net Oil Exporters   ─●─ Net Oil Importers   ─── Africa

cent recorded in the previous three years. Nevertheless, per capita income among this group of countries is two and half times below that of the continental average.

Political instability and civil conflict had a negative impact on a number of countries, including Angola, Democratic Republic of Congo, Côte d'Ivoire, Eritrea, Ethiopia, Sierra Leone and Zimbabwe. In Angola, the benefits of higher oil revenues were partly offset by the continuing civil war, while the combined ravages of drought and war in the horn of Africa led to a 10 percent contraction in Eritrea's GDP. In Zimbabwe, output fell some 6 percent as business confidence

collapsed and the land resettlement dispute continues. Investment fell sharply and tourism arrivals dropped by two thirds, resulting in a foreign
currency crisis. In contrast, successful political transitions in Ghana and Senegal boosted investor confidence, while among the larger countries, Algeria, Nigeria and South Africa made further head-
way in restoring political stability, with positive implications for investment and growth.

South Africa gained momentum

Output growth in South Africa, the region's largest economy, accelerated from 2 percent in 1999
to 3.1 percent in 2000 reflecting stronger expansion in agriculture and manufacturing and increased earnings from platinum, now the country's
chief export, having overtaken gold and diamonds.
Manufacturing growth picked up in the second
half of the year on the back of stronger foreign
as well as domestic demand.

Mining output fell as the long-run decline in
gold production continued, though this was partly
offset by increased output of platinum group
metals which were buoyed by stronger world
demand and high prices. Contagion from the crisis
of governance in Zimbabwe undermined the
South African rand, especially in the first half of
2000; over the year as a whole the currency lost
20 percent of its value against the US dollar.

The External Sector

A striking feature of Africa's balance-of-payments
at the beginning of the new millennium was the
remarkable 25 percent increase in merchandise
exports which reached the $150 billion mark for
the first time. The bulk of this export expansion
was restricted to the oil exporting nations, reflecting terms-of-trade gains more than volume

growth.

Terms of Trade. The region's terms-of-trade
improved by an estimated 15 percent, while some
of the major oil exporters, such as Algeria and
Nigeria, improved by as much as 50 percent (Table
1.4). The price of oil averaged $30 per barrel, a
sharp increase from $18 in 1999 and $13 in 1998.
In the third quarter, oil prices reached a 15-year
high (excluding the Gulf war period) in both real
and nominal terms. The recent run-up in oil prices
reflected buoyant current and expected world demand growth as well as the limited capacity of
oil producers, apart from a few major members
of OPEC, to increase production.

During 2000, African commodity exporters
and fuel importers were affected considerably by
commodity price swings. Non-oil commodity
prices, as a whole, were virtually unchanged from
their 1999 levels, but beverages were sharply lower
while metals firmed modestly with aluminium,
copper, nickel and platinum all showing useful
gains.

But agricultural commodities, especially beverages, were particularly weak (Table 1.5). Beverage prices fell some 30 percent, reflecting the sharp
drop in prices of cocoa and robusta coffee. Of
other exports important to African countries, cotton recovered some lost ground as did timber,
though prices remained well below their 1990 levels. Gold, a major export for South Africa, Ghana,
Zimbabwe and Tanzania, stayed depressed losing further ground early in 2001.

Trade Volumes. Export volumes are estimated
to have increased 7.3 percent, while import volumes rose 4.8 percent. Africa's trade volumes were
influenced by supply factors discussed below under sectoral developments as well as by demand
factors emanating from the growth of world
output and global trade.

Table 1.4.: Oil Exporters: Export Dependency and Terms of Trade (%)

Country	Export Dependency[1] Oil (Net Exports)	Change in Terms of Trade[2]		
		1998	1999	2000[3]
Nigeria	92	-28	-4	38
Libya	91	-28	-4	37
Angola	87	-27	-4	36
Congo, Republic of	84	-26	-4	34
Gabon	73	-23	-3	30
Equatorial Guinea	72	-22	-3	30
Algeria	63	-24	-12	30
Cameroon	30	-10	-6	4

1. Export dependency refers to net oil exports (averaged over 1995–97) as a percentage of total exports of goods and services (averaged over 1995 - 97).
2. The change in the terms of trade is the average of the price change of each commodity listed relative to the 1995-97 base period, weighted by that commodity's share of total exports of goods and services in the base period. Changes are shown as a percent of total exports for countries for which oil exports were at least 20 percent of total exports in the base period.
3. Through June 2000.
Source: World Economic Outlook (Oct. 2000).

World output growth accelerated to 4.7 percent in 2000 from 3.4 percent in 1999 and the trough of 2.6 percent recorded during the global financial crisis of 1998. Growth in world trade doubled to 10.4 percent as exports and imports among developed countries, particularly in Europe, expanded vigorously. The sharp turnaround in Asian exports from the depressed levels of 1998 also contributed to the expanded world trade values and volumes. Driven by the recovery of exports and by strong domestic demand, economic expansion in the European Union, Africa's major trading partner, gathered momentum as GDP grew 3.4 percent, up from 2.4 percent in 1999.

In 2000, two major policy initiatives that are likely to affect Africa's export prospects came into effect. First, the European Union and the African, Caribbean and Pacific States Group (ACP) of countries reached agreement on a successor arrangement to the Lomé Convention (Box 1.1). This agreement sets out a framework for a new 20-year partnership between the EU and the ACP Group. Similarly, the Africa Growth Opportunity Act which was designed to improve trade and investment opportunities between the US and selected low-income African countries was approved. These initiatives are important as market access needs to improve for exports of African countries. It is estimated that since the 1970s

Table 1.5: Selected Primary Commodities: Recent Price Movements[1]

	1998	1999	2000
Commodities with prices in 2000 much higher than in 1995–97			
Energy			
Crude petroleum ($/mt)[a/]	-30.92	-4.49	26.85
Natural gas ($/mmbtu)[b/]	-9.52	-1.73	21.21
Commodities with prices in 2000 much lower than in 1995–97			
Agricultural Commodities			
Wheat($/mt)[d/]	-30.47	-38.25	-33.84
Rice($/mt)[e/]	-5.27	-11.44	-22.15
Soybeans($/mt)	-15.08	-29.61	-23.21
Fish meal[f/]	17.61	-30.28	-27.69
Sugar (world)	-26.88	-48.66	-50.00
Coffee (arabica)	-12.27	-54.68	-28.49
Coffee (robusta)	-13.37	-29.24	-47.63
Cocoa beans	11.56	-24.43	-6.66
Cotton(c/kg)	-23.26	-37.81	-34.41
Jute($/mt)	-30.72	-26.29	-19.97
Tea(c/kg)[c/]	17.81	5.89	7.10
Metals			
Copper($/mt)	-33.91	-37.15	-28.08
Nickel ($/mt)	-38.69	-20.41	19.17
Gold($/toz)	-19.98	-24.17	-22.48

1: Percentage change from 1995-97 level.
a/ avg spot
b/ us
c/ 3-auction average
d/ us, hrw
e/ tai, 5%
f/ any origin
Source: Global Commodity Markets (2000), April 2000; January 2000; April 1999
IFS: January 2001; Yearbook 2000

Box 1.1: The Post-Lomé Convention Partnership Agreement between the ACP Countries and the European Union

A new 20-year successor Partnership Agreement to the Lomé Convention between the African, Caribbean and Pacific (ACP) States and the European Union (EU) was signed in Cotonou on 23 June 2000. The new Agreement covers 77 countries, with African countries making up 48 of the total number. The major aim of the new Agreement is to promote and expedite the economic, cultural and social development of the ACP States, with a view to contributing to peace and security and to promoting a stable and democratic political environment. Specifically, the objective of the Agreement is to reduce and eventually eradicate poverty, consistent with the objectives of sustainable development and the gradual integration of the ACP States into the world economy. The issues that form an integral part of the common and comprehensive strategy are equitable growth, the role of the private sector, access to productive resources, social development, regional integration and co-operation processes, gender equality, environmental sustainability, institutional reforms, and capacity building.

The new Partnership Agreement (ACP-EU Convention), has four main components:

- Reinforcement of the political dimension of relations between ACP States and the EU;
- Poverty reduction within the context of the objectives and strategies agreed at international level;
- An innovative economic and trade co-operation framework; and
- Rationalisation of financial instruments and a new system of "rolling programming".

The political dimension involves regular political dialogue to promote the consistency and relevance of ACP-EU co-operation strategies and to make it possible to address all issues of mutual interest. Peace-building policies, conflict-prevention and resolution and migration are important issues, which have been expressly introduced into the new Partnership Agreement. Respect for human rights and fundamental freedoms, democratic principles and the rule of law, and good governance are subjects for regular dialogue between regional and sub-regional organisations and representatives of civil society. New consultation procedures are envisaged in the event of violation of the basic principles.

The development strategies focus on poverty reduction in the short-run and poverty eradication in the long run, pursued through integrated strategies that incorporate economic, social, cultural, environmental and institutional elements, which must be country-owned. To achieve this, areas of support include economic development (investment and private sector development, macroeconomic and structural reforms and policies, economic sector development, and tourism); and social and human development (social sector development, youth issues, and cultural development). Others are regional co-operation and integration, and thematic and crosscutting issues (gender, environmental and natural resources, and institutional development and capacity building). The strategies will be reviewed on a regular basis by means of the annual publication of a Compendium of reference texts, which will allow the partnership to take account of best development practices.

Unlike the Lomé Convention under which trade co-operation was based essentially on preferential tariffs, the new Agreement's economic and trade co-operation will consist of a more complete set of arrangements. Its objective is to promote the progressive integration of the ACP countries into the global economy, by enhancing production and the capacity to attract investment, and ensuring conformity with WTO rules, while taking into cognisance individual countries' levels of development. The new approach, which aims at establishing new trade agreements will lead to the liberalisation of trade between the parties. This includes co-operation in areas linked with trade, such as competition policy, the protection of intellectual property rights, standardisation and certification, sanitary and phytosanitary measures, trade and environment, trade and labour standards, and consumer policy and protection of consumer

Box 1.1: (continued)

health. There are also provisions for co-operation in international fora, fishery agreements, and food security. The strategy for achieving this establishes a clear link between development aid, particularly support for modernisation of the economy, and the setting up of a regulatory and trade policy framework to favour the development of trade and private investment.

The Agreement makes provision for the introduction of new trade agreements after a preparatory period during which the current trade regime will be maintained. The latest date for commencing negotiation of economic partnership agreements is September 2002. Before this, there would have been preparations, support for regional integration processes and the enhancement of public and private capacities. In 2004, the parties will carry out an assessment of the situation of non-LDC ACP countries not in a position to enter into economic partnership agreements, so as to find alternatives. The EU has undertaken to liberalise virtually all imports of products from the less developed countries by 2005. An evaluation of progress made in the negotiation of economic partnership agreements will be carried out in 2006. This is to ensure that no additional time is needed for the negotiations. Latest by 1 January 2008 the new trade agreements would enter into force while trade liberalisation will be attained during a transitional period of at least 12 years.

Financial co-operation, which is to be based on assessment of need and policy performance, will cover debt (support for debt relief) and structural adjustment support; support in cases of short-term fluctuations in export earnings; sup-

port for sectoral policies; and microprojects and decentralised co-operation. Others are humanitarian and emergency assistance; investment (promotion, finance and support, guarantees, and protection) and private sector development; and technical co-operation. A system of rolling programming accompanied by regular review will allow the support strategy to be continually adapted as the situation in the country or region evolves. The 20-year Partnership Agreement also provides for new financial protocol at 5-year intervals. Financial resources to support the development strategies in the ACP States amount to €25.1 billion for the period, 2000-2007. Under this new Agreement, the Stabex Fund (which covered losses of earnings caused by a fall in prices or a decline in production of the main ACP agricultural exports) and Sysmin (a special financing facility for countries reliant on the export of minerals) are phased out.

Though the new Partnership Agreement fell short of sweeping reforms for a comprehensive restructuring of the Lomé Convention, it reflected the objective of modernising, streamlining, and updating EU's development assistance activities along the lines of the 1996 proposals. In addition, the Agreement preserved the ACP Group as a legal entity, promised faster disbursement of allocated funds, and provided for transitional arrangements that would give countries more time to adapt to globalization and the requirements of the international trading system.

Source: EC(2000).

Africa's agricultural exports have lost some $70 billion in market share due to inefficiency and protectionism by its major trading partners. Agricultural subsidies in the developed countries cost some $300 billion a year or about 100 times current aid levels to Africa.

External Financing Declined Marginally

Trade and Current Account Balances. Africa's trade surplus strengthened to $11 billion or 1.2 percent of GDP. Oil producers recorded trade surpluses of more than a quarter of GDP compared to only 7 percent of GDP during the oil crisis of 1998. The significant improvement in the balance of trade for Africa was driven largely by oil trends, masking the developments in many of the region's economies. While the oil exporting nations made major trade gains that led to trade surpluses, a large number of nations experienced severe trade deficits. Overall, thirty two countries recorded trade deficits with some fifteen countries experiencing trade deficits of more than 10 percent of GDP. Only a handful of net fuel importers, including Botswana, Guinea and Mauritania, managed to improve their trade balances, partly reflecting firmer export prices but also the depressed level of imports.

Africa's current account deficit declined dramatically to only $1.96 billion in 2000 (0.3 percent of GDP), from $18.6 billion (3.4 percent of GDP) in 1999, with major oil exporters and South Africa accounting for the improvements. The region's net reserves increased by some $14 billion in 2000.

Foreign Capital Inflows. Net external financing to the region declined from $27.3 billion in 1999 to $26.3 billion in 2000. While capital transfers increased from $5.4 billion to $8.3 billion (53 percent) between 1999 and 2000, direct investment declined marginally by 5 percent to $9.3 billion.

In 1999, the bulk (70 percent) of the $9 billion FDI inflow into Africa went to a handful of countries, most of them energy exporters— Angola, Nigeria, South Africa, Morocco, Mozambique and Tunisia. An UNCTAD survey in 2000 found that multinationals are less inclined to invest in Africa's smaller economies or in globally integrated industries such as textiles or mechanical/electrical equipment. Privatization is an increasingly important determinant of FDI in Africa. The main recipients of privatization capital between 1990-1998 were South Africa ($1.38 billion), Ghana ($770 million), Nigeria ($500 million), Zambia ($420 million) and Côte d'Ivoire ($373 million). Most of these inflows went to the telecommunication and mining sectors.

The UK, France, and US are the main sources of FDI in Africa. Investment from the U.S. and France focuses on natural resource industries while that from Germany, Switzerland and the Netherlands has targeted manufacturing and the U.K has targeted services. The sources of new FDI now vary considerably. In the past, it was investment by the former colonial power that tended to dominate, but recently a number of new players have taken the field, including Malaysia, which has become an important source of FDI in a number of African countries, including South Africa. Australian and Canadian firms have also become significant players in the mining sector, just as South African firms have moved into the brewery and service sectors—tourism, finance, retail, satellite broadcasting—in many African countries.

As global investor and lender confidence returned, private flows to emerging market economies recovered, especially portfolio investment, bond issues and loans. Net private capital flows to major emerging market economies strengthened to $154 billion in 2000 from around $148 billion in 1999. Equity investment was estimated at $151 billion, down from $163 billion in 1999, and foreign direct investment also slowed somewhat to $128 billion, with evidence of increased merger and acquisition activity relative to new greenfield investment (IIF, 2001). Direct investment flows have grown very strongly in recent years proving to be less vulnerable to international financial volatility than portfolio flows and bank and trade-related lending.

Portfolio equity flows recovered marginally to an estimated $22 billion in 2000, as emerging market equity prices consolidated after their exceptionally strong performance in 1999, when prices rose 66 percent in dollar terms on average. Flows in 2000 were sensitive to developments in developed country financial markets. However, the strengthening of policy frameworks, improved transparency and the more widespread adoption of floating exchange rates will continue to make emerging market equity attractive. Although progress has been made in recent years, Africa continues to lag far behind the rest of the developing world in attracting private capital.

Debt stock and debt service also went down

Heavy reliance by African countries on foreign financing, especially bilateral and multilateral loans, contributed to the rapid build-up of the continent's external debt, especially in the 1970s and 1980s. For many countries in the region the external debt burden has reached unsustainable levels. Large foreign debt and high interest rates have combined with adverse terms of trade to make debt service payments simply unmanageable for many countries, which is why 31 African states are now classified as Heavily Indebted Poor Countries.

The continent's debt stock declined marginally from $337.2 billion in 1999 to $334.3 billion in 2000. This was made up of $38.9 billion of short-term obligations and $295.3 billion long-term. This maturity structure is explained by the preponderance of official borrowing - some 70 percent of Africa's debt is owed to official creditors. Only 12 percent was owed to banks and financial institutions in 2000 and the balance of 18 percent to other private creditors. With GDP increasing while the debt stock declined, Africa's total debt to GDP ratio fell from 61.4 percent in 1999 to 58 percent in 2000. Similarly, improvement in the region's export meant that the ratio of foreign debt to exports of goods and services decreased significantly from 225.3 percent to 182.6 percent over the same period. Despite this, in many countries the present value of debt as a proportion of exports of goods and services exceeds 200 percent.

In 2000, though with a small debt stock of only $300 million, Sao Tomé and Principé had the highest debt-GDP ratio of 573.6 percent in the continent. Zambia, whose external debt in 2000 was $5.1 billion represented 174.9 percent of GDP, has obtained debt relief under the HIPC program, becoming the eleventh country to qualify under the initiative. South AFrica has the largest debt stock in the continent at $38.91 billion (though only 30 percent of GDP) followed by Nigeria with $31.4 billion (81.4 percent of GDP). Debt relief for Nigeria is under discussion at a number of international fora and during 2000, the Paris Club of commercial creditors agreed to reschedule $23.4 billion or 80 percent of Nigeria's external debt over the next 20 years with 3 years moratorium on interest. This rescheduling will enable Nigeria to redirect revenues that would have been used to pay interest to improve the living standard of its people and rebuild the country's deteriorating infrastructure.

Partly because of the highly concessional nature of external financing provided to Africa, debt-service ratios have declined from 19.3 percent of exports in 1999 to 16.2 percent in 2000. Despite this, many countries in the region have been unable to service their debt without recourse to rescheduling under Paris Club arrangements or by accumulating arrears.

Increasing capital flight from the region has exacerbated the detrimental effects on investment and growth of the debt overhang arising from the rapid accumulation of foreign borrowing in the 1970s and 1980s. Thus, Africa was simultaneously an exporter as well as an importer of capital.

The sustainability of African debt has for long been one of the critical issues on the international development agenda as most countries have had to continuously deal with several intractable external debt issues. The Highly Indebted Poor Country Initiative (HIPC) was launched in 1996 to relieve developing countries of their high debt burdens. The initial conditions for eligibility were perceived to be difficult and thus the initiative was received with little enthusiasm in Africa.

Phase one of HIPC required a three-year record of compliance with an IMF program that leds to a decision point. Acceptance at this stage required countries to show they were beyond debt sustainability by having a debt service ratio of 20-25 percent and a present value of debt to export ratio of 200-250 percent. This entitled them to two-thirds reduction of all external debt. The HIPC conditions were revised in 1999 with the requirement for the present value of debt to export ratio reduced to 150 percent while debt relief commences at the decision point (Box 1.2).

Domestic Policy Developments

Macroeconomic strategy in most African countries has emphasized restrictive monetary and fiscal policies to achieve internal and external balances as well as structural, institutional and governance reforms in order to provide a conducive environment for private sector-led growth. While the attainment of fiscal balance and monetary stability in the short to medium term continues to be constrained by external shocks, structural policy reform should help to lay the foundation for sustained long-term economic growth.

Fiscal Balance. In 2000, Africa's overall budget deficit declined to one percent of GDP from an average of 3.5 percent in the previous two years. Higher oil revenues in the major oil-exporting countries, as well as continued fiscal restraint in some of the smaller economies, drove improvements in the overall fiscal position in the region. Increased oil prices enabled oil exporting countries to run a surplus, while the others were forced to keep a tight rein on public spending. A fiscal surplus of 7 percent of GDP was recorded by oil producing countries.

Government revenue as a percentage of GDP averaged about a quarter of GDP. In general, government revenue as a ratio of GDP is lower in countries within the CFA zone. In the CFA zone, public revenues fell with the loss of tariff revenues in some countries as a result of their compliance with the WAEMU Common External Tariff. To compensate for this, several countries including Mali and Senegal introduced value added tax in 2000. Increased military and defence spending contributed to fiscal deterioration in countries involved in civil and regional conflicts, including the Democratic Republic of Congo (DRC), Eritrea, Ethiopia, Zimbabwe and Sierra Leone.

Box 1.2: Bank Group Participation in the HIPC Initiative

The HIPC Initiative commenced in 1996 in response to the inadequacies of the earlier international approaches to addressing the external indebtedness of low-income countries. The main objective of this comprehensive approach is to reduce the debt stocks of eligible countries to a sustainable level subject to satisfactory policy performance.

Following a consultative review of the HIPC implementation in 1998/99, coordinated by the Bretton Woods Institutions (BWIs), new proposals emerged for an enhanced HIPC framework. The enhanced HIPC framework offers a deeper, broader, and faster debt relief linked to a comprehensive program for poverty reduction in eligible countries; and, it is retroactive, by reassessing countries that have already qualified for HIPC assistance under the original framework for additional relief based on the new eligibility benchmark. The new benchmarks for the enhanced framework include: an NPV debt-to-export ratio target of 150 percent – instead of a range of 200 to 250 percent in the original framework – and an NPV debt-to-revenue ratio target of 250 percent – instead of 280 percent.

Costs
These enhancements have increased the number of eligible African countries from 25 to 31, while the total costs more than doubled to US $28.6 billion in 1999 NPV terms compared to US $12.5 billion in 1998 NPV terms, under the original framework. The costs to multilateral creditors stand at US$14 billion. The Bank Group's total contribution is currently estimated at US$ 2.3 billion (in 1999 NPV terms) for 27 countries (i.e. excluding Central African Republic, Congo Republic, Democratic Republic of Congo, Ghana, Liberia, Somalia and Sudan, which have yet to be assessed).

Financing
The Bank Group has mobilized internal resources amounting to US$ 320 million to fund its share of debt relief under the new initiative. These include: US$ 74 million from the ADB net income (1997-2003), US$ 156 million from ADF loan cancellations, and US$ 90 million from ADF reflows (1997-2003). Following the request by donors on the need for a maximum internal effort by MDBs, management has proposed an additional US$ 50 million from the net income of ADB beyond 2003. This would bring the total internal contributions to US$ 370 million.

In addition to Bank Group internal resources, a total of US$ 1.4 billion is available to the Bank Group in pledges and contributions through the HIPC Trust Fund.

Bank Group Delivery Modality
The modality endorsed by ADF Deputies and approved by the Bank Group Boards of Directors for the delivery of debt relief to eligible countries under the enhanced HIPC framework, has the following characteristics:

- Delivery of debt relief through annual debt service reductions, by releasing up to 80 percent of annual debt service obligations as they come due, until the total debt relief is provided;
- Interim financing of up to 40 percent of total debt relief, between decision point and the point of irrevocable delivery of debt relief (completion point);
- Debt service to be provided, whenever possible, within a 15-year time horizon to assist countries attain the internationally agreed development goals for the year 2015.

Implementation
Under the original HIPC framework, the Bank Group delivered debt relief, amounting to US$ 141.7 million, to Uganda and Mozambique, which reached their completion points, in 1998 and 1999 respectively. Of this, the Bank Group financed US$ 57.3 million from its internal resources, and the balance of US$ 84.7 million came from bilateral contributions through the HIPC Trust Fund.

As at the end of 2000, the Bank's Board of Directors had approved the Bank's debt relief to the following ten countries under the enhanced HIPC Initiative: Benin, Burkina Faso, Cameroon, Guinea Bissau, Mali, Mauritania, Mozambique, Sénégal, Tanzania and Uganda. The total Bank Group debt relief for these countries amounts to US $635.84 million (in 1999 NPV terms), or US$ 845.43 million in nominal terms. The total contribution of the Bank Group from its internal resources amounts to US$127.00 million in 1999 NPV terms, with the balance from bilateral contributions through the HIPC Trust Fund.

Approvals in 2001
Since the beginning of 2001, debt relief has been extended to eight additional countries which reached their decision points in December 2000. These are The

Box 1.2: continued

Zambia, all of which, with the exception of Chad, reached their decision points in December 2000. Total Bank Group debt relief contribution to this second group of countries would amount to US$476.63 million (in 1999 NPV terms), or US$ 799.5 million in nominal terms, of which US$95.33 million (in 1999 NPV terms) would be financed from its internal resources.

Total Bank Group debt relief for all the 17 countries would amount to US$ 1.12 billion (in 1999 NPV terms), or US $1.83 billion in nominal terms, out of which the Bank Group would finance US $224.30 million (in 1999 NPV terms) from its internal resources, and the balance from bilateral contributions.

A further seven countries - Burundi, Côte d'Ivoire, Ethiopia, Madagascar, Sao Tome and Principe, Sierra Leone, and Togo could reach their decision points sometime in 2001. The Bank Group's debt relief to these countries is estimated at US$558.3 million in 1999 NPV terms.

There are other countries which are eligible for debt relief under the enhanced HIPC Initiative. However, they have not been assessed for assistance. These include three countries in chronic arrears and/or conflict (Central African Republic, Congo Republic, and the Democratic Republic of Congo) whose assistance is expected to cost US$ 560 million in 1999 NPV terms; and four other countries – Ghana, Liberia, Somalia and Sudan – which are for the time being are not considered for HIPC assistance.

Source: African Development Bank Group (2000).

For example, overall fiscal balance excluding grants ran into a deficit of more than 40 percent of GDP in Eritrea. In Ethiopia, defense spending alone consumed more than a third of government expenditure. Recent peace efforts in the horn of Africa should enable these countries to reduce their huge budgetary deficits through the reduction of military spending and increased revenue as economic activity rebounds.

Money Supply, Inflation and Exchange Rates. Broad money supply growth slowed to 13.4 percent in 2000 from 17.9 percent in 1999 and 18.7 percent in 1998. More than thirty countries recorded money supply growth below the regional average. In general, broad money supply growth is lower among CFA zone countries at about half of the continental average. Most countries have consistently pursued conservative monetary policies designed to control inflation. In the West African Economic and Monetary Union (WAEMU), monetary policy is dictated by the common central bank of WAEMU, Banque centrale des Etats de l'Afrique de l'ouest (BCEAO), which raised the rediscount and repurchase agreement rates by 0.75 percentage points in 2000. Reserve ratio requirements were also tightened in many member countries.

Although the region's average inflation rate at 12.7 percent was only marginally higher than in 1999, it was almost four times lower than the peak reached in 1994 as restrictive fiscal and monetary measures outweighed higher energy costs. Consumer prices remained subdued with forty countries registering single digit inflation rates. The median inflation rate for the 53 African countries was less than 5 percent. Inflation rates among CFA-zone countries averaged 2.6 percent, while the average inflation rate in the non-CFA zone countries was marginally down to 14 percent.

The larger economies too managed to keep inflation in check. Consumer prices increased 2.9 percent in Egypt during 2000 and 4 percent in South Africa, while greater financial discipline contributed to declining inflation rates in Algeria and Nigeria. Only a handful of countries experienced double-digit inflation—Angola, Burundi, DRC,

Ghana, Malawi, Sudan, Zambia and Zimbabwe. At more than 80 percent, inflation remained a major problem among the conflict countries. Higher imported petroleum costs allied with a rapid cedi depreciation put upward pressure on price levels in Ghana, while in Malawi similar pressures accounted for high inflation. In Zimbabwe, consumer inflation increased to 55.8 percent in 2000, despite the introduction of informal price controls on certain commodities. Inflation was driven by rapid monetary expansion, currency depreciation, rising energy and food prices and growing shortages due to the foreign currency crisis.

Almost all African currencies depreciated to some extent during 2000, though this was partly explained by the strength of the US dollar in global financial markets. Developments with respect to exchange rates in Egypt, Nigeria and South Africa—three of the major economies— are illustrated in the following paragraphs.

Egypt has maintained for sometime that a sharp devaluation would discourage foreign investors and could result in sudden, and massive, capital flight. However, the inflation differential with its partners resulted in an appreciation of the pound, making Egyptian goods more expensive overseas. In 2000, the exchange rate was allowed to depreciate gradually, declining an estimated 5.1 percent over the year. Recognizing that economic growth might be hampered if the monetary squeeze remained tight, Egypt adopted a more flexible monetary policy in 2000. Despite this increased flexibility, monetary policy remained cautious as the government sought to control the pound's depreciation by selling dollars, while seeking to avoid draining pound liquidity and raising interest rates.

The Nigerian naira experienced a sharp depreciation in 2000 despite higher oil export earnings, higher foreign remittances, and a relatively lower inflation rate. This has been attributed to large net outflow of short term capital to finance imports. The gap between official exchange rate and the parallel market rate remained high at about 10 to 15 percent. The South African rand experienced increased volatility, losing almost 20 percent of its value against the US dollar due to the dollars' strength and the contagion effect of the deteriorating political situation in Zimbabwe.

The CFA franc, which depreciated against the dollar by 14 percent in 1999, weakened further as a direct result of the slide in the euro to which the Franc Zone currency is linked through its peg to the French franc. The European Central Bank raised interest rates partly to shore up the Euro, which hit record lows against the dollar.

Financial market developments. African Stock markets declined in the year 2000 following their impressive upswing in 1999. Stock markets ended 1999 with a market capitalization of $249 billion, more than double the 1990 total of $144.6 billion. In contrast, by the end of 2000, market capitalization had declined somewhat to $240 billion, though this figure was distorted to some degree by the strength of the dollar.

By the end of December 2000, only the Tunisian and Nigerian Stock Exchanges had kept ahead of the surging dollar. Tunisia was up 50 percent and Nigeria 30 percent, while in contrast, the capitalization of the Ghanaian market, rose 15 percent in Cedi terms, but fell 40 percent in dollar terms.

More seriously, the Johannesburg Stock Exchange (JSE), accounting for 89 percent of regional market capitalization saw the value of its market plunge from $245 billion in January 2000 to $213 billion in December 2000. The 15 percent decline in the JSE took place against a background of relatively strong economic fundamentals, reflecting the strength of the dollar along with concerns over regional stability, emanating from the Zimbabwean crisis. Similarly, the Mauritius Stock exchange experienced a 7 percent fall in local currency terms and a 10 percent decline in dollar terms while the Namibian Stock Exchange was down 30 percent in local currency and 42 percent in dollars.

Although the Zimbabwe Stock Exchange (ZSE) had risen to a new record high of 19,570—up more than 30 percent in local currency terms by September—it retreated in the final months to close the year at 18,000, down only marginally in local currency terms. This was explained by excess market liquidity in the face of 58 percent money supply growth as well as by the scarcity of alternative investment opportunities. Furthermore, the markets might have read the political situation better than the analysts. If Zimbabwe is closer to far-reaching political change than many believe stocks might actually be cheap.

There is a trend toward the regionalization of stock markets in Africa to take advantage of economies of scale. West Africa was the first area to test the concept of a regional exchange. In 1998 the Abidjan-based Bourse régionale des valeurs mobilières (BRVM) became the world's first regional stock exchange, linking the equity markets of Benin, Burkina Faso, Côte d'Ivoire, Guinea-Bissau, Mali, Niger, Senegal and Togo. There are now plans by the countries of the proposed Second West African Monetary Zone (Nigeria, Ghana, Sierra Leone, Guinea, The Gambia and Liberia) to establish a common Stock Exchange along with a common currency. Link-ups have also been mooted between exchanges in Kenya, Uganda and Tanzania, and between the JSE and smaller Southern African Development Community exchanges.

The challenges faced by African financial systems are characteristics of those in emerging markets as a whole—fragmentation, illiquidity, informational inefficiency, limited size and capacity, underdevelopment of human capital, inefficient regulatory schemes, excessive risk factors, dearth of risk-sharing and hedging mechanisms and legal and contract enforceability issues. The urgency of change and of dealing with these challenges is accentuated by the speed with which capital and money markets are globalizing.

Although African stock markets remain small and illiquid—with the single exception of the JSE in South Africa—they still provide potential for the faster integration of Africa into the global economy.

Sectoral Developments

The natural resource endowment of Africa's economies is an important determinant of the relative importance of the four main sectors—agriculture, industry (comprising manufacturing and mining), energy, and services—and their impact on macroeconomic aggregates. The performance of the four main sectors is provided in Table 1.6. Growth in the industrial sectors averaged 4.4 percent while agriculture grew by less than 1 percent in 2000.

Agriculture

Agriculture dominates most African economies (South Africa and Mauritius being the major exceptions), employing about two-thirds of Africa's total labor force and accounting for about one-third of GDP and one half of exports.

Table 1.6: Sectoral Growth Rates, 1996-2000 (Percentage changes from preceeding year)					
	1996	1997	1998	1999	2000[a/]
Agriculture	10.6	1.1	3.6	1.1	0.6
Industry	4.0	4.5	3.1	3.1	4.4
Manufacturing	2.7	4.4	3.1	3.5	4.5
Services	4.0	3.1	3.1	3.3	4.0
GDP at constant Market prices	5.3	3.2	3.2	2.7	3.2

Notes: a/ Preliminary Estimates.
Source: ADB Statistics Division.

Agriculture's value-added in Africa's GDP was 17 percent in 2000, compared with 50 percent for the services sector and 33 percent for the industrial sector. Agriculture's low value-added reflects the inefficient nature of agricultural production, with a high dependence on rain-fed farming and limited use of fertilizers and modern inputs (Table 1.7). The performance of agriculture is central to food security and poverty reduction since the majority of the region's poor live in rural areas.

Food production worsens

In 2000, food security in the region was seriously threatened as many countries, particularly in Eastern Africa were unable to meet production targets. The number of people facing food shortages is estimated to have risen from 19 million in 1999 to 28 million in 2000 (FAO, 2000).

In much of **East Africa** the food situation was precarious throughout 2000, with some 20 million people requiring emergency food assistance. Total cereal production was estimated at 10,480 million tonnes which was 91 percent of the average output for the previous five years. Worst affected countries were Eritrea, Ethiopia and Kenya. In Kenya, where only 72 percent of the previous five-year average output was produced, the crisis was largely due to the lengthy drought, which only began to ease towards the end of 2000. As many as 3.3 million people were estimated to be in urgent need of food assistance in Kenya during the drought, with conditions in the north and east of the country resulting in major livestock losses.

In some other East African countries, the impact of adverse weather was compounded by civil strife. Mass displacement of farmers in Eritrea from the main cereal producing regions of Gash Barka and Debub, which account for more than 70 percent of cereal production, jeopardized production in 2000. Nearly 1.5 million people were displaced by war and another 300 000 were affected by drought. The situation in Ethiopia was no better despite rains towards the end of the year and an estimated 10.2 million people required food assistance. Even though Somalia produced 119 percent of the cereals it had produced on average for the previous five years, emergency food assistance was still required for an estimated 750 000 people. This resulted from a succession of droughts and a high degree of insecurity in a state with barely any government structures.

The situation in Uganda was most acute in the north-east due to drought and in Bundibugyo District in the west, due to civil strife. About 1.2 million people were estimated to be in need of assistance.

Table 1.7: Sub-Saharan Africa Cereal Import and Food Aid Requirements by Sub-Region
(In thousand tonnes)

Sub-Region	1999 Production	Cereal Import Requirements	1999/2000 or 2000 Anticipated Commercial Imports	Food Aid Requirements
Eastern Africa	19627	5398	3349	2049
Southern Africa	19287	4919	4597	322
Western Africa	38520	5874	5407	467
Central Africa	2952	800	770	30
Total	80386	16991	14123	2868

Source: FAO (2000).

In **Southern Africa**, cereal production improved in a number of countries but worsened in some others. For the sub-region as a whole, the output of 22.8 million tonnes was 114 percent of the average cereal production in the previous five years. Countries that recorded significant gains over the previous five-year average included Zambia, South Africa, Namibia and Malawi. Those that suffered less than average production included Angola, Botswana, Lesotho, Madagascar, Mozambique and Swaziland.

Food production in Zimbabwe and Angola, two countries whose significant agricultural potential is constrained by inappropriate domestic policies and governance crises, is illustrated. In Zimbabwe, value added in agriculture is estimated to have increased by 3 percent in 2000 following a 1 percent rise in 1999. Disruption on commercial farms, where wheat is grown under irrigation, led to a 20 percent fall in the winter wheat harvest. But production of other crops planted in 1999—before the land invasions by former liberation war veterans started in February 2000—increased, with maize harvest up 40 percent over 1999 levels due to an increase in acreage planted and above average rainfall. The total cereal output of 2.4 million tonnes was above average. There was also a record cotton harvest of 330,000 tons in the 1999/2000 year, up from 286,000 tons in 1998/99.

Future prospects are clouded by the uncertainties surrounding the government's land reform program which involves taking over 5 million hectares of commercially-owned farmland—more than half the commercial area —and allocating it to smallscale farmers. Since the bulk of export production (tobacco, soyabeans, horticulture and beef), is produced on commercial farms, the planned land redistribution could change Zimbabwe's pattern of foreign trade radically.

Cereal production in Angola in 1999/2000 is estimated at 504,000 tons, 5 percent lower than the previous year. This was because of unfavorable rainfall and the fact that the main planting season—September to November—coincided with an increase in government military activity across the country. Maize production fell by 8 percent, whereas sorghum and millet rose by 3 percent. Commercial agriculture has effectively collapsed in Angola, except in some coastal areas where crops are grown under irrigation. Marketing surpluses from the subsistence sector have also declined sharply owing to continuing insecurity.

Predictably, given the conflict in the **Great Lakes Region**, agriculture is in crisis. The civil war in the DRC has led to the displacement of some 2 million people, making it impossible for them to produce any food, while at the same time making it very difficult for aid agencies to deliver food supplies. Kinshasa's food deficit was estimated at 1 million tonnes in 2000, compared to 954,000 tonnes in 1999. Aside from poor transport infrastructure, the inability to supply Kinshasa with food is a consequence of the collapse of government structures.

In Burundi, it is estimated that production of cereals in 2000 was 97 percent of the five-year average, while in Rwanda, cereal output increased 23 percent from 1999 levels. But other crops, including bananas and coffee, failed in some parts of the country where there were prolonged dry spells. By October, 267,000 people were estimated to be in need of food assistance.

Some **West African** countries reported significant improvements in cereal production, including Cape Verde, Gambia, Guinea Bissau and Senegal. But several others reported marginal declines in cereal output, with output in Chad declining to 85 percent of the previous five-year average. For the Sahelian countries, cereal output was 97 percent of the average for the previous five years. In Senegal, cereal production grew 14 percent in 2000.

Sierra Leone continued to be of major concern in the sub-region with an estimated half million persons internally displaced in government controlled areas, while another million are believed to be held in rebel controlled areas. While there is no clear indication of how much food was produced, the number of displaced persons is used to project a food import requirement that was 27 percent higher than in 1999. Liberia, on the other hand, was expected to record significant increases in food production.

Food supply in Nigeria was satisfactory with no major deviation from average production. But in Ghana, irregular rains affected food production marginally, with food imports expected to rise by some 9 percent. Côte d'Ivoire's food production was expected to follow a similar pattern to that in Ghana given the similarity of rainfall patterns, but food supplies were expected to be disrupted on the marketing side due to civil disturbances in the country. As a result, food import requirements were forecast to have increased 56 percent in 2000.

In **North Africa**, agricultural production in Morocco and Tunisia is susceptible to drought. Farm production in Tunisia is highly dependent on the rainfall pattern with only one million hectares of fertile arable land available for cropping. The 1994-98 period was characterized by persistent drought, which affected output and water levels in the dams. During the VIII Plan (1992-1996), the agricultural and fishery sectors experienced a decline of 1.1 percent at constant prices against an estimated increase of 2 percent and drought deterred new investment in the industry.

This situation has however been reversed with a 15 percent increase in investment in the 1997-1999 period. But agricultural production continues to suffer from drought with output falling 15 percent in 2000, which limited GDP growth to 5 percent.

Morocco's second drought-inflicted recession in agriculture in two years led to a contraction in agricultural output of 17 percent in 2000. In Egypt, agricultural production growth slowed from 3.7 percent in 1999 to 3 percent in 2000. Production and export of the country's major export, cotton, has declined with the removal of state subsidies, resulting in sharply higher production costs. As a result, many farmers switched to other cash crops.

In Sudan, despite the fact that in 2000 cereal output was 113 percent of average output in the previous five years, serious food shortages emerged in several areas following prolonged dry spells. As a result, food prices more than doubled over the same period in 1999.

Agricultural exports remain unstable

With two thirds of agricultural export earnings derived from only six commodities—cocoa, coffee, cotton, sugar, tobacco and tea—African economies are largely dependent on a narrow range of export crops. Coffee and cocoa accounted for over half of total export earnings in the mid-1990s. While some agricultural exports (cotton, rubber and tea) enjoyed significant price recoveries in 2000, others (coffee, cocoa and tobacco) experienced further major declines.

West Africa produces some 4.7 percent of global cotton output, with another 0.3 percent coming from the rest of the region. Cotton prices

are estimated to have averaged 128 cents a kilogram in 2000, up from 117 cents the previous year. They are expected to rise again in 2001 to 137 cents.

The commodity to suffer most from global price declines in recent years is cocoa whose price fell to a 30-year low in the first quarter of 2000 when the prices were a third of their early 1999 levels. With an output of 1.25 million tonnes or 42.5 percent of global production, Côte d'Ivoire was severely affected—followed by Ghana, which produces 410,000 tonnes.

Under a plan aimed at boosting world prices, Côte d'Ivoire, Ghana, Cameroon and Nigeria agreed in July 2000 to destroy 250,000 tons of cocoa beans in the 2000/01 season in an attempt to reduce oversupply. Because no details were given of what percentage each country would destroy and who would pay for the scheme, the market response has been sceptical.

Producers of robusta coffee experienced similarly adverse world market conditions. Côte d'Ivoire, Uganda and Cameroon saw prices fall to a seven-year low at 102 cents/kg early in 2000. At the end of the year, prices averaged 95 cents/kg—little more than half their 1998 levels of over 180 cents.

Manufacturing

One of the most significant problems facing African economies remains the difficulty of increasing the share of manufacturing output in overall growth. UNIDO (2000) estimates that growth in manufacturing value-added (MVA) slowed from 5.7 percent in 1998 to 4.1 percent in 1999 and 2.7 percent in 2000.

Excluding South Africa, MVA growth is estimated at only 1.7 percent in 2000, while sub-Saharan Africa's share of global MVA was only 0.4 percent— unchanged for four years—and compared to 23.6 percent in other developing economies. Africa's share of manufactured exports, excluding South Africa, was 0.2 percent in 1995 and is reckoned not to have changed since then.

Aside from the slow growth of manufacturing activity and its insignificant share of total exports, the distribution of manufacturing activity in the region is extremely skewed. In sub-Saharan Africa, South Africa accounts for 54.5 percent of MVA with the other significant players being Côte d'Ivoire with 4.7 percent, Cameroon (4.6 percent), Zimbabwe (3.8), Nigeria (3.7), Kenya (2.4), Mauritius (1.7) and Ghana with 1.6 percent.

Excluding South Africa, the MVA of all these countries is less than that in Egypt ($15billion). However, some of the fastest MVA growth rates have come, not in the larger industrialized economies, but in the smaller ones. Uganda's industrial sector has been growing at 13 percent a year, while Lesotho grew at 10.

In Tunisia, which has one of the most advanced manufacturing sectors in the region, industry plays a key role in GDP growth and employment creation. Manufacturing industry's share in total value-added was 20.2 percent in 2000, an increase of 4.5 percent from 1994 levels. Textiles play a dominant role in the country's economy accounting for one-third of the value-added of manufacturing industry and 50 percent of employment and exports of the sector. The average growth of manufacturing (5.6 percent) in the 1997-1999 period exceeded the average growth of GDP of 5.2 percent. The average annual increase of 12 percent in manufacturing investment—84 percent of which come from the private sector—points to a bright future for manufacturing.

Manufacturing output in Senegal increased 5.6 percent in 2000 and an average of 6 percent in the previous five years driven largely by the agrofood sub-sectors and the chemical and cement industries. Government policy gives priority to industries with a high value-added and export potential, such as chemicals, textiles, agro-processing, leather goods and mechanical industries.

In Zimbabwe, industry has been hit by foreign currency and fuel shortages as well as by the slump in domestic demand. Manufactured exports declined due to the overvalued exchange rate, relative to the South African rand, while the steep decline in tourism and construction activity undermined domestic spending power. With manufacturing operating at only half of its installed capacity, the volume of production fell 10 percent in 2000 to its lowest level since the 1970s.

In Kenya, MVA also declined reflecting the water and energy crises that necessitated drastic power-shedding. In Ghana, MVA growth slowed fractionally to 4.6 percent in 2000 from 4.8 percent in 1999, largely as a result of reduced exports, currency depreciation and faster inflation.

One of the most striking developments in African manufacturing in 2000 was the attempt by a section of the textile manufacturing industry in Mauritius to relocate to other African countries. Countries that have benefited from this relocation are Madagascar, Mozambique and Botswana. While Mauritian textile firms were relocating, some of their Zimbabwean counterparts were closing shop. Since 1997, a number of Zimbabwean textile firms have been forced to close and output has declined by a third in response to weak domestic demand and growing difficulty in accessing and competing in the South African market.

Industry structure

Sub-Saharan manufacturing industry, excluding South Africa, is dominated by production for domestic demand and the processing of raw materials for export. Three broad sectors account for over two-thirds of valued-added, with food, beverages and tobacco products contributing the largest share (40.6 percent), followed by clothing, textiles, footwear and leather products (14.3 percent) and chemicals, petroleum refining and coal products (13.9 percent). Food processing is the largest single branch, accounting for 22.9 percent of total MVA in 1996, followed by beverages (13 percent) and textiles (8.9 percent).

Not only do high-technology and capital-intensive activities—other than the processing of raw materials, such as petroleum refining—account for less than 15 percent of MVA, but there has been little expansion of such activities. In 1970, industries such as machinery, transport equipment and professional and scientific equipment, accounted for 5.6 percent of regional MVA, but by 1996 their share had grown by only 1.2 percentage points to 6.8 percent and this was mainly because of increased activity in the transport equipment sector.

There is a consensus that the main problem facing manufacturing in Africa is declining productivity and the non-competitiveness of many activities. The differing productivity outcomes in African and other emerging economies, especially in Asia, may be explained by different patterns of industrial growth. In developed economies, the rapid growth of labor productivity is a reflection of investment in new plant and machinery, the adoption of modern technologies, the restructuring of manufacturing and the focus on skills- and knowledge-intensive production techniques.

Work by Collier and Gunning (1999) suggests that labor productivity in four African countries declined between 1992 and 1996. In Ghana, value-added per worker in the machinery industry declined by 60 percent in 1991-93, while in the furniture industry, productivity declined 39 percent. There is also evidence that low task efficiency is also a major problem for African manufacturing. This is particularly striking when compared to some Asian economies with studies of manufacturing in Ghana, Kenya and Zimbabwe showing that the number of garments produced per 8-hour shift is much lower than in China and India (Biggs and Ratauri 1997).

Mining

Mining continues to be a significant source of foreign exchange in many African countries and indeed drives economic performance in mineral-dependent states like Botswana, Namibia, Zambia and the DRC. Diamonds provide 30 percent of GDP in Botswana, 50 percent of government tax revenues and 75 percent of foreign exchange earnings. In Namibia, diamonds account for 30 percent of export earnings. Gold is the largest foreign exchange earner for Ghana at around 30 percent of the total while in Zambia, copper exports provide 80 percent of foreign earnings.

Despite this, it has long been accepted that Africa's mining output falls well short of its real potential, reflecting a scarcity of capital. Thus, while Africa has 50 percent of known world bauxite reserves it delivers less than 15 percent of world bauxite output. Similarly, with 53 percent of the world's manganese reserves, it produces only 33 percent of the manganese sold on the market.

Although many African countries are significantly endowed with a limited range of mineral ores, they usually lack the other inputs required for the development of strong and broadly-based metals industry. Accordingly, integration is essential for the development of an industrial base that will attract mining investment. In the absence of such industrial integration the fortunes of mining-dependent economies will continue to depend on the vagaries of the unstable global metal markets.

Unfortunately, although many African countries are well endowed with mineral deposits their significance in the world market is diminishing. In 1976, Africa accounted for 61 percent of world gold output but by 2000 its share had slumped to 23 percent—largely reflecting the decline in South African production, whose share of world output has fallen to only 18.5 percent. Ghana, Africa's second largest producer, accounts for just 3 percent of world output while Zimbabwe's market share is only one percent. Output in all these countries is nowhere near its 1970s levels.

A similar decline in production is evident in copper. Zambia and the DRC are currently producing 260,000 tonnes and 30,000 tonnes, respectively—down from 500,000 tonnes and 356,000 tonnes 30 years ago, with enormous reserves still untapped.

In 2000, developments in global prices for metals varied considerably with price of gold stabilizing while the prices of other metals recovered. Gold-dependent countries—Ghana, Mali, Zimbabwe, South Africa and, increasingly, Tanzania —all suffered as a result.

In Zimbabwe, six gold mines ceased operations in 2000 and gold production fell 20 percent. Mining companies blamed the overvalued exchange rate of the Zimbabwe dollar as well as escalating production costs and shortages of elec-

tricity and diesel fuel. Gold producers are required to sell their production to the Reserve Bank, which then exports the gold. Until June, the Bank paid gold producers at the official exchange rate of Z$38:$1, but the mines had to pay parallel market rates of up to Z$70:$1 to buy essential imports such as cyanide. To stem the decline in gold output, the Zimbabwe government announced a new policy to allow gold miners to retain 20 percent of their foreign currency earnings and this was followed by the 24 percent devaluation of the currency in August. Output is estimated to have declined to 22 tonnes in 2000 from 27 tonnes in 1999.

South Africa is well endowed with natural minerals including gold, manganese, platinum, metals, chromium, vanadium and alumino-silicates, as well as sizeable reserves of iron ore, coal, diamonds, uranium, titanium and nickel. A significant proportion of manufacturing activity involves minerals processing and manufacturing contributes 25 percent of GDP, more than any other sector. Although South Africa remains the world's leading producer it is losing market share largely due to high extraction costs.

Though the cost of producing an ounce of gold fell to $240 in 2000, this was achieved only by closing marginal mines with a consequential loss of production. In 2000, output averaged 105 tonnes per quarter which was 13 percent lower than in 1998. Because of this, the industry is restructuring rapidly and seeking lower cost gold deposits elsewhere in Africa in countries such as Mali and Tanzania.

Fortunately, gold price's continued decline was more than offset by major positive developments in other commodities. Platinum and diamond earnings continued to rise and platinum group metals have now displaced gold as the country's largest foreign exchange earner, with estimated earnings of $1.3 billion in 2000. Other metals, including nickel, palladium and zinc are set to become more significant earners, particularly with increased investment in these sectors.

Zambia benefitted from the 16.7 percent recovery in the copper price in 2000 but, despite this, production fell marginally to a low of 256 000 tonnes. The infusion of new capital, following copper privatization in March 2000 is expected to lead to increased production in the region of 300 000 tonnes in 2001. The DRC, which today produces only one-tenth of its 1970 output, was unable to take full advantage of the higher copper price due largely to the civil war.

Energy

Crude oil prices increased from an average of $18 per barrel in 1999 to average $28.5 per barrel in 2000, with divergent impacts on African economies. Net oil exporters gained enormously from increased export earnings and higher government revenues, but importers experienced sharp terms-of-trade deterioration which led to currency depreciation and increased inflation (Table 1.8).

Nigeria, the region's largest producer, raised its exports from 1,699,000 bbl/d in 1996 to 2,198,000 bbl/d at the end of 2000, resulting in total production of 101.06 million metric tonnes at the end of the year (Table 1.8). The 29 percent rise in production combined with more than 50 percent increase in the country's terms of trade was a tremendous boost for the Nigerian economy, leading to faster GDP growth and healthier fiscal and current account balances. Nigeria plans to increase crude oil production by as much as 50 percent by 2002 by providing better funding for the development of new oil and gas fields. At the same time, contracts have been awarded for the repair and maintenance of its

petroleum refineries, which should ensure that downstream supplies return to normal.

In Algeria, crude oil production rose from 783,000 bbl/d in 1996 to 853,000 bbl/d in 2000, with exports increasing more than 50 percent in 2000, propelled largely by sales of oil and natural gas. Similarly, Libya raised its crude oil production from 1,119,000 bbl/day to 1,431,000 bbl/d in the same period and its total exports increased in value by more than 21 percent in 2000. Egypt has expanded its oil refinery capacity and is currently the largest refiner in the region. Not surprisingly, net oil exporting nations enjoyed faster GDP expansion of 4.3 percent in 2000, while in the oil importing countries, growth was only 2.7 percent.

A number of credible exploratory activities in West and Central Africa, particularly offshore, suggest that more discoveries of oil and gas are likely in the near future. Substantial new discoveries of oil have been made in Angola, where an estimated 1.35 billion barrels of oil were discovered in 1999—the third highest in the world after Iran and Saudi Arabia. Angola stands first among non-OPEC nations in terms of new discoveries during the 1990s, with a reserve replacement rate of 397 percent.

South Africa is the region's largest net crude oil importer, followed by Morocco while other major net importers include Côte d'Ivoire, Ghana and Kenya. Rising crude oil prices caused serious economic problems for all these countries. For instance, in Ghana total oil imports rose from $333 million in 1999 to $564 million without any significant change in import volumes. Because the government was reluctant to pass on the increased oil price to consumers in the run-up to elections, it was forced to borrow extensively both domestically and internationally to subsidize fuel supplies. The fall-out from this strategy included a steep

Table 1.8: Crude Oil Production, 1993-2000
(in millions of metric tonnes)

Country	1993	1994	1995	1996	1997	1998	1999	2000[b]
Algeria[a]	36.75	37.24	37.74	40.72	42.21	41.22	37.24	40.06
Angola	24.98	27.61	30.79	34.27	36.25	36.75	38.29	39.40
Cameroon	6.34	6.54	5.05	5.46	6.16	5.07	4.97	4.75
Congo	9.05	9.01	8.77	10.43	12.12	11.82	11.67	11.45
Egypt	46.76	44.79	44.20	45.69	45.69	43.90	42.31	40.97
Equ. Guinea	0.25	0.30	0.40	1.74	2.38	4.12	4.47	...
Gabon	14.90	15.89	17.38	17.83	18.37	17.88	16.88	16.69
Libya[a]	68.03	68.53	70.02	69.03	70.52	69.52	67.04	70.81
Nigeria[a]	94.85	94.35	95.84	106.77	113.22	105.28	97.83	101.06
Tunisia	4.50	4.50	4.17	5.31	5.36	4.02	4.17	3.73
Total Africa	307.78	310.20	316.00	338.48	353.43	340.72	326.02	332.57
OPEC	1,297.02	1,246.91	1,266.57	1,293.14	1,360.75	1,383.03	1,457.52	1,452.11
World[a]	3,233.60	3,278.35	3,342.01	3,465.51	3,580.48	3,648.01	3,587.93	3,737.68

...   Not available
a/ Crude oil and Condensates (excluding Natural Gas Liquids).
b/ Estimates
Source: Petroleum Economist, December 2000, Economist Intelligence Unit and ADB Statistics Division estimates

cedi depreciation in anticipation of a policy reversal, rising inflation and macroeconomic instability.

Although crude oil remains the dominant source of revenue in the energy sector, the energy resources of Africa are immense; they include natural gas, coal, nuclear, tar sand, hydro-electricity, geo-thermal, bio-mass, solar, wind and other renewable energy resources. It is estimated that the region has up to 10.5 billion metric tons of recoverable oil reserves, approximately 8 percent of the world's crude oil reserves in 1994 and 10.2 trillion cubic metres or 7.2 percent of global recoverable natural gas reserves. Africa's uranium deposits are estimated at 431,570 tons or 28.2 percent of world reserves, second only to Australia. Coal reserves are estimated at 61.7 billion tons or 6 percent of world reserves, while exploitable hydro-electric potential is about 1,589 GW, which is about a third of the world's total hydro potential.

Services

In a number of African countries, services are the fastest growing sector of the economy. In the early 1990s, financial services, transport and distribution were the leaders but more recently, tourism and telecommunication have attracted increased interest and investment, some of it, especially in telecommunications, due to privatization.

In North Africa tourism plays a vital role not only in Egypt, which has a long tradition of attracting tourists to its pyramids and other ancient Egyptian monuments, but also in Morocco and Tunisia. These three countries are the largest markets for tourism in North Africa, accounting for more than 99 percent of the region's tourism revenues. Egypt's tourism industry continued to recover from the negative impact of the Luxor attack of November 1997 (see Chapter 2). The contribution of the sector to GDP has reached about 5.6 percent, while the demand for tourism and travel and tourism-related investment accounts for 9 percent of GDP. In Morocco, the tourism sector is flourishing, despite the relative appreciation of the Dirham against the euro. In Tunisia, tourism revenues continued to improve with significant contribution to economic growth. The tourism industry is expected to benefit further from the privatisation of public enterprises, particularly those in construction and tourism.

East Africa is also a major tourist destination, with the industry leaders being Kenya, Uganda, Tanzania, Mauritius, and Seychelles. All the other countries in the sub-region, with the exception of those that are torn by civil strife (such as Somalia) and those that recently engaged in war (Ethiopia and Eritrea), are striving to develop viable tourist sectors. Tourism as an industry is the largest single employer in the world in addition to being a major source of foreign exchange and a growing number of African countries are making efforts to exploit it.

Kenya, Tanzania, Uganda and Mauritius, account for an overwhelming share of the sub-region's tourism revenues. Total tourism receipts

from these countries increased steadily from $1.2 billion in 1995 to $1.6 billion in 2000, though Kenya suffered a setback in the wake of the terrorist bombings that killed and maimed scores of people in 1998. The number of tourist arrivals has since rebounded, with tourism revenues increasing by almost 11 percent in 2000. In Mauritius, tourism revenues increased by 12.2 percent following the end of the drought and the riots that affected the country in 1999. The 1998 terrorist bombings also affected tourism in Tanzania, slowing the rate of industry growth, while Uganda suffered from the adverse publicity surrounding the mass suicides in 1999.

In spite of a huge potential in Madagascar, stemming from its beautiful sights and beaches, tourists have yet to arrive en masse. The country is able to attract only a fraction of the number of tourists that go to Kenya or Mauritius. Weak promotion and international air links with major markets account for the limited tourist interest. However, the government is taking bold steps to reverse this situation, including the establishment of a tourism development committee and tourism agency and allowing freer access to Madagascar by foreign air carriers.

Ethiopia, like Madagascar, has huge tourism potential. In the 1990s, the government adopted policies designed to return tourist levels to those of the 1970s, but the conflict with Eritrea has set back hopes for an early recovery in tourist numbers.

Seychelles, which relies heavily on tourist earnings, is trying to rejuvenate the sector, which has stagnated recently. Earlier development plans projecting a huge increase in tourism failed to achieve their goal and the government is now taking steps to eliminate bureaucratic obstacles that make it difficult for hotels to import food and beverages.

It has also established an advisory board on tourism, including members of the private sector.

To boost productivity and increase competitiveness, African economies must exploit the knowledge revolution. Information and Communications Technology (ICT) services are a promising sources of income and employment generation for countries that are positioned to harness the opportunities arising from the rapidly-changing global ICT market. The value of the global ICT market passed $2 trillion in 1999 and at a growth rate of 10 percent annually is expected to reach $3 trillion by 2004. Telecommunications are now the world's fastest growing sector but African countries account for less than one percent of this burgeoning market.

In Africa as a whole, growth in electronic business has been very slow, with activity concentrated in a handful of markets, dominated by South Africa which has almost 90 percent of the total number of internet hosts in the region. Egypt follows a long way behind with 3 percent and Botswana with 1 percent. Six countries—South Africa, Egypt, Botswana, Zimbabwe, Namibia and Morocco—account for 98 percent of the total number of internet hosts (Table 1.9).

This situation is not dissimilar to telephone line density, mobile telephone density, personal computer density and other yardsticks of electronic market penetration. While, on average, there are 18 main telephone lines per 1000 persons throughout Africa, in South Africa the ratio is much higher at 100 telephone lines. Despite this, less than 5 percent of the population has access to internet services. In North Africa, there are 47 telephone lines per 1000 persons.

While Africa's share of global ICT is small, there are a number of countries where the industry is growing rapidly, including Ghana, Côte

Table 1.9: Internet Users and Services Providers

	Internet Users[1]	% of Population	Internet Services[2] Providers
Algeria	20,000	0.06	2
Botswana	12,000	0.76	6
Cameroon	20,000	0.13	7
Côte d'Ivoire	20,000	0.13	5
Egypt	440,000	0.65	30
Ghana	20,000	0.1	5
Kenya	45,000	0.16	8
Mauritius	55,000	4.66	3
Morocco	120,000	0.4	36
Mozambique	15,000	0.08	4
Nigeria	100,000	0.08	6
Senegal	30,000	0.3	10
South Africa	1,820,000	4.19	61
Tanzania	25,000	0.07	10
Tunisia	110,000	1.16	4
Uganda	25,000	0.11	4
Zambia	15,000	0.16	3
Zimbabwe	30,000	0.27	15

Notes: 1: Estimates, March-June 2000.
             2: April 2000.
Source: Various, Compiled by NUA Internet Surveys;
Mike Jensen: mike@sn.apc.org

d'Ivoire and Kenya. They are expanding their ICT infrastructure at a fast pace, partly as a result of the privatization of telecommunications services. Indeed, in Cape Verde, Central African Republic, Guinea-Bissau, Ghana, Côte d'Ivoire, Madagascar, Sao Tome, South Africa and Senegal, parts of the telecommunications service have been privatised. Sixty percent of the service in Guinea is now in private hands as 30 percent in Ghana.

In the last five years, mobile cellular telephony has grown very rapidly and the service is now available in 42 African countries. Outside South Africa, mobile phone services constitute 20 percent of the total number of telephone connections in the region. In some countries, these services are provided by monopolies, as in Ethiopia and Mauritius, while in others there is significant competition from a number of service providers.

The number of countries providing internet services has increased from 12 in 1996 to cover almost the entire continent. There are currently almost 400 service providers, double the 1998 figure. In several countries, internet service providers (ISPs) enjoy a monopoly, though in a growing number of economies the service is highly competitive with increasing participation from new small private sector ISPs.

E-commerce statistics for South Africa point to rapid expansion with revenues estimated at $1.1 billion in 2000 compared with only $84.7 million in 1997. In many countries, e-commerce has not caught on largely because of limited access to internet facilities and the poor infrastructure for the delivery of goods. Other problems include the limited understanding of the new information economy and the skills required to operate in it erratic power supplies and a poorly developed banking sector that cannot facilitate electronic payments.

Africa's ability to develop and exploit the new information economy depends on increased investment in physical infrastructure on the one hand, allied with substantial investment in skills and technology development on the other. For Africa to cross the digital divide that has opened up, governments must focus on capacity and institution-building programs designed to keep abreast of technological developments in the world. Strategic alliances with overseas partners will play a crucial role backed by the formulation of a supportive, robust and appropriate public policy environment for e-business.

Future Prospects

The Medium-Term Outlook

In 2001, the African economy is to grow 4.1 percent, while real per capita incomes increase 1.8 percent. Stronger expansion in South Africa, steady growth in the other larger economies and the continued strength of some of the continent's smaller economies will underpin this growth. In the continent's largest economy, South Africa, economic recovery is gaining momentum, with the rate of output growth on track to accelerate to 3.5 percent in 2001 from 3 percent in 2000. South Africa's rebound will be driven by robust growth in world output, an improvement in its external competitiveness and the strengthening of its public finances.

Modest economic growth in three other larger economies – Algeria, Egypt and Nigeria – should also contribute to overall regional growth in 2001. Algeria and Nigeria's growth rates are projected to remain slightly above those registered in 2000 at 3.8 percent and 3 percent, respectively. Both countries will continue to benefit from high oil prices and strong oil output growth, though demand pressures and prices will slacken with the anticipated slowdown in global economic growth. The price of oil is expected to average $23 per barrel as against an average of $28.5 per barrel in 2000.

In Nigeria, growth will consolidate in line with the civilian administration's efforts to restore macroeconomic stability, tackle corruption and improve relations with creditors. Performance in

Algeria will be boosted by rapid private sector expansion as well as the positive developments in the oil sector. The new government is poised to accelerate reforms, including the restructuring and privatization of state-owned enterprises, restructuring the banking sector and reducing government's intervention in the economy. Judicial, housing, and land reforms are also envisaged. In Egypt, increased non-traditional exports and the government's commitment to continue economic liberalisation and enhancement of external competitiveness will enable the economy to grow at rough 5 percent as in 2000.

In some of the smaller economies - Botswana, Cameroon, Senegal, Uganda and Tanzania - economic growth is forecast to remain buoyant as macroeconomic and structural reforms impact positively on output and export growth.

Even in conflict countries, growth is expected to accelerate significantly from 2.8 percent in 2000 to 4.8 percent in 2001 following the end of the war between Ethiopia and Eritrea and improved peace prospects in some other conflict areas, particularly the Democratic Republic of Congo. However, the conflict situations in Guinea, Liberia and Burundi remain uncertain and may undermine this optimistic outlook to some degree.

In 2001, the Southern African region will be spared the devastating damage suffered in 2000 from severe flooding, though Mozambique has again experienced abnormally heavy rainfall. Following the reconstruction efforts and emergency assistance projects in Mozambique in the wake of the 2000 flood, the economy is expected to regain the spectacular rates of 8 to10 percent recorded over the preceding four years. The SADC area should benefit from the South Africa-EU free trade agreement, which will facilitate SADC exports to major world markets while improv-

ing access to cheaper, better-quality inputs from the EU. It should also lead to increased flows of European foreign direct investment to the SADC region.

In North Africa, although Morocco remains vulnerable to the vagaries of weather (especially drought), the economy is projected to grow more than six times its 2000 growth rate of 0.8 percent in 2001. Tunisia is projected to grow at 6 percent in 2001, up from 5 percent in 2000, on the strength of good macroeconomic management, better-than-expected rainfall and higher tourism revenues.

Africa's growth will continue to be shaped by developments in commodity prices and export market performance. Continued recovery in prices of non-fuel commodities, especially industrial metals, is expected in 2001, reflecting stronger growth in the EU, though this will be offset to some extent by a weaker US economy and ongoing sluggishness in Japan. The post-Lome Convention Partnership Agreement between the EU and the African, Caribbean and Pacific Group of States (ACP), and improved African access to the US market through the Africa Growth and Opportunity Act (AGOA), should also boost regional export expansion.

Cotton prices should improve in 2001 as all major producers, with the exception of the US, reduce output, while consumption increases, benefiting Mali, Chad, Burkina Faso, Benin, Sudan, Uganda and Tanzania, all of which are expected to have improved growth rates in 2001. Prices for metals such as copper are likely to strengthen on the back of firmer global demand especially in the EU and Asia, benefiting countries like Zambia and the DRC.

The 1999 agreement of 15 European central banks to limit gold sales over the 5 years to 2004 and the decision that gold should remain an important element of global monetary reserves may help to stabilise gold prices in 2001, though prices remained weak early in the year. Potential beneficiaries include South Africa, Mali, Ghana, Tanzania and Zimbabwe. Botswana, Angola, DRC, Namibia and Sierra Leone will continue to benefit from higher diamond prices and strong global demand.

Reduced production, the agreement between Malaysia and Thailand following the demise of the International Natural Rubber Organisation (INRO), higher prices for competing products, such as petroleum, and a seasonal fall in supplies, should combine to push up rubber prices in 2001.

Beverage prices seem destined to remain depressed. Improved weather conditions point to increased coffee supply in 2001 and prices are unlikely to recover significantly, despite the recent agreement among major exporters to withhold surpluses from global markets. Leading coffee exporters, including Burundi, Ethiopia, Kenya, Uganda, Rwanda and Madagascar, will be adversely affected. Although the price of cocoa is expected to recover slowly over the next few years from the lows experienced in 2000, cocoa earnings of major exporters like Cote d'Ivoire, Ghana and Sao Tome and Principe will remain depressed.

Higher growth rates in Africa in the medium to long term depend on the continued commitment of governments to economic reform programs. Inconsistent and delayed responses to reform initiatives put pressure on governments to adopt more short-termist policies, especially when economic and political reforms are undertaken in tandem. A good example is Zimbabwe where, in the face of political instability caused by the land reform program, the government abandoned some of its macroeconomic reforms, notably in respect of exchange rate management and interest rate policy.

In South Africa, there are concerns that the government will come under considerable pressure from trade unions to move away from its liberal macroeconomic policies in an attempt to secure rapid improvements in living standards and accelerated job creation. While the South African government is committed to maintaining the reform process, it is uncertain how institutional change in such areas as privatization will be managed. Thus, while a policy reversal in South Africa is unlikely (especially with improvements in external competitiveness and expected inflows of foreign investment), the speed with which reform will be carried out will be largely determined by the relative strengths of the various interest groups.

Despite the brighter economic outlook for the continent, the fact remains that the expected recovery still falls far short of what is needed to improve the living conditions of millions of Africans and sustain the region's structural transformation. Over 50 percent of the African population, or some 300 million people, live below the poverty line. The overriding objective of development in Africa is poverty reduction, with the international community having set a target of halving the incidence of poverty by 2015.

Reducing poverty will require actions on three major fronts:

- promoting broad based growth through mobilising resources for development;
- tackling issues related to human development, particularly HIV/AIDS; and
- promoting good governance.

Key issues for medium- to long-term growth and development

Mobilizing resources for development

It has been calculated that for *per capita* consumption to rise to a minimum of $1 per day within the next fifteen years, countries must, on the average, grow at 7 to 8 percent annually. For Africa to grow at 6 percent a year over ten years, investment ratios will have to rise sharply (Box 1.3). Using varying investment/GDP ratios (22-25 percent) and an initial savings rate of 13 percent (rising to 18 percent) it is estimated that net official capital inflows must at least double from the current $9.5 billion a year. This calculation assumes that the proportion of the capital inflows used for real resource transfers would be around 62 percent with the balance utilized to finance financial transactions and reserve accumulation. Doubling net capital inflows to $20 billion will increase the investment ratio to 27 percent of GDP which would be enough to halve the number of Africans living in poverty by 2015.

In the absence of radical policy and institutional developments, rising poverty rates would mean that the growth of domestic financial assets among households will be far slower in the coming years than it is presently and also far less than is required for the acceptable growth rates. The situation is made worse by the fact that various structural and institutional factors keep households from monetizing their assets. There is ample evidence that financial sector reforms of the last decade have failed to achieve the projected increase in resource mobilization in most countries. Fragmented market structures and high transaction costs constrain the processes of financial intermediation and savings mobilization – a situation unlikely to improve in the absence of far-reaching structural change in the African economies.

Over the medium-term, prospects for significantly increased official development assistance are poor. Despite the very strong case made for a doubling of aid to Africa in order to generate the growth that will attract private capital flows, there is still widespread skepticism over the willingness and capacity of donors and multilateral institutions to respond positively to that call. Frequent reference to aid fatigue and the aid dependency syndrome are perceived as indicators of a growing unwillingness to raise aid volumes significantly in the medium term.

The prospects for foreign direct investment (FDI) and other private capital flows vary between countries. Only a handful of African countries – mostly South Africa and those with rich energy oil and gas resources - have in the past managed to attract significant inflows of private capital. The combination of perceived high levels of risk and weak institutions has deterred foreign investors and lenders. While the reversal of capital flight would provide increased finance for a number of countries, this will only be achieved after the necessary reforms have been undertaken. The conditions that will lead to the attraction of private foreign capital are the same as those necessary to reverse capital flight.

Increasingly, many groups both within and outside of Africa are focusing on debt relief as a major source of finance. Debt relief for Africa has been placed on the agenda of most major international meetings to discuss global development, including those of the G-7 countries. During the UN Millennium General Assembly, debt relief for impoverished nations was one of the highest profile issues. The focus on debt relief in

Box 1.3: Issues on the Determinants and Productivity of Investment in Africa

Over the past two-and-a half decades, African countries have recorded declining investment rates. Gross domestic investment declined steadily from about 26.5 percent of GDP in 1980 to 22 percent in 1990. After more than a decade of donor-supported market-oriented reforms aimed at improving both the macro and microeconomic environments, investment rates remained as low as 20 percent of GDP in Africa with low-income countries averaging 16 percent investment rate. The desire to explain the weak response of investment to economic reforms in the 1980s and 1990s, and to diagnose the failure of international assistance to improve investment, generated a sizeable amount of research that explore the determines of investment and issues pertaining to its productivity. This Box provides a summary of some of the most recent papers on these issues.

Investment Determinants

A paper by Mlambo and Oshikoya (2001) argues that Africa's investment ratio is still not sufficient to replace depreciated physical and human capital, and that both domestic and foreign investment must be mobilised if the Continent is to be recapitalised to the level which is compatible with sustained economic growth. The paper states that low investment rates are a problem not only because investment matters for growth, but also because low investment rates increase vulnerability. Drawing on both the theoretical literature and empirical evidence, the paper examines whether standard macroeconomic factors can explain why Africa is undercapitalised relative to other developing regions. By performing a standard cross-country investment regression for the 1970-96 period, the paper shows that macroeconomic factors robustly affect private investment growth. It is found that the standard macroeconomic policy variables, such as exchange rates and trade policy, fiscal and monetary policies, and public service provision explain a substantial part of the weak investment performance. Particularly, there is some strong evidence on the impact of fiscal deficit, domestic credit to the private sector, the real exchange rate and macroeconomic uncertainty.

The paper concludes that the establishment of a sound macroeconomic framework is a prerequisite for sustained investment recovery in Africa. It argues that in order to encourage investment, the stability and predictability of the incentive framework—relative prices, interest rates, exchange rate, etc.—might be more important than the level of incentives themselves. The paper points out the need for accelerating public sector policy reforms, especially in enhancing the privatisation and divestiture process, and for enhancing financial sector reform by restructuring the banking system, strengthening prudential regulation and supervision, as well as deepening the capital markets.

The Productivity of Investment

While the paper by Mlambo and Oshikoya focuses on the macroeconomic determinants of low investment in Africa, the paper by Devarajan, Easterly and Pack (2001) challenges the notion that investment in Africa is too low. Rather, the paper argues that it is the productivity of investment that is too low, and this is symptomatic of low capacity utilisation and shortage of skills. The paper investigates the productivity of investment in Africa using macro and micro evidence, and concludes that the direct and indirect evidence of overall poor returns to investment in Africa contradicts the notion that investment was too low in Africa. Higher investment would not have had a high payoff.

The paper by Devarajan et. al (2001) uses cross-country regressions for 29 African countries to explore whether public and private investment had a positive and significant effect on growth in Africa. The paper finds that public investment is not correlated with growth in Africa, as there is no discernible association between growth and public investment. The only country with high public investment and exceptional growth is Lesotho. According to the paper, the unproductive nature of public investment appears to be across the board. On the other hand, private investment has a significant positive and strong effect on growth, even after controlling for its endogeneity. However, this result is also not robust if Botswana is excluded from the sample. As Botswana is the only country

Box 1.3: (Continued)

in Africa to have high private investment rates and high growth, private investment is also not correlated with growth unless Botswana is included in the sample.

To further investigate the low returns to investment in Africa, the paper focuses on the productivity of manufacturing investment in Tanzania. It is argued that the problem in Tanzania is that of low productivity, and if this result could be generalised, it this factor which may help explain why the correlation between investment (both private and public) and growth in cross-country regressions turns out to be weak. The paper concludes that several factors, including public policies, insulation from market forces, weak technological capacity rendered manufacturing capital in Tanzania unproductive. The suggestion here is that unless the factors behind the low productivity of investment are understood, calling for increased investment to achieve higher growth rates in Africa may be misplaced.

The Foreign Exchange Productivity of Investment

A paper by Hussain (2000) argues that, in African countries where foreign exchange is the binding constraint, emphasis must not be placed on the productivity of investment per se, but rather on the foreign exchange productivity of investment. In contrast to the dominant development philosophy that emphasizes investment in human and physical capital, the paper argues that in the absence of strong export performance, such investments will be curtailed by the lack of sufficient foreign exchange. Hence, a growth strategy that concentrates on expanding investment in human and physical capital without due regard to the 'the foreign exchange productivity of investment' will be short-lived because the balance of payments constraint will eventually put an end to such an expansion, rendering domestic resources, including human capital, underutilized.

The paper postulates that fast and sustained growth necessitates lifting the balance of payments constraint on growth by producing the goods and services that are attractive to the domestic as well as foreign markets. The fundamental objective for countries striving for growth and poverty reduction is to adopt macroeconomic and sectoral policies that reduce the income elasticity of demand for imports and/or increase the income elasticity of demand for exports. This suggests a model of socio-economic development, which is firmly anchored on the promotion of income-attractive importable and exportable goods. Regulatory, investment and trade policies, the pursuit of good governance, institutional building, infrastructure development, and human capital formation, all must be designed and implemented with this fundamental objective in mind.

The paper concludes that if the ultimate goal of foreign assistance is to help poor countries graduate to a self-sustaining growth path, the effectiveness of foreign assistance must be assessed with reference to two yardsticks. First, the development effectiveness of foreign aid should be measured in terms of its ability to promote export growth relative to that of imports in the recipient country and/or create the conditions that will attract private long-term capital. The second is that, even in the case of private capital its development effectiveness must also be measured in terms of their contribution to expanding export earnings relative to imports.

Source: Mlambo and Oshikoya (2001); Devarajan, Easterly and Pack (2001); Hussain (2000).

different forms, including debt forgiveness, has received considerable attention largely as a result of the pressures from NGOs, governments and humanitarian international agencies.

Despite this, the resulting initiatives such as the original HIPC and its enhanced successor are often perceived to be inadequate for addressing the problems, in view of the magnitude and scope of the problem. Accordingly, unless debt relief is structured in such a way as to reduce significantly the external debt burden of African countries, while promoting growth and poverty alleviation, it is unlikely that significant additional finance for African development will be found.

Although it is essential to mobilize domestic resources in order to reduce the size of the financial resource gap facing most countries, the extent of structural constraints within African economies suggest that this is likely to prove feasible only in the long term. The implication is that there is an urgent need to increase the flow of external resources. (see Box 1.4).

HIV/AIDS threatens Africa's future growth

Rapid and sustained economic growth is necessary to attain the goal of reducing by half the number of people living in poverty by 2015. Efforts to achieve broad-based economic growth must be complemented by high and sustained investment in social capital (especially in basic education, public health and nutrition, housing and sanitation), productive activities and infrastructure. Investing in the enhancement of human capital is crucial both to reduce poverty and to directly improve people's living standards.

The socio-economic impact of the HIV/AIDS pandemic in Africa is increasingly severe. By the end of 2000, there were 36.1 million people

around the world living with HIV/AIDS, of which 70 percent (25.3 million) were in Africa south of the Sahara (Table 1.10). Sub-Saharan Africa is home to 80 percent of the children living with HIV in the world and three-quarters of the more than 20 million people world-wide who have died of AIDS since the epidemic began, lived in Africa.

In 2000 alone, 3.8 million people in Sub-Saharan Africa were infected with the HIV while 2.4 million people at a more advanced stage of infection died of HIV-related illnesses. The most seriously affected regions are Southern and Eastern Africa, with infection rates ranging from 8 percent of the adult population in Tanzania to 20 percent in South Africa and Zambia, 25 percent in Swaziland and Zimbabwe and 36 percent in Botswana. In the Central and Western regions, with the exception of the Central African Republic (13.8 percent) and Côte d'Ivoire (10.7 percent), prevalence rates are far lower, ranging from 6.4 percent in Burkina Faso to 1.3 percent in Niger. In North Africa, HIV prevalence rates are very low, varying between 0.9 percent in Sudan and 0.2 percent in Egypt.

The implications of this for African countries are ominous. The epidemic is reversing progress in human capital formation by affecting individuals at ages when they are most industrious and productive. It is undermining education and hence the potential to expand skills as quickly as they are needed. Already, Botswana is being forced to import white-collar skills as a result of the impact of AIDS on the supply of trained workers. Also Botswana's Human Development Index (HDI) declined 9 percent during the 1990s despite growth of 15 percent in income per head.

The disease is also changing the age and sex structure of the population. At the end of 1999 there were 8.2 million children aged less than 15

Box1.4: Innovative Ways to Finance Development In Africa

In order to reduce the domestic resource gap in Africa and then attract the required external resources, African Finance Ministers meeting at the behest of the ECA in Addis Ababa in November 2000 agreed on the following innovative measures:

1. Improve the generation of financial resources from domestic assets in the medium to long term. Governments should take steps to:
    -   Reduce the risks associated with rural production (e.g. seasonality of rainfall) possibly through improved irrigation and other infrastructure, and the application of improved and appropriate technology. This will reduce significantly the higher liquidity preference of households, at the same time raising incomes in the medium term.
    -   Stabilize the macroeconomic environment that ensures that the returns on financial assets are relatively stable and predictable.
    -   Reduce the transaction costs of holding financial assets through the development of appropriate institutions such as microfinance institutions.

2. Facilitate the growth of exports in the short to medium term. To achieve this African governments should pay attention to:
    -   The pace, sequencing and phasing of trade liberalization with a view to generating early supply response.
    -   The development of export promotion and import substitution policies in a complementary manner.
    -   The re-building of the primary commodity export sector and creating of capacity for processing export commodities.
    -   The raising of the competitiveness and technological capability of industrial firms in view of the pressing need for export diversification.
    -   Pursuing a temporary and strictly time bound protection for selected industries.
    -   Designing forward-looking industrialization strategies with a well-formulated and coherently executed industrial and technology policy.
    -   Pursuing regional integration, which offers significant opportunity for the expansion of exports for most countries.

3. Attract additional official development assistance. The objective is to make aid provide about 95% of the new required external finance after reducing the resource gap through trade, while the remainder is drawn from the private sector. At the end of 15 years, most inflows should have private origins and aid would be entirely absent. African governments and their development partners need to do the following in order to expand aid inflows:
    -   Improve aid effectiveness while institutions for aid management must be made transparent.
    -   Increase specialisation among donors which will see the World Bank, African Development Bank and the European Union pay greater attention to the finance of regional infrastructure projects, based on the understanding that regional integration is the most feasible path to the transformation of economic structures in the region.

4. Attract Increasing Foreign Direct Investment and Other Private Capital. While this can immediately make up for the remaining 5% of required external funds, the objective is to make private capital provide 70% of external finance in the medium term and 100% in the long term. Concerted actions need to be taken by African governments on many fronts, including:
    -   Improving infrastructure, strengthening banking systems, developing capital markets by accelerating the pace of privatization and broadening the domestic investor base, and developing an appropriate regulatory framework and a more liberal investment regime.
    -   Introducing competitive labor market policies while creating and maintaining institutions for upgrading human capital, and

Box1.4: (Continued)

reforming the judiciary system and containing corruption. It is important that these are carried out in a comprehensive framework and not in a piecemeal manner.

- Countries must have a strategic framework for industrial development and make clear choices about where and how they want foreign participation; these choices can then be reflected in the various incentive packages that countries may offer.

- Countries must have fairly stable macroeconomic regimes, governed in a transparent manner that keeps exchange rates stable. Exchange rate determination must not be dogmatic but based on country capacity and its position in the world market.

- Financial systems must be made more robust and in tune with global developments. There is no question about whether capital accounts should be opened. It is more a question of the extent and the conditions under which this should take place.

5. Let Debt Relief Enhance Growth. It is observed from the enhanced HIPC initiative that countries will continue to borrow even as they receive relief in order to settle other obligations in the pursuit of poverty-reduction goals. It is important that payments on these do not slow down growth. The main issue is how to make debt relief growth enhancing in order to facilitate the achievement of sustained poverty-reduction. To this end,

- Creditor countries must recognize debt-relief as additional to new and increased ODA with a focus on enhancing and sustaining both growth and poverty-reduction explicitly.

- Making debt-relief pro-growth requires that relief must come early rather than later. There is a tension between quick debt relief and comprehensive country-owned poverty-reduction strategies. The solution to this problem is to make countries focus on their medium and long term development frameworks, showing the anticipated growth paths and how these provide for poverty reduction.

- A part of the freed-up resources from debt relief must be channeled to the private sector for job creation purposes. Governments have to exploit such mechanisms as debt-equity swaps inasmuch as they promote private investment.

- Improved debt management in African countries is very essential. Governments need to monitor closely future borrowing in order to prevent a re-occurrence of the debt problems.

6. Encourage A New Financial Architecture that Addresses Africa's Peculiar Problems. The reform of international financial institutions must be done with a view to developing a more level playing field in the implementation of a rule-based system for managing international capital flows. African countries must also have a greater say in the functioning of a more transparent International Financial Institutions' structure.

Source: ECA (2000).

Table 1.10: Estimation (%) of HIV/AIDS Prevalence
Among Adults (15-45 years) by Country

Country	2000
Algeria	0.07
Angola	2.78
Benin	2.45
Botswana	35.8
Burkina Faso	6.44
Burundi	11.32
Chad	2.69
Cameroon	7.73
Cape Verde	..
Central African Republic	13.8
Comoros	0.12
Congo	6.43
Congo (DRC)	5.07
Côte d'Ivoire	10.76
Djibouti	11.75
Egypt	0.02
Equat. Guinea	0.51
Eritrea	2.87
Ethiopia	10.63
Gabon	4.16
Gambia	1.95
Ghana	3.6
Guinea	1.54
Guinea Bissau	2.5
Kenya	13.95
Lesotho	23.57
Liberia	2.8
Libya	0.05
Madagascar	0.15
Malawi	15.96
Mali	2.03
Mauritania	0.52
Mauritius	0.08
Morocco	0.03
Mozambique	13.22
Namibia	19.54
Niger	1.35
Nigeria	5.06
Rwanda	11.21
São T. & Principe	..
Senegal	1.77
Seychelles	..
Sierra Leone	2.99
Somalia	..
South Africa	19.94
Sudan	0.99
Swaziland	.25
Tanzania	58.09
Togo	5.98
Tunisia	0.04
Uganda	8.3
Zambia	19.95
Zimbabwe	25.06

.. no data.
Source: UNAIDS (2000), Report on the Global HIV/AIDS
Epidemic.

years who were AIDS orphans - 90 percent of them in Sub-Saharan Africa. This has contributed to the problem of street children and the social consequences of begging, theft, delinquency, violence, alcoholism, drug abuse, prostitution and rape. Africa's hard-won gains in life expectancy, an important measure of human development, are being eroded in the severely affected countries, where life expectancy has declined from 45-60 years in 1985 to 38-50 years in 2000. By 2010, life expectancy in the most seriously affected countries will have halved to around 30 years from 60 years in the mid-1980s.

HIV/AIDS will also have a significant impact on social service delivery system. In Ethiopia, keeping a child in an orphanage costs between $300 and $500 a year – more than three times the present national income per capita. Due to an estimated 5 to 10-year time lag between infection and death, the number of people infected with AIDS will continue to grow even assuming a decline in new HIV infections. The burden will be extremely heavy, both in terms of direct costs for treatment as well as the indirect impact on productivity and human suffering.

Direct costs of the epidemic are the huge medical expenses necessary to care for AIDS patients, while indirect costs include the increasing number of young people who can no longer participate in productive activities. The demands on the health sector for treatments of AIDS-related illnesses will overstretch already-inadequate healthcare budgets in most African countries, accounting for between 20 and 90 percent of health budgets.

The losses from absenteeism, in labor productivity and income will ultimately affect savings at all levels of the economy, in turn slowing long-term investment. In South Africa, estimates show that overall economic growth rate over the next decade will be 0.3 to 0.4 percentage points a year lower than it would have been without AIDS. Cumulating the impact by 2010, real GDP will be 17 percent below what it would have been in the absence of AIDS. In 2000 values, this represents a loss of some $22 billion - more than twice the entire national production of any other country in the region except Nigeria.

If countries with low HIV infection rates are able to avoid the worst of the epidemic, then there may well be a shift of investment from Southern and East Africa to the North and West over the next 20 years. If the spread of the disease is not checked and reversed, the continent will lose qualified employees who are already in scarce supply, thereby slowing economic growth and denting productivity. Estimates indicate that in the most seriously affected countries, GDP per capita will be 5 percent lower by 2010 than would have been the case without AIDS.

The impact of AIDS on Africa's agricultural sector, in particular, is likely to be severe. The Zimbabwe Commercial Farmers Union estimates that the AIDS-related reduction in maize output could reach 60 percent, while in cotton it is projected at 50 percent. There have been forecasts suggesting that African GDP growth could be lowered by as much as 25 percent over the next 20 years or approximately one percent annually.

By 2020, the labour force in high HIV-prevalence countries would be between 10 and 22 percent lower than it would have been without the disease. Furthermore, productivity will decline as younger, less experienced employees replace experienced workers, while the shortage of skills will lead to higher production costs. Business costs will rise as firms are forced to pick up an increased proportion of employee healthcare costs and deal with the impact of absenteeism and lower productivity.

Some countries, notably Senegal and Uganda, have demonstrated that it is possible to control the spread of the epidemic through effective prevention and AIDS awareness programs, provided this is driven by political commitment at the highest level. In contrast to the response in many African countries, Senegalese leaders did not deny the existence of the HIV/AIDS pandemic and hence faced the challenge from the start. The country enlisted all major sectors as allies in a timely and aggressive prevention campaign, as a result of which Senegal now has one of the lowest HIV infection rates in Africa of 1.8 percent of the adult population (as at June 2000).

Estimates indicate that at least $1.5 billion a year is needed to achieve massively higher levels of implementation of all the major components of successful prevention programs for the whole of Sub-Saharan Africa. While action at the international level to develop an AIDS vaccine is crucial for the future, experience has shown that what will really make a difference in the short term is effective leadership and societal change to prevent the spread of HIV, along with effective healthcare for those already infected. This involves confronting taboos about sexuality, while targeting information and support to high-risk groups, such as prostitutes, and providing compassionate care for AIDS sufferers. This is where international assistance is urgently needed. The African Development Bank Group has formulated an HIV/AIDS strategy for its operations, involving the mainstreaming of HIV/AIDS preventive and care activities in relevant social sector policies, programs and projects.

CHAPTER 2
Regional Economic Profiles

Introduction

Chapter 1 reviews economic performance in Africa from an overall continental perspective. To complement this review, Chapter 2 focuses on regional economic perspectives with an analysis of the five sub-regional groupings into which Bank Group operations are classified—Central Africa, East Africa, North Africa, Southern Africa and West Africa. It provides an overview of the five sub-regional economies, recent economic trends, policy developments and the outlook for the years immediately ahead.

Table 2.1 summarizes the sub-regions' real GDP growth rates showing that the pace of expansion accelerated in four of the five sub-regions—the exception being East Africa. North Africa recorded the highest growth in 2000 at 4.1 percent, up from 3.8 percent in 1999, but in East Africa expansion slowed to 3.8 percent in 2000 from 4.5 percent the previous year. Growth in West Africa accelerated to 3.1 percent from 2.8 percent in 1999. Southern Africa's GDP increased 2.6 percent in 2000, up from 2.1 percent the previous year, but in Central Africa output increased only 0.0 percent in 2000, though this was a significant improvement from the 4 percent contraction experienced in 1999.

Table 2.1: Real GDP Growth Rates by Sub-Region, 1996-2000

	1996	1997	1998	1999	2000[a/]
Central	1.7	0.6	2.2	-4.0	0.0
Eastern	6.4	3.9	2.5	4.5	3.8
Northern	6.1	2.8	4.5	3.8	4.1
Southern	5.0	3.2	1.6	2.1	2.6
Western	4.9	4.5	3.5	2.8	3.1
Franc Zone	4.8	5.7	4.8	2.7	2.9
Net Oil Exporters	4.6	3.6	3.6	3.7	4.1
Net Oil Importers	5.8	2.8	2.9	2.1	2.6
ALL RMCs	5.3	3.2	3.2	2.7	3.2

Note: a/ Preliminary estimates.
Source: ADB Statistics Division.

Central Africa

Central Africa is made up of ten countries— Burundi, Cameroon, Central African Republic (CAR), Chad, Congo, the Democratic Republic of Congo (DRC), Equatorial Guinea, Gabon, Rwanda and Sao Tome and Principe. Six of them—Cameroon, CAR, Chad, Congo, Gabon, and, Equatorial Guinea belong to the Communauté économique et monétaire de l'Afrique centrale (CEMAC), which is part of CFA franc zone. CEMAC has a regional central bank, the Banque des états de l'Afrique centrale (BEAC), based in Yaounde, while the other countries have their own national central banks. With the launch of the Euro in January 1999, the CFA franc's peg was automatically switched from the French franc to the euro at a fixed rate of CFAfr656: €1. Three countries—Burundi, Democratic Republic of Congo, and Rwanda—are members of the Com-

mon Market for Eastern and Southern Africa, COMESA.

The Central Africa region has a combined population of 97.2 million people and accounted for 5.7 percent of Africa's GDP in 2000. Per capita GDP in the region fell from $289.3 in 1999 to $269.8 in 2000, mainly due to the intensification of conflict that is undermining economic performance in most countries in the region. The most serious of these conflicts has been the DRC civil war—known as "Africa's seven-nation war" — but Congo, Guinea Bissau, and Burundi have also been embroiled in military campaigns.

As a result, the region has failed to fully exploit its abundant natural resources and rich agricultural land. Gabon and Cameroon are substantial oil exporters, while the DRC used to be a major exporter of minerals, notably copper, cobalt, and diamonds. Rwanda and Burundi rely on coffee exports, while the recent discovery of rich oil deposits in Equatorial Guinea and Chad has the po-

Table 2.2: Central Africa: Macroeconomic Indicators, 1990-2000

Indicators	1990	1995	1996	1997	1998	1999	2000[a/]
Real GDP Growth Rate (%)	-4.6	3.4	1.7	0.6	2.2	-4.0	0.0
GDP Per Capita (US $)	494.3	318.7	329.6	323.5	309.0	289.3	269.8
Inflation (%)	10.8	48.7	36.6	19.8	14.4	17.6	28.4
Fiscal Balance (% of GDP)	-7.6	-3.9	-3.8	-3.7	-7.4	-6.2	-2.9
Gross Domestic Investment (% of GDP)	15.0	17.0	17.5	17.9	21.1	17.5	16.2
Gross National Savings (% of GDP)	15.7	13.3	12.4	11.8	8.9	13.0	13.3
Real Export Growth (%)	1.9	1.8	1.9	1.8	1.6	1.9	1.7
Trade Balance (% GDP)	9.8	11.9	13.7	13.8	7.4	13.0	24.6
Current Account (% GDP)	-5.6	-3.9	-4.6	-5.9	-11.4	-6.2	-4.2
Terms of Trade (%)	-3.6	0.2	12.7	-1.1	-17.9	16.4	25.4
Total External Debt (% GDP)	69.7	130.1	121.2	122.2	134.6	139.1	128.6
Debt Service (% of Exports)	17.4	22.5	25.8	25.1	21.9	15.4	...

Note: a/ Preliminary estimates.
Source: ADB Statistics Division and IMF.

tential of transforming these countries from aid-dependence to self-sustained growth. However, political problems and armed conflict continue to divert resources from productive endeavors, threatening to derail the region's economic and social progress for some time to come.

Recent Economic Trends

Following a severe recession in 1999 when real GDP declined by 4 percent, the region's economy recorded no growth in 2000 (see Table 2.2 and Figure 2.1). Coming out of contraction was attributable to a strong performance by oil exporters in the region whose export revenues were boosted by buoyant prices on the global market in 2000, which more than offset the slowdown in conflict countries. The combined economies of the oil exporters—Cameroon, Gabon, Congo, and Equatorial Guinea—represent some 80 percent of the regional economy.

In 2000, Cameroon, the region's largest economy, accounting for more than 44 percent of GDP, grew by an estimated 4.2 percent, slightly down from 4.4 percent recorded in 1999 (Figure 2.2). This was due largely to the sharp increase in oil prices, increased investment in the privatized industries and public investment in infrastructure, along with the continued recovery in timber prices. These two commodities contribute more than a third of Cameroon's export earnings, but these gains were partially offset by the slump in prices of its other leading exports—coffee and cocoa. Economic growth was boosted also by the successful completion of a three-year adjustment program that has led to increased international confidence and improved access to global financial markets.

On international markets, cocoa prices have halved in the last two years. In an effort to stabi-

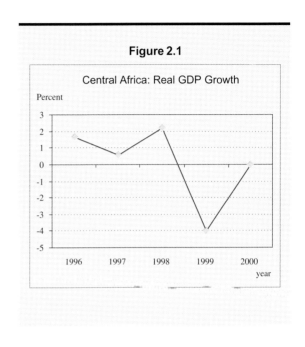

Figure 2.1

Central Africa: Real GDP Growth

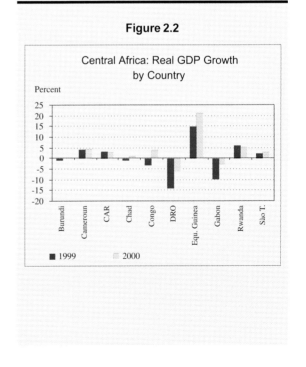

Figure 2.2

Central Africa: Real GDP Growth by Country

lize the market, Cameroon, Ghana, Côte d'Ivoire, and Nigeria (which together produce two-thirds of the world's supply of cocoa), agreed to destroy some of next season's output. Under this agreement, each country will receive a fixed quota and reduce its excess output. However, negotiations were temporarily disrupted because of the political crisis in Côte d'Ivoire. Meanwhile, Cameroon has developed its own plan to deal with the crisis which involves a tax on cocoa processors, with the proceeds being used to purchase and destroy surplus cocoa.

In 1999, Gabon, the region's second largest economy, contracted by 9.6 percent following the severe depression of 1998, reduced oil output, the fall in timber prices and drastic cuts in public investment. Despite higher oil prices and the robust performance of the forestry and wood-processing sector, the depression continued in 2000, particularly in construction and public works, leading to a further 2.9 percent contraction in real GDP.

The decline in non-oil activities arose from the drastic cutback in public investment spending necessitated by government overspending in the run-up to the 1998 elections. Oil production declined further, which together with weak domestic demand and the sluggish performance of the non-oil sector during the first half of the year —also the result of lower levels of public investment— contributed to the disappointing economic performance in 2000.

The third largest economy in the region, Congo, recovered strongly in 2000, when GDP is estimated to have increased 3.8 percent compared with a decline of 3 percent the previous year. The surge in oil prices boosted government revenues and encouraged oil companies to step up their spending on exploration and development. The timber sector also expanded as world market prices recovered and as domestic concern over the en-

vironmental impact of large-scale logging diminished. Non-oil sectors benefited also from the resumption of transport activities and the improved security in the country.

Equatorial Guinea continued its stellar performance in 2000. Ever since the discovery of oil, economic activity has expanded at phenomenal rates, with an average annual growth rate of more than 20 percent during the mid 1990s. In 2000, this trend was maintained with GDP expanding 21.3 percent compared with 15.1 percent in 1999. Growth was driven by increased oil production and higher prices as well as by substantial oil industry investment, which had positive spillover effects on the construction and service sectors.

Rwanda has recently recorded high growth rates due to growing interest from foreign investors, particularly from South Africa, as well as increased foreign aid. Both agriculture and services grew strongly in 2000 and after virtually halving in the early 1990s due to domestic conflict, GDP has expanded at the impressive average annual rate of 14.6 percent between 1995 and 1999. In 2000, however, the economy lost momentum with growth slowing to 5.5 percent from 6.1 percent in 1999. The main culprit was the depressed price of Rwanda's chief export, coffee.

In Chad, GDP reversed the 0.7 percent decline experienced in 1999, growing one percent in 2000 reflecting increased cotton production and prices as well as a strong investment recovery after the sharp contraction in 1999. The recent discovery of oil is expected to boost economic growth considerably in the early years of the 21st century. Burundi has underperformed relative to other countries in the region due to the civil war. Output stagnated in 2000 with zero growth following a one percent decline in 1999 and 4.8 percent growth in 1998. Drought and insecurity adversely affected the farming sector in 2000, but there was a modest upturn in manufacturing and services.

Sao Tome and Principe also recorded modest growth due partly to low prices for its main export commodity, cocoa. In 2000, its economy is estimated to have expanded by 3 percent against 2.5 percent in 1999, driven by expansion in the services sector and increased development assistance.

With the exception of 1996, the CAR has performed impressively since the 1994 devaluation of the CFA franc, benefitting from the implementation of reforms. However, in 2000 the economy was adversely affected by the high oil price, further compounded by trade disruption as a result of war in neighboring Congo. This growth in the CAR in 2000 is estimated to have fallen to 2.9 percent from 3.4 percent in 1999.

GDP in the Democratic Republic of Congo (DRC), is estimated to have declined some 6.5 percent in 2000 after a 14 percent slump in 1999 caused by the civil war that broke out in mid-1998. The simmering conflict is to blame for the loss of business confidence, a chronic shortage of foreign exchange and disarray in the diamond sector. Despite the conflict, cobalt and copper production increased modestly in 2000.

The External Accounts

Central Africa's exports are made up almost entirely of primary commodities—oil, cocoa, cotton, timber, copper and cobalt. After the price slide in 1998/99, oil exporters are enjoying the fruits of one of the fastest and steepest recoveries in oil prices in years, though the signs are that the price has now peaked and lower average prices are expected through 2001.

Exporters of primary agricultural commodities have been less fortunate, especially those that rely on coffee and cocoa, whose prices continued to decline during 2000. Because the positive oil price effect outweighed the downturn in beverage prices, the region's trade balance improved sharply in 2000 to 24.6 percent of GDP from 13 percent in 1999 (Figure 2.3). But both the trade balance and the current account deficit of agricultural exporters deteriorated in 2000.

All the oil exporters were in surplus on visible trade. Cameroon recorded a trade surplus of $0.43 billion (5.1 percent of GDP), while in Equatorial Guinea the surplus was $0.87 billion (79.9 percent of GDP), Gabon $2.04 (41 percent of GDP), Congo $1.53 billion (56.7 percent of GDP), and the DRC $0.54 billion (12 percent of GDP). Burundi ran a trade deficit of $0.06 billion (8.8 percent of GDP), Chad $0.04 billion (3 percent of GDP), Rwanda $0.16 billion (9 percent of GDP), and Sao Tome and Principe $0.02 billion (44 percent of GDP).

The entire region was in deficit on the current account of its balance-of-payments in 2000 to the extent of -4.2 percent of GDP, down slightly from 6.2 percent the previous year (Figure 2.4). All the countries in the region recorded current account deficits except Equatorial Guinea and Gabon. Equatorial Guinea built up a current account surplus of 17.2 percent of GDP, up dramatically from only 2.7 percent in 1999, while Gabon's current account surplus was 4.3 percent in 2000 compared with 1.9 percent the previous year.

Sao Tome and Principe registered the largest current account deficit at 48.8 percent of GDP, followed by the DRC (16 percent), Rwanda (12.6 percent), Chad (11.7 percent), Burundi (7.9 percent), Central African Republic (6.4 percent), Cameroon (2.4 percent) and Congo with 2.1 percent.

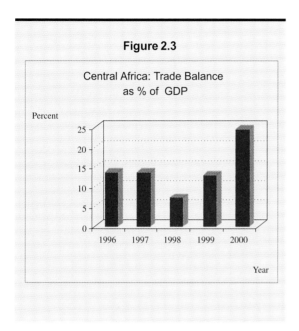

Figure 2.3

Central Africa: Trade Balance
as % of GDP

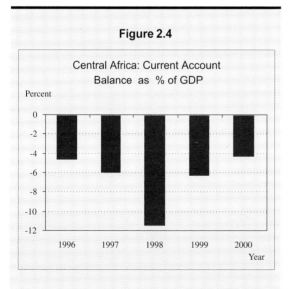

Figure 2.4

Central Africa: Current Account
Balance as % of GDP

External Debt

The region's foreign debt declined from $38.16 billion in 1999 to $34.17 billion in 2000 (128.6 percent of GDP as against 139.1 percent in 1999) (Figure 2.5), partly reflecting the inability to borrow offshore and low levels of foreign aid. As the largest economy in the region, the DRC has the largest external debt estimated at $14.01 billion in 2000 (309.4 percent of the GDP) a marginal decrease from $15.90 billion in 1999.

Sao Tome and Principe's debt stood at $270 million in 2000 (573.6 percent of GDP), down from $310 million in 1999. Its low foreign reserves and continuing current account shortfall explain its high level of external indebtedness. Congo's external debt of $5.22 billion ($5.48 billion in 1999) is more than twice its GDP, reflecting an unsustainable debt burden, while Burundi's debt amounts to 152 percent of GDP, and in Gabon the debt burden was 69 percent of GDP. The least indebted country in the region is Equatorial Guinea with a debt-to-GDP ratio of only 13.4 percent, which is extremely low by African standards.

Policy Developments

Civil strife, war and commodity price fluctuations have negated some of the beneficial results achieved in those Central African countries that have maintained their commitment to economic reform. Despite this, the region has made great strides in its fight against inflation, fiscal consolidation and exchange rate adjustment.

Monetary Policy, Inflation and Exchange Rates

The CFA franc zone's stability depends on the maintenance of tight monetary policies and credit

Figure 2.5

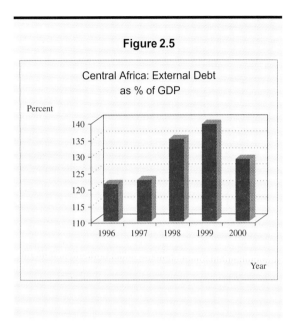

Central Africa: External Debt
as % of GDP

Figure 2.6

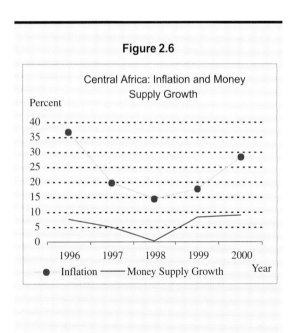

Central Africa: Inflation and Money
Supply Growth

restraint underpinned by two safeguards. These are: i) Zone central banks are required to maintain 20 percent foreign exchange to cover their sight liabilities; and, ii) governments are only allowed to draw a maximum of 20 percent of the previous year's budget receipts from regional banks. Countries which have their own central banks formulate and implement individual monetary policy measures, while still subject to the overall guidelines that prevail across the franc Zone.

Money supply growth in the region remained modest at 8.9 percent in 2000 compared with 8.3 percent in 1999. Despite this monetary restraint, inflation accelerated to average 28.4 percent in 2000 compared with 17.6 percent in 1999 (Figure 2.6). In the CFA zone money supply growth in 2000 varied between a high of almost 14.6 percent in Equatorial Guinea and a fall of less than one percent in Gabon. In Cameroon money supply grew 15.6 percent while in Chad the increase was 5.9 percent.

Since the aftershock of CFA franc devaluation in 1994, inflation has not been a major concern for CFA zone countries and in 2000 inflation in CFA economies averaged 2.6 percent compared with the non-CFA zone's 14 percent. In the CFA zone, exchange rates fluctuate with the Euro—via the French franc—to which the CFA franc has been pegged since January 1999. Although the Euro started on a firm footing, it depreciated substantially against a powerful US dollar over the next 18 months before recovering towards the end of 2000. As a result, the CFA franc depreciated from CFA615.7/US$ to CFA700/US$1 in 2000, which was a favorable development for non-oil exporters in Central Africa. However, given the fixed parity with the Euro, the CFA countries have little influence on the movements of their currency.

Sao Tome and Principe's monetary objective in 2000 was to reduce inflation to an annual average of 5 percent, which it achieved. However, it recorded a monetary growth rate of 8.5 percent. In Burundi, money supply growth recorded 20.2 percent in 2000. The main increase was in the circulation of notes and coins, indicating strong inflationary pressures in the economy and inflation averaged 27.4 percent in 2000 against only 3.3 percent the previous year. Exchange rate policy targeted convergence between the official and parallel rates for the Burundian franc through foreign currency auctions. During 2000, the policy succeeded in stabilizing the exchange rate, which fluctuated between Bufr760 and Bufr790:US$1 for most of the year, rising to Bufr800:US$1 in early October. The parallel exchange rate moved closer to the official rate, having fallen from Bufr1,200:US$1 immediately prior to the auctions to about Bufr985:US$1 in October 2000. Overall, the currency lost an estimated 23 percent of its value against the US dollar in 2000.

In Rwanda, monetary policy seeks to keep inflation below 5 percent. Money supply growth in 2000 averaged 8.1 percent, up from 6.6 percent in 1999 but despite this, inflation increased only modestly to 2.5 percent, compared with a price decline of 2.4 percent in 1999 - the main reason being higher fuel prices. The exchange rate of the Rwandan franc against the US dollar lost some 14.4 percent of its value in terms of the US dollar during the year to Rwfr413:US$1. Money supply growth remained out of control in the DRC during 2000 with hyperinflation of 540 percent, up from 333 percent in 1999. Its money supply, however, grew by 4.2 percent in 2000 compared to 20 percent in 1999.

Fiscal Policy

Most countries in the region are committed to fiscal consolidation by broadening their tax base, enhancing the efficiency of tax collection and administration, and improving the monitoring and control of public spending. In 2000, the region incurred a fiscal deficit of 2.9 percent of GDP, compared with 6.2 percent in 1999 (Figure 2.7). With the exception of Equatorial Guinea, Gabon, and Congo, all countries in the region recorded fiscal deficits in 2000. Equatorial Guinea, however, achieved a fiscal surplus of 16.5 percent while Gabon's budget surplus was 8.5 percent thanks to increased revenues from higher oil prices. Congo's fiscal surplus was 4.5 percent of GDP, a significant improvement from a deficit of 8.1 percent recorded in 1999.

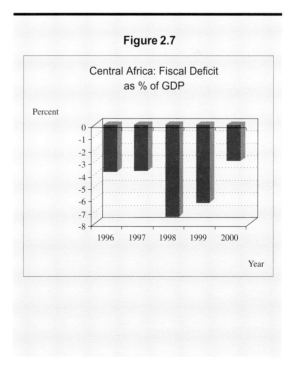

Figure 2.7

Sao Tome and Principe recorded the largest fiscal deficit in 2000 at 19 percent of GDP compared with 25.8 percent in 1999. The DRC's fiscal deficit was 16.7 percent of GDP, while in Burundi the fiscal shortfall was 5.7 percent, largely the result of parastatal losses. The budget deficit was 5.8 percent in Rwanda and less than one percent in Cameroon.

Central African Republic's deficit declined to 0.8 percent of GDP partly reflecting progress in trimming its public sector employment. In Chad, the deficit was 5.6 percent of GDP notwithstanding government efforts to streamline tax procedures, broaden its tax base and improve tax administration. However, the delay in the introduction of VAT until January 2001 forced the government to slow down the planned payment of accumulated arrears.

Cameroon has a successful record of fiscal discipline, assisted by higher oil prices and improved revenues. The 2000/2001 budget gave more priority to social spending and education while maintaining fiscal balance, and it is possible that the country will achieve a small budget surplus in 2001. The budget projects total spending at CFA1,476 billion, which is 13 percent more than in 1999/2000. Social spending, especially education, is receiving a larger share, increasing nearly 50 percent, while the share devoted to debt service will decline to 32 percent of the total budget. The Government is also taking steps to increase transparency and fight corruption.

Privatization

The progress of privatization varies depending on the political situation in individual countries and their economic priorities. Pockets of resistance remain throughout the region due to concerns over job losses and ordinary citizen's exclusion from the process.

Cameroon has sold 51 percent of the national Water Company and listed the government-owned cellphone company for sale in the near future. The national electricity company, Societé nationale d'electricite du Cameroon (Sonel) is also to be privatized with the assistance of the International Finance Corporation. In Gabon, although privatization has fallen behind schedule, the government has sold or is in the process of selling, government-owned or partially-owned enterprises including the public utilities (water and telecommunications), railways and milling companies. In the last quarter of 2000 the government of Gabon privatized the national cement company, Ciments du Gabon (Cimgabon), in which Norway's Scancem International now holds a 75 percent stake. The new owners have promised to double cement production to 400,000 tonnes per year within ten years. The national airline, Air Gabon, has been restructured and is now ready for sale.

In the Central African Republic, privatization is on course with progress in the sale of Petroca. Foreign private investors are taking over the retail and distribution network, while imports and stockpiling of petroleum products will be in the hands of Sogal, a specially created joint venture in which oil multinationals Shell and TotalFina-Elf hold the majority of the shares. However, the government has still to settle financial obligations left behind by Petroca, in the form of loans from local banks. In Chad, the state-owned Telecom Company is to be sold early in 2001 and negotiations for the sale of the Sugar Company will start soon. But progress has been slow in Burundi, where only a handful of parastatals have been prepared for privatization.

Rwanda has promised that it will accelerate the sale of a majority stake in the Telecom Company. It also plans to sell 51 percent of the telecommunications parastatal, Rwandatel, to a strategic partner in early 2001. The Rwandan public will be offered a 20 percent share while 5 percent will be offered to employees and the remaining 24 percent will remain in the government's hands. In the Republic of Congo, the government intends to privatize the management of the national Railway Company, CFCO. In Sao Tome and Principe, the government has dismantled and sold all but four state-owned companies that it considers strategic.

Outlook

Macroeconomic and structural reforms implemented to date have failed to reduce Central Africa's heavy dependence on raw material exports, especially oil. Part of the blame for this state of affairs lies with the high level of regional political instability which is deterring the foreign investor interest necessary for the diversification of production and exports. Recently, some countries, most notably Equatorial Guinea, achieved phenomenal growth rates due to the discovery of oil, but it is important for governments to avoid the classic Dutch Disease woes that affected other oil-producing countries in the past. Oil exporting nations must ensure that the economic rents from the exploitation of natural resources are spread across the country and used to invest in human capital as well as agriculture, manufacturing and services.

In the near to medium term, the region is poised to grow more rapidly than in the recent past, due to firmer oil prices and a recovery in the prices of some other primary commodities. Growth of between 4 and 6 percent a year is forecast over the near to medium term, with oil exporters possibly managing to grow even faster, especially when starting from a very low base. However, this scenario depends on a quick reso-

lution of the internal and external conflicts that have plagued the region of late.

Equatorial Guinea is likely to retain its star status, growing at double digit rates, barring a sudden collapse in oil prices. Increased investment and forecast strong growth in non-oil sectors, especially forestry, construction and services will also help boost economic expansion over the next few years in Equatorial Guinea. Chad is set to grow at 3-4 percent annually over the short term, assuming that its oil resources are developed and both external assistance and foreign investment increase in line with anticipations. However, it will take time before the effects of the vagaries of the Sahelian climate are overcome, while a shortage of energy is likely to constrain productive activities.

The second tier of high performers will include Rwanda and Cameroon, with the latter benefitting from firmer oil prices and Rwanda enjoying continued foreign assistance designed to prevent a recurrence of ethnic strife. Barring unforeseen adverse climatic conditions, the combination of economic reform and accelerated privatization in Rwanda should ensure real GDP growth of at least 5 percent a year in the 2001-2002 period. In Cameroon, fuelled by a rise in external assistance and by firmer oil prices, GDP growth of 4-5 percent will be sustained over the 2001-2002 period.

Growth in Burundi's economy is expected to accelerate in 2001-2002 to around 4 percent a year reflecting the resumption in international assistance, policy reforms, some private sector recovery, and increased social expenditure.

In Gabon, the clearance of debt arrears will free resources to finance economic expansion while, providing the momentum of reform is maintained, the privatization program, especially of the main public utilities, should attract foreign support. However, the continuing fall in oil production underscores the need for policymakers to promote a new development path. The decline in production largely reflects falling output at the Rabi-Kounga field, which is responsible for some 60 percent of national output. Government's estimates indicate that oil production will fall to 223,900 barrels per day in 2001 and 195,400 barrels per day in 2002, against 266,900 barrels per day in 2000.

With anticipated political stability and the return of investor confidence and donor enthusiasm, real GDP growth in the Central African Republic is expected to increase to 4 percent a year in 2001-2002, fuelled by higher external assistance and a recovery in consumer spending.

So long as the war continues in the Democratic Republic of Congo, the economy will continue to contract. Economic deterioration may be worsened by the chronic shortage of foreign exchange caused by disarray in the diamond sector. Firm oil prices will boost government revenue but, as long as the conflict continues, there is a very real risk that these funds will not be used to finance the ambitious three-year "programme interimaire post-conflit", launched in May 2000. The program has not yet taken off because of financing constraints.

In Sao Tome and Principe, success in the promotion of macroeconomic stability and market reform will underpin a rise in donor confidence and increased inflow of foreign assistance. This is likely to translate into faster growth in the services sector as well as fostering greater diversification of the economy in the 2001-2002 period.

East Africa

Overview

Eleven countries make up the Eastern Africa Region: Comoros, Djibouti, Eritrea, Ethiopia, Kenya, Madagascar, Mauritius, Seychelles, Somalia, Tanzania, and Uganda. The sub-region's population stood at 180.4 million in 2000, representing 23 percent of Africa's total. Blessed with lush vegetation, clement weather and rich agricultural land, the sub-region is heavily dependent on agricultural production, which accounts for about 43 percent of GDP, with coffee and tea, as the dominant crops.

Relative to countries in other sub-regions, few East African economies rely on mineral and energy resources. Although relatively poor in natural resources, East Africa is slowly emerging as a region that is able to grow and thrive despite its narrow natural resource base.

At $234.2, per capita GDP in 2000 was little more than a third of the continental average of $645.5. Per capita income declined slightly in 2000 from its 1999 level of $238.6, thereby reversing the upward trend that started in 1993. Currency devaluation was partly to blame for this reversal, as also was the severe drought experienced in the sub-region's largest economy, Kenya.

Recent Economic Trends

During 2000, regional GDP expanded at 3.8 percent, down from its 1999 growth rate of 4.5 percent (Table 2.3 and Figure 2.8), but still slightly above the African growth rate of 3.2 percent in 2000. Growth was constrained by the aftermath of the terrorist attacks that seriously damaged the economies of Kenya and Tanzania in 1998, and the drought that affected the whole region.

The economy of Kenya, accounting for a quarter of East African GDP, stagnated in 2000 with output growing at 0.3 percent (Figure 2.9). The

Indicators	1990	1995	1996	1997	1998	1999	2000[a]
Real GDP Growth Rate (%)	4.2	5.4	6.4	3.9	2.5	4.5	3.8
GDP Per Capita (US $)	229.1	228.5	232.3	242.1	250.1	238.6	234.2
Inflation (%)	29.7	12.2	9.1	6.5	4.7	5.2	5.3
Fiscal Balance (% of GDP)	-5.5	-3.1	-3.6	-2.2	-2.0	-2.5	-2.5
Gross Domestic Investment (% of GDP)	19.1	19.8	18.4	17.5	17.3	17.1	17.2
Gross National Savings (% of GDP)	13.9	12.7	12.7	11.9	10.7	10.9	10.4
Real Export Growth (%)	0.8	1.2	1.4	1.3	1.3	1.2	1.5
Trade Balance (% GDP)	-12.2	-10.3	-9.8	-9.7	-11.2	-11.2	-12.3
Current Account (% GDP)	-5.0	-7.1	-5.8	-5.9	-7.0	-6.7	-7.0
Terms of Trade (%)	-10.9	1.7	-5.9	-0.4	4.1	-0.4	-2.4
Total External Debt (% GDP)	86.8	99.8	94.2	87.0	82.9	82.9	70.9
Debt Service (% of Exports)	26.7	21.6	19.1	18.1	18.4	16.8	...

Table 2.3: East Africa: Macroeconomic Indicators, 1990-2000

Note: a/ Preliminary estimates.
Source: ADB Statistics Division and IMF.

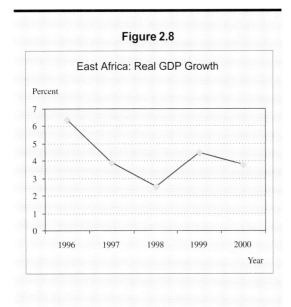

Figure 2.8

East Africa: Real GDP Growth

Percent

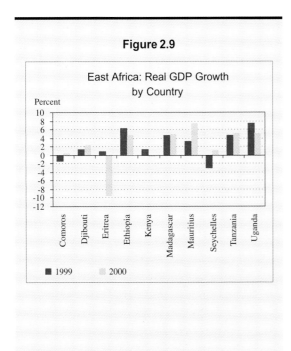

Figure 2.9

East Africa: Real GDP Growth
by Country

Percent

■ 1999   ▨ 2000

country is currently in the grip of one of the worst droughts in its history with the result that some 3.3 million Kenyans—16 percent of the population—are in desperate need of food assistance. Kenya relies on hydroelectric power for much of its electricity and low water levels in the major dams forced the government to impose power rationing, which had particularly severe ramifications for the manufacturing sector.

Tanzania too was hit by drought, as a result of which agricultural production, contributing more than half of GDP, declined. As in Kenya, food shortages forced the government to dip into its strategic grain reserve to alleviate shortages. Despite this setback, output growth accelerated in 2000 to 5.2 percent from 4.6 percent in 1999, driven by increased mining output and investment and a recovery in tourism.

In Uganda, the sub-region's third largest economy, drought also affected agricultural production adversely. Both exports and government revenue weakened due to the combined impact of reduced output and lower prices for coffee and some other agricultural commodities. Despite increased public sector investment, GDP is estimated to have slowed to 5.1 percent in 2000, from 7.4 percent in 1999.

Drought had a devastating impact on Ethiopia, particularly the south-eastern part, resulting in the death of scores of people and cattle. The border conflict with Eritrea also had an adverse effect, diverting precious resources away from development. Consequently, growth slowed to 4.6 percent in 2000 from 6.2 percent the previous year.

After growing at over 5 percent annually through the 1990s, output in Eritrea fell sharply 9.5 percent in 2000, due mainly to the war with Ethiopia and the adverse impact of the drought. Growth in Djibouti accelerated to 2.3 percent in 2000, up from 1.4 percent in 1999, reflecting increased port and transport activities. Because of the border conflict with Eritrea and the closure of Eritrean ports to Ethiopian trade, Ethiopia switched to using ports in Djibouti for its external trade needs.

Economic activity in Mauritius rebounded strongly in 2000 to grow at 7.4 percent compared with a below-average 3.3 percent in 1999. The upsurge was led by a 28.6 percent increase in agricultural output, especially sugar production, where value-added surged 56 percent in real terms. The drought, which depressed agricultural GDP in 1999, had little impact on output in 2000. The economy was also boosted also by increased tourism, while manufacturing value-added in the Export Processing Zone increased 6 percent in real terms and construction output was up 8 percent.

Growth in Madagascar rose marginally in 2000 to 4.8 percent from 4.7 percent the previous year, due to increased agricultural output and a strong rebound in the tourist in sector. Increased construction activity, necessary to repair the damage inflicted by the cyclone early in 2000, also contributed to stronger expansion.

The Seychelles economy continued to underperform with growth of only 1.2 percent in 2000, up from a contraction of 3 percent in 1999. Tourist arrivals were disappointing, reflecting increased competition from cheaper destinations. The economy continues to suffer from the negative image of its offshore financial sector, which the government is taking steps to reform with the aim of developing it into a regional financial center. In Comoros, economic activity suffered recently due partly to political uncertainty and partly to the failure to push ahead with structural reform. After sliding 1.4 percent in 1999, output recovered marginally to grow 0.5 percent in 2000.

The External Accounts

Coffee remains the major source of foreign exchange in Ethiopia, Uganda, and Kenya, while also an important export for Tanzania and Madagascar. However, in two East African countries, Mauritius and Seychelles, manufactures and services dominate foreign currency earnings. Mauritius is sub-Saharan Africa's second largest exporter of manufactured goods—after South Africa. Clothing accounts for some 55 percent of exports while manufacturing as a whole contributes two thirds. Both Seychelles and Mauritius are also heavily reliant on earnings from tourism, while Seychelles exports processed fish.

Traditionally, the sub-region runs a visible trade deficit, partly offset by invisible earnings from tourism - a major source of income for Kenya, Tanzania, Mauritius and Seychelles. Imports are dominated by capital and other manufactured goods. After shrinking in 1996, the trade gap has since widened resulting in an estimated $5.08 billion deficit in 2000, partly reflecting the 50 percent decline since 1995 in the price of the sub-region's main export, coffee. East Africa's terms of trade deteriorated dramatically during 2000 as the price of coffee continued to weaken, while oil prices rose to their highest levels in a decade. As a result the regional trade deficit increased to 12.3 percent of GDP (Figure 2.10).

Tanzania's trade deficit deteriorated to $1.17 billion in 2000 (12.9 percent of GDP) as a result of increased imports and lower output and hence lower exports, brought about by drought. Ethiopia's experience was similar as were those of other countries affected by the drought. Ethiopia's trade gap widened also, due to heavy imports of armaments because of the border conflict with Eritrea. The trade deficit grew to 19.2 percent of GDP in 2000, up from 16.6 percent in

Figure 2.10

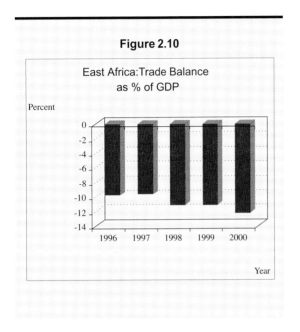

East Africa: Trade Balance as % of GDP

1999. Eritrea runs a substantial trade deficit due to its small export base consisting mainly of raw materials and live animals. Its trade balance deteriorated further in 2000, reflecting increased military imports.

Kenya's trade performance continued to deteriorate in 2000 with the trade deficit rising sharply to $970 million (9.6 percent of GDP), from $870 million (8.4 percent of GDP) in 1999. Adverse weather conditions and poor international prices led to a decline in commodity exports—coffee and tea—while imports fell too reflecting the depressed state of the domestic economy. Fuel imports, however, were up in value because of the higher oil prices during 2000.

In Uganda and Madagascar, lower coffee prices and exports and higher imports also resulted in bigger trade deficits. However, the deteriora-

tion in the trade balance of Madagascar was less pronounced due to the rebound in cotton prices, one of its main exports. In Djibouti, both exports and imports rose substantially due to the use of its ports by Ethiopia for its exports and imports. Djibouti's service-based economy enabled it to run a trade deficit throughout the 1990s, which in 2000 stood at 28.3 percent of GDP.

Countries less dependent on primary commodity exports showed either a slight deterioration in their trade balance (Mauritius) or a largely unchanged situation, as in Seychelles and Comoros. In Mauritius, the trade deficit increased to $200 million in 2000 (4.6 percent of GDP) from $150 million (3.8 percent of GDP) in 1999, in spite of faster expansion in exports than imports. Since the Euro-zone is a major trading partner, the weak Euro impacted negatively on Mauritian exports to Europe. In Seychelles, higher tuna exports were offset by increased fuel and capital goods imports, while in Comoros, the shortage of foreign exchange reduced import demand, thereby preventing a substantial deterioration of the trade balance, which was 22.3 percent of GDP in 2000.

East Africa's trade deficit of 12.3 percent of GDP in 2000 was partly funded by invisible earnings, primarily from tourism, along with increased remittances and net transfers—East Africa is a major recipient of foreign aid. These inflows reduced the current account deficit to $3.09 billion in 2000 or 7.0 percent of GDP (Figure 2.11).

The region's international reserves (excluding gold) decreased in 2000 by 8.3 percent to $3.5 billion or the equivalent of 4.1 months of imports, down from 4.8 months in 1999. Increased energy imports and the resulting rise in both the trade and current account deficits forced East African countries to dip into their reserves.

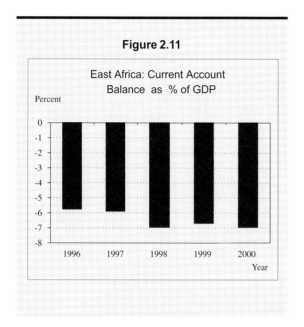

Figure 2.11

East Africa: Current Account Balance as % of GDP

External Debt

Since 1993, East Africa's foreign debt has fallen from 112.5 percent of GDP to 82.9 percent in 1999 and 70.9 percent in 2000 (Figure 2.12). Despite this improvement, foreign debt remains a severe constraint on growth and development and no fewer than eight of the eleven—the exceptions being Eritrea, Seychelles and Mauritius—are classified as HIPC countries, entitled to debt relief.

In absolute terms, Tanzania was the most heavily indebted country in the region in 2000 with a debt of $7.49 billion (82.9 percent of GDP). As a percentage of GDP, Somalia with 131.2 percent, had the largest debt burden, followed by Madagascar with 103.2 percent out of its debt of $3.94 billion. Ethiopia is the second most heavily indebted country in the sub-region in absolute

In 2000, Kenya held the largest foreign exchange reserves in the region with an estimated $830 million followed by Tanzania with $760 million and Uganda with $770 million. However, in relative terms, Uganda's reserves represented 7.2 months of imports followed by Tanzania's 6 months of imports. Ethiopia experienced the sharpest drop in reserves (45.5 percent) due to increased food imports following the drought and import of weapons because of the Eritrean war. Mauritius recorded the second largest drop of 11.5 percent while Comoros registered the largest increase of 7.7 percent.

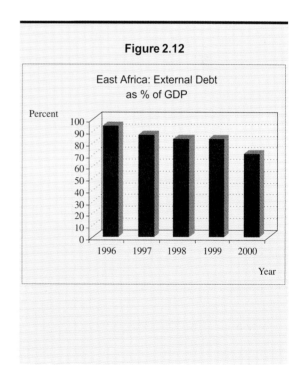

Figure 2.12

East Africa: External Debt as % of GDP

terms with debt of $5.46 billion (79.5 percent of GDP) in 2000. A major part of this total debt, estimated at $10.0 billion at the end of 1999, is owed to bilateral creditors, especially the former Soviet Union. Uganda's external debt is $3.48 billion (60.3 percent of GDP in 2000) and Kenya's is $5.3 billion (52.8 percent of GDP). Mauritius had $1.51 billion of debt (34.9 percent of GDP), and Seychelles $140 million.

Policy Developments

Monetary Policy, Inflation and Exchange Rates

Tight monetary policies in the sub-region kept inflation under control again during 2000, when the rate of consumer price increases accelerated somewhat to 5.3 percent from 5.2 percent in 1999. (Figure 2.13) Higher inflation resulted in the main from drought-induced shortages, higher energy prices and currency depreciation. East African governments have maintained market-determined exchange rates to stay competitive in international markets and avoid real exchange rate appreciation.

While the broad money supply growth increased markedly in Kenya from 2.8 percent in 1999 to 7.4 percent a 2000, inflation doubled to 5.4 percent in 2000 from 2.7 percent the previous year. In 2001, the Central Bank of Kenya is targeting an inflation rate of below 5 percent and money supply growth of no more than 8 percent. Since 1995, the Kenyan shilling has depreciated losing more than a quarter of its value against the US dollar in the last two years alone. It fell 14.2 percent in 1999 and a further 10.5 percent in 2000.

In Ethiopia, money supply remained unchanged at 11.4 percent in 2000 as in 1999. Despite this, inflation more than halved to 3.7 per-

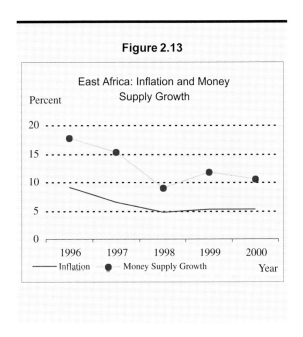

Figure 2.13

East Africa: Inflation and Money Supply Growth

cent in 2000, from its 1999 level of 8.8 percent. The Ethiopian currency, the birr, which weakened against the US dollar during the 1990s, after being pegged at a fixed rate before then, continued to depreciate in 2000. It fell 8.7 percent against the dollar compared with a 10.4 percent decline in 1999.

Inflation in Madagascar fell marginally from 9.9 percent in 1999 to 9.5 percent in 2000, reflecting a relatively lower monetary growth of 10 percent in 2000. The Malagasy franc stabilized in 2000, depreciating only 7 percent compared with almost double that amount - 13.4 percent - in 1999.

Uganda has maintained a tight monetary stance, with the result that inflation slowed from 6.4 percent in 1999 to 2.9 percent in 2000. Money supply grew 15.9 percent in 2000. Currency depreciation accelerated reflecting the terms-of-trade shock from weak coffee prices and escalating energy import costs. The shilling lost a further 19.4 percent of its value against the US dollar in 2000 after 14.7 percent depreciation in 1999.

The new tighter fiscal stance in Tanzania, following the introduction of cash budgeting, contributed to slower monetary expansion and reduced inflation. Although inflation declined to 6.1 percent in 2000 from 7.9 percent in 1999, the Tanzanian shilling continued its gradual depreciation against the US dollar, falling 7 percent in 2000 after a 10.8 decline in 1999.

Mauritius maintains a prudent monetary policy designed to ensure price and exchange rate stability. Money supply growth remained virtually unchanged at 10 percent in 2000 as in 1999, while inflation rate slowed to 4 percent in 2000 from 6.9 percent in 1999. The rupee stabilized in 2000, depreciating only 6 percent following a 4.8 percent decline against the US dollar in 1999.

In Seychelles, inflation accelerated in 2000 to 6.8 percent from its 1999 level of 2.7 percent. In line with this, the rupee depreciated 6.3 percent during 2000 after a decline of only 1.5 percent in 1999.

Broad money supply and credit in Comoros grew by only 4 percent in 1999, reflecting the decline in economic activity. The rate of monetary expansion doubled to 4 percent at the end of 2000 from its 1999 level. In January 2000, the Central Bank of Comoros adopted a more flexible interest rate policy, linking rates for the country's single commercial bank to those prevailing in the Euro zone. Inflation remains subdued, largely due to its membership of the franc zone, increasing modestly to 5 percent in 2000 from 3.5 percent the previous year. The currency depreciated 11.3 percent in 2000 in line with the decline in the CFA Franc against the strong US dollar.

As part of its ongoing economic reforms, the government of Djibouti continues to maintain a very tight monetary policy. Broad money growth increased very marginally from -0.1 percent in 1999 to 0.1 percent in 2000. Inflation remained low at 2.5 percent, up slightly from 2.3 percent in 1999. Djibouti is the only country in the region that maintains a fixed exchange rate against the US dollar, following a currency board regime, with the result that its nominal exchange rate has appreciated significantly in recent years in tandem with the US currency.

Fiscal Policy

While East African governments have maintained broadly uniform monetary policies designed to curb inflation and stabilize the exchange rate, fiscal policies have varied in line with the different economic circumstances in individual countries. Nonetheless, budget deficits remain modest by African standards, averaging 2.5 percent of GDP in 2000—unchanged from 1999 (Figure 2.14).

Kenya is committed to a strategy of fiscal consolidation as the government inches its way towards a balanced budget. Indeed, in fiscal 2000, the budget was in marginal surplus at 0.2 percent of GDP compared with a balanced budget the previous year. To boost revenues, the VAT rate has been raised to 18 percent from 15 percent, though to cushion the impact on the low-paid, this was partly offset by an increase in the income tax threshold to sh9 400 a month from sh8,000, thereby removing 200,000 Kenyans from the tax net. To help overcome the electricity supply crisis, new incentives were introduced in the 2000 budget that allow companies to import electric generators without paying duty or VAT. Firms with generators with over 100 KVA capacity will receive compensation from the Kenya Power and Lighting Company. The government also formalized the duty reduction of raw materials imported from COMESA countries.

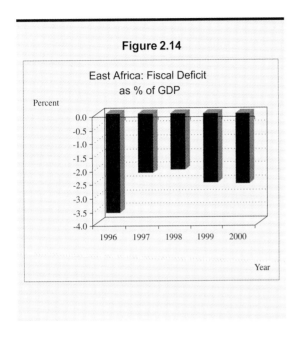

Figure 2.14

East Africa: Fiscal Deficit as % of GDP

Following the budget, the IMF lent Kenya $198 million over three years subject to strict conditions; these have since been temporarily suspended because of slippage in meeting the conditionalities. Resumed lending by the multilateral financial institutions (MFIs), backed by assistance from some bilateral donors, should boost business confidence and strengthen the economic recovery. The resumption of lending by the MFIs followed a three-year freeze on support for Kenya because of donor dissatisfaction with Nairobi's economic management and slow progress in tackling corruption and public sector reform.

In Ethiopia, war and drought jeopardized the progress made in recent years toward a balanced budget, resulting in a steep increase in the budget deficit in 2000 to 8.2 percent of GDP from 4.9 percent in 1999. In Mauritius, the budget deficit decreased in 2000 to 0.8 percent of GDP from

1.9 percent in 1999. After taking office, the new administration cut the projected deficit to 7.8 percent of GDP by raising electricity and fuel prices which had been subsidized. Underspending, especially on capital projects, is likely to mean a somewhat smaller deficit in the region of 6 percent of GDP. Privatization of Mauritius Telecom will boost revenues, but the new government has warned that further revenue-raising measures are likely to be needed in 2001

In Madagascar, in spite of the broadening of the tax base and a more aggressive tax collection the budget deficit increased from 2.8 percent of GDP in 1999 to 4.1 percent in 2000. The introduction of VAT also helped increase revenues, while public spending was kept under control. Progress towards fiscal consolidation was slowed as a result of the damage suffered by the island from Cyclone Eline early in 2000. The MFIs have responded by extending the country's deficit reduction timetable.

In Uganda, the 2000/2001 fiscal budget gives more priority to domestic spending and industry relief programs. It limits the share of defense spending to a maximum of 2 percent of GDP, despite Uganda's military intervention in the Democratic Republic of Congo. In order to boost domestic industry, the 2000 budget eliminates the 4 percent withholding tax and the 2 percent import commission previously imposed on imported raw materials. In 2000, the country's budget deficit stood at 3.7 percent of the GDP, up from 1.3 percent in 1999.

Privatization

Although East African countries are committed to broad privatization programs, progress in individual states has been mixed, reflecting bureaucratic bottlenecks and a lack of interest on the part of potential buyers.

To date Kenya has privatized only six parastatals out of a list of more than 30. The sale of a 49 percent stake in Telkom Kenya was delayed in December 2000 when the government rejected bids on the ground that they were too low. In January 2001, the government announced the sale of a 49 percent stake in Telkom Kenya to a South African-led consortium for $305 million. Ahead of the sale, Telkom Kenya had laid off 10,000 workers.

In 2000, Tanzania sold 51 percent of the Dar Es Salaam Airport Handling Company (DAHACO) to a Swiss company, while a management contract for the country's largest port, Dar es Salaam, was awarded to a company from the Philippines. Enterprises targeted for privatization include the Dar es Salaam Water and Sanitation Authority and Tanzania Petroleum Development Corporation. A major state-owned company that has attracted interest from foreign investors is the Tanzania Telecommunications Company. However, the privatization of some parastatals, such as the National Bank of Commerce (NBC), was delayed due to strong opposition from its employees.

In Mauritius, France Telecom bought a 40 percent stake in the country's state-owned telecommunications company, Mauritius Telecom (MT). Among the state-owned enterprises that are scheduled for sale to the private sector in Uganda, is the Uganda Electricity Board, which is to be broken up into two entities before privatization. In Madagascar, the national Airline Company, Air Madagascar, and the national telecommunications company were slated for privatization during 2000, but the sale of Air Madagascar stalled due to financing problems with the US Eximbank. The hurdle was only cleared recently, with the sale of the company now being authorized. In Ethiopia,

commitment to privatization remains strong but progress has been slow. Few of the more than 163 parastatals have actually been privatized though some small retail outlets and hotels have been sold to the private sector. However, bureaucratic obstacles continue to delay the privatization of state farms and industrial plants.

In Seychelles, the government has slated several hotels for privatization to foreign investors, while in Djibouti privatization is seen as a mechanism for helping to revive the sluggish economy. Heavily indebted public utilities are to be sold first along with the national railways, while management of the port is to be privatized. In Eritrea, the privatization of a small number of public enterprises has proceeded very slowly, partly reflecting the relatively high prices sought by the government.

Emerging Regional Economic Relations

The Common Market for Eastern and Southern Africa (COMESA) is the largest regional economic organization in Africa in terms of country membership (20 nations) and its population of about 385 million people. In GDP terms though, it is smaller than the Southern African Development Community (SADC). COMESA members are Angola, Burundi, Comoros, Democratic Republic of Congo (D.R.C.), Djibouti, Egypt, Eritrea, Ethiopia, Kenya, Madagascar, Malawi, Mauritius, Namibia, Rwanda, Seychelles, Sudan, Swaziland, Uganda, Zambia, and Zimbabwe. Tanzania, which belongs to SADC and EAC, withdrew its membership in 2000.

The most important goal of COMESA in recent years has been the creation of a Free Trade Area. In 1992, tariff reduction was extended to all goods originating in the member states, on the basis of 10 percent average annual reductions. In October of 2000, nine member states formally launched the COMESA Free Trade Area providing for zero tariff rates on all intra-COMESA trade. In the last two months of 2000, Zimbabwe, Zambia, and Madagascar implemented the agreement while several other countries, including Djibouti, Kenya, Malawi and Mauritius, were in the final stages of its implementation. If successfully implemented, this initiative will qualify COMESA as a free-trade area under WTO guidelines.

In order to attract foreign investment into the region, COMESA is working towards harmonization of investment codes in the member states. It is also trying to improve the region's economic infrastructure by financing road, water, power supply and telecommunication projects through the Preferential Trading Area (COMESA) Bank. Another important step is a regional export credit guarantee facility, which is essential for the promotion of trade given the fact that COMESA region is rated as one prone to high levels of political and country risk. COMESA has therefore proposed the creation of the Africa Guarantee Fund (AFG) to address political risk. There are plans to finance AFG using a $200 million IDA credit along with similar loans from other donors.

Outlook

Although the region remains precariously dependent on favorable weather conditions for agriculture and the level of commodity prices for key exports, notably coffee and tea, growth prospects for the short and medium term are promising. The sub-region is strongly committed to further economic reforms that will diversify economies, reducing dependence on agriculture, through increased investment in manufacturing and tourism,

where several East African countries have a strong competitive advantage.

But formidable obstacles must be overcome for East Africa to exploit its full potential - including a poorly developed and maintained infrastructure, widespread poverty, scarce human capital and a heavy external debt burden. For GDP growth to reach the levels needed to alleviate poverty, of 6 percent and above annually, these bottlenecks must be tackled urgently.

Barring adverse weather conditions, the subregion economy will continue to grow in the range of 4 to 6 percent annually over the near to medium term. It should be possible to achieve even higher rates in the longer run, if countries such as Uganda, Ethiopia, Mauritius and Tanzania can maintain their recent strong growth performance. This scenario, however, assumes a quick resolution of the internal as well as external conflicts that have plagued the region recently. The lead economies in the region will continue to be Uganda, Mauritius and Tanzania because of their steadfast commitment to economic reforms and in the case of Mauritius, exploitation of manufacturing and service sector growth opportunities.

Assuming Kenya manages to stay on track in its reform programs, and given reasonably favorable climatic conditions and commodity prices along with continued growth in the tourism industry, the economy should recover over the next two years. Economic growth prospects are good for Tanzania due to heavy investment in mining, faster export expansion, privatization and expected strong growth in agriculture and tourism. Mauritius is forecast to continue to grow at 7 percent in 2001 and 6.6 percent in 2002 on the strength of continuing tourist expansion and exploitation by exporters of the tariff-free entry to the US market under the Africa Growth and Opportunity Act.

In Uganda, given normal weather conditions and continuing economic reforms and donor inflows, economic growth is forecast to accelerate to 6.8 percent in 2001, just below the official target of 7 percent. With its drive for increased tax revenue, accompanied by further market liberalization, Madagascar's growth prospects for the 2001-2002 period are encouraging. But although continued expansion is expected in the fishing sector, continuing foreign exchange shortages point to GDP growth in the next two years of no more than 2 percent a year.

In Ethiopia, if new agreements with the MFIs can be finalized so that the country obtains debt relief under the enhanced HIPC Initiative, growth should increase over the next two years, especially if military spending is reduced as planned. In Eritrea, foreign assistance and normal weather conditions will be essential to underpin growth in 2001-2002, while in Djibouti, the economy is unlikely to grow rapidly given the slowness of economic reforms. In Somalia, the ban imposed by several Gulf states on imports of Somali livestock will adversely affect the economy. Economic recovery will be hard to achieve in Comoros given the political problems in Anjouan and Grand Comoro, economic hardships in Moroni, and the shortage of foreign capital.

North Africa

Overview of the Economy

North Africa comprises Algeria, Egypt, Libya, Mauritania, Morocco, Sudan, and Tunisia. They have a combined population of 175.6 million people. The region accounted for 38.6 percent of Africa's GDP in 2000. Per capita GDP in the region increased 2.0 percent in 2000 to $1,145.6 from $1,123.1 in 1999, explained partly by higher oil prices and the continuing structural reform. A further plus factor was the reduction of political violence in Algeria, that improved the environment for investment and growth.

Regional per capita GDP numbers mask the vast disparities that exist in the region, with per capita incomes varying from a high of almost $5829 in Libya to a low of only $346 in Mauritania.

Sudan is the second poorest country in North Africa with a per capita GDP of $379 while Tunisia, with a per capita GDP of $2,067, ranks second to Libya in terms of average prosperity.

Recent Economic Trends

With growth of 4.1 percent in 2000, economic activity expanded at a slightly faster pace than in 1999 (3.8 percent) reflecting higher growth rates across the region, except in Tunisia (Figure 2.15 and Table 2.4). Buoyant crude oil prices account for stronger growth in oil exporting countries—Algeria, Libya, and Sudan—with Sudan achieving the highest rate of growth of 6.8 percent, compared with 5.9 percent in 1999 (Figure2.16). 2000 was the first full year of oil production in Sudan and the country benefited from the high oil prices that prevailed during the year as well as from agriculture's strong performance.

Table 2.4: North Africa: Macroeconomic Indicators, 1990- 2000

Indicators	1990	1995	1996	1997	1998	1999	2000[a]
Real GDP Growth Rate (%)	3.5	2.0	6.1	2.8	4.5	3.8	4.1
GDP Per Capita (US $)	1,292.3	1,196.3	1,058.4	1,067.9	1,104.5	1,123.1	1,145.6
Inflation (%)	16.6	20.3	22.1	10.0	6.6	4.7	5.0
Fiscal Balance (% of GDP)	-5.0	-2.6	-1.3	-0.8	-2.2	-2.0	-0.4
Gross Domestic Investment (% of GDP)	24.3	22.8	20.8	20.6	23.4	25.1	23.9
Gross National Savings (% of GDP)	22.8	22.0	22.0	22.2	21.0	23.6	23.2
Real Export Growth (%)	14.4	7.5	7.3	7.4	6.8	8.0	9.3
Trade Balance (% GDP)	-6.7	-8.0	-5.4	-4.7	-8.0	-7.2	-3.5
Current Account (% GDP)	-3.4	-2.6	0.2	1.6	-2.3	-1.3	1.7
Terms of Trade (%)	6.7	5.5	6.1	6.9	-14.2	7.1	17.1
Total External Debt (% GDP)	79.6	66.2	58.5	52.7	49.5	45.7	40.0
Debt Service (% of Exports)	14.2	38.1	30.9	26.5	26.3	24.2	...

Note: a/ Preliminary estimates.
Source: ADB Statistics Division and IMF.

Figure 2.15

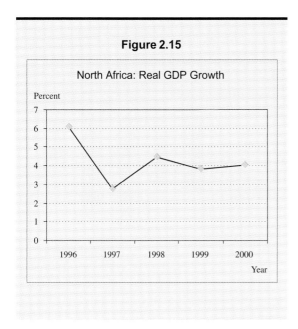

North Africa: Real GDP Growth

Figure 2.16

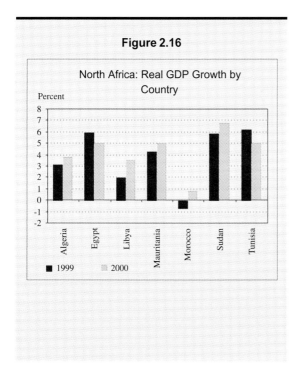

North Africa: Real GDP Growth by Country

GDP growth rate in Egypt in 2000 although robust at 5 percent, was lower than the 6 percent recorded the previous year. Expansion was driven by the good performance of exports of both goods and services, especially tourism, while increased foreign direct investment (FDI) inflows provided added momentum.. The energy sector continues to be the main beneficiary of FDI as foreign investors target new contracts for crude oil prospecting, natural gas development and increasing refinery capacity. Travel and tourism, including all travel and tourism-related spending, accounted for 9 percent of GDP.

Both Mauritania and Tunisia are estimated to have grown by 5 percent in 2000. The acceleration in Mauritania from 4.3 percent in 1999 was driven by a strong agricultural performance allied with higher prices for the country's main exports, iron ore and fish. In Tunisia, although growth slowed from the 6.2 percent achieved in 1999, strong performances by manufacturing, construction and tourism offset the negative effects of drought which affected the country adversely during the year.

Growth in Algeria increased to 3.8 percent in 2000 from 3.2 percent, due largely to high oil prices, increased activity in the hydrocarbon sector and higher exports of other goods and services. Although political violence and sabotage of economic facilities abated significantly, with the exception of the oil and gas sector, foreign investors shied away from investing in the country citing continuing security problems in the countryside. Agriculture was hit by drought which reduced its growth rate while inadequate funding of Algeria's state enterprises constrained performance in the manufacturing sector.

The Libyan economy grew 3.5 percent in 2000, up from 2 percent in 1999, Here too, increased oil output and higher prices were the main drivers, while in Morocco there was a limp recovery with output rising marginally (0.8 percent) following the 0.7 percent contraction in 1999, as the economy suffered from drought for the second consecutive year. However, the decline of some 16 percent in agricultural output was offset by growth in other sectors, including manufacturing and especially the services sector led by tourism.

External Accounts

North Africa's exports continue to be dominated by primary products—notably oil, natural gas, and phosphates. However, the share of processed and manufactured products is increasing gradually, while tourism is a major revenue earner in Egypt, Tunisia and Morocco. Most countries in the region have stepped up efforts to diversify their exports with varying degrees of success.

Reflecting the strength of energy prices, the region's trade deficit declined by about 40 percent in 2000 to $8.11 billion from $13.83 billion, falling to 3.5 percent of GDP from almost 7.2 percent in 1999 (Figure 2.17). Due to the sharp rise in oil prices, Algeria's trade surplus increased from $3.36 billion in 1999 to $9.7 billion in 2000 or 18.7 percent of GDP. Exports rose by almost 50 percent reflecting increased oil and natural gas production and exports as well as firmer prices.

The second largest trade balance improvement in the region was recorded by another oil producing country, Libya, whose exports increased over 21 percent, also due to higher oil production and exports. Consequently, Libya's trade surplus improved from $2.8 billion in 1999 to $4 billion in 2000 or 13.8 percent of GDP. For the same reasons, Sudan's trade surplus increased to 3.5 percent of GDP from a deficit of 6.2 percent of GDP.

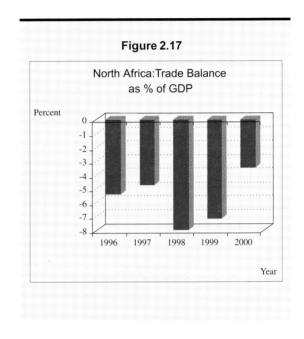

Figure 2.17

North Africa: Trade Balance as % of GDP

Tunisia's exports decreased almost seven percent in spite of increased sales of textiles and other manufactures, resulting in a trade deficit of $2.2 billion or 10.9 percent of GDP, compared with $2.11 billion in 1999. Mauritania's trade balance remained unchanged at $10 million, (0.8 percent of GDP). This relatively weak performance was attributable mainly to the unchanged prices and stagnant exports of iron ore and fish. Both Egypt and Morocco recorded huge trade deficits in 2000 of 13.3 and 9.1 percent of GDP, respectively.

The region's current account swung from a deficit of $2.51 billion in 1999 to a surplus of $3.32 billion (1.7 percent of GDP), the highest in almost 10 years (Figure 2.18). Algeria recorded the largest current account surplus (12.58 percent of GDP), followed by Libya with 10 percent and Sudan with 3 percent. The other countries in the region had current account deficits -2.3 percent

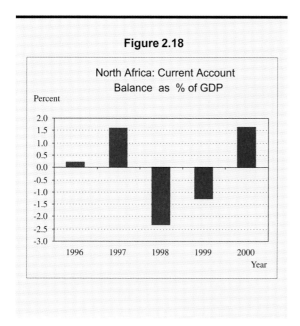

Figure 2.18

North Africa: Current Account Balance as % of GDP

percent in 2000, falling steadily since the mid-1990s to $80.26 billion at the end of 2000.

Egypt is the region's largest debtor accounting for a third (33.7 percent) of the regional total in 2000. (Figure 2.19). After decreasing in the first half of the 1990s, Egypt's foreign debt increased from 1994 to 1996 before falling to $28.8 billion in 1998 and to $27.02 billion in 2000. Foreign exchange reserves have declined in line with the government's policy of seeking to maintain an overvalued exchange rate. This and persistent current account payments deficits forced the authorities to borrow overseas. Nonetheless, at 28.6 percent of GDP in 2000, Egypt's foreign debt situation is manageable.

Algeria, with an external debt of $25.84 billion in 2000, accounts for a quarter of the regional total. Unlike Egypt, however, Algeria's debt has

of GDP in Morocco, -3.4 percent in Tunisia, and about -1.75 percent in Egypt.

The region's services balance improved only slightly from 1999 as did the net transfers balance with the exception of Libya where the transfer balance deteriorated slightly, reflecting higher levels of foreign remittances. All the other countries, however, recorded positive transfer balances, as a result of inward remittances from nationals working abroad. In 2000, Egypt was the largest beneficiary of remittances in the region, amounting to almost $5 billion, followed by Morocco with $2.7 billion.

External Debt

Foreign borrowing fell in line with the region's improved current account situation. External debt declined from 70 percent of GDP in 1992 to 40

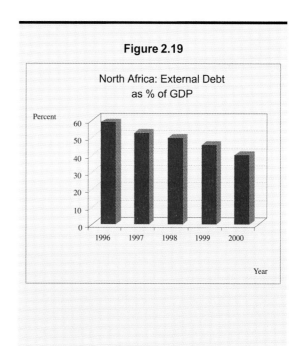

Figure 2.19

North Africa: External Debt as % of GDP

declined in the last four years on the back of the improved current account balance resulting from higher oil prices, as well as the healthy foreign exchange reserves position built-up in recent years. Algeria has also promoted debt-for-equity swaps, though only with limited success as yet. Despite this, the debt/GDP ratio fell to 49.8 percent in 2000, a marked improvement on the 79.5 percent recorded in 1995.

Morocco's debt is the third largest in the region, representing 20 percent of the total. Although it has declined from the early 1990s levels, it was $16.16 billion in 2000—48.5 percent of GDP, down substantially from 91 percent in 1990. In recent years, Morocco has used offshore borrowings to finance a current account deficit arising from higher oil prices, increased drought-related food imports and the need to finance investment. Tunisia's debt has also declined in recent years to $9.61 billion or 47.5 percent of GDP.

Two North African countries—Mauritania and Sudan—are classified as Heavily Indebted Poor Countries. Although Sudan's foreign debt of $16 billion in 2000 (134 percent of GDP) is high, its debt burden has declined steeply from 370 percent of GDP in the early 1990s to its present level. Given Mauritania's qualification for HIPC debt relief, its debt fell to $1.63 billion in 2000. To ensure that this debt relief is translated into poverty reduction, Mauritania is expected to continue with its economic, social and governance reforms.

Policy Developments

In addition to specific measures designed to encourage savings and investment, all governments in the region are committed to reform programs that have resulted in the recent improved economic performance. Although a few countries remain hesitant about the wisdom of across-the-board

reform, most have recognized the necessity for far-reaching structural change to meet the challenges of globalization.

Monetary Policy, Inflation and Exchange Rates

Since the early 1990s, most North African governments have consistently pursued conservative monetary policies designed to control inflation. Figure 2.20 shows that the inflation rate in the region declined from 22.1 percent in 1996 to 4.7 percent in 1999. In 2000, inflation edged slightly higher to 5 percent. Monetary restraint was the key to the decline in inflation in the late 1990s. After moderate increases or decreases during the past decade, M1 expanded 5.7 percent in 2000 while M2 expanded by 11.6 percent.

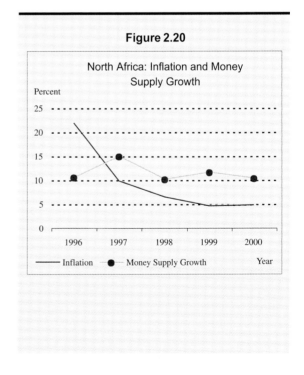

Figure 2.20

North Africa: Inflation and Money Supply Growth

With the exception of Egypt, which has resisted devaluation until recently, countries in the region have devalued their currencies not only to compensate for the differential between domestic inflation and that in trading partner countries, thereby preventing real exchange rate appreciation, but also to enhance international competitive position.

Algeria maintains a prudent monetary policy, designed to keep inflation in check while devaluing down the dinar to make the country more competitive internationally. Growth in narrow money slowed to 14 percent in 1999 from 20 percent in 1993, while in 1999, broad money increased by 14 percent rising to 16.6 percent in 2000. Since the early 1990s, when Algeria embarked on policy reforms, it has devalued its currency to mitigate a growing balance of payments crisis caused by weak oil prices. Between 1990 and 1999 the dinar was devalued by almost 87 percent to AD66.6:US$. During 2000, the dinar depreciated a further 8.9 percent. While successive devaluations have failed to generate any noticeable increase in non-oil exports, they have slowed the rate of increase in imports thereby helping restoring balance-of-payment viability.

Recognizing the risk that economic growth might be constrained by a tight money strategy, Egypt loosened monetary policy in 2000. At the same time, the authorities maintained a reactive stance as they sought to manage the depreciation of the pound, without draining domestic market liquidity and raising interest rates. Though money supply growth fell marginally to 8.4 percent in the second quarter of 2000 from 9.4 percent in the previous quarter, the average lending rate remained unchanged at 13 percent. At the end of 2000 M2 had fallen to 8.8 percent from 11.4 percent in 1999. The government has also focussed on a closer

alignment of bank and informal market rates. This has made the banks, rather than the exchange bureaus, the "market-makers".

Inflation in Egypt remained at 3 percent in 2000. The long-run slowdown in inflation—from 15.7 percent in 1995—is largely a result of the deflationary effects of tight fiscal policy, a stable currency and continued price controls on some basic goods and services. For some time, Egypt has maintained that rapid currency devaluation would discourage foreign investors and could lead to massive capital flight. However, the inflation differential with its partners resulted in an appreciation of the real effective exchange rate for the pound. The authorities responded by allowing the exchange rate to depreciate some 5 percent during 2000.

In Libya, money supply growth declined to -5.9 percent and -3.7 percent in the first and second quarters of 2000 from 15.1 percent and 12.1 percent during the corresponding period of 1999. Money supply growth has been moderate since 1993 and over 2000 as a whole money supply is estimated to have increased 3.1 percent. Discount and money-market rates have remained unchanged at 5 percent and 4 percent, respectively since 1998, despite the fact that inflation has been in double digits. The UN sanctions have been the major cause of inflation because of the shortages of goods and services that they created.

In Mauritania, money supply growth surged from 4.2 percent in the second quarter of 1999 to 38.2 percent in the corresponding period in 2000, chiefly because of demand deposit growth. However, money supply rose by 7 percent at the end of 2000. Mauritania has been relatively successful in controlling inflation, (from 4.1 percent in 1999 to 2.7 percent in 2000) and money supply—from 8 percent in 1997 to 3.5 percent in 1999 and then doubling at 7 percent in 2000. One consequence of relative monetary expansion in recent years was currency depreciation. The exchange rate of the Mauritanian ouguiya lost two-thirds of its value against the dollar between 1990 and 2000 and that had the beneficial side effect of increasing the competitiveness of iron ore and fish exports.

Monetary policy in Morocco has been cautious. Both the narrow and broad money supply measures grew less than 10 percent during the 1990s, with narrow money supply (M1) slowing to an estimated 6.5 percent and the broad money supply to 7.4 percent in 2000. Lending rates have remained steady at 13.5 percent while other interest rates stayed below 10 percent. Though reserve requirements for commercial banks have been reduced from 20 percent to 15 percent of deposit liabilities, there is little need to alter monetary policy, given relatively low inflation (1.9 percent in 2000) and a stable exchange rate. The government continues to use the pegged exchange rate as an anchor for maintaining price stability.

In Sudan, one of the objectives of the structural reform program is monetary stability. Money supply growth has moderated slightly from 33.8 percent in the second quarter of 1998 to 30.3 percent in the corresponding period in 1999. In 2000, monetary growth slowed substantially to average an estimated 25 percent compared with over 50 percent in the first half of the 1990s. As a result, inflation slowed dramatically from a high of 133 percent in 1996 to a low of 14.4 percent in 2000. High inflation throughout the 1990s (up to 132.8 percent in 1996) forced Sudan to sharply devalue its currency.

Intervention by the central bank, Banque centrale de Tunisie (BCT) in the money market is the main instrument of monetary policy in Tunisia. BCT uses the weekly auction of the fixed amounts of seven-day funds and the *prise en pension* seven-day repo facility to keep the money supply growth below the nominal GDP growth rate. While money supply growth increased from 11.9 percent in the first quarter of 1999 to 19.1 percent in the corresponding period of 2000, the average money market rate remained below 10 percent. During 2000, money supply is estimated to have increased 6.8 percent—down from the expansion rate of 9.6 percent in 1999. Inflation remained low (3.1 percent in 2000), due partly to the removal of duties on most items imported from EU, along with a tight fiscal policy.

Fiscal Policy

Relative to sub-Saharan Africa and other less developed regions, North Africa has maintained a healthy fiscal balance in recent years as governments acknowledged the value of economic reforms and the necessity of avoiding large high budget deficits that would spur inflation and crowd out private investment. Since the mid-1990s, North Africa's budget deficit has stayed below 2 percent of GDP and in 2000 the region came close to achieving a balanced budget (Figure 2.21). Buoyant oil prices enabled oil exporting countries to run a surplus, while non-oil countries kept public spending under tight control. Furthermore, healthy economic growth also contributed to a reduction in the deficit-to-GDP ratio.

Egypt aims at achieving a budget deficit ratio less than 1.5 percent of GDP in the 2000/2001 fiscal year, while the Algerian budget for 2000 projected a deficit of AD220 billion, or 6.3 percent of GDP. Estimates suggest however that the oil price boom translated into a substantial budget surplus of the order of 6.7 percent of GDP for Algeria but a deficit of 1.3 percent of GDP for Egypt. For Algeria, despite strong, though

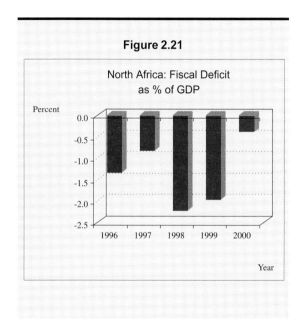

Figure 2.21

North Africa: Fiscal Deficit
as % of GDP

The government has announced a three-year plan to reduce the impact of cyclical droughts on the Moroccan economy. The plan includes a number of fiscal consolidation measures designed to reduce the budget deficit, including phasing out subsidies on foodstuffs and utilities, with power and water prices the first to be increased. It also aims to abolish tax exemptions for capital gains, agriculture and housing and freeze civil service salaries to reduce wage costs to 8 percent of GDP from 10 percent at present.

On the revenue side, the tax rate on capital gains from equities and mutual funds has been increased with the tax on mutual fund gains from the bond market increased from 10 percent to 30 percent. Capital gains from equity, which were tax-free until recently, will now be taxed at 10 percent. The government is also counting on revenues from privatization. In fiscal 1998/1999 fiscal period, privatization auctions raised MD16.7 billion, while in 2001 the proposed sale of Morocco's Royal Airline is expected to generate sizable revenue for the government.

Fiscal prudence characterized Tunisian budgets during the 1990s. The government sought to control the rise of expenditure while at the same time simplifying the tax collection system to broaden the tax base. As a result, Tunisia has maintained a budget deficit of less than 4 percent of GDP since 1997, reaching 2.3 percent of GDP in 2000. In the 2000 budget the government raised VAT and personal income tax rates to offset the loss of customs revenue following the reduction in trade tariffs as part of the trade agreement with the EU.

Both Mauritania and Sudan have made great progress in fiscal consolidation. Mauritania has been successful in controlling the budget deficit that increased during the 1980s and early 1990s, reaching a surplus of 5.3 percent of GDP in 1999 and

lower, energy prices the budget for fiscal 2001 is conservative. Oil revenues are expected to contribute 60 percent of total government revenue, with non-oil sources providing only 10.4 percent of GDP, which is relatively low for a country at Algeria's stage of development. The clear implication is that the authorities need to broaden the tax base to reduce revenue reliance on the energy sector.

Despite government's long-term plans to curb public spending and reduce the fiscal deficit, Morocco's budget deficit increased from 5.5 percent of GDP in 1999 to 6.6 percent of GDP in 2000. Drought and the need to spend more on grain imports are partly to blame for the marginal deterioration in the budget balance. Due to the drought, the July–December 2000 transitional budget, allocated MD6.5 billion to agricultural assistance and cereal imports.

1.3 percent in 2000. The introduction of VAT as a revenue enhancing measure played a major part in this process. In the past, Sudan ran large budget deficits, partly due to high levels of military spending on the civil war. The deficit was exacerbated by the country's narrow tax base. To correct this, the government cut capital project spending drastically while increasing indirect taxes especially VAT. The net effect has been to bring the budget closer to the government's target of budget balance.

Privatization

North African countries are committed to a rigorous privatization program designed to sell most, if not all, of the ailing state firms. However, the privatization process has not been even throughout the region as countries such as Algeria are still debating internally the breadth of the program, while others have made great strides.

Algeria has worked towards reducing its budget deficit and hence subsidies of all kinds, especially to enterprises under government control. However, opposition to massive privatization was, and remains, strong because it is feared that it will affect the livelihood of many workers who may have to be laid off. Although the government has been particularly sensitive to this issue, it recently opened the door to a comprehensive privatization effort. No state enterprise will be off limit to the privatization effort, including the highly profitable oil company, Sonatrach. A law has already been approved in parliament to split and privatize the national post and telephone company.

The sale of 15,000 medium-sized and small parastatals will accelerate. These will require much smaller investment and will result in fewer layoffs. Plans have been set up to first sell about 1,300 small and medium-sized companies to their employees through tender. The stock exchange was set up to help expedite the privatization process but with limited success so far. The privatization efforts have attracted the attention of a number of foreign investors, mainly in the oil and natural gas industry. Investment plans are being considered in several other sectors.

In Egypt, about 40 percent of the total number of companies targeted for privatization has been partially privatized during the past four years. Estimated at 1.5 percent of GDP per year, the rate of privatization in Egypt has been ranked fourth in the world, only lower than Hungary, Malaysia, and the Czech Republic. Sixty-five of the offerings were conducted through the stock market, while 21 companies were sold to workers and 27 to private sector investors. Privatization of utilities will take longer but Egypt will continue to seek some participation from private investors in sectors not subject to outright privatization. The privatization process is expected to be broadened to sectors such as energy and banking.

Morocco has also made great progress in its privatization program. Since the privatization program was launched in 1993, Morocco has privatized 58 companies. According to the program, the total number of companies to be privatized by the end of 1998 was 114. In 2000, the government planned to privatize the car assembly plant, Somaca and the tobacco firm, Regie des Tabacs. Earlier plans for privatization of Moroccan national airline (Royal Air Maroc) in 2000/2001 have been postponed. The new target is 2002. RAM is one of the largest state owned enterprises. Government has announced that it needed more time to improve the standing of the company before it is offered for sale to private investors. Several other privatization projects are on target. Morocco is now moving cautiously on the privatization pro-

gram and, simultaneously, applying policies to provide a supportive framework for private investment. The privatization receipts for 1998/1999
amounted to 2 billion dirhams. The receipts for
1999/2000 were 3.5 billion dirhams, a 75 percent
increase. In the approved six-month transitional
budget (July–December 2000), the privatization
receipts are expected to grow by 63 percent. In
the most recent auction, GSM Mobile (cellular
phone service license) was sold to a consortium
led by Spain's Telefonica for $1.1 billion dollars.
The government planned to auction two large
state-owned hotels as part of its privatization program in 2000. Since 1993, Morocco has sold 21
state-owned hotels.

Tunisia has sold a number of state enterprises
since it launched its privatization program in 1987,
mostly in the construction, commerce and tourism sectors. Foreign investors own the majority
of the assets sold to the private sector. The government wants also to sell parastatals in agriculture, banking and textile, as well Tunis Air, the national airline.

In Mauritania, the government has divested
from more than three-quarters of the companies
it owned. Air Mauritanie is now in the hands of
the private sector and the electricity and water utility
is due to be privatized in the near future. The post
and telephone state company is being split into
two separate entities in order to sell the phone
business to private concerns.

In Sudan, the government had sold several
parastatals in order to alleviate the drain they represent on government resources and at the same
time raise the necessary revenues to restore more
balance to the budget. In the early 1990s, the government slated 190 companies for privatization.
While many of the state enterprises have been sold,
including the phone company, others have remained on the selling block due to the lack of

interest. The perception is that they are not suffi-
ciently viable to be profitable in the future. Among
the assets that the government plans to privatize
are the national airline company and the national
shipping company.

Outlook

With the commitment of the majority of the governments in the region to the continuation of economic reforms and to a privatization program,
the region is poised to continue to perform well
in the near future, barring a collapse of the prices
of the region's main export commodities or adverse weather conditions. In the longer term the
region will be less vulnerable to weather uncertainties or fluctuations of export commodity prices
as it diversifies. Inflation in the region is likely to
remain under control because of the pursuit of
conservative monetary policies. All countries in the
region are likely to continue to devalue their exchange rates to prevent a real appreciation.

For the short-term (one to two years), growth
in the region is likely to be lower than in 2000.
For Algeria, because of lower oil prices and production, economic growth is likely to be lower.
Also, because of the continued political uncertainty,
foreign investors are likely to stay away at least
until there are signs that a final political settlement
has been reached. The current account is likely to
remain in surplus as exports of hydrocarbons (particularly of natural gas) increase. Inflation will remain low due to tight monetary policy.

Growth prospects in Egypt remain promising. Increased export revenues, tourism receipts,
Suez Canal receipts and remittances from Egyptian nationals working abroad provide the bulk
of Egypt's foreign exchange earnings. The continuation of economic reforms and a relatively
stable environment will increase the flow of for-

eign direct investment. Increases in exports of non-traditional commodities will also be a major contributor to growth in the future.

Barring continuation of the drought and continued political stability, growth in Morocco is likely to rebound strongly, as has been the case in the past. While the lower oil prices will mean a lower energy bill, increased imports caused by higher economic activity will mean that both the trade and the current account balances will deteriorate but only slightly. Inflation will remain under control due to the conservative monetary policy.

In Tunisia, good macroeconomic management, better-than-expected rainfall and improved tourism revenues will cause economic growth to be higher in the short- to medium-term. As in the case of Morocco, the economy, however, remains vulnerable to climate, competition and world prices. Greater liberalization of the economy will enable Tunisia to take greater advantage of the new economic relationship with EU and attract more direct investment to develop other sectors of the economy. This will reduce the dependence on agriculture and improve long-term prospects for growth. Inflation is likely to remain under control.

Libya's economic prospects are also brighter, in spite of lower oil prices in the short-term. The lifting of UN sanctions has allowed the country to import the necessary raw materials and capital goods necessary for further economic expansion. Libya will continue to make progress on the inflation front now that the shortages caused by the sanctions are a thing of the past.

Because of the continuation of economic reforms, both Sudan and Mauritania are likely to continue a healthy growth pattern in the future. While Mauritania will maintain a tight control on inflation, Sudan will have to make more determined effort to sustain the lower inflation rate.

Southern Africa

Overview

Ten countries make up the Southern Africa Region: Angola, Botswana, Lesotho, Malawi, Mozambique, Namibia, South Africa, Swaziland, Zambia, and Zimbabwe. The sub-region's population was estimated at 111.2 million in 2000, representing 14.2 percent of Africa's total. With a total GDP of $162.5 billion in 1999 the sub-region accounts for almost a third (32 percent) of the continent's total GDP. On a per capita income basis, Southern Africa's average of $1,463.9 in 2000 ranks among the highest in the continent, though this masks enormous disparities between different countries in the sub-region. Botswana's per capita GDP of $3,986, which is the highest in Southern Africa, is almost thrice the average for

Southern Africa and almost twelve times that of Zambia.

Recent economic trends

During 2000, regional GDP grew 2.6 percent—a modest increase on its 1999 rate of 2.1 percent, though this remained well below the African average of 3.2 percent (Figure 2.22 and Table 2.5). Growth rates in the region varied from a high of 6 percent in Botswana to –5.5 percent in Zimbabwe (Figure 2.23). Because of South Africa's dominance in the region's economy (more than 80 percent of the region's total GDP), the overall growth pattern for the region is largely determined by South Africa's economic performance.

Hopes that South Africa's economy would rebound strongly from its lackluster performance in the previous two years, did not materialize. Provisional estimates suggest that GDP grew 3 per-

Table 2.5: Southern Africa: Macroeconomic Indicators, 1990- 2000

Indicators	1990	1995	1996	1997	1998	1999	2000[a/]
Real GDP Growth Rate (%)	0.6	3.2	5.0	3.2	1.5	2.1	2.6
GDP Per Capita (US $)	1,640.5	1,801.5	1,739.2	1,768.4	1,544.7	1,510.6	1463.9
Inflation (%)	33.9	70.7	72.0	23.5	18.9	30.3	23.0
Fiscal Balance (% of GDP)	-4.4	-5.7	-4.6	-4.2	-2.9	-2.8	-2.6
Gross Domestic Investment (% of GDP)	17.5	18.3	16.9	17.1	17.1	17.4	17.3
Gross National Savings (% of GDP)	18.3	16.7	16.5	14.5	13.9	15.1	15.1
Real Export Growth (%)	10.4	20.6	23.0	25.6	30.8	25.5	29.0
Trade Balance (% GDP)	5.6	1.9	2.8	2.0	0.9	2.8	3.9
Current Account (% GDP)	0.7	-2.3	-1.6	-2.4	-3.3	-2.1	-0.8
Terms of Trade (%)	1.0	-0.4	4.4	-0.2	-3.0	4.1	7.4
Total External Debt (% GDP)	32.8	39.7	37.9	38.8	42.2	43.9	42.0
Debt Service (% of Exports)	8.9	18.1	22.4	16.6	18.8	17.9	...

Note: a/ Preliminary estimates.
Source: ADB Statistics Division and IMF.

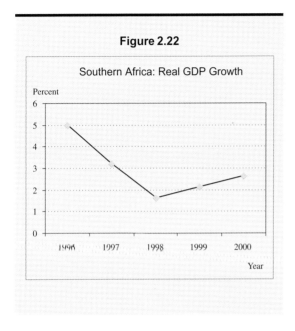

Figure 2.22

Southern Africa: Real GDP Growth

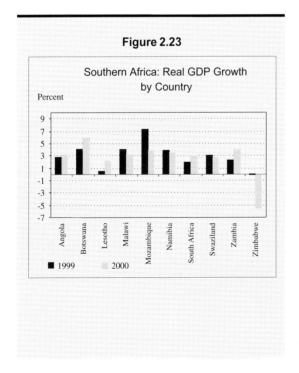

Figure 2.23

Southern Africa: Real GDP Growth by Country

cent in 2000, compared with 1.9 percent in 1999 and the fastest such growth rate since 1996 (4.2 percent). A strengthening of public finances, improved external competitiveness and the strong global economy contributed to the modest acceleration in economic growth.

Two events were responsible for slower-than-forecast expansion in the first half of 2000. The devastating floods that hit parts of Southern Africa in the first quarter undermined GDP growth, while South Africa was also adversely affected by the contagion effects from the deteriorating economic situation in neighboring Zimbabwe. As a result, the rand came under pressure in the foreign currency markets in April-May and the authorities were unable to reduce interest rates as early and as much as had been anticipated. Investor sentiment towards South Africa, which had been expected to improve, remained negative for much of the year, partly due to the Zimbabwean situation.

In the domestic capital market, the repo-rate declined from 19.32 percent in the first week of January 1999 to 11.75 percent a year later, leading to a reduction in the prime rate from a relatively high 22 percent in January 1999 to 14.5 percent in January 2000. However, the contagion effects of the crisis in Zimbabwe, declining gold production and weak investor confidence contributed to an outflow of capital from the economy during the year. There was also a sharp rise in the outward foreign direct investment (FDI) by South African companies, much of it linked to take-over activity in the southern African region and abroad. Capital outflows were affected also by the decision of some leading corporates bodies to move their primary stock market listing from the Johannesburg to the London Stock Exchange.

Agricultural output fell some 10 percent in the first half of the year, chiefly reflecting the impact of the floods, while mining volumes also declined marginally. These falls were more than offset by the recovery in manufacturing and a buoyant tertiary sector. Exports benefitted from the weak rand and strong platinum prices, as a result of which platinum group metal exports exceeded those of gold in 2000. There was also a sharp increase in manufactured exports, especially motor vehicles and textiles.

Zimbabwe's economy has been slowing since 1998 when growth exceeded two percent. In 1999, output fell by 0.2 percent, while in 2000 GDP is estimated to have fallen by 5.5 percent. At US dollar values, Zimbabwe is now the third largest economy in the sub-region after South Africa and Angola, accounting for 3.5 percent of regional GDP. On present form, however, it could well be overtaken by Botswana in the next year or two.

Several factors account for this poor recent economic performance. The political crisis associated with the government's "fast track" land resettlement programme, frightened off foreign investors and investment approvals by the Zimbabwe Investment Centre fell by almost 90 percent. Tourism, one of the country's leading sources of foreign currency, is estimated to have declined 16 percent, while mining fell 14 percent and manufacturing over 10 percent. Industrial production is now lower than at independence in 1980.

Despite the dislocation of commercial agriculture caused by the threatened takeover of some 5 million hectares of commercial farming land, value-added in agriculture actually increased 3 percent. This reflected good rains, bumper maize and cotton harvests, especially those by smallholder farmers, and a 23 percent increase in tobacco production, mainly on large commercial properties.

But the economy as a whole was undermined by the collapse in business confidence reflecting concerns over property rights, an acute shortage of foreign exchange manifested in power ration-

ing, periodic fuel shortages and inadequate supplies of essential inputs needed in the productive sector. A number of gold mines were forced to close and production of gold, the country's second largest export after tobacco, declined almost 20 percent in volume.

Exports, which have now fallen by a quarter since 1997, were constrained by an overvalued exchange rate. The authorities devalued the Zimbabwe dollar by 24 percent in August 2000, a move followed by several smaller adjustments. Despite this, the IMF warned that on its calculations the currency was some 56 percent overvalued at the end of 2000, pointing to a substantial adjustment during 2001.

With virtually no international funding available to Zimbabwe, following the withdrawal of support by multilateral institutions, the government resorted to the local money market for most of its borrowing requirements. As a result, interest rates were driven up to record levels, which crowded out private investment by making the cost of borrowing prohibitively high. Consequently, gross fixed investment is estimated to have shrunk by almost 8 percent in 2000.

Botswana, the sub-region's fourth largest economy maintained its stellar performance in 2000. With a growth rate averaging above 6 percent in the last four years, Botswana has emerged as a role model for other African countries, though its success has been heavily reliant on its diamond sector. GDP growth accelerated to 6 percent in 2000 from 4 percent the previous year, driven largely by increased diamond demand and production. Other positive influences at work included higher social spending, increased FDI inflows and a competitive exchange rate. The construction sector has also expanded rapidly reflecting high levels of public sector development spending.

The government's economic diversification strategy received a sharp setback with the closure of the country's motor vehicle assembly plant. Motor vehicles had become Botswana's second largest export, after diamonds, and the shut-down of the Hyundai assembly plant will impact adversely on foreign currency earnings.

Growth in Southern Africa's most dynamic economy—Mozambique—virtually halved during 2000 due to the devastating floods in the south and centre of the country in the first quarter of the year (Box 2.1). After expanding almost 12 percent in 1998 and more than 7 percent in 1999, GDP growth slowed to 3.8 percent in 2000.

While agriculture employs the vast majority of the people in Mozambique and represents approximately one-third of GDP, other sectors of the economy such as the budding industrial sector, the construction and energy sub-sectors and the services sectors, were able to sustain economic activity. Part of the expansion of the economy resulted from reconstruction efforts after the floods.

The commissioning—ahead of schedule—of the Mozal aluminum smelter was a major boost for the economy. Exports from the plant are estimated at over $100 million in 2000 rising to average almost $500 million a year over the next few years. The country benefitted also from exceptionally large aid inflows needed to finance the rebuilding of infrastructure destroyed or damaged by the floods, as well as from debt relief under the Heavily Indebted Poor Countries Initiative.

GDP in Namibia expanded 3.5 percent in 2000 largely due to a good grain harvest, good performance of the fishing and construction sectors and growth in the mining sector. Output of diamonds increased with the new NamSSol II diamond mine coming on stream. The fishing sector also grew strongly with the recovery of the Southeast Asian economies and increased EU demand for Namibia's fish exports.

Zambia's GDP growth increased from 2.2 percent in 1999 to 4 percent in 2000, well on target. Agricultural production, especially maize, improved following good rains while the tourist sector, though still tiny, benefited from the switch of business away from Zimbabwe to Zambia. It was hoped, however, that the successful completion of the privatization of Zambia Consolidated Copper Mines would lead to a rapid turnaround in production and exports, but figures for the first nine months of 2000 show a 20 percent decline to a new low of 155 000 tonnes. Both the two new groups that took over the main copper mines, Konkola Copper Mines and Mopani Copper Mines, have warned that they will miss their production targets for the financial year to March 2001, though thereafter they expect output to rise sharply.

Growth in the Angolan economy—now the second largest in the sub-region—accelerated to 3.2 percent in 2000 from 2.7 percent the previous year. Expansion was driven mainly by the combination of soaring oil prices, rising oil production and increased inflows of FDI mostly targeting offshore oil exploration and development. But the combination of political uncertainty in the region, the ongoing civil war and rampant inflation, constrained economic performance and are likely to do so again in 2001.

Agriculture remains the main economic sector in Malawi, and in spite of an increase in tobacco production, albeit of lesser quality than in the previous years, GDP growth slowed to 3.2 percent from 4 percent the previous year. Poor weather and lower tobacco prices accounted for the slowdown in the economy.

Lesotho's growth is estimated to have risen to 2.2 percent in 2000 from 0.5 percent in 1999. With

Box 2.1: The Mozambique Flood

With a population of 19.7 million people, the Republic of Mozambique lies on the southeast coast of Africa. It achieved independence from Portugal in 1975. Between 1977 and 1992 about a million Mozambicans died from famine and war that ruined the economy and much of the countryside. The country was also left with a legacy of landmines, amputees, substantially destroyed infrastructure, and as one of the most impoverished nations in the world. A series of structural adjustment programs initiated in 1987 had led to an upsurge in domestic production, leading to the acceleration of real GDP growth rate from 4.3 percent in 1995 to 12 percent in 1998 and 8.8 percent in 1999. However, the economy suffered a serious setback in 2000 when floods, accompanied by Cyclone Eline, which affected a quarter of the population and destroyed much of its rebuilt infrastructure, hit the country.

The country has a long history of floods, which usually occur during the rainy seasons of October and April. However, the floods with Cyclone Eline, which lasted for three weeks in February 2000 was Mozambique's worst in 50 years. It left major devastating trails on the economy, properties, farming, infrastructure and people. More than 700 people lost their lives, 800,000 others were displaced out of over one million directly affected, and crops and livestock were wiped out. The total cost to the country is estimated at $600 million, representing 14.8 percent of GDP and 52 percent of total government expenditure in 2000. The damage was worst in seven Southern and Central provinces (especially Maputo, Gaza and Cabo Delgado), where about 27 percent of planted crops were lost, representing over 6 percent of the national total.

The destruction of agricultural output and seeds means severe food shortages and seed (especially maize and rice) availability for subsequent agricultural seasons represents a major problem, particularly in Central and Southern provinces. Estimates indicate that 172,000 food insecure people in Mozambique, including those most affected by the flood damage, require food aid until the next harvest season. For reconstruction, therefore, the country needs seeds and agricultural implements to plough and plant again.

Displaced people were living in overcrowded conditions and this aided the outbreak of health epidemics, including increased incidence of cholera, other diarrhoeal diseases and malaria. Moreover, due to damaged bridges and roads, both rescue operations and humanitarian assistance were made difficult. The United Nations put the estimate of the financial requirements for urgent food, medical supplies, and plastic sheeting for people worst affected at $13 million. While a number of emergency appeal funds have been launched, donors pledged a total of $453 million in humanitarian aid to the country at an international reconstruction conference in Rome in mid-2000 though many of the pledges are yet to be fulfilled. Delays in the release of donor funds had slowed down economic activity and left thousands of people in dire social and economic conditions.

The floods also temporarily reversed the stellar economic growth of Mozambique in 2000. Following the implementation of sound economic reforms the economy had grown at above 7 percent since 1996, reaching 12 percent in 1998. But due mainly to the flood-induced losses in 2000, economic growth nose-dived to 6.1 percent. However, with increased international assistance for reconstruction activities and anticipated full recovery of the agricultural sector, economic growth is expected to accelerate to over 10 percent in 2001.

Given Mozambique's vulnerability to disasters caused by climatic irregularities, more permanent and enduring measures should be taken to minimize future losses. A strengthened early warning system should be put in place, complemented by the setting up of a Disaster Preparedness, Relief and Rehabilitation body, which should work in coordination with relevant UN agencies. People inhabiting lowlands where damages and losses are usually very severe should be relocated permanently to highlands. Also, grain storage in more protected areas after each harvest season has become very imperative.

Box 2.1: (Continued)

These will not only help reduce damages and losses to the economy, but will also minimize external dependence for both overall economic development and during the occurrence of national disasters. However, given the enormity of resources required to achieve these in the face of government's lean financial resources, the international community should come to Mozambique's aid by setting up a Disaster Prevention Fund. Both multilateral and bilateral donors as well as international NGOs should contribute to the fund since it is superior to *ad hoc* relief measures usually adopted after disasters and losses have occurred. Greater external debt relief for such a poor, disaster-prone but reforming economy should also be top on the agenda of international financial institutions. But the important lesson for Mozambique, other African countries, and the donor community is that external factors such as natural disasters can deal a setback to a well-intentioned economic recovery program.

Source: FAO (2000).

---

the government committed to maintain tight budgetary restraint, public spending is no longer a major growth stimulus. Businessmen say that political uncertainty is holding back private investment spending by both domestic and foreign-owned firms. Lesotho remains dependent on developments in the South African economy, with private consumer spending remaining depressed following the downsizing of migrant worker jobs on the South African gold mines.

In Swaziland, also dependent on the South African economy, GDP expanded by 2.7 percent in 2000 against the 1999 growth rate of 3.1 percent. The heavy rains, which fell in early 2000, adversely affected yields and production of maize. However, the manufacturing sector fared better with increased production of refrigerators and woodpulp. The construction sector also expanded its output with the construction of the Maguga dam and new roads.

External accounts

Southern Africa is heavily dependent on exports of primary products with the most important being oil from Angola, diamonds from Botswana, Namibia and South Africa, platinum (South Africa), gold, copper and agricultural produce - tobacco, horticulture, cotton and beef. Imports are dominated by capital and intermediate goods and other semi-finished products.

In the latter part of the 1990s, both exports and imports declined up to and including 1999, reflecting weak commodity prices, especially oil and minerals, and slower economic growth. But as economic growth picked up in 2000 and commodity prices recovered some of their lost ground, exports rose 29 percent while imports increased 10 percent.

As a result of the faster increase in exports than imports, the trade surplus for the region increased from $4.48 billion in 1999 to $6.16 billion (or 3.9 percent of the GDP) in 2000 (Figure 2.24). The trade surplus recorded in 2000 was accounted for overwhelmingly by South Africa, which registered a $3.3 billion surplus or 2.6 percent of GDP. South Africa accounts for almost 80 percent of the region's exports and three quarters of its imports.

Exports grew strongly during 2000 stimulated by improved world economic growth, the depreciation of the rand—especially against the US

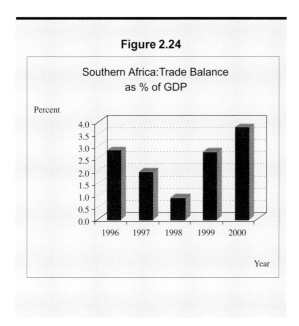

Figure 2.24

Southern Africa:Trade Balance
as % of GDP

terms of trade shock was cushioned by the surge in the price of platinum

Botswana registered $970 million trade surplus (16.3 percent of GDP) in 2000. Botswana represents 5.5 percent of the region's exports and 5.8 percent of its imports. Other countries to record trade surpluses in the region were Angola and Zimbabwe. Angola's foreign trade showed a surplus of some $3.59 billion (54.2 percent of GDP) compared to $2.08 billion in 1999, due largely to the sharp rise in oil prices. In Zimbabwe, trade surplus rose from $250 million in 1999 to $450 million in 2000, representing 5.9 percent of GDP. Despite softer prices on the Harare auction floors, tobacco exports increased following favorable climatic conditions and a bumper harvest of 236 million kilograms, but gold exports were sharply lower as were manufactured goods, reflecting an overvalued currency and supply-side constraints, especially fuel, electricity and the availability of imported inputs.

For Swaziland, stronger international demand for the country's main exports (textiles, refrigerators, wood pulp and sugar) translated into an export increase of 8.5 percent over 1999. Imports also increased due to demand generated by large public sector capital projects. As a result, the trade deficit increased to $140 million (11 percent of GDP).

Mozambique recorded an estimated $950 million deficit (23.4 percent of GDP) due to continued high levels of imports which outstripped exports because of the purchase of capital goods for major projects. These imports totalled more than $200 million in 2000, though this was partly offset by the $120 million earned from new large projects—notably the Mozal aluminum smelter. Exports are forecast to more than double in 2001 to $685 million from $312 million, as a result of

dollar which boosted competitiveness—and increased output and prices of platinum. As a result, real exports of goods and services expanded by 8.5 percent in 2000—a significant improvement after the stagnation experienced in 1999.

Import demand was driven by a recovery in consumer spending after a decline in gross domestic expenditure of 0.5 percent in 1999 and a slight recovery in gross fixed capital formation after a 7 percent fall the previous year. Domestic demand growth accelerated in the latter half of the year as interest rates fell and the impact of the February floods diminished with the result that import volumes grew some 8.8 percent.

South Africa was less severely affected by the oil price shock during 1999/2000 than most other oil-importing emerging markets because of its dependence on domestic energy sources notably coal and oil from coal. Furthermore, the adverse

which the trade deficit will fall steeply to less than $500 million from $950 million in 2000.

Similarly, in Lesotho, the trade balance deteriorated to a deficit of $510 million (61.8 percent of GDP) due to increased imports of capital goods and raw materials to maintain its budding manufacturing sector. The manufacturing sector is also responsible for a growing share of exports, mainly to South Africa.

Depressed prices for Malawi's main export commodity, tobacco, and the lower quality of its crops translated into a weak export performance in 2000, but currency depreciation cushioned the impact on the trade balance to some degree by discouraging non essential imports. Despite this, the trade deficit widened from $10 million in 1999 to an estimated $30 million (1.7 percent of GDP) in 2000.

In Namibia, increased demand for diamonds and fish, the country's main export commodities, resulted in a 9 percent increase in exports. However, increased oil prices were the main factor behind a 7 percent increase in imports, resulting in an estimated trade deficit of $230 million (7.7 percent of GDP).

The current account deficit for the region was $1.35 billion (or 0.83 percent of GDP) in 2000, down from $3.32 billion or 2.1 percent of GDP in 1999 (Figure 2.25). Botswana contributed in a significant way to the overall improvement, with an increase in its surplus to $0.86 billion (or 14.54 percent of GDP), a rise from $540 million in 1999. As a percentage of GDP, the other countries in the region recorded current account balances as follows: -21.8 percent for Mozambique, 0.38 percent for Angola, 6.03 percent for Namibia, -5.71 percent for Malawi, -1.52 percent for Swaziland, 0.74 percent for Zimbabwe, and -13.38 percent for Zambia.

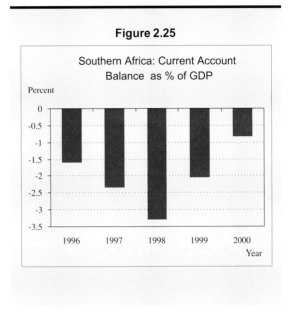

Figure 2.25

Southern Africa: Current Account Balance as % of GDP

External debt

As a result of the sub-region's past persistent current account deficit and insufficient foreign investment to finance the shortfall, its foreign debt increased steadily between 1994 and 2000, reaching $68.47 billion or 42 percent of total GDP (Figure 2.26). South Africa accounts for the lion's share, with an external debt of $38.91 billion or 57 percent of the regional total. However, at only 30.1 percent of GDP, South Africa's external debt is very modest by international standards.

Four of the ten Southern African countries are classified as Heavily Indebted Poor Countries (HIPC) - Angola, Malawi, Mozambique and Zambia, with Zambia having an external debt of $5.09 billion or 174.9 percent of GDP. In the last quarter of 2000, Zambia became the eleventh country to obtain debt relief (US$3.3 billion) under the enhanced HIPC program. Without the HIPC deal,

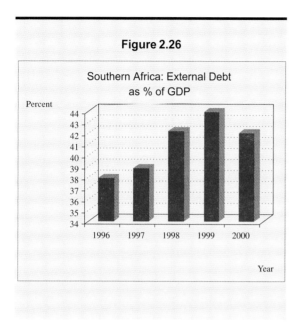

Figure 2.26

Southern Africa: External Debt
as % of GDP

Zambia would have been unable to pay debt service of some $230 million due to the IMF alone in 2000, together with further large amounts arising from series of bridging loans made during the 1990s.

Zimbabwe has its external debt as $6.85 billion, representing almost 89.5 percent of GDP in 2000. Debt service consumes 29 percent of revenues from exports of goods and services. The main growth in external debt in 2000 arose from the accumulation of external payments arrears of some $600 million.

Lesotho's external debt of $0.72 billion represented 87.9 percent of GDP in 2000, but despite this high level of indebtedness its debt-service ratio was only 7.1 percent of exports. The first country in the region to obtain debt relief of some US$4 billion under the HIPC facility was Mozambique. As a result, its debt-service ratio fell

dramatically from 26 percent of exports in 1999 to just 4.4 percent in 2000. It will increase to 5.8 percent in 2001 before falling back to average 4 percent over the subsequent five years. Its total external debt in 2000 was $773 million or 190.6 percent of GDP.

Angola's external debt decreased to $6.44 billion (97.3 percent of GDP) in 2000, while Malawi's was $1.91 billion (114.9 percent of GDP). Namibia's external debt was $100 million (3.3 of GDP), while that of Swaziland was $250 million (19.7 of GDP).

Policy developments

For the region to successfully integrate into the global economy, meaningful reforms (both political and economic) must be implemented fully. With the exceptions of Zimbabwe and Angola, countries in the region heeded the call from multilateral organizations for the pursuit and continuation of sound economic reforms in 2000. Governments acknowledge that this must be an ongoing process and much remains to be done in respect of restoring macroeconomic stability in some countries as well as carrying out far-reaching structural and institutional reforms, including privatization.

Monetary Policy, inflation and exchange rates

Most Southern Africa countries maintained relatively tight monetary policies during 2000 in an attempt to further reduce inflation and encourage savings and investment. Inflation in the Common Monetary Area (CMA), comprising South Africa, Lesotho, Namibia and Swaziland declined during the 1990s, primarily as a result of the orthodox and cautious monetary stance of the South African authorities. It is not possible to calculate a single inflation rate for the CMA, but since South Africa accounts for some 90 percent of CMA GDP, its inflation rate is a relatively accurate indicator of the average for the rand monetary area. Consumer inflation in South Africa fell to an estimated 4 percent in 2000 from 14.4 percent in 1990. For the entire region it fell to 23 percent from 30.3 percent in 1999, while money supply remained virtually unchanged at 12 percent (Figure 2.27).

Governments in Southern Africa have recognized the need to maintain realistic exchange rates, considering the inflation differentials with major trading partners. Countries in the region have devalued their currencies not only to reflect their respective inflation rates (thus preventing an appreciation of their real exchange rates) but also to enhance their international competitive positions.

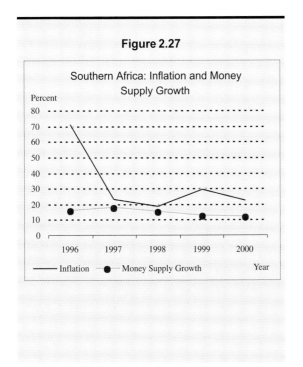

Figure 2.27

Southern Africa: Inflation and Money Supply Growth

In 2000, the South African Reserve Bank (SARB) followed a neutral monetary policy stance, in spite of the inflationary pressures from oil and food prices. Money supply growth, however, rose from 8.9 percent in the first quarter of 1999 to 14.1 percent in the first quarter of 2000. The annual average for 2000 was 9.4 percent, down from 10.2 percent in 1999. It also introduced a system of inflation targeting which tracks CPIX (CPI inflation less mortgages). This, together with the tight monetary policy, is largely accountable for the country's relatively low inflation rate of 5.3 percent recorded in 2000. The SARB's target is to bring CPIX between 3 percent and 6 percent by 2002.

High real interest rates played a key role in helping curb inflation and mitigate inflationary expectations. Prime lending rate was driven up to a high of 23 percent in 1998 in an attempt to slow inflation and stabilize the rand at the time of the Asian financial crisis. By the end of 2000, prime rate had been reduced to 14.5 percent and while the authorities are anxious to cut rates further during 2001, monetary policy has been constrained by the steep rise in oil import costs and the weakness of the rand.

The rand fell nearly 20 percent against the US dollar during 2000, largely reflecting the strength of the US currency. It was hit also by nervousness in the international markets over the political and economic crisis in neighboring Zimbabwe.

The Reserve Bank of Zimbabwe has tried to operate a tight monetary policy to maintain price and exchange rate stability. Unfortunately, its room for manoeuvre has been constrained by low foreign exchange reserves and pressures to finance government expenditure, especially the fiscal deficit. Thus, monetary policy had been in the form of local borrowing through Treasury bills with a 91 day maturity or monetary financing (printing money). This resulted in extremely high rates of money supply growth (57.9 percent in 2000) and high real interest rates. Consumer inflation increased to 56.3 percent in 2000 from 49.9 percent in 1999. Food prices fell significantly in the latter half of the year, but underlying (non-food) inflation continued to rise reaching 64 percent in December, as wage pressures intensified and the authorities raised administered prices for fuel, electricity and tele-communications.

The Zimbabwean dollar was devalued by 24.1 percent on August 1, 2000 to Z$50:US$1 after having been pegged at approximately Z$38:US$1 since the beginning of 1999. The government has adopted an exchange rate policy based on inflation differentials between Zimbabwe and her trading partners. Although this is a move in the right direction, the local currency is still considerably overvalued, with the IMF calculating that at the end of 2000, the Zimbabwe currency was more than 50 percent overvalued.

The central bank of Botswana has traditionally maintained a tight monetary policy that explains the slowdown in money supply growth to 11.9 percent in 2000 from 18.4 percent in 1999. The average lending rate remained close to 15 percent, while inflation accelerated from 7.1 percent in 1999 to 8.2 percent in 2000, so that real lending rates remained substantially positive. The exchange rate of the pula, which is linked to a trade-weighted basket of currencies, in which the South African rand is dominant, depreciated through 2000, dragged down by the weak rand, losing 6.5 percent of its value against the US dollar during the year.

Throughout the 1990s, the Bank of Zambia sought to use monetary restraint to curb inflation and stabilize the exchange rate for the Kwacha. However, in 2000, the policy shifted to bringing down interest rates through the reduction of yields on Treasury bills and short-term bonds. Money supply growth fell to 16.5 percent in 2000 from 21.5 percent in 1999 while inflation, which had fallen to 20.6 percent in 1999 rose to 24.5 percent in 2000. The kwacha depreciated sharply in the second half of 2000 falling from K2600 to the US dollar at the end of 1999 to K4500 a year later. The government responded by announcing plans to re-impose limited exchange controls from January 2001.

The civil war and huge budget deficits have forced Angola into a very loose monetary stance with extra-budgetary expenditure being funded by uncontrolled monetary growth. Consequently, money supply growth surged from 63 percent in the first quarter of 1999 to 708 percent a year later. In the same vein, the average lending rate rose from 45 percent in the first quarter of 1999 to 1,336.55 percent in the corresponding period in 2000. Although inflation is estimated at 120 percent during the year 2000, this marked a major improvement on the 1996 figure of 4145 percent. The new currency, the Kwanza, issued in December 1999, continued to depreciate in line with the differential between Angolan inflation and that in its main trading partners.

Malawi's main monetary policy instrument is the Reserve Bank of Malawi's management of the money stock through Treasury bill auctions. The banking sector maintains a cautious stance towards new loans which has made it difficult for private sector to access bank loans for working capital and investment. Although inflation has shown signs of slowing recently as the effects of currency devaluation wear off, the rate of price increases remained high at 27 percent in 2000 due to increased utility charges and higher prices for basic goods. During 2000, the Petroleum Control Commission of Malawi increased prices on several occasions because of the higher oil import prices and costs and the depreciation of the Malawi kwacha against the US dollar.

In Mozambique, the combination of an easier monetary policy in 1999 and severe flooding leading to higher food prices in February-March 2000 resulted in a sharp increase in consumer inflation. Broad money grew 35 percent in 1999 and fell to 16 percent in 2000. Consumer inflation, which had averaged only 1.5 percent a year in 1998/99 rose steeply to 16.8 percent in October 2000, before subsiding somewhat and averaging 12 percent over the year. Monetary policy was tightened in mid-year and broad money growth is forecast to remained at 16 percent in 2001, bringing inflation down to 7 percent by the end of the year. The exchange rate depreciated by 19 percent against the US dollar in 2000, due mainly to exogenous shock of the flooding, higher inflation and the strengthening of the dollar against the rand, the currency of Mozambique's main trading partner.

In Lesotho, monetary policy is heavily influenced by monetary and inflation developments in South Africa. The currency, the maloti, is pegged to the rand, which effectively forces the Lesotho authorities to follow very similar monetary policies to that of South Africa. Monetary policy was tightened in 1999 so that by the end of that year, broad money had actually fallen 2.8 percent. This strategy was maintained through 2000 and money supply continued to decline marginally and, while prime lending rates also decreased slightly to 17 percent, they remained very high in real terms—some eleven-percentage points above the inflation rate of 6 percent.

Namibia's bank rate closely shadows the repurchase (repo) rate set by the South African Reserve Bank. However, although the SARB increased the repo rate in October 2000 by 25 basis points to 12 percent, the Bank of Namibia kept its bank rate unchanged at 11.25 percent. Money market rates maintained a gradual downward trend during the year, in line with development in South Africa.

As a member of the CMA, Swaziland's monetary policy is effectively determined in South Africa. While the rand is not legal tender in Swaziland and Lesotho, it is still widely accepted as a means of transaction. In Namibia, the South African currency will remain legal tender for a transitory period of a few years, though there are no plans to alter the pegged exchange rate relationship between the Namibian dollar, Swaziland's lilangeni, and Lesotho's maloti.

Fiscal policy

There is now a general consensus in the sub-region that to achieve macroeconomic stability budget deficits must be reduced to sustainable levels. With two notable exceptions—Angola and Zimbabwe —Southern African countries have already made significant progress in this direction. For the region as a whole, the fiscal deficit as a percentage of GDP decreased slightly in 2000 to 2.6 percent from 2.8 percent in 1999 (Figure 2.28).

However, given the commitment of governments in the region to alleviate poverty through increased public provision of health and education facilities, further deficit reduction will be difficult, if not impossible, to achieve without increasing taxes. There is, however, considerable scope for Southern African states to increase their tax-GDP ratios by widening their tax bases. As in many developing economies, much of the sub-region remains under-taxed because tax collection systems are weak, compliance levels are low and tax exemptions widespread. A number of governments are tackling these problems through the establishment of autonomous national revenue au-

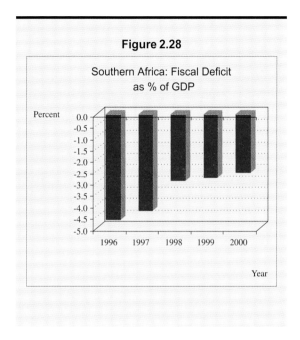

Figure 2.28

Southern Africa: Fiscal Deficit
as % of GDP

thorities, by simplifying tax systems, thereby reducing exemptions, and introducing value-added taxation. Most countries also have active privatization and public sector reform programs.

In 2000, South Africa recorded a budget deficit of 2.6 percent of GDP. The deficit was financed partly from foreign loans to the tune of R6.5 billion, an increase in government's net domestic short-term debt of R3.5 billion, and partly from a reduction in the cash balance of R2 billion. Total expenditure figure of R233.5 billion was proposed for the 2000/2001 fiscal year, representing an increase of 8.1 percent on the revised expenditure figure for 1999/2000. It also represents 26.4 percent of the Department of Finance's forecast GDP of R885.2 billion.

Zimbabwe's fiscal situation deteriorated dramatically during 2000 with the budget deficit increasing from 9 percent of GDP in 1999 to an estimated 11.4 percent. As a result, and because multilateral lenders and donors had withdrawn support due to the problematic land resettlement program, the authorities were forced to fund the deficit from short-term domestic borrowing. Consequently, domestic debt doubled from Z$78 billion at the end of 1999 to Z$162 billion (US$2.9 billion) a year later.

In the 2000 fiscal year, government spending was 67 percent above budget with wages and interest costs each accounting for a third of total expenditure. Defence spending was also above budget due to Zimbabwe's military involvement in the civil conflict in the Democratic Republic if Congo. The 182 percent increase in salaries for ministers and members of parliament coupled with a 69 to 90 percent wage hike for civil servants were also not provided for in the budget.

In Angola, because of the past loose fiscal policy and the high and unsustainable budget deficits (reaching 15.2 percent of GDP in 1999 and averaging more than 20 percent for most of 1990s), the government has come under increasing pressure from multilateral financial institutions to reduce its expenditures. The government agreed to not only eliminate the deficit in 2000, but also to achieve a surplus equivalent to 2 percent of GDP in 2000 and 4 percent in 2001. In 2000, it recorded a budget surplus of 7.9 percent of GDP.

Zambia's fiscal deficit fell from 8.2 percent of GDP in 1993 to 2 percent in 1999. However, estimates put the budget deficit at 3.6 percent of the GDP in 2000. The target is to achieve a balanced budget by 2002 by reining in expenditures and increasing revenues.

Malawi is striving to increase government revenues by diversifying and broadening its tax base, assisted by the setting up of the semi-autonomous Malawi Revenue Authority. Civil service reform is also being implemented though this is being met with resistance in the public sector. In 2000, the country's fiscal deficit fell to 2.4 percent of GDP from 4.1 percent in 1999. The level of the budget deficit will continue to depend on donor assistance.

In Mozambique, the government aimed to cut the budget deficit in 2000 mostly by increasing revenues and broadening the tax base. This objective proved elusive, partly because of the severe flooding and, while revenue did increase marginally to 12.7 percent of GDP from 12.2 percent in 1999, expenditure rose far faster, reflecting the need to spend heavily on reconstruction. With spending exceeding 29 percent of GDP, the deficit widened to 4.5 percent (from 1.5 percent in 1999), most of which was financed from foreign grants of 10.5 percent of GDP. While the imposition of a value-added tax (VAT) successfully boosted revenue, the devastation caused by the floods has increased Mozambique's dependence on foreign assistance, which may again be necessary in 2001.

Namibia continues to suffer from high levels of public spending, brought about by a bloated civil service. Because of the stiff resistance from public servants to any effort to rein in salary increases, the government has tried to increase revenues by replacing the sales tax with VAT. VAT is levied at 15 percent on basic goods and 30 percent for luxury items such as top-of-the-market vehicles, jewelry, alcohol and most electronic equipment. Certain services such as financial services, education, public transport, water and electricity are exempted. The fiscal deficit, however, decreased marginally from 4.9 percent in 1999 to 4 percent in 2000.

Swaziland received a US$5 million grant for fiscal reform from the European Union (EU) to help expand its revenue base as receipts from the Southern African Customs Unions (SACU) fall. SACU receipts, which make up more than half of the Swazi revenue budget, are expected to dwindle over the next few years as new World Trade Organization and Southern African Development Community trade pacts take effect. The grant was intended to boost the government's revenue collection and budget preparation capabilities and reduce its expenditure. However, its fiscal deficit increased from 3.1 percent in 1999 to 4.1 percent in 2000.

Botswana is one of very few African countries that managed to maintain a budget surplus through most of the 1990s. In spite of damages caused by the floods and lower than expected diamond revenues budget surplus of 0.6 percent of GDP was recorded in 2000 compared to 0.1 percent of GDP in 1999. Also, several tax incentives have been offered to international financial companies to set up branches in Botswana.

In 1999, Lesotho experienced a sharp reversal of the great progress it had made in streamlining its fiscal accounts. It had succeeded in increasing revenues while keeping spending under control. However, recapitalization of the Lesotho Bank prior to its privatization increased public spending and gave rise to a deficit. But in 2000, fiscal deficit decreased to 1.6 percent of GDP from 16.5 percent in 1999.

Privatization

All countries in the sub-region acknowledge the need for privatization to boost government revenues, reduce spending on loss-making parastatals and increase economy-wide efficiency. However, there is considerable policy divergence in respect of the timing and magnitude of such programs. For some governments, the loss of jobs due to post-privatization rationalization is a serious problem, while others are concerned at losing control of some of the "commanding heights" of their economy.

South Africa has announced plans to accelerate privatization in 2001/2 with the sale of assets estimated to be worth up to $24 billion. Among the assets to be privatized are the state forestry company (Safcol) the aerospace company (Denel), South African Airways, and the telecommunications utility, Telkom, which has already been partially privatized.

After years of delay, the privatization of Zambia's three main copper mines was concluded in March 2000. The bulk of the program is now complete, except for a handful of relatively minor assets, such as the New Savoy Hotel and a number of strategic businesses including the utilities - electricity, the railways, telecommunications - and the state-owned commercial bank and insurance company.

With parastatals having Z$52 billion in debt and generating a negative net worth of about Z$6.7 billion in Zimbabwe, acceleration of privatization has become urgent. In 2000, the Privatization Agency of Zimbabwe was officially launched and the Cabinet approved an accelerated privatization program. This includes fast-track divestiture of the Forestry Commission, the Cold Storage Commission, Zimbabwe Reinsurance Company, Agribank, Wankie Colliery, Affretair, the Industrial Development Corporation, industrial conglomerate Astra, Air Zimbabwe, and the National Oil Company of Zimbabwe. The 2001 budget includes revenues of Z$22 billion to be obtained from the sale of state assets.

Although privatization has been on the agenda in Angola since 1990, progress has been slow with the government retaining control of key industries, including oil and diamonds. However, recently, the government pledged to sell up to 49 percent of the downstream distribution division of the state oil company, Sonangol, to private national interests. Upstream oil and gas production assets of the company are not part of the deal. Lesotho has shown its commitment to privatization with the sale of the Lesotho Airways, Lesotho Flour Mills, International Freight and Travel Services, Loti Brick, Government Motor Vehicle Pool, and Marakabeki Lodge. Moreover, 70 percent of the Lesotho's Telecom Corporation is to be sold to a private consortium from South Africa, Mauritius and Zimbabwe.

In Botswana, the sale of Air Botswana is moving ahead and the government has demonstrated its commitment to privatization by setting up an autonomous Public Enterprise Evaluation and Privatization Authority to monitor privatization and to identify candidates for sale to the private sector. Malawi is taking the preliminary steps necessary to privatize its national carrier, Air Malawi, and has begun to rationalize operations of the carrier to make it profitable in the near future.

In Namibia, although there is strong opposition to a total sale of the assets of state-owned companies, the government has adopted its first privatization guidelines for the sale of Namibia Power Corporation (Namcor), Air Namibia, and Telecom Namibia. However, a full list of candidates for privatization will not be finalized for at least another year. Swaziland has privatized its airline, water and dairy companies. However, the sale of other state concerns is proceeding at an extremely slow pace.

Mozambique has so far privatized more than 900 parastatals - many of them very small. More recently, it has moved beyond the sale of assets with the negotiation of concession agreements for its railways and ports. Swaziland is seeking technical assistance to strengthen its rather weak privatization unit.

Emerging Regional Economic Relationships

International trading relationships in Southern Africa will change over the next few years following the launch in 2000 of three important trading agreements. These include the Southern African Development Community's free trade protocol, launched in September 2000, the Common Market for Eastern and Southern Africa (Comesa) free trade area, established in October and - potentially the most important - the South Africa-European Union free trade area that took effect from January 2000.

SADC-SACU Free Trade Agreement

The joint free-trade agreement of the Southern African Development Community (SADC) and the Southern Africa Customs Union (SACU) came into effect on 1st September 2000 following the ratification of the protocol by all member states. The agreement covers eleven of SADC's fourteen members – Angola, the Democratic Republic of Congo and Seychelles are not participating at this stage.

The protocol is an asymmetric agreement that aims at removing all tariff and non-tariff barriers on intra-regional trade within eight years. South Africa, as the sub-region's most developed and most industrialized economy, is lowering most of its barriers to imports from other SADC states immediately. Other SADC states will eliminate

trade barriers progressively over the next eight years, though special arrangements are in place for sensitive industries.

The broad liberalization strategy classifies goods into three, with trade on sugar as a special category. Category "A" goods, which constitute about 47 percent of the goods traded in the region, will have their duties reduced to zero as soon as they have been gazetted with individual parliaments. Category "B" goods will have their tariffs gradually reduced over the eight-year period at the end of which 85 percent of goods traded within the region will be exempted from tariffs or trade taxes. Given the sensitivity of category "C" goods their tariffs will not be reduced until 2012.

For sugar, initially all SADC producers will have access to the SACU market based on their share of the total world market. Their share of the SACU market will then be gradually increased up to 2012, when the total liberalization of the SADC market is expected to take place. However, with a free trade agreement just concluded between EU and South Africa, many of the other SADC countries, particularly members of the SACU (including Botswana), are worried they may be flooded with cheap European imports.

Outlook

Because of South Africa's dominance and the influence it has on the other Southern Africa economies, the outlook for the region depends very much on the performance of the region's biggest economy. GDP growth in South Africa in 2001 is projected at 3.5 percent, due mainly to a strong rebound in investment, further interest rate reductions and increased exports as firms exploit the free trade area with the EU and the US Africa Growth and Opportunity Act. The main impetus for faster South African growth will come from consumption spending, expected to rise 3 percent in 2001 and fixed investment, predicted to expand 5.8 percent.

In Zimbabwe the continued uncertain political environment and the absence of meaningful economic reforms will mean that the economy will contract further (by another 10 percent) in 2001. This is due to continued political uncertainty, economic mismanagement, growing social unrest, illegal land seizures, reduced agricultural activities, business failures and withdrawal of external financial support.

The Botswana economy is again expected to perform well during 2001, growing by 5.3 percent with growth driven mainly by the diamond industry, which will be buoyed by rising international demand for gems. Social spending, stronger direct foreign investment and a competitive currency will further spur growth.

Growth in Angola will be lower at 2.1 percent in 2001 compared to 2000 due to a reduction in the pace of oil industry expansion, a decline in oil prices and the ongoing civil war. In Mozambique, the reconstruction efforts to repair damage from the floods, full-capacity production at the Mozal aluminum plant and the full recovery of the agricultural sector will push GDP expansion to more than 10 percent in 2001. Investment levels will remain very high by African standards at 27 percent of GDP, of which nearly half will be government spending, much of it on reconstruction and infrastructure rehabilitation.

Its investment rate is expected to increase substantially in the near future with the implementation of the industrial projects. The construction, mining and utilities sub-sectors are expected to

record significant improvements in economic performance in the years ahead. Mozambique can expect further increases in foreign capital in the short- to medium-term. In the long run, the rate of economic growth will remain between 5 and 10 percent.

In Namibia, GDP is expected to show strong growth of 5 percent in 2001 largely due to expansion in mining and fishing. Continuing investments to rebuild the capital, Maseru, will be the momentum behind real GDP growth in both the short and medium term for Lesotho. Real GDP is projected to grow by 2.8 percent in 2001 but, as reconstruction efforts wind down, we anticipate that growth will stabilize at 2.7 percent in 2005. Much of the growth will come from increased private and public consumption, with investment growth varying between 4 and 5 percent between 2002 and 2004.

In Swaziland, sluggish international demand, especially from South Africa, for the country's main exports will constrain growth, which is expected to be maintained at recent levels of around 3.5 percent annually. In Malawi, an anticipated upturn in tobacco prices and more favorable weather conditions should result in higher growth of around 4 percent annually over the next few years. In the medium term, the manufacturing sector is expected to contribute more significantly to economic growth as tax incentives encourage production. For Zambia, the privatization of the copper mines is expected to increase copper production in 2001 and beyond. Tourism will become increasingly important, but the main impetus will come from the spillover effects of substantially higher copper production between 2001 and 2004.

West Africa

Overview

West Africa is home to fifteen countries, divided into two distinct groups. The first group, the CFA zone, comprises Benin, Burkina Faso, Côte d'Ivoire, Guinea Bissau, Mali, Niger, Senegal and Togo, whose currencies were pegged to the French franc (and to the Euro since January 1999). These eight countries are also members of the West African Economic and Monetary Union (WAEMU). The exchange rate of CFA franc was devalued by 50 percent against the French franc in January 1994 and has been maintained at a fixed rate ever since.

The second group, the non-CFA zone, is made up of Cape Verde, Ghana, Guinea, Liberia, Nigeria, Sierra Leone, and The Gambia. The combined population of West Africa was 219 million in 1999. Nigeria, the most populous African nation in the region, plays a crucial role in the regional economy.

While Côte d'Ivoire dominates the economies of the CFA zone, Nigeria and Ghana are the dominant economic powers of the non-CFA zone. In 2000, the per capita income in the CFA zone was estimated at $436 (in 1995 constant dollars) compared with $311 in the non-CFA zone. Cape Verde with a per capita income of $1,299.9 and Sierra Leone with $131.6 are the richest and poorest nations, respectively in the region. Per capita income in West Africa at $334.4 in 2000 lags behind North ($1,145.6) and Southern Africa ($1,463.9) but is higher than in East ($234.2) and Central Africa ($269.8). Cocoa, coffee, timber, cotton and oil are the region's main sources of export revenues. Consequently, the international market prices of these commodities influence the speed and pattern of regional economic growth.

Table 2.6: West Africa: Macroeconomic Indicators, 1990-2000

Indicators	1990	1995	1996	1997	1998	1999	2000[a]
Real GDP Growth Rate (%)	3.7	3.6	4.9	4.6	3.5	2.8	3.1
GDP Per Capita (US $)	395.3	335.7	375.8	365.9	350.2	353.1	334.4
Inflation (%)	13.3	20.5	12.8	9.0	7.1	4.1	3.3
Fiscal Balance (% of GDP)	-2.8	-1.0	-0.8	-2.7	-5.9	-6.1	2.1
Gross Domestic Investment (% of GDP)	17.1	16.9	16.6	18.1	23.2	20.8	21.0
Gross National Savings (% of GDP)	16.6	13.7	15.2	15.7	19.7	13.5	16.5
Real Export Growth (%)	2.9	7.1	9.0	9.2	5.7	10.0	12.7
Trade Balance (% GDP)	9.2	5.1	9.2	6.9	0.9	0.2	8.0
Current Account (% GDP)	-0.9	-4.9	0.8	-0.6	-6.5	-8.3	-1.9
Terms of Trade (%)	17.5	2.4	12.5	2.7	-19.2	11.3	25.0
Total External Debt (% GDP)	97.6	115.4	100.0	93.7	93.1	96.1	91.0
Debt Service (% of Exports)	21.4	23.2	17.8	15.0	16.3	18.6	...

Note: a/ Preliminary estimates.
Source: ADB Statistics Division and IMF.

Recent Economic Trends

Annual output growth in West Africa strengthened to 3.1 percent in 2000, (Figure 2.29 and Table 2.6) spurred by a sharp rebound in Nigeria, the largest economy in the region and the continent's largest energy exporter, as well as by continued strength in smaller economies in the CFA zone (Figure 2.30). The recovery of oil prices in 1999 boosted Nigeria's economic growth rate from 1.1 percent in 1999 to an estimated 3 percent in 2000.

Apart from buoyant oil prices, several other factors contributed to the sharp acceleration in Nigeria's growth rate, including the restoration of macroeconomic stability, the intensified campaign against corruption, the return of private and foreign investor confidence, and an improved relationship with creditors and the donor community. Growth in Ghana, the region's second largest economy, was constrained by the depressed prices of its two leading exports, gold and cocoa. As a result, output expansion slowed slightly to 4 percent, down from 4.4 percent in 1999. Sharply higher inflation and the steep fall in the Cedi also constrained growth in the manufacturing and services sectors.

In the CFA sub-region the largest economy, Côte d'Ivoire, suffered a severe setback in 1999 because of depressed cocoa and coffee prices and the military coup in December of that year. This same combination of depressed export prices, the steep rise in the price of oil imports and ongoing political instability, also undermined economic performance throughout the year 2000. Donor assistance and lending was put on hold and private foreign investors stayed on the sidelines while they waited for the political situation to clarify and stabilize. As a result, the economic downturn that began in 1999 worsened with the country sliding into a recession as real GDP contracted by 2 per-

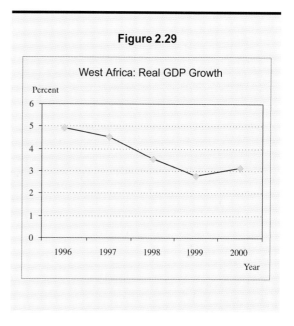

Figure 2.29

West Africa: Real GDP Growth

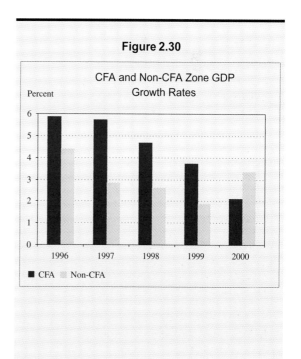

Figure 2.30

CFA and Non-CFA Zone GDP Growth Rates

cent in 2000.

Growth rates in other major CFA zone countries stayed above the continental average with Benin, Burkina Faso and Senegal recording 5 percent or more. These countries continued to benefit from stable macroeconomic conditions, political stability and improved export performances. Burkina Faso, Mali and Niger recorded fairly good economic growth in spite of harsh weather conditions, which adversely affected agricultural output in 2000. Niger recorded growth of 3 percent up from a contraction of less than 1 percent in the previous year, while Mali grew by 4.5 percent in 2000.

As a result of a devastating armed conflict, Guinea-Bissau's economic output collapsed by 28 percent in 1998. The agricultural sector, which is the source of livelihood for the majority of the population, declined by more than 17 percent in that year. The change of government in February 1999 led to a new initiative for reconstruction and economic recovery, as a result of which economic growth in 1999 and 2000 rose to 7.8 percent and 7.5 percent, respectively.

Cape Verde, which is the most prosperous country of the region in terms of per capita income, also had the best growth performance during the 1998-2000 period. Driven by a strong export performance, GDP increased 8 percent a year in both 1998 and 1999, slowing somewhat to 5 percent in 2000. Liberia's rapid economic growth from above 20 percent since 1997 dropped to 7 percent in 2000. High growth rates were also recorded in Guinea and The Gambia. In Guinea, GDP grew 4 percent in 2000 against 3.2 percent in 1999 but the Gambia experienced a marginal drop in its growth rate to 5.3 percent in 2000 from 5.6 percent. After a steep 8 percent decline in 1999, Sierra Leone's economy recovered some lost

ground, expanding 3.8 percent in 2000 due to a slight reduction in the level of hostilities in the civil war.

External Accounts

The depreciation of the Euro against the US dollar did not boost CFA Zone exports enough to improve their trade and current account balances in 2000. Not only did the markets for their primary exports (cocoa, coffee, and timber) remain depressed but the cost of their petroleum imports nearly doubled. As a result, the number of countries with trade deficits exceeded those that managed to record trade surpluses. As a whole, the West Africa region's trade surplus stood at 8 percent of GDP in 2000, up from 0.2 percent recorded in 1999. Estimates indicate that only Nigeria, Côte d'Ivoire, and Guinea, recorded trade surpluses in 2000 (Figure 2.31).

An important factor affecting import volumes in West Africa's CFA Zone countries was the implementation of a Common External Tariff (CET) from January 1, 2000. Since the CET rates are lower than previous tariff rates in most of these countries, there was an increase in import volumes often associated with reduced import tariff revenues.

Nigeria's huge trade surplus —16.8 percent of GDP —was driven by buoyant oil prices and the commencement of gas exports but in Côte d'Ivoire imports fell sharply reflecting depressed private and government consumption resulting in a trade surplus of 11 percent of GDP. In Ghana, the trade deficit represented 16.8 percent of GDP, while it was 7 percent in Senegal.

The current account deficit for the entire region fell to an estimated 1.9 percent of GDP from 8.32 percent in 1999 (Figure 2.32). Côte d'Ivoire's current account external payments gap fell to 5.42

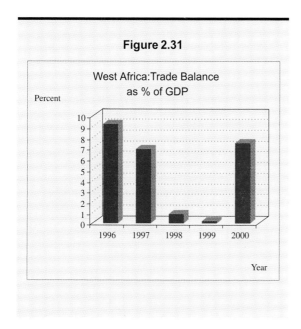

Figure 2.31

West Africa:Trade Balance as % of GDP

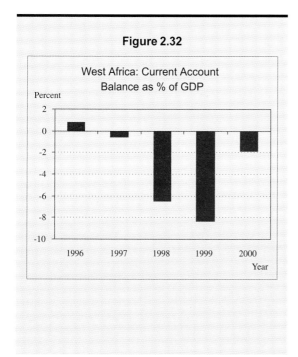

Figure 2.32

West Africa: Current Account Balance as % of GDP

percent of GDP in 2000 from 3.99 percent, largely attributable to a sharp fall in cocoa exports, higher oil import prices and reduced aid inflows.

Mali's terms-of-trade deteriorated for the second successive year, falling 8.8 percent in 2000 after a 10.8 percent decline the previous year, leading to a current account deficit of 14.92 percent of GDP, up from 10.84 percent of GDP in 1999. Exports declined 1.7 percent while import volumes were up 2.7 percent.

The current account deficit of the non-CFA sub-region has been much more volatile mainly due to Nigeria's fluctuating oil export revenues. In 1998, when the price of oil (OPEC basket) declined to $12.5 a barrel, the non-CFA current account deficit rose to 8.7 percent of GDP. Higher oil revenues improved Nigeria's current account balance from 10.96 percent of GDP in 1999 to an estimated surplus of 2.35 percent in 2000. As a result the non-CFA bloc's current account deficit declined from 8.7 percent of GDP in 1998 to 1.2 percent in 2000. Ghana's current account balance moved in the opposite direction over this period— a reflection of the sharp worsening in its terms-of-trade, as cocoa and gold prices weakened and oil prices soared. Revenues from its two leading exports, gold and cocoa, declined sharply in the 1999-2000 period, leading to a marginal fall in the current account deficit from 10.65 percent of GDP in 1999 to 8.54 percent in 2000.

Concern over the declining price of cocoa in international markets motivated Ghana, Côte d'Ivoire, Nigeria and the central African nation of Cameroon to take joint action to restrict the supply of cocoa. These four nations pledged to withdraw 250,000 tons of cocoa beans during the 2000/2001-harvest season from the market. Effective implementation of this plan, however, is a major challenge and requires a high degree of coordination and monitoring.

Among the other West African nations, Cape Verde and Liberia have enjoyed improvements in their current account balances. In 1999 Cape Verde's exports and imports grew by 18.5 percent and 14.5 percent respectively and resulted in a balance to the current account. Liberia's current accounts position remained balanced in 2000 as in 1999.

External Debt

West Africa's total external debt is gradually declining, partly reflecting the impact of debt relief but foreign debt still remained very high at 91 percent of GDP in 2000.

The region's external debt reached a peak of $77.28 billion in 1995, declining to $69.55 billion in 2000—a fall of 10 percent. Figure 2.33 shows that both CFA and non-CFA sub-regions have reduced their external debt as a percentage of GDP. In the CFA Zone external debt has fallen by almost a quarter (23 percent) since 1995, but in non-CFA countries the decline was only 10.3 percent —largely the result of a 17 percent reduction to $31.44 billion in Nigeria, the most heavily indebted country in the region.

The lower external debt of CFA sub-region is primarily due to a sharp decline in Côte d'Ivoire's foreign debt. Côte d'Ivoire, which accounts for almost one third of the sub-region's debt, reduced its external debt by 20 percent between 1995 and 1999, due mostly to a reduction in amounts owed to commercial banks after the 1998 debt restructuring agreement with the London Club. In 2000, however, its foreign debt profile deteriorated as relations with donors were strained by governance problems.

Nigeria accounts for more than three-quarters of non-CFA debt. Higher oil revenues in the last two years have helped Nigeria realize a positive current account balance, reducing its external

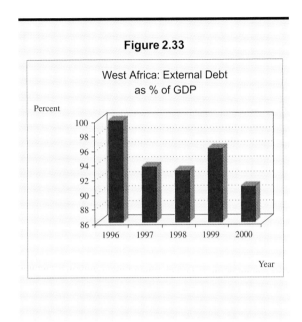

Figure 2.33

West Africa: External Debt as % of GDP

debt from $31.93 billion in 1995 to an estimated $31.44 billion in 2000. Despite this, the debt burden is unsustainable at 81.4 percent of GDP and 169 percent of exports. In 2000, Nigeria reached a new agreement with the Paris Club of official creditors under which its annual debt service obligations were reduced, enabling it to divert substantially increased resources to economic rehabilitation and development programs. Guinea-Bissau has the heaviest debt burden in the entire region. Its external debt represented 328.5 percent of GDP in 2000. Liberia's external debt of $2.04 billion represented 60.2 percent of GDP in 2000.

In most West African nations at the end of 2000, the debt burden was estimated at between 60 percent and 120 percent of GDP. Accordingly, 12 of the 15 West African countries— the exceptions are Cape Verde, Nigeria and the Gambia — are classified as Heavily Indebted Poor Countries

(HIPC) and as such are eligible for debt relief under the HIPC initiative.

Under this program, which began in 1996, HIPC countries that improve their economic track records by implementing effective social and governance reforms with a focus on poverty alleviation qualify for debt relief. The HIPC Initiative was enhanced in October 1999 to cover a larger number of countries and provide increased and faster relief. The enhanced HIPC also added poverty reduction and strengthening of civil society as two new conditions for eligibility.

In West Africa, six countries —Benin, Burkina Faso, the Gambia, Guinea-Bissau, Mali and Senegal —met the required conditions and became eligible for debt relief under this program in December 2000. The relief package will be disbursed over a two to five year period with the aim of reducing debt/GDP ratios in these countries to sustainable levels. Rather than reducing the debt directly, this program returns part of the debt payment as grants for specific developmental and poverty reducing projects. Social services such as health and education are top priorities for allocation of these grants.

Policy Developments

Monetary policy, inflation and exchange rates

Monetary discipline in West Africa has increased significantly in recent years, partly to meet the reform program targets of multilateral financial institutions. The monetary policies of member states of the West African Economic and Monetary Union (WAEMU), are dictated by the regional central bank, Banque centrale des états de l'Afrique de l'ouest (BCEAO). In 2000, the BCEAO raised rediscount and repurchase agreement rates by 0.75 percentage points while the reserve requirements

ratio was tightened in many member countries.

Figure 2.34 shows that since 1995 inflation in West Africa has declined, reaching 3.3 percent in 2000 from 4.1 percent in 1999. In the CFA sub-region inflation has stayed below 4 percent since 1998, slowing to 0.8 percent in 1999 and rising to 2.6 percent in 2000, as three countries—Burkina Faso, Mali and Togo—experienced mild deflation. The inflation rate in the CFA zone is influenced to some extent by the exchange rate of the Euro to which the CFA franc is pegged at a fixed rate. The depreciation of the Euro in 1999/2000, along with political turmoil in Côte d'Ivoire, led to increased inflation and the regional rate rose from less than one percent in 1999 to 2.6 percent in 2000. In some CFA Zone countries, however, consumer inflation remained subdued with Burkina Faso and Mali recording negative inflation rates.

Average inflation in the non-CFA sub-region has been higher than in the CFA. Nonetheless, it declined from a high of 39.6 percent in 1995 to 15.3 percent in 1999 and 14 percent in 2000. This remarkable success was largely due to the committed implementation of structural adjustment programs one of whose main goals is monetary stability. The growth of money supply in the region slowed to 16.5 percent in 2000 from 27.4 percent in 1999 (Figure 2.34).

In the largest non-CFA Zone economy, Nigeria following the sharp fall in inflation in 1999, the Central Bank loosened monetary policy in the first half of 2000, reducing the minimum discount rate three times to its year-end level of 14 percent. Minimum cash reserve requirements were also reduced in August 2000 but the authorities subsequently tightened their monetary stance when excess market liquidity drove interbank interest rates down and the exchange rate of the naira weakened. Despite the naira's depreciation, the gap between the market and parallel exchange rates re-

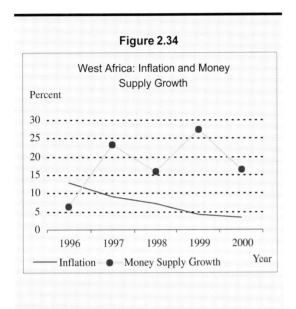

Figure 2.34

West Africa: Inflation and Money Supply Growth

inflation of 4.9 percent in 2000 but in the remaining non-CFA countries inflation slowed from its 1999 levels. Sierra Leone managed to reduce the inflation rate from 34 percent in 1999 to a negative rate of 2.6 percent in 2000.

Fiscal Policy

West Africa's overall fiscal surplus was 2.1 percent of GDP in 2000 against a deficit of 6.1 percent recorded in 1999, in spite of the political instability and the high cost of defense spending. Figure 2.35 shows that the fiscal deficit as a ratio of GDP increased in both the CFA and non-CFA countries. In the CFA sub-region, the weighted average budget deficit grew from 1.9 percent of GDP in 1999 to an estimated 2.5 percent in 2000. Increased deficits in the sub-region were partly due to the

mained at between 10 to 15 percent, indicating sharper depreciation of the currency in the short term which will have a knock-on effect on inflation. Indeed, during 2000, inflation accelerated to 9.5 percent from 6.7 percent in 1999.

In Ghana, the main objective of monetary policy remains price stability. The steep depreciation of the cedi and rising inflation forced the authorities to tighten monetary policy in 2000. Specific measures included raising Treasury bill rates from 34.2 percent in 1999 to 42.6 percent in December 2000, increasing the reserve ratio of commercial banks from 8 percent to 9 percent of deposits, and limiting large over-the-counter withdrawals. Inflation increased from 12.4 percent in 1999 to an estimated 16.9 percent in 2000, partly reflecting the impact of higher petroleum prices. This followed the decline from 46.6 percent in 1996 to 12.4 percent in 1999. Guinea had higher

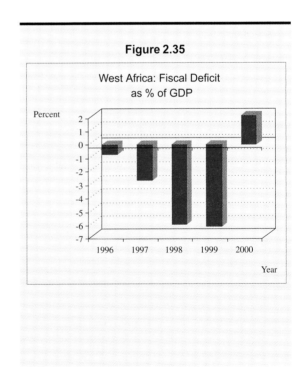

Figure 2.35

West Africa: Fiscal Deficit as % of GDP

loss of tariff revenues in some countries as a result of compliance with the Common External Tariff rates introduced in January 2000. Although, as a remedy, Senegal introduced VAT in July 2000, its estimated fiscal deficit for 2000 was 1.6 percent of GDP, up from 1.4 percent in 1999.

Mali also introduced VAT in 2000 at a single rate of 18 percent to compensate for the loss of tariff revenues, recording a fiscal deficit of 4.6 percent of GDP. Along with a number of other countries, Mali also raised the price of petroleum products. In Côte d'Ivoire, government revenues suffered largely because of low agricultural commodity prices and because the interim military regime also increased the government's wage bill in response to protests by soldiers and civil servants. The budget deficit/GDP ratio fell marginally from 2.9 percent in 1999 to 2.2 percent in 2000.

In the non-CFA sub-region, which has historically had higher deficit/GDP ratios in recent years, the average increased marginally from 4 percent in 1999 to 4.1 percent in 2000. In Nigeria, higher oil revenues contributed to improvements in fiscal conditions with budget balance, reaching a surplus of 7.7 percent of GDP in 2000 from a deficit of 8.4 percent in 1999. Government revenue is estimated to have risen 15 percent, while expenditure rose only 12.2 percent. Ghana and Sierra Leone had significantly higher deficits in 2000 with Ghana's budget deficit standing at 7.2 percent of GDP while Sierra Leone's rose to 14.1 percent from 10.3 percent in 1999. But Liberia improved its fiscal stance with tax revenues rising strongly from 3.9 percent of GDP in 1997 to 9.3 percent in 1999. As a result, Liberia's budget deficit remained below 0.5 percent of GDP.

West African countries with ongoing conditional loan agreements with multilateral institutions are giving greater priority to social programs in health, education and housing. This pattern is particularly apparent in the budgets of those countries that have qualified for debt relief under the enhanced HIPC initiative. Such countries must prepare a Poverty Reduction Strategy Paper before they qualify for the enhanced HIPC debt relief scheme.

As part of their program of fiscal consolidation most West African countries are working to broaden the tax base, by introducing taxes such as VAT, while closing loopholes and reducing tax exemptions in an attempt to increase public revenues. A growing number of countries too, are committed to more active and effective anti-corruption campaigns and to public sector restructuring designed to improve the delivery of public services, especially to the poor and disadvantaged.

Privatization

Privatization is high on the policy agenda in most West African economies as part of the overall thrust of structural reform and fiscal consolidation. Progress has, however, been slow in some countries reflecting political concerns and unanticipated economic crises. In Cape Verde privatization of port facilities and the national airline were delayed but several smaller projects were privatized in 2000. Similarly, the privatization of 10 state-owned enterprises in Senegal was delayed because of the country's 2000 presidential elections. The electricity company and the national airline were privatized in 1999.

In The Gambia a privatization bill, setting up an agency to oversee the process, was approved in 2000 while some of the revenue from asset sales in 2000 was used to reduce the government's domestic debt. Along with privatization, the Gambian government is also improving the financial accountability of existing public enterprises, and it has established an independent agency to oversee its privatization program.

Benin has targeted the cotton sector, the country's main export, for privatization and deregulation. In June 2000, the government ended the cottonseed marketing monopoly of SONAPRA, while also approving a plan for SONAPRA's partial privatization as well as participation of the private sector in the importation of fertilizers and pesticides. The initial steps towards privatization of Benin's telecommunications sector were taken in 2000 and a final sale is expected in the first half of 2001. Preparation is also underway for transfer of port management services of the Port of Cotonou to the private sector. Benin is using part of the privatization proceeds for public investment programs and emergency assistance to cotton farmers.

Since the mid-1990's, Côte d'Ivoire has carried out a successful privatization program with 13 enterprises including a major bank, BIAO, having been privatized since 1998. The state's shares in seven other firms were sold on Abidjan's regional stock market, the BVRM. In 2000, the process was slowed by the interim military administration but the new elected government is expected to resume the privatization of larger enterprises such as the SIR petroleum refinery in 2001.

In Guinea, several inefficient public enterprises were placed under liquidation during 2000 while the government's shares in seven other enterprises were sold to the private sector. Burkina Faso has set in motion plans for the partial privatization of Air Burkina, while relaunching the full privatization of the Societe des hotels de la gare, which owns and operates two Ranhotels, in Ouagadougou and Bobo-Dioulasso. Ghana is deregulating electricity supply by ending the Volta River Authority's (VRA) electricity generating monopoly prior to its privatization. Telekom Malaysia has bought a 15 percent stake in Ghana Telecommunications Company, which controls over 73 percent of telephone lines in the country.

In 1999, Nigeria drew up a three-stage privatization schedule designed to help rehabilitate the country's rundown physical infrastructure, attract new investment and new economic players and reduce operating costs and the size of government while creating a more investment friendly business environment. Unfortunately, the privatization program, which could yield as much as $20 billion in revenue for the Federal government, is progressing very slowly and by the end of 2000 was well behind schedule.

The first phase, involving the sale of government holdings in 14 firms in the banking, cement and petroleum marketing sectors, which had a June 2000 completion deadline, had not been completed by the end of the year. However, core investors had been chosen for five of the firms while substantial stakes in another five were either sold to investors or listed for public offers.

The second phase with an end-of-2000 deadline was also missed. This will be dominated by the sale of 39 state-owned hotels, insurance firms, vehicle assembly plants and paper mills. Phase three, which should be completed by December 2001 deadline, involves the partial sale of the state-owned oil and gas firms and utilities, including power firm NEPA, Nigerian Telecommunications (NITEL) and Nigeria Airways. NITEL and M-Tel have already been merged preparatory to their proposed sale in March 2001.

Emerging regional economic relations

The main vehicle for regional integration in the West African region is the Economic Community of West Africa (ECOWAS), established in 1975. During 2000, one member state, Mauritania, withdrew from ECOWAS, having given notice of its intentions in 1999. According to the ECOWAS Secretariat, Mauritania has a year to reconsider its decision, after which its name will be taken off the regional group's membership list.

The long-term goal of ECOWAS is to achieve complete market integration and a single customs union for the entire region within 15 years. ECOWAS states are pursuing this goal through a number of intermediate steps and strategies. In December 1999 the member states approved the creation of a Common External Tariff, though this has not yet been implemented. Another important long-term goal is creating a single currency and harmonizing the economic and financial policies of the member states, paving the way for creation of a unified monetary zone (Box 2.2).

In 2000, the leaders of ECOWAS agreed on the composition of a common court and currency. A budget of $1 billion was proposed for the common currency while another $400 million was proposed for its study, research and design.

ECOWAS is also working towards integrating and developing the region's infrastructure. Work is already underway to interconnect the existing national networks in areas of transportation, communication and energy.

Two major Trans West Africa highways are currently under construction. The 4,560-kilometer Trans Coastal Highway is nearly 83 percent complete while the 4,460 km Trans-Sahelian Highway is 87 percent complete. Plans to set up a regional airline, ECOAIR with the initial capital of $25 million have also been announced. All ECOWAS members own ECOAIR which has its headquarters in Abuja, Nigeria.

In the field of energy, ECOWAS member states have approved a plan to interconnect the region's national electricity grids. An estimated 5600 kilometers of electricity lines will be used for this purpose. The goal is to supply the region with an installed electric capacity of 10,000 MW by the year 2015.

Tax and customs harmonization and coordination is an important step towards economic integration of WAEMU members. Already, WAEMU has agreed to harmonize tax policies, with all members agreeing to adopt common Value Added Tax (VAT) rates ranging from 15 to 20 percent. They are also expected to adopt a common list of exempted goods and services and dismantle VAT exemptions for investment, mining and petroleum codes while broadening the tax base. The deadline for tax harmonization is January 1, 2002 but Côte d'Ivoire expects to achieve this target in early 2001.

In 2000, WAEMU member states took an important step towards tariff harmonization by replacing the previous tariff system with a common external tariff (CET). Under CET, there are four tariff categories —zero, 5 percent, 10 percent and a top rate of 20 percent. Member states are expected to adopt a minimum 5 percent tariff on previously exempted goods and services under investment, mining and petroleum codes. Côte d'Ivoire took the lead in introducing CET by taking two transitional measures in March 1998, when the maximum rate was lowered to 25 percent from 35 percent. This was followed in July 1999 with the reclassification of goods according to four WAEMU categories.

Box: 2.2: The ECOWAS Monetary Zone

Ghana and Nigeria are leading a fast-track initiative toward monetary union with The Gambia, Sierra Leone, Guinea and Liberia. The objective is to establish a single currency by 2003 that will then be merged with the CFA Zone countries in 2004 to create a common currency for ECOWAS member states.

Nigeria, Ghana, Guinea, Sierra Leone and The Gambia signed the agreement establishing the West African Monetary Zone (WAMZ) on 14th December 2000 in Bamako, Mali. Liberia was not a signatory. The agreement establishes a West African Monetary Institute that will begin operation in January 2001. The WAMI will serve as the forerunner for a regional West African Central Bank to be established in 2003 with the launch of the single currency.

The countries of the West African Monetary Zone have agreed a set of convergence criteria, similar to those applied in Euro Zone countries prior to the launch of the Euro.

The convergence criteria include:

- Single-digit inflation by end-2000 and a rate of no more than five percent by 2003
- Gross foreign currency reserves covering at least three months of imports by end-2000 and six months by end-2003
- Central bank financing of the budget deficit limited to ten percent of the previous year's tax revenue; and,

- A maximum budget deficit (excluding grants) of five percent of Gross Domestic Product by 2000 and four percent by 2003.

At the end of 2000, progress towards meeting the convergence criteria varied considerably across the region. Three countries – The Gambia, Guinea and Nigeria - had met the single-digit inflation criterion, but only two, The Gambia and Guinea, had managed to reduce their budget deficits to less than five percent of GDP.

Two countries - The Gambia and Nigeria - met the limit on central bank financing of the budget deficit while another three - The Gambia, Nigeria, and Sierra Leone - satisfied the foreign reserves to import cover ratio.

Overall, at the end of 2000, The Gambia met all four criteria, while Nigeria attained three. The republic of Guinea attained two and Sierra Leone one. Ghana did not meet any of the criteria.

It seems clear that meeting the convergence criteria by 2003 will pose serious challenges for Ghana, Sierra Leone and Guinea, raising doubts over whether the single currency zone will, in fact, take off in 2003 as planned. Nonetheless the WAMZ agreement provides that any two countries that meet the criteria by the set date may begin the single currency process. It may well be that by 2003 only Nigeria and The Gambia will be ready to adopt the common currency agreement.

Source: Adapted from Buabeng C.S. (2000).

Other Western African countries have also undertaken trade policy reforms during the past two years. Cape Verde reduced its average tariff rate to 26 percent in 1999 while also terminating the monopoly of the state-owned trade-company

EMPA on sugar, oil, maize and rice. The Gambia has approved a plan that will allow the central bank to introduce foreign currency deposits starting in 2001 with the aim of reducing the cost of foreign exchange transactions and facilitating trade.

Outlook

The economic outlook for West Africa is at best mixed. Most countries in the region are currently in the throes of far-reaching economic and political transitions and their structural reforms and macroeconomic stabilization programs are expected to have a positive impact on economic growth and human development. Of particular importance is the recent Africa-wide reorientation of such programs towards a greater focus on reducing poverty and inequality. These measures will have a secondary reinforcing effect on economic growth in the sense that reduction of poverty increases social and political stability which is essential for sustainable economic growth.

Also positive is the gradual decline in the region's external debt, partly due to the HIPC debt reduction initiative. Under the enhanced HIPC program, the debt burden of eligible countries will decline by more than 25 percent over the next few years, enabling them to divert additional resources to investment and poverty alleviation.

Market conditions for the region's leading exports—cocoa, coffee, oil and gold—will influence substantially the speed and pattern of economic growth. Assuming some modest improvement in non-oil commodity prices, the CFA Zone is expected to grow 4.1 percent over the medium term and the non-CFA sub-region 3.9 percent.

The price of cocoa, which was at its lowest in two decades in 2000, is expected to recover slowly over the 2001-2003 period with a similar trend predicted for coffee. The slow pace of forecast commodity price improvements is not very encouraging for Côte d'Ivoire and other main exporters of soft commodities in the region, pointing to only a modest improvement in the external accounts of these countries over the next few years.

Efforts are under way by major African cocoa and coffee growers to reduce the annual supply of these commodities by curbing production—efforts which may help strengthen prices to some degree over the next few years.

Oil market prospects are more encouraging. Although the price of oil is expected to be lower in the 2001-2003 period than its 2000 average, it is still forecast to remain above $20 per barrel. This will help Nigeria achieve a positive external balance over the next few years and sustain economic growth in the 3 to 5 percent range. But West African oil importers will continue to feel the heat from the heavy cost of fuel imports and those countries that have been slow to raise the domestic price of petroleum products may eventually be forced to do so.

Political instability and border conflicts are the two main downside risks that could dent the relatively positive outlook of 4 percent annual growth. In 2000 West African countries like Côte d'Ivoire, Guinea, Liberia and Sierra Leone experienced civil turmoil, but greater stability is forecast for 2001. To avoid future conflicts, ECOWAS has taken an active political role in the region, setting up a regional peacekeeping force which is currently present in several West African countries including Sierra Leone, Guinea and Liberia.

Fortunately, several countries have conducted peaceful and successful democratic elections in the past two years, demonstrating to the international community the region's capacity to operate within democratic norms. The successful elections in Ghana and Senegal along with continuation of civilian rule in Nigeria are expected to promote a conducive business environment that will attract foreign investors and capital to the region in the short- to medium-term.

Nigeria's growth outlook for the period, 2001-2002 is promising despite concerns over ethnic tensions, the slow pace of privatization and widespread corruption. Ghana will benefit from the return of political certainty after the uncertainty of the elections, as well as from some improvement in cocoa and timber prices, though gold seems set to remain weak. Donor inflows should recover and recent investment in infrastructure should start to pay dividends in the form of an improved operating environment for business. While the Gambia and Benin are expected to continue with their good track record on economic reforms, fiscal discipline may be jeopardized in 2001 in the run up to presidential elections during the year.

Continued disputes with neighboring countries will most likely deter growth in Liberia, as foreign investors may be wary of committing themselves until this situation improves. In Sierra Leone, despite the resumption of diamond exports, economic growth and development will depend entirely on the establishment of peace. In Senegal, continuing projects in construction and public works will help the economy to grow above 5 percent annually over the period 2001-2002.

Though elections have been successfully concluded in Côte d'Ivoire, continued political violence and instability as well as external debt arrears will undermine investor and donor confidence in the country in the short- to medium-term. This may also damage the sub-region's economic performance. Despite continued aid inflows to Burkina Faso, growth will slow down in the short term due to political crises and poor agricultural harvests. In Niger, political instability and harsh weather conditions will lead to further deterioration of economic growth.

PART TWO

FOSTERING GOOD GOVERNANCE IN AFRICA

Fostering Good Governance in Africa

This year's theme, *Fostering Good Governance in Africa* is motivated by the realization that good governance, in its political, social, and economic dimensions, underpins sustainable human development and the reduction of poverty. Poverty reduction programs are very often undermined by conflicts, a lack of public accountability, corruption, and the exclusion of beneficiaries in the program processes. Several factors have combined in recent years to give new impetus to the issue of governance in the development debate. Pervasive corruption for example weakens government's ability to function effectively and severely detracts from the equity goal in the provision of public services. Another driving force has been the rise of pro-democracy movements on the continent demanding good governance and more responsive forms of government, as has the rising disquiet over the cost of corruption in terms of both domestic and external resources. Similarly the unparalleled increase in globalization and its even stronger imperatives for sound domestic policy environment and economic management have been motivating factors behind the quest for good governance.

Chapter 3 of the Report reviews the related questions of *Politics, Conflicts and Corruption* and their linkage with development and poverty reduction. While good politics foster economic development and social cohesion, and reduce corruption, bad politics breed corruption, retard socio-economic development and may lead to civil conflicts and wars. This chapter views good politics from the perspective of the three axioms of citizens influence and oversight, i.e. participation in the political process; responsive and responsible leadership; and social reciprocities of respect and tolerance between citizens or groups of citizens in the pursuit of politics. Without the first two the environment will be ripe for political instability, underdevelopment, corruption and socio-economic decay while the non-adherence to the axiom of social reciprocities where social groups and their leaders are incapable of transcending the boundaries of religion, kinship, ethnicity, or race is a prescription for violent conflicts and civil war. Against this framework, the chapter examines Africa's record with reference to the political environment, the prevalence of corruption and the incidence of conflicts. The chapter also explores the measures that need to be taken in order to establish participatory democracy in Africa with the aim of building the political foundation of socio-economic development, reducing corruption and promoting social cohesion.

Chapter 4 discusses the importance of *Promoting Economic and Corporate Governance* in the pursuit of economic development. The chapter recognizes that the importance of good governance for economic development in Africa relates not only to creating the right economic environment but also to adopting a clear development vision that stipulates the strategic choices that define the economic paradigm the government would adopt. It also relates to building accountable and transparent economic management and to equipping the government apparatus with the capacity to design and implement policies that aim at realizing that shared development vision. The chapter emphasizes the desired improvements that need to be reflected in effective and transparent systems of financial supervision and legal accountability, effective public administration systems, a functioning legal framework, predictable regulatory structures and socially responsible corporate governance. The prevention of monetary instrument being used for political or material gain, which hampers economic growth can be enhanced by making the Central Bank an independent agency. The creation of debt management units that manage the process of borrowing and repayment is necessary for avoiding debt crises and promoting economic development. Fiscal management that adheres to the three principles of efficiency, fairness and adminstarability of tax regimes is an important instrument for enhancing broad based economic growth and reducing poverty.

Chapter 5 examines the implications of the *Global Dimensions of Governance* for African countries and what can be done at the international level to address the challenges of governance. The trend toward democratic governance has for some time now been a global phenomenon with this century often described as the democratic century. Globalization is altering the world economic landscape in fundamental ways driven by a widespread push towards the liberalization of trade and capital markets, increasing internationalization of corporate production and distribution strategies, and technological change, which is rapidly dismantling barriers to the international tradability of goods and services and the mobility of capital. Globalization has profound implications for governance, including the erosion of state sovereignty as transnational bodies increasingly mediate national concerns and press for universal laws. This chapter specifically explores key areas such as the impact of development aid on governance in Africa; the global trading system; global financial architecture, international responses to corruption, conflict prevention and the potential uses of ICTs for improved governance by African countries. The findings indicate that the new global and interconnected world poses some challenges for governance and development in Africa. Critical among the challenges uncovered is the lack of expertise and institutional capacity to participate effectively in the globalization process. The new rules-based trading system under the WTO is a major challenge for African countries, as most African countries do not have representation at trade negotiations and discussions. Yet, African countries must abide by the rules and standards. Many countries are not adequately represented and their negotiators may not have the required expertise or the government support that is needed.

International financial institutions in collaboration with bilateral donors can assist African countries to ensure that the continent benefits from the new global order to improve governance and facilitate development. Chapter 6 discusses the *Bank Group Policy on Good Governance* in line with the Bank's Vision for sustained African development in the 21st Century. The Bank Group's interest in good governance arises from its mandate to ensure the effectiveness of the development efforts it supports. Using its financing instruments namely, policy based lending, and non-financing programs such as economic policy support, capacity-building and institutional development programs, the Bank Group has now focused on mainstreaming governance into its operations as a way to facilitate sustained long-term growth and development in Africa.

CHAPTER 3

Politics, Conflicts and Corruption

Introduction

The issues of politics, conflict and corruption are closely interrelated with each other as well as with the issues of development and poverty reduction. While good politics foster economic development and social cohesion, and reduce corruption, bad politics breed corruption, retard socio-economic development and may lead to civil conflicts and wars.

As conceptualized by Hyden (1992), good politics can be empirically looked into with reference to three axioms.

- *Citizens' influence and oversight*, which relates to the means available for individual citizens to participate in the political process and to hold their governors accountable for their decisions and actions.

- *Responsive and responsible leadership*, which refers to the attitudes of political leaders toward their role as public trustees and their adherence to the rule of law as well as their readiness to share information with citizens.

- *Social reciprocities*, which refer to the degree to which citizens or groups of citizens treat each other in an equal fashion, and how far such groups demonstrate tolerance of each other in the pursuit of politics. It also speaks of how far the different groups in a country are ca-

pable of transcending the boundaries of religion, kinship, ethnicity, and race.

These three axioms are interlinked. If citizens have no influence and oversight and the political leadership is irresponsible and not responsive to the voice of the people, the environment will be ripe for political instability, underdevelopment, corruption and socio-economic decay. Non-adherence to the axiom of social reciprocities—where social groups and their leaders are incapable of transcending the boundaries of religion, kinship, ethnicity, or race—is a recipe for violent conflicts and civil war (see Figure 3.1). With this framework in the background, this Chapter examines Africa's record with reference to the political environment, the prevalence of corruption and the incidence of conflict. The Chapter also explores the measures that need to be taken in order to establish participatory democracy in Africa with the aim of building the political foundation of socio-economic development, reducing corruption and promoting social cohesion.

The Political Context

It is generally recognized that socio-economic development cannot take place without stable political and civil conditions and institutions that would secure private property rights, ensure personal liberty, enforce contracts, and provide responsive, transparent and accountable governments.

Figure 3.1: The Destructive Mechanism of Bad Governance

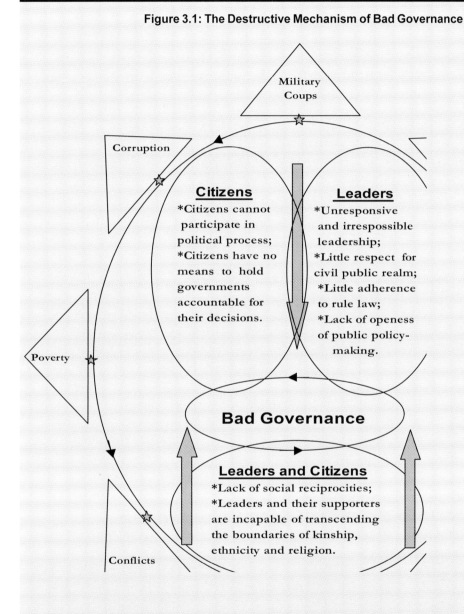

Source: ADB Research Division.

Since independence, African countries have experienced widely differing forms of political governance, ranging from extreme totalitarianism to liberal democracy. The attributes of the political leadership and the state with respect to the overall economic management, rule of law, and respect for private property have been influenced significantly by the prevailing political governance regimes. Box 3.1 provides some insights on the question of political leadership in Africa and its evolving nature in an era where economic reforms and democracy are becoming the norm.

In the early post independence period, most African countries adopted, to some measure, various forms of democratic governance with competitive parties, elections, independent judiciaries, and in some cases with innovations designed to facilitate national unity and to provide a major push for social development. There were, however, some notable exceptions. A major setback for the region, for instance, was the collapse of the democratic experience in Nigeria and national unity was threatened as the country plunged into civil war in the late 1960s. From mid-1970s and through most of the 1980s, however, military rule and dictatorships were prevalent in Africa. During this period, the continent witnessed rampant civil unrest, wars and politicization of government bureaucracies. The results included a weakening of institutional capacity and serious economic regression. Combined with external shocks during this period, it is not surprising that the early progress both on the economic and social fronts were undermined and in some cases reversed.

In the 1990s, and most notably following the end of the Cold War, the political environment in Africa began to change dramatically. The period was characterized by popular demand for democracy and the subsequent collapse of most military and autocratic regimes on the continent. After years of military rule, one-party states and authoritarian regimes, there was a resurgence of democracy and popular participation in governance.

Africa's record in politics is documented in a recent study by the United Nations Economic Commission for Africa (UNECA, 2000). According to this study, political regimes in Africa fall into 11 different types. The most important five types include, first, what is called "dominant party rule", which is practised by 22 countries, covering a population of 325 million and accounting for 41.8 per cent of Africa's population. Second, there is the "presidential parliamentary" type of regime, which is adopted by 12 countries with a population of 199.9 million, accounting for 25.7 per cent of Africa's population. Third, there is the "presidential-legislative democracy", practised by six countries, covering a population of 81.3 million, and accounting for 10.5 per cent of the population of Africa. Fourth, there is the "military-backed dictatorship", adopted by three countries with a population of 58 million, accounting for 7.5 per cent of the population of Africa. Fifth, there is the "civilian-military" system, adopted by three countries with a population of 65.3 million, accounting for 8.4 per cent of the population of Africa (see Table 3.1).

About 42 countries covered in this study have held multiparty presidential elections or parliamentary elections since the early 1990s. The detailed analysis by Ali (2001) further confirms the improvement in Africa's political environment. The study shows that for the period 1998-1999 about 68 per cent of the population of Sub-Saharan Africa was living under "partly free" conditions compared with the 1980s where about 88 per cent of the population was living under "not free" conditions (Ali, 2001).

Box 3.1: Political Leadership and Economic Reforms in Africa

Leadership Transitions, Risk and Behavior

Political economy offers a theory of micro-level behavior in which an overly-cautious or corrupt leader attempts to maximize his utility under conditions of personal and political uncertainty. A leader's intertemporal choices include future events with a present value, which one can calculate by using a political discount rate. That rate of discount rises with risk and uncertainty. When an outcome is doubtful over time, it makes sense to mark down its present value.

The probability of leaving office and the likely mode of exit are two factors that plausibly affect African leaders' intertemporal risk estimates, which, in turn, may influence the way they exercise power. Table 1 summarizes how independent Africa's 180 leadership successions took place. By far the most common means for African leaders to lose power is through a coup d'état or similar extra-constitutional event. Between 1963 and 2000 over 200 regimes ended with a coup, civil war or invasion. The large proportion of coups can be construed as a sign that leaders in Africa typically employ high political discount rates. High political discount rates are also a possible explanation for the extensive and destructive political corruption seen in Africa.

At the same time, Africa is famous for leaders with long tenure. Fourteen present national heads in the region have been in office for between ten and 20 years; nine have served more than 20 years. The mean tenure for all former African leaders is 7.2 years, and about twice that for leaders who died in office or retired. For comparison, European national leaders served an aver-age of 3.2 years over the past four decades, with Finland having the shortest average duration and Luxembourg the longest. At first, the relative lack of turnover would seem to contradict the hypothesis that the political environment for leaders is unstable or insecure. Yet, another interpretation is plausible. In the field of finance, risk is associated with volatility. The same may be true in politics. For the individual ruler who wants to weigh his prospects of retaining power, the average term of office may be a less meaningful statistic than is the variation around the mean. As an indication of how much volatility exists, three recently independent countries have had no leadership transitions. Another 11 countries have had just one transition since independence. At the far end of the spectrum, Nigeria has had 11 transitions and Benin has had 12.

The rational leader also needs to anticipate what may happen to him were he to lose power. Of the 101 past leaders who left office due to a coup or similar unauthorized event, roughly two-thirds were killed, imprisoned, or banished to a foreign country. Twenty-seven former rulers died violently, counting five whose deaths appear to have been independent of a coup or coup attempt. The remaining 22 leaders in this category clearly perished as a direct result of coups. Of Africa's overthrown leaders who were not executed or assassinated, 37 were detained and held in jail or placed under house arrest. Twenty-nine other ex-leaders were forced into exile, at least temporarily. That figure does not include nine ex-leaders who experienced periods of both imprisonment and banishment. Some rulers may look for reassurance in the region's declining rate of

Table 1: How Leaders Leave Office in Africa, 1960-1999

	Number of Incidents					Mean Time in Office Years
	1960-69	1970-79	1980-89	1990-99	Total	
Overthrown in coup, war or invasion	27	30	22	22	101	5.7
Die of natural or accidental causes	2	3	4	3	12	11.7
Assassination (not part of coup)	1	0	1	3	5	7.8
Retire	1	2	5	9	17	11.7
Lose election	0	0	1	12	13	14.8
Other (interim or caretaker regime, impeachment)	6	8	4	14	32	1.2
All regime transitions	37	43	37	63	180	7.2

Box 3.1: (continued)

coups. The rate of military takeovers has dropped steadily, falling from 0.087 per country year in the 1960s to 0.046 per country year in the 1990s. So, the region-wide probability of being overthrown is currently about half what it was in earlier years.

There is little doubt, therefore, that holding high office in Africa poses acute risks. To what extent do those risks affect leaders' behavior, specifically their behavior in the areas of economic reform and corruption? That question is difficult to answer fully without detailed case studies of the individuals' involved, but aggregate data may give us clues about how these leaders conduct themselves. Low-risk environments would tend to produce more reform-minded leaders. Table 2 provides some evidence that such may be the case in Africa. A correlation exists between the hazards of leadership and the degree of economic freedom. Leaders in the so-called "mostly free" countries were the least likely to be overthrown, killed, arrested, or exiled. Leaders in the mostly unfree and repressed countries, by contrast, experienced a greater number of negative outcomes. Correlation does not prove causation, especially in making inferences about micro-level behavior based on macro-level data, but the results are consistent with political economy theory. Low political risk and economic reform seem to go together in Africa. The predicament facing any individual national leader is that the payoffs to most economic reforms lie in the future, but he also has to hold on to power now. An insecure power base is likely to encourage either reckless gambling for immediate returns or highly cautious strategies to preserve political capital; it is unlikely to promote measured actions to obtain long-range returns.

Democratization and Improved Leadership

Better leadership is not the cure-all for Africa's lack of development, but it would be an important step in the right direction. Political economy theory also suggests that one solution to poor leadership is to make the political environment less hazardous. A safer environment would reduce the incentives to engage in political misbehavior and, in principle, encourage responsible and forward-looking activity. In this context, Africa's recent moves toward democracy and competitive elections are reasons for hope. Since 1982, 13 incumbents have been turned out of office by voters – accounting for about one-sixth of the leadership transitions in the 1990s. The threat of losing an election also may account for the increasing rate of leader retirements – nine in the 1990s versus only eight in the previous three decades.

Democratization appears to be altering the outcomes of the many coups that still occur. In the past, the new heads of military juntas often declared themselves permanent leaders (sometimes after doffing their uniforms and becoming "civilians"). Now, it is becoming the norm for coup leaders quickly to organize internationally acceptable elections. More importantly, the people of Côte d'Ivoire have demonstrated the consequences of failing to honor the election results afterwards. African elections have not yet produced marked beneficial effects. Still, the rise of orderly political competition does offer hope for encouraging African leaders to act positively and redress decades of oppression and economic decline.

Table 2: Hazards of Leadership, by Economic Policy Category

Policy category (1995-2000)	Leaders overthrown	Leaders Killed	Leaders Arrested	Leaders Exiled
Mostly free countries	1.0	0.2	0.2	0.5
Mostly unfree countries	2.5	0.6	1.0	0.7
Repressed countries	1.5	0.5	0.6	0.6

Note: The economic policy categories are based on the Heritage Foundation economic freedom ranking for 1995-2000.
Source: Adapted from Goldsmith (2000).

Table: 3.1. Political Freedoms, Civil Liberties and Type of Government in Africa

Type of Government	Number of Countries	Status as Group	Population (million 1998)
Dominant Party	22	PF (5.2)	325
Presidential-Parliamentary Democracy	12	PF (3.2)	200
Presidential-Legislative Democracy	6	PF (3.4)	81
Civilian Military	3	NF	65
Military Backed Dictatorship	3	NF	58
Monarchy and Limited Parliament	1	PF	28
Rival Ethnic Based Militias	1	NF	11
Parliamentary Democracy and Traditional Chiefs	2	PF(3)	3.7
One-Party Transitional	1	PF	3.5
Legislative Democracy	1	Free	1.1
Traditional Monarchy	1	NF	0.9
All Government Types	**53**		**778**

Notes: F = Free, PF = Partly Free, NF = Not Free.
Source: UNECA (2000).

Since the path-breaking national conference and multiparty elections in Benin (1989), most African states have undergone some form of competitive multiparty elections. Even though the results are at best mixed, there are success stories that have banished terror and dictatorship, widening the scope of good economic governance (Chege, 1999). These cases include South Africa, Uganda, Nigeria, Malawi, Ghana, Botswana, Mauritius and Senegal. In other cases, competitive party politics has been inappropriately pursued, resulting in sharpening ethnic and regional cleavages, even inducing warfare between win-ners and losers when the gains are so obviously confided to one side ethnically. In some cases, it is feared that the phenomenon of one-party rule might give way to one-party ethnic groups or cultural coalitions (Chege, 1999). This fear is instigated by the mismatch between the ethnic expression of voters and the failure of constitutional structures to cater for such ethnic expressions. There are, however, some cases where ethnic expressions were reflected in the construction of the constitution. Ethnically-inclusive local systems include those of South Africa especially, Namibia (1989) and Zimbabwe (1980).

Overall, African countries have made some progress towards democracy. Notwithstanding these positive developments, much remains to be done to improve citizens' influence and oversight over the conduct of the government, elect responsive and responsible leadership and promote social reciprocities. For one thing, there are still many parts in Africa where progress would need to be made towards greater adherence to the axioms of good politics including basic political order, political legitimacy and rule of law. Furthermore, there are still cases where democracy is superficially based on ethnic elections that do not reflect the judgement of the people on the performance of the government. This may explain the puzzle of limited achievements in turning electoral democracy into a tool for political liberalism and efficient economic governance. More will need to be done to improve the degree of political equality, inter-group tolerance, inclusiveness, and popular participation. Related to these, the existence of societal peace and the promotion of an environment that respects human rights are at an insufficient level, as evidenced by the number of African countries mired in instability and conflicts.

Civil Wars and Conflicts

Civil wars and armed conflicts are closely linked to the unwillingness or inability of social groups and their leaders to transcend the boundaries of religion, ethnicity and race. Civil wars and armed conflicts have figured prominently in the political history of Africa. Starting with the early days of independence when the accent was on nation building and socio-economic transformation, Africa experienced various forms of institutions and strategies. While an enduring stability emerged in some countries a good many encountered civil strife and conflicts generated by dissatisfaction with the economic, social and political arrangements.

According to the Organization of African Unity (OAU), 26 African conflicts took place from the establishment of the organization in 1963 to the end of 1998. Some of the world's longest civil wars were in Africa (Ethiopia, Mozambique and Sudan) and some older civil wars are still raging. All in all, 474 million Africans, representing 61 per cent of the population of the continent, were affected by these conflicts. No region was spared the agony of the suffering caused. East Africa was the region with the highest percentage of affected population (79.4 per cent of the population, or 189 million). Followed by Central Africa region (73 per cent of the population, or 21 million), West Africa (64 per cent of the population, or 144 million) and North Africa (51 per cent of the population or 87 million). The Southern African region recorded the lowest share of civil conflict-affected population (29 per cent of the population, or 33 million).

Of the 26 listed conflicts, the OAU classifies seven as inter-state. While six of these were related to border disputes, the OAU classifies three of them as border conflicts: Algeria/Morocco (1964-65), Somalia/Kenya (1965-80) and Cameroon/Nigeria (1996). The other three are classified as territorial claims relating to disagreement over the interpretation of colonial legal documents: Ethiopia/Somalia (1964-65 and 1976-77), Morocco (involving Algeria in the context of Western Sahara, continuing up to now) and Ethiopia/Eritrea (1998 to the present). The seventh is the conflict between Uganda and Tanzania in 1979.

The remaining 19 conflicts are classified as occurring within countries. In Central Africa, these include Democratic Republic of Congo (1964 and 1998), Republic of Congo (1998), Chad

(1977-80), Burundi (1993-98), Rwanda (1992-94) and Sao Tome and Principe (1994). In East Africa, they include Uganda (1970-79), Somalia (1991-99) and Comoros (1995-98). In North Africa, Sudan (1983-98) was the only case in this category. And in West Africa, they include Guinea (1970), Benin (1977), Liberia (1990-97), Sierra Leone (1993-98) and Guinea-Bissau (1998). Finally in Southern Africa, they include Angola (1975-99), Lesotho (1998) and Mozambique (1975-92).

The factors that trigger civil wars are complex, but one of the root causes is often found in the inability to respect social reciprocities: political inequality, inter-group intolerance, and the lack of inclusiveness in associational membership. In the OAU's summary analysis of the causes of African civil wars, at least six causes are identified. *Ethnicity* was identified as the triggering factor for the wars in Burundi in 1993 and Rwanda during 1992-94. Problems related to *power-sharing* were the reasons for the war in DRC since 1998, Sudan since 1983, Sao Tome and Principe in 1994, and Comoros since 1995. *Inter-clan* and other factional rivalries and their contagion were responsible for the wars in Somalia since 1991, Liberia during 1990-97 and Guinea-Bissau since 1998. *Destabilization by mercenaries* was identified to be behind the wars in DRC in 1964 and Guinea in 1970 and Benin in 1977. *Human rights violations* were identified as the cause in Uganda from 1970-79. *Geopolitics and the Cold War* were behind the wars in Chad during 1977-80 and Mozambique during 1975-92.

Elbadawi and Sambanis (2000) explored the major characteristics of Africa's civil wars compared to other regions in the world. They found that Africa has the highest incidence of civil wars among world regions, and that the incidence of war has increased in Africa in the last two de-

cades while it has fallen or remained constant in other regions. They also concluded that wars in Africa tend to be relatively short in duration but relatively intense in terms of military casualties per unit of time. The intensity of casualties of wars in Africa would exceed, by far, that of other regions if civilian war-related deaths and other loss of life caused by war are included.

While it is difficult to provide a complete account of the negative impact of civil strife and conflict on economic performance some obvious effects are generally known. Collier (1999) identified five effects of a civil war. These include the destruction of physical and human capital, reduction of savings, diversion of portfolios from domestic investment to capital flight, disruption of economic transactions, and distortion of government expenditure from the provision of public services to military expenditure. The combined impact of these negative effects is likely to be on the growth rate of the economy rather than a once-and-for-all reduction in the level of output.

Ali (2001) estimated the cost of civil conflicts by looking at the economic performance of 15 African countries afflicted by war in a sample of 45 African countries. The study measures economic performance in terms of real per capita GDP growth rates. It found that the group of countries in war always under-performed in relation to the rest of the continent in all periods under consideration (see Table 3.2). For instance, in the post-independence period, which was characterized with relatively high growth, it would have taken countries in war 40 years to double per capita income in contrast to 30 years for the continent as a whole. Likewise, during the recovery period of the second half of the 1990s, per capita GDP for the countries in war declined by about 0.35 per cent per annum, while per capita income for

Table 3.2: The Real Cost of Conflict in Africa ($ in 1985 PPP)

Country	1973 Per Capita GDP	Actual 1999 Per Capita GDP	No Civil War 1999 Per Capita GDP	Per Capita Cost of Conflict
Angola	1203	472	963	491
Benin	1142	1077	1271	194
Burundi	447	412	489	77
Chad	717	381	545	164
Comoros	747	439	572	133
Congo, D.R.	688	171	343	172
Congo, Rep.	1715	2001	2233	231
Guinea	574	792	814	22
G.Bissau	857	818	836	18
Lesotho	643	1156	1180	24
Liboria	NA	NA	NA	NA
Mozambique	1681	837	1619	782
Rwanda	621	1093	1133	40
S. T& P	NA	NA	NA	NA
S. Leone	1182	479	676	197
Somalia	778	862	1045	183
Sudan	763	831	1409	578
Uganda	634	723	1368	645
Average	900	784	1031	247

Source: Ali (2001).

the continent increased by about 0.8 per cent per annum. The cumulative effect of the above pattern of growth is that by the end of 1999 there were nine countries out of a sample of 15 countries in conflict with real per capita income less than that in 1973. These include Angola, Benin, Burundi, Chad, Comoros, Congo Democratic Republic, Guinea-Bissau, Mozambique and Sierra Leone.

The analysis of the impact of conflicts shows clearly that war and civil strife can and do hamper economic development for decades. No accurate value can be assigned to the cost of war, in terms of loss of human life and deprivation and destitution for those who endure war. About one in five Africans live in countries severely affected by war or conflict in 1999. Also, 90 per cent of the casualties of civil conflicts in Africa are civilians and 3 million Africans are refugees while 16 million are internally displaced as a result of various civil wars and conflicts (ADB et al., 2000). Box 3.2 provides an account of the impact of war on children in Rwanda.

Box 3.2: The Impact of War on Children: The Case of Rwanda

Children in Rwandan society traditionally occupied a central and key position. The child was seen as the hope and future of the family. According to custom in Rwanda, children were supposed to enjoy love, care, and the protection of the family and the community. The genocide turned these values completely upside down. The following is a brief account of how the genocide afflicted Rwandan Children.

- UNICEF reports that a very large number of children were killed during the genocide. Maternity clinics, orphanages, children's homes, and schools were all systematically targeted. An additional 100,000 children were separated from their families. Not all the orphans or separated children were Tutsi, although no exact ethnic breakdown is available.

- When hundreds of thousands of Hutu fled into Zaire and Tanzania, thousands of children were abandoned along the route, whether lost in the shuffle or deliberately left behind. All over the country people were put into the position of looking after relatives' or other peoples' children, while the camps for the displaced were filled with children living on their own.

- By late 1995, only 12,000 children in Rwanda and 11,700 in eastern Zaire had been reunified with their families. In the same period, over 12,000 children were crowded into 56 centres that had been turned into temporary orphanages, while more than 300,000 children had been taken in by families. Even now many children still have not been reunified with their families.

- A study of 3030 children, found that virtually all of them had witnessed some kind of violence during the genocide. More than two-thirds had actually seen someone being injured or killed, and 79 per cent had experienced death in their immediate families.

Twenty per cent witnessed rape and sexual abuse, almost all had seen dead bodies, and more than half had watched people being killed with machetes and beaten with sticks. Children killed other children, forced or encouraged by adults. Almost half of surviving children witnessed killings by other children.

- Almost all of the children interviewed had believed that they themselves would die during the war and 16 per cent reported that they had hidden under dead bodies to survive. The majority of the children continue to have intrusive images, thoughts, and feeling despite attempts to remove the events from their memories. They also suffer continuing physical reactions, such as trembling, sweating, or increased heart rates. About 20 per cent of Rwandan children are still traumatized.

- Five years after the genocide, somewhere between 45,000 and 60,000 households were still headed by children under 18, with some 300,000 children living in such households. According to recent estimates, 90 per cent of these households were headed by girls with no regular source of income. They were the legacy of the genocide and the subsequent mass migrations of people into neighboring nations and back again.

- There has been precious little help for the children taking on this role. Communities, unable to decide whether to treat them as adults or children, have tended to leave them to fend for themselves. Inevitably, these children become vulnerable to many problems: they are abused sexually and used as slave laborers; their land is stolen by adults and they often wind up forsaking their education.

Source: IPEP (2000).

Effects of Corruption on Development

Corruption is closely linked to the absence of citizens' influence and oversight and to unresponsive and irresponsible political leadership. Corruption becomes prevalent when the people are not empowered to participate in the political process and have no means to hold political leaders and their administrations accountable for their decisions and actions. Corruption takes hold in society when political leaders do not honor their role as public trustees, do not adhere to the rule of law, and are not ready to share information with citizens. In such environments, failures in economic policy create rent-seeking opportunities, and the weaknesses in public administration provide public servants the opportunities to engage in corrupt practices. All these factors, in addition to the inadequacy of legislative and judicial oversight, provide a nurturing environment for corruption.

Corruption is often narrowly defined as "the abuse of public office for private gain" (Gray and Kaufman, 1998). It involves using a position of power to seek or extort an advantage by a public servant in consideration of the performance or omission of an act. As the scope of corruption widens, the definition has been enlarged to cover the abuse of all offices of trust for private gain, whether in the public or private sectors (Ofosu-Amaah et al., 1999). There are various forms of corruption. Personal corruption is motivated by personal gain while political corruption is motivated by political gain. A distinction can also be made between individual corruption and institutional corruption. State corruption refers to criminal or otherwise unlawful conduct by government agencies, or by officials of these agencies acting in the course of their employment.

Corruption undermines development. It is both a symptom and an outcome of poor governance. Despite the interrelationship between corruption and broader governance, conclusions regarding the connection between corruption and any particular set of political institutions or societies cannot easily be made. Corruption has reached global proportions and is present in all societies (Ofosu-Amaah et al., 1999) and it occurs in poor, emerging and developed countries, regardless of the level of social and economic development. It also occurs in countries with diverse forms of government ranging from dictatorships to established democracies. However, a defining distinction between countries can be made when corruption becomes the rule rather than the exception. The corrosive effects of corruption are much more problematic for developing countries, as it comes at a high cost for those that are poor (Rose-Ackerman, 1997).

Corruption in Africa, as in other parts of the world, takes many forms, including embezzlement of public funds, theft of state property, bribery to obtain services or shorten processing time, and bribery in procurement. Corruption occurs at all levels, from major pay-offs at the top of the system, to petty bribes to local officials for the delivery of services and evasion of regulations (Box 3.3). In some cases, the gains from corruption are siphoned off into foreign bank accounts, while in other cases proceeds are recycled in the local economy.

It is apparent that in many countries, much of the corruption in society occurs at the nexus between the public and private sectors, with actors in the private sector interacting with holders of offices of trust in the public sector. Corruption in this regard manifests itself when private sector officials bribe government officials to make deci-

Box 3.3: Nigeria: Fighting the Cumulative Impact of Corruption Under Democratic Dispensation

Corruption is a global phenomenon, intelligible only in its social context. In Nigeria corruption is known to be rife, pervasive and deeply entrenched. To most outsiders, Nigeria conjures up images of rampant corruption, business fraud and nepotism. Not surprisingly, Nigeria consistently fare poorly on Transparency International's Corruption Perception Index, a league table of nations ranked according to the perceived levels of corruption in public service and government (see Table 3.3).

Corruption is not just endemic but an integral part of the social fabric of life in Nigeria. It had in the last decade, especially under the military regimes, increased to the extent that it began to be asserted that in Nigeria, *it is not simply that officials are corrupt, but corruption is official.* Rampant corruption among the ruling class has, over time, sent the dangerous lesson that being honest and law-abiding does not pay. Consequently those among the ordinary people who have learnt this lesson from the top then try to replicate such corrupt practices at their own levels in the form of petty acts of bribery, peculation and embezzlement of public funds. Particularly under military regimes, corruption permeated all strata of Nigerian society and became accepted as the norm. Ranging from the post office clerk who sells stamps at a premium to the army general who arranges the filling of an oil tanker at night in exchange for hard currency, systematic looting and corruption became the order of the day, an expected element of every social transaction.

The habitual and systematic pilfering of public resources in Nigeria can be accounted for by the neo-patrimonial nature of society. Neo-patrimonialism is the cross-fertilization between patrimonialism and legal-rational mode of governance. This dual form combines the logic of bureaucracy and patrimonialism: the formal structure of the state is bureaucratic, a written law exists, civil servants are recruited through examinations, but there is no real state of law. Within this neo-patrimonial setup, the public sector is in reality appropriated by private interest - military and civilian hangers-on of the various regimes. The consequence is that public service remains personalized by way of clientelism and nepotism and

access to the public institutions of the state is not only seen but also taken as the main means of personal enrichment. This peculiar logic of governance has in turn generated well-organized predatory networks based upon personal loyalty and patron-client ties. It is this institutional and political environment that accounts for the level of corruption in Nigeria. In such an atmosphere everything was for sale and holding any slice of public power constituted a veritable exchange instrument, convertible into illicit acquisition of money or other goods.

Fighting corruption in Nigeria is as old as the phenomenon itself. Whatever the strength and limitations of their underlying commitment, Nigerian leaders in the various regimes have constantly extolled the virtues and absolute indispensability of efficient and honest government. Accordingly, the fight against corruption has more or less been a permanent feature of the political scene in Nigeria. The search for appropriate reform measures has taken a wide variety of forms. The first such measure was the attempt to rid the nation of corruption by termination of appointment and administrative purges. An example of this was the massive purge of the public service in 1975 in which over 10,000 public servants lost their jobs for corrupt activities, inefficiency and ineffectiveness. A second strategy was the setting up of anti-corruption boards, commissions, and panels and the like. Third was the attempt to locate the root of corruption in politics and the antics of politicians. The fourth main strategy was to situate corruption and the abuse of office within the larger problem of a general social malaise or moral vacuum, the remedy for which is some form of moral regeneration. The promulgation of a Code of Conduct and the principle of public accountability for public officers were another anti-corruption device. There were also the civil service based measures like the General Orders and the Financial Instructions, which were meant to provide guidance for the effective performance and the development of positive attitudes among public servants. The General Orders later re-christened the Civil Service Rules contained procedural instructions on operations in the civil service. It defined what was

Box 3.3: (Continued)

misconduct and what was not. The Financial In-
struction outlined procedures for government financial transactions to avoid abuse. Through
training, a civil servant was supposedly equipped
in not only becoming technically proficient but also
highly aware of his responsibility to serve the public fairly, objectively and impartially.

In spite of the various wars, crusades, and
ethical revolutions against corruption in Nigeria,
the epidemic remains seemingly uncontainable.
Several reasons account for this. First, a lot of the
remedial actions of these regimes were back-
ward looking and self-protective. The anti-corruption measures adopted by an incumbent regime
to sweep away the sins of its predecessors were
often taken without touching its own. Second, government approach to the question of public accountability has mainly been ad hoc and non-in-
stitutional. The very institutions that were to promote public accountability were stifled by military
decrees. For example, Decree 4 restrained the
press by stipulating as an offence, any article by a
journalist and his publisher that was critical of the
government. Similarly, another decree(13) made
it impossible for government activities and decrees to be brought before the judiciary. The result was that the very government that committed
itself to 'upholding the principles of public accountability' suppressed the two critical institutions of
public accountability. In another example, the report of the Panel of enquiry into the accounts of
the Central Bank of Nigeria remains largely a
mystery to the Nigerian people in spite of a rev-
elation during its presentation that $12.4 billion of
Nigeria's revenue from crude petroleum sales
disappeared into a black hole, dedication accounts and was not reflected in the official government accounts kept by the Central Bank of Nigeria.

Fighting corruption requires institutions, laws,
conventions and practices, which effectively discourage and punish corrupters and corruptees.

Effective sanctions - moral, social, political and
legal - are an essential part of the antidote against
corruption. In the final analysis, the quality of institutional structures which limits the temptations of
elected leaders and bureaucrats will be the most
effective anti-dote against corruption in Nigeria. A
necessary expedient of empowering the Nigerian
people can be facilitated by pursuing the constitutional entrenchment of the principles of honest
representation by politicians, a code of conduct
for civil servants, freedom of information, freedom
of the press as the watchdog of the people's interest, and judicial independence.

The advent of democracy brought renewed
hope and expectation for solving the entrenched
problem of corruption in Nigeria. As a first step in
the right direction the current administration in
Nigeria has pledged and proceeded to tackle corruption head-on at all levels as well as to ensure
good governance in an attempt to overturn the
country's notoriety as one of the worlds most corrupt nations. Its first bill through parliament was
the anti-corruption bill aimed at ending widespread corruption among officials and civil servants and since then the state-owned oil company NNPC has had to publish its accounts. The
war on corruption, among other things, has
changed Nigeria's image abroad with the international community vesting a lot of trust in the
Nigerian president considering him as one of the
most promising African leaders. Within Nigeria
the administration has made considerable
strides in attempting to restore public confidence
in government and for the most part while it may
be too early to evaluate the effect of the new Bill, it
is however evident that most Nigerians see the
civilian regime's crusade as being sincere.

Source: Adapted from Daniel Edevbaro (1998) and S.O.
Osoba (1996).

sions which are favorable to their interests. Another aspect of corruption, which is quite prevalent in Africa, is fraudulent misappropriation of assets or funds. Depending on the circumstances, this phenomenon can occur entirely within the private or public sectors.

In some countries, it is difficult to demand routine services from officials, especially in the public sector, without paying a bribe. In countries where corruption is pervasive, it has greatly distorted government actions and undermined the effectiveness of public interventions. In those countries, graft amongst government officials is quite high. Funds are embezzled from state accounts, enterprises or projects without legal penalty. In these countries, corruption has grown into a major problem as it is hampering development efforts. In some other societies, corruption is not pervasive enough to affect resource allocation decisions in any significant manner.

A measure of the extent to which corruption is prevalent in African countries can be obtained from the Corruption Index of Transparency International (CITI). The CITI measures the perception of corruption as seen by business people, risk analysts and the general public. The CITI ranges between ten (highly clean) and zero (highly corrupt). The classification of country CITI scores by regions reveals that the degree of corruption in Africa is similar to that of Eastern Europe. The 22 African countries covered by the CITI scored an average of 3.4 points— the same score for the 21 East European countries covered by the CITI (see Table 3.3). The CITI averages for the other regions are Latin America 3.9, Asia 4.5, Western Europe 7.8 and the US and Canada 8.5.

Turning to individual cases in Africa, there are only four countries (Botswana, Namibia, Tunisia and South Africa) that passed the middle mark on the road towards a highly corruption-clean environment, with Mauritius, and Morocco bordering that mark. The best score among African countries of 6 points for Botswana is comparable to the scores of Belgium (6.1) and, with a stretch, to Japan (6.4). However, the score for Botswana has a relatively high standard deviation – with the lowest score of 4.3 and highest score of 8.2 – indicating greater differences among the surveyors with regard to their perception of corruption in the country. Nigeria registers the worst record among all the countries covered by the survey (1.2), but its score is comparable to that of Yugoslavia (1.3).

In a nutshell, although the degree of corruption in Africa must not be underplayed, the comparison with other developing countries in Eastern Europe and Latin American countries supports the argument that the extent of corruption in Africa is often overstated. In this respect, it might be remarked that the average score for Africa fairs better in comparison with the scores of individual countries that are highly regarded by international investors—for instance, Mexico (3.3), Thailand (3.2), China (3.1), Romania (2.9), India (2.8), Russia (2.1), and Indonesia (1.7).

The Causes of Corruption

The distribution of incidence shown by the CITI suggests that corruption thrives in emerging and transitional economies where the political system is immature. The complexity, overregulation, and lack of predictability serve as incubators for corruption in emerging economies. Too many controls and too much political and administrative discretion encourage the creation of rent-seeking "colonies", as do inappropriate pricing policies, which encourage the development of parallel markets. In general, the government imposes regulations, levies taxes and enforces criminal laws, but

Table 3.3: Corruption Perceptions in Africa Compared to Other Regions (2000)

Country Rank	Country	2000 CPI Score	Surveys Used	Standard Deviation	High-Low Range
African Countries					
1	Botswana	**6**	4	1.6	4.3 - 8.2
2	Namibia	**5.4**	4	0.8	4.3 - 6.1
3	Tunisia	**5.2**	4	1.5	3.8 - 7.1
4	South Africa	**5**	10	0.9	3.8 - 6.6
5	Mauritius	**4.7**	5	0.8	3.9 - 5.6
6	Morocco	**4.7**	4	0.7	4.2 - 5.6
7	Malawi	**4.1**	4	0.4	3.8 - 4.8
8	Ghana	**3.5**	4	0.0	2.5 - 4.7
9	Senegal	**3.5**	3	0.8	2.8 - 4.3
10	Zambia	**3.4**	4	1.4	2.1 - 5.1
11	Ethiopia	**3.2**	3	0.8	2.5 - 3.9
12	Egypt	**3.1**	7	0.7	2.3 - 4.1
13	Burkina Faso	**3**	3	1	2.5 - 4.4
14	Zimbabwe	**3**	7	1.5	0.6 - 4.9
15	Côte-d'Ivoire	**2.7**	4	0.8	2.1 - 3.6
16	Tanzania	**2.5**	4	0.6	2.1 - 3.5
17	Uganda	**2.3**	4	0.6	2.1 - 3.5
18	Mozambique	**2.2**	3	0.2	2.4 - 2.7
19	Kenya	**2.1**	4	0.3	2.1 - 2.7
20	Cameroon	**2**	4	0.6	1.6 - 3.0
21	Angola	**1.7**	3	0.4	1.6 - 2.5
22	Nigeria	**1.2**	4	0.6	0.6 - 2.1
	Average	**3.4**	**4.4**	**0.8**	**2.6 - 3.5**

Other Regions	Number of Countries		Averages		
Eastern Europe	21	**3.4**	4.1	0.7	2.5 - 4.7
Latin America	11	**3.9**	3.8	0.5	3.0 - 5.3
Asia	12	**4.5**	3.8	0.5	2.8 - 5.8
Western Europe	18	**7.8**	4.2	0.7	6.3 - 8.9
North America	2	**8.5**	4.0	0.6	7.2 -9.6

Notes: 2000 CPI Score: Relates to perceptions of the degree of corruption as seen by business people, risk analyst and the general public and ranges between 10 (highly clean) and 0 (highly corrupt). **Survey Used**: Refers to the number of surveys that assessed a country's performance. 16 survey used and at least 3 surveys were required for a country to be try to be included in the CPI. **Standard Deviation:** Indicates differences in the values of the sources: the greater the Standard deviation, the greater the differences of perceptions of a countries among the sources. **High-Low Range**: Provides the highest and lowest values of the sources.
Source: Compiled by the Research Division from Transparency International, Corruption Perceptions Index 2000.

when the underlying legal framework is inefficient, individuals and firms are emboldened to pay for relief from these costs. For example, individuals and firms may collude with tax authorities to perpetuate fraud and reduce their taxation by bribing tax collectors (Commonwealth, 2000).

Beyond collecting levies, governments also engage in a large number of economic activities involving transactions with the private sector. These range from procurement of goods and services and delivery of public services from transportation, health, education to implementing regulations in a variety of areas such as the environment. Therefore, reducing excessive economic control will not eliminate corruption, as there are other opportunities, especially in government procurement. Paradoxically, the transition from a controlled to a liberalized economy may increase the opportunities for corruption. As economies liberalize, the liberalization process itself provides new areas for corruption to flourish. A case in point, here, is the process of privatization – where the selling of government assets provides opportunities for government officials to receive bribes from would-be buyers. This phenomenon of rising corruption during liberalization is closely related to the lack of transparency in the liberalization process.

The low real wages for civil service in many African countries constitute another factor encouraging corruption. Over the last three decades the real incomes for many public service employees have declined significantly (Gray and Kaufman, 1998). Low pay forces highly-skilled people to depart to the private sector or emigrate to developed countries, leaving behind weak institutions and administrative systems. Those that stay may be tempted to engage in corrupt practices to supplement their incomes. In some cases, government employees actually believe that corruption is the only rational behavior available to earn enough income to satisfy the needs of their families. Other coping mechanisms include using a public office and telephone line and other available assets for running private business activities. This might explain why in some cases civil servants continue to go to 'work' whereas they claim that their salaries are not enough to cover their transport cost to the office (Hussain, 1991).

The Costs of Corruption

The exact cost of corruption may not be known and probably will never be known simply because it is a secret crime, which goes unreported and is never meant to be discovered. Despite the lack of exactness, the uncertainty and the complexity of the issues involved, the implications of corruption for governance and development are clear. Corruption is bad for both. It hinders proper resource management, undermines efforts to enhance growth and reduce poverty, and obstructs sound and sustainable private sector growth (ADB, 2000).

Corruption has a crippling effect on development through undermining the rule of law and weakening the foundations of national institutions on which economic development depends. The negative impact of corruption falls mostly on the poor who are hardest hit when there is an economic decline (Kaufman et al., 1998). Widespread corruption also reinforces existing economic and social inequalities, and it undermines the credibility of government and public institutions.

The intention of the state to provide all citizens access to education, health and the legal system will be thwarted if bribery determines the allocation of these resources and services. The poor are the most reliant on public services and are the least capable of paying the extra costs associated with corruption. Also when officials embezzle state funds, which are meant to provide services such as education and health care, the poor suffer the most.

Perceptions of widespread corruption reduce donor assistance, as public support in donor countries is undermined. Corruption in aid programs reduces their benefits to recipients. Where programs are funded through loans, the burden of external debt is increased without commensurate social returns. Likewise, foreign direct investment is reduced as corruption undermines confidence of private foreign investors. Widespread corruption provides a poor environment, which discourages those investors most likely to make a long-term contribution to development, and encourages those who seek quick profits through dubious ventures. As a result, needed capital that could lead to sustained growth is directed to other places, undermining economic development. The costs of corruption are, therefore, particularly high for poor African countries in great need of inflows of productive foreign capital (Commonwealth, 2000).

Corruption also hinders the development of small and medium-sized businesses, which are the engine of job creation and economic growth in emerging economies (Eizenstat, 1999). Corruption costs force small businesses into the unofficial economy while also undermining the ability of government to collect tax revenues and balance budgets. Corruption in the private sector can cause as much harm to the health of the economy as corruption in the public sector. The distinction between the two sectors is becoming increasingly blurred. Within the private sector, weak corporate governance could engender corrupt practices

(Iskander and Chamlou, 2000). The recent financial crisis in East Asia and the banking crises in several African countries highlight the negative effects that crony capitalism and insider lending within the banking industry could have on the economy. In many cases in Africa, depositors' money was badly invested or simply embezzled by banking officials in the private sector. It led to banking crises and hurt the confidence in the banking sector in affected countries.

On the political scene, bribery can undermine the government and lead to cynicism. Politicians may purchase votes and political campaigns may be funded illegally by big business or crime syndicates (Rose-Ackerman, 1997). In some countries, the votes of parliamentarians may be bought by the executive branch or by private corporations to get favorable decisions. This undermines democracy, as elected officials then become only accountable to the highest bidder. The result is poor governance and a vicious circle of sluggish growth and underdevelopment. The potential impact of corruption on the economy is summarized in Box 3.4.

Combating Corruption

Unless comprehensive and systematic actions are taken to combat corruption the vicious circle of rising poverty, poor governance and corruption is likely to continue unabated. Corruption transcends national borders and must be combated both at the national and global levels (see Chapter 6). Actions are needed at both levels to successfully address the corruption problem. The basis of any effective national action against corruption is a clear sense of national purpose, ownership and strategy. Without this, the efforts are not likely to yield effective long-term solutions. The

Box 3.4 : The Cost of Corruption

When corruption grows, it can help perpetuate development problems. Corruption thrives in emerging and transitional economies where entrenched corruption becomes one of a constellation of development problems that is endogenous to societies. Corruption is both worrisome on its own right and also a symptom of deeper developmental problems, as Johnston (1997) pointed out.

Corruption is associated with slow economic growth and poor competitiveness, low domestic and foreign investment, poor property and contract rights, weak institutions, weak rule of law, ethnic divisions, low educational attainment, violation of civil liberties and low citizen participation in governance. Because of the perverse nature of corruption, its growth further weakens the state and erodes the authority and effectiveness of public institutions.

Corruption is both a prime effect of poor governance and a major cause of poor governance. This vicious circle sustains rent-seeking vested interests, which tend to act as barriers to reform. The impact of corruption on socio-economic development might be summarized as follows:

- Increases the costs of development programs;

- Encourages government officials to spawn projects of little economic merit;

- Undermines revenue collection and contributes to fiscal deficits and macroeconomic imbalance;

- Acts as a strong disincentive to genuine foreign investors, while attracting more rent-seeking dubious enterprises;

- Leads to the diversion of resources from their intended purposes and distorts public policy;

- Undermines allocation priorities of public services in favor of the only those that can afford the extra costs to the detriment of the poor;

- Subverts essential public regulatory systems, which in turn affects markets and in some cases public safety;

- Brings government into disrepute and encourages widespread cynicism about politics and public policy.

Source: Adapted from: Johnston (1997) and (Commonwealth, 2000).

sense of national purpose requires the development of a new culture with zero tolerance for corruption. There must be a new dispensation that abhors corruption both in public and private life.

None of these, however, can take place without a strong political champion (Heilbrum and Keefer, 1999). The political leaders and others with the power to act and influence must be committed to the fight and must lead the efforts. The first

step is to secure a strong commitment at the highest political level, as it is often the most difficult hurdle. When corruption is widespread and involves the political establishment, fighting will involve political risks (Heilbrum and Keefer, 1999).

To sustain a new culture that is corruption-free, the people must be empowered by making leaders accountable to them and other stakeholders, providing access to information and providing the people with the education needed to understand issues and make informed decisions. A strong and independent press will be indispensable to this effort as will the supremacy of the rule of law.

Opportunities for decision-makers to engage in corrupt practices must be reduced. This will involve creating small yet strong and effective state establishments, where the discretionary powers of government officials are reduced while keeping the public administration effective and efficient. An effective civil service with well-paid civil servants, and democratic processes in political parties are important factors that could help to promote good governance and reduce corruption. The key economic reform measures that are required to combat corruption are summarized in Box 3.5.

The tendency to focus only on the symptoms of corruption must be avoided. This means that the actions taken should focus not only on corrupt activities but also address their underlying causes. Since these factors are likely to differ amongst countries, each national situation must inform a nation's strategy to combat corruption. It is crucial for national policy-makers to uncover the underlying causes of corruption in order to develop appropriate national responses. This does not preclude learning from the experiences of other countries; it only precludes copying what others have done without regard to the nation's situation and circumstances.

A piecemeal approach will not work. An all-out approach should be adopted from the outset, demonstrating a serious political commitment to the fight corruption within all segments of society. The fight to eliminate corruption must permeate national policies and legislative frameworks. The judiciary must also be geared up to participate in this fight against corruption. The ultimate goal must be the development of value systems that have zero tolerance for all types of corruption, including corruption at the highest levels.

The fight against corruption should go hand-in-hand with more general efforts to improve economic and corporate governance. The larger issues can help close the avenues for corruption by improving regulatory oversight, building the capacity of the administration, and enhancing enforcement capabilities. As part of such efforts to improve the governance environment, sustained action has to be directed at the root causes of corruption by targeting the underlying weaknesses in economic policy, public administration and politics and to reduce rent-seeking opportunities. Other areas of action may include reform to improve the effectiveness and probity of the public service, reforms in tax policy and administration, and tightening of controls over public expenditure. All these are important ingredients for a corruption prevention strategy (Commonwealth, 2000).

Prevention efforts must focus on the holders of offices of trust and also those who offer bribes. A code of conduct for private business should spell out what corruption practice and what is legitimate business promotion. Similarly, a public code of ethics should be developed to address the issue of corruption. A good prevention strategy requires strong enforcement to provide effective deterrence. Laws against corrupt behavior at all levels must be enforced without favor. Laws and regulations should be reviewed to remove any ambiguities that create incentives for corrupt behavior. In addition, the judiciary must be built up to ensure the probity and effectiveness of these agents. Box 3.6 outlines key reform measures in the judicial and legal systems that might be necessary for combating corruption.

Box 3.5: Key Economic Reforms for Combating Corruption

While the content of national strategies will vary, depending on national circumstances, there are areas of reform which must be examined and addressed, based on the prevailing conditions in each country. Some of these areas for evaluation and reforms in governance are:

Economic Reforms – to reduce rent-seeking opportunities by reducing bureaucratic controls that allow undue scope for the exercise of administrative discretion, as well as simplified economic regulations.

Fiscal Reforms – to increase the efficiency of the public sector, thus permitting adequate funding of public services.

Reform of Subsidized Public Lending Programs (which readily become vehicles for corruption) – by better targeting, enhancing transparency in the operation of the programs, strengthening the criteria for entitlement and reducing reliance on political and administrative discretion in their operation.

Reforms to Improve the Management, Efficiency and Delivery of Public Services — measures to improve management and efficiency should encompass all those who have responsibilities for providing goods and services in the public interest whether in the public or private sector.

Civil Service Reform – to restore the morale and integrity of the public service through merit-based recruitment, promotion, and a good reward system (better pay).

Strengthening the Regulatory Systems — Especially with regard to financial markets and privatized utilities, it is vital to establish regulatory regimes that, whilst not stifling free enterprise, are nonetheless firm regulators to ensure transparency, equity and fairness in private market transactions.

Legal Reform – to commit sufficient resources for the judiciary to investigative and prosecute offenders, and also ensure the autonomy of the judiciary from political interference.

Local Government Reform – to empower people to combat corruption, to decentralize power to the local government and to get the people involved in governance.

Monitoring of Privatization – to ensure misappropriation of public assets does not create opportunities for the illicit accumulation of wealth.

Opening Up – so that the administrative and political systems are subject to greater public scrutiny through parliamentary questioning and freedom of information provisions.

Reforms in the Funding of Political Parties – to prevent conflicts of interest and the exercise of improper influence and to preserve the integrity of democratic political structures and processes.

Capacity-Building – to enhance the capacity of core economic management institutions (e.g. Ministries of Finance, revenue collection agencies and auditor generals' departments) for effective and efficient public sector management.

Source: Adapted from: Commonwealth, (2000); Ofosu-Amaah et al. (1999).

Box 3.6 : Reforming the Judiciary and Legal System

The legal system is crucial to the success of any national anti-corruption strategy. As the third arm of government, with the power to enforce the law, the judiciary plays a key role in maintaining the rule of law.

Adequate enforcement of the law serves as the best deterrent against corruption. In an environment where there is a strong legal framework and enforcement of laws without favor, it is difficult for corruption to thrive or to become widespread.

The independence and integrity of the judiciary is of vital importance and it determines whether or not the judiciary can fulfil its duties under the constitution. The independence of the judiciary from political control and integrity of the members of the judiciary are key factors.

Similarly, the quality and integrity of public agencies responsible for investigating corruption and prosecuting offenders need to be ensured. Critical components of a strategy of legal reform should include:

Entrenching an Independent Judiciary: Restoration of the protections enjoyed by judges, including financial independence and security of tenure, is an important defence against improper interference. Judicial independence does not imply a lack of accountability, as judges should act properly and in accordance with their office and there should be transparent and publicly administered procedures to discipline or dismiss them if they do not.

Court Systems: An efficient court system is an essential component of an effective governance and anti-corruption strategy. The courts must not be overburdened and should be able to dispense unbiased judgements.

Detecting and Dealing with Corrupt Conduct: Many countries have enacted laws which permit the investigation of persons whose apparent assets exceed their known lawful sources of income. This permits relevant authorities (such as anti-corruption commissions) to require persons to explain the sources of their assets and where the assets cannot be attributed to lawful acquisition, the person can be charged with a corruption offence. In addition to laws which criminalize corrupt conduct, laws which permit the confiscation of the proceeds of corruption are an essential weapon in the fight against corruption. It is also important to have legal provisions to protect witnesses and whistle blowers in cases involving corruption.

Corporate Liability: The concept of corporate criminal liability, where corporations are involved in particular forms of criminal conduct or are used to facilitate or disguise criminal conduct, should be recognized within the legal system.

Non-criminal Legal Remedies in Corruption Cases: Effective anti-corruption legal strategies cannot rely on the criminal law alone. Civil, administrative and regulatory laws all have a place in a comprehensive strategy.

Source: Adapted from: Commonwealth (2000) and Ofosu-Amaah et al. (1999).

To create a new culture there is a need for massive mobilization of popular support for the involvement of civil society (Johnston, 1997). This is important in changing public values. It also exerts pressure on governments to take the necessary actions to formulate and implement anti-corruption programs. Public resentment of corruption and the burdens it places on citizens are perhaps the greatest potential capital for reforms to combat corruption. This can provide an important basis of political support for anti-corruption actions and challenging vested interests. Popular pressures can ensure accountability in the management of public resources. The role of the media and a free press is critical, as is the government's commitment to freedom of expression (see Box 3.7).

Combating corruption requires a consistent effort over a long-term period. The national efforts should generally involve both a long-term strategy and a series of short-term programs with some decisive time-bound actions. Because of the nature of corruption, there is a need to move on a number of fronts simultaneously, but at varying speeds, as some reforms are easier to implement than others and also, because resources will be limited. The sequencing will be crucial and must depend on a thorough analysis of the national situation.

National anti-corruption strategies should encompass both the public and private sectors. Corruption in the private sector can be as corrosive to economic performance as public sector corruption. Public sector corruption typically involves actors from the private sector. A national culture opposed to corruption requires high standards of behavior from all sections of society, but especially from political leaders. In addition, national efforts should be reinforced with appropriate

Box 3.7: The Media and Good Governance

It is now increasingly recognized that development demands good governance. Without good governance – based on key principles such as participation, rule of law and respect for human rights, transparency, accountability and legitimacy – development is likely to be stalled or aborted. At the base of good governance are representative government, an ongoing dialogue between the "governed" and "governors" and an active participation by the people. These basic facts bring to the fore the importance of a vigilant and free media, which must provide a bedrock for democratic exchange and respect for human rights.

The significant contribution made by media in the creation, nourishment and development of democracy and good governance is clear. It exposes violation of human rights and can improve the climate of democratic debate. A media sensitive to the importance of human rights and the need for good governance can provide reliable sources of information through which citizens, civil society groups, private organizations, and public authorities can work together to promote development and to eliminate arbitrary abuse. As a "surrogate sovereign", the media can be a watchdog on behalf of the electorate and can potentially assist in entrenching democratic and good governance. In such a capacity, the media can be expected to ferret out corruption, malfeasance and misuse of power and public resources, thus facilitating accountability, transparency and legitimacy.

News and information media provide a very important framework for factoring and articulating the demands, actions and orientations of the people and civil groups, in particular, and the civil society, at large. Given the manifest weakness of other vectors of the civil society in Africa, media resources can be massively deployed to strengthen and build democratic capacity of the people and their civil organizations. Thus, the consolidation of the emerging process of democratic governance in Africa requires a free and active mass media.

Box 3.7: (continued)

It has been well established that radio and television can have significant impact on political participation. Electronic media, especially the Internet, could play a crucial role in institutionalizing democratic governance. The Internet's ability to support simultaneous, interactive communications among many people is its greatest strength. Unlike the telephone, which primarily supports one-to-one communications, or radio and television, where information flows in only one direction from a single source to an audience that can only listen passively, the Internet allows information to flow back and forth among millions of people at practically the same time. This is changing the rules of the game, and people's power has been increased infinitely.

Interactive telecommunications now make it possible for millions of widely-dispersed citizens to receive the information they need to carry out the business of government themselves, gain admission to the political realm, and retrieve some powers from elected leaders. The electronic media has given a larger percentage of constituents than ever before the ability to easily and quickly transmit their opinions on public policy issues to their representatives, mobilize public opinion, and form pressure groups to lobby and defend personal or group interests.

The danger however is that electronic media such as the Internet or the print media disproportionately favor the educated and rich citizens, because the cost of acquiring the necessary equipment and services is prohibitive to the poor. The ownership of even television sets is still limited by poverty and the lack of adequate infrastructure. The result is the dominance of the elite in the access to the media, a factor which could have repercussions for democratic governance in the African context.

Despite the significant contributions that media can make towards realizing good governance, the single most important obstacle in Africa and elsewhere is the failure to recognize the role played by free media in the creation, nourishment and development of democracy. In many African countries where the democratic culture is not well established and where respect for democratic pluralism and human rights is not firmly entrenched, restrictions on the media tend to be severe and are profoundly damaging to the project of public engagement in democracy and development.

The lack of recognition of the important role of the media is reflected in active censorship, restrictive regulation of the media, lack of rights of access to official information, and an extensive legal landscape which inhibits the ability of the members of the media to inquire freely (e.g. the application of draconian libel and sedition laws). Essential media services, including broadcasting, printing facilities and distribution systems, in many cases, becomes part of the state administration.

The goal of the government or the ruling elite, in many circumstances, is to ensure that the media expresses only the values and preferences of the power elite. Crucial is the state control of radio, television and print media. It is only in the last decade that private radio and television has been allowed to exist in many African countries, and in many of these states the cost of licensing is enormous and the regulatory hurdles are immense. Coupled with set-up costs and inadequate infrastructure, the result is an underdeveloped and non-competitive media controlled by certain groups in society.

Despite these constraints, the development of the media in Africa has been broadly positive. The persecution of journalists and those involved in the media has reduced progressively since the 1990s. In many African countries, the media (especially the print media and radio) are vibrant and quite active. In these countries, the media are playing an active role in the consolidation of the recent gains in democratic governance.

Sources: International Federation of Journalists (1999); Clement D. Ebri (2000); Dana Ott (1998).

support at the international level (see Chapter 6). Corruption originating within national boundaries and that resulting from international transactions must be tackled with the same vigor. The international community has a crucial role to play in eliminating corruption in Africa, especially in aid administration and procurement. Along these lines, many African countries have already embarked on creating specialized agencies for combating corruption with donor support (see Box 3.8).

Building the Political Context for Development

While there is no disputing the fact that good governance and societal peace are a *sine qua non* for the pursuit of sustainable socio-economic development, one cannot speak of a single ideal model of political governance that African states should aspire to emulate. Even among developed liberal democracies around the world there are wide variations in approach and in forms of governance. Successful democracies differ in many ways and, as noted earlier, the OAU has identified about 11 political modes in efforts to institutionalize liberal democracies in Africa.

Despite the differences in approach, effective political governance tends to have some fundamental characteristics, which African countries must endeavor to establish if they are to build good public administrations. These characteristics include: popular participation in regular elections; maintenance of peace, law and order; individual liberty; political equality; inter-group tolerance; inclusiveness in associational membership; and workable checks and balances to avoid abuse of power.

Without nationwide peace, government functions are either compromised or impossible. Liberty and equality before the law are important for

securing property rights, which play a key role in investment decisions. Absence of checks and balances may lead to arbitrary exercise of power, and lack of transparency and accountability. Without a reasonable level of these fundamental characteristics, sustained rapid growth and development is unlikely.

Empowering citizens will entail their active participation in governance through the right to select their leaders in competitive elections and fair electoral systems. Additionally, governments must be close to the people through decentralization of government functions and devolution of power to local communities. Effective participation also requires that citizens be able to form their own associations and pressure groups to facilitate political activism. Good political governance needs a civil society that is able to articulate popular interests, facilitate participation in governance and monitor government performance. Citizens must be educated and endowed with the necessary civic knowledge in order to be able to effectively participate in the political process.

Particular attention would need to be devoted to raising the status of women, who represent about half of the voters in Africa, through general awareness, civic education, and the participation of women's groups in promoting equal rights for women at all levels. Until recently, efforts to raise the status of women were mainly restricted to increasing their electoral participation. Even within the electoral process, women are seriously manipulated through bribery, violence, and intimidation, owing to their illiteracy, civic ignorance, poverty, and cultural marginalization. The introduction of multiparty politics has provided the opportunity to enhance women's civic knowledge and increase their participation in governance. Current endeavors by national governments, the

---

Box 3.8: Specialized Corruption Investigation Agencies

Partly to mitigate the shortcomings of the adversarial investigative procedure, and partly in recognition of the limited capability of conventional police forces, many African countries have opted to establish specialized corruption agencies to investigate and combat economic crimes and corruption.

Ghana. In response to the problem of widespread corruption, the government of Ghana established a Serious Fraud Office (SFO) and developed an anti-corruption work plan. This is in addition to the Economic Crime Unit of the Ghana Police Service. Ghana is among seven African countries that are piloting the new integrated strategy to fighting corruption. The approach is preventive. The aim is to attack the root causes of corruption and fight it with a coalition of internal forces. The methodology requires a countrywide diagnostic survey to delineate problem areas and identify priority actions. This initiative was strengthened by a number of governance programs under the National Institutional Renewal Program (NIRP) supported by donors such as the African Development Bank, Konrad Adenauer Foundation and the World Bank.

Kenya. The Prevention of Corruption Act gives the director of the Anti-Corruption Authority wide-ranging powers to investigate and prosecute offences involving corruption. It vests employees of the authority with powers similar to those of the police. It confers upon officers the powers necessary for the prevention, investigation, and prosecution of corrupt offences. The Prevention of Corruption Act provides the director with some degree of security of tenure and, in so doing, isolates the office from political interference. The Act expressly provided that the director can be removed from office but only if he is incapacitated, bankrupt, or convicted of a criminal offence, or if he absents himself from office. When it is intended to remove the director, the Act provides for the appointment of a tribunal of judges to investigate the allegations against him and make recommendations accordingly to the President.

Malawi. The Corrupt Practices Act of 1995 established the Anti-Corruption Bureau, which consists of a director, a deputy director, and such other

officers as may be appointed from time to time. The director is appointed by the President, but he is subject to the direction and control of the relevant government minister on all masters of policy, and the appointment is subject to confirmation by the Public Appointments Committee (PAC). The Anti-Corruption Bureau has extensive powers of arrest and search and seizure, as well as access to books, records, and other documents relevant to its functions. Under certain circumstances, the director is empowered to issue an order directing an officer of the bureau to investigate any account in any bank and issue subpoenas

Mauritius. The Unified Revenue Board in Mauritius was established pursuant to the Unified Revenue Act of 1993. The functions of the board are, among other things, to "determine the steps to be taken to counteract fraud and other forms of fiscal evasion." Subject to the overall authority of the board, the Commissioner of Fiscal Investigations has authority to "take such steps as may be necessary with a view to expediting revenue collection or combating fraud and other forms of fiscal evasion." In the discharge of its functions under the Act, the board is required to act in accordance with such directions of a general character as the minister may issue from time to time. All the board's members either report to or are designated by the minister.

Tanzania. The Tanzanian Prevention of Corruption Bureau was established by the President pursuant to the Prevention of Corruption Act. It consists of a director-general and directors, and other officers as the President may determine. Its functions are to take measures to prevent corruption in the public, parastatal, and private sectors, investigate and prosecute for offences involving corruption, and advise on ways to prevent corruption. The bureau is subject to the control and supervision of the President. In the exercise of its powers to prosecute offences under the Prevention of Corruption Act, it is also subject to the directions of the Director of Public Prosecutions.

Source: Ofosu-Amaah, Soopramanien and Uprety (1999).

UNDP and NGOs concentrate on training women candidates who plan to run for parliament or other governance bodies. Box 3.9 outlines some women governance projects in Kenya.

Democratic governance requires more than elections and citizens' participation. The state must also be able to respond to the needs of the citizens. All three branches of government—the executive, the legislature and the judiciary—have crucial roles to play and must be effective in undertaking their assigned functions. Separation and balance of powers must be established in order to ensure a well-functioning state. Each arm of government must be accountable. In addition, each must have the technical expertise and institutional capacity to fulfil its mandate under the constitution. The judiciary and other public institutions must serve as the watchdog to ensure fair enforcement of the rule of law, transparency and accountability for individuals and institutions.

Human rights violations, ethnicity, exclusion in power sharing arrangements and inter-clan and other factional rivalries are some of the factors that have been blamed for wars and civil conflicts in Africa. These challenges can be addressed by building a durable and inclusive political representation. The governance structures and systems must facilitate political pluralism, tolerance and inclusion, given the ethnic diversity of African societies.

To achieve this, the Western liberal democratic practice of winner-takes-all may need to be tailored to the need of African societies. Power-sharing will have to be encouraged to ensure that minorities are not left out. Proportional representation, acknowledgment of ethnic nationalities through instituting bicameral legislatures with one house representing diverse or regional groups, confederacy, regional autonomy, and federalism are just some of the ideas which have been ad-

---

Box 3.9: The Women and Governance Project in Kenya

The Family Support Institute (FASI), an NGO, has been implementing the Women and Governance project in Central Isukha, which is in Kakamega District, in Western Province; and in Nguumo, which is in Makueni District, in Eastern Province. Rural women's group members and their leaders in the communities in the two localities make up the target population for the project. Kenya has more than 30 000 women's groups with memberships totaling more than 1 million. The catchment area for the Central Isukha project has 500 women's groups, with a total membership of 15 000. In Nguumo, the project targets another 500 women's groups, also with a total membership of about 15 000.

The broad objective of the project is to build on the existing infrastructure in community-based resource centers so that the women in the two rural localities will be able to access, generate, and use civic information to enhance their participation in governance. Its specific objectives are to:

- Increase women's awareness of their civic rights and responsibilities;
- Increase the pool of informed women who can participate in the electoral process as candidates and voters;
- Increase women's representation in decision-making positions in the public and private sectors;
- Increase community members' control of the electoral process and promote the principles of free and fair elections;
- Create awareness of the virtues of accountability, transparency, and good governance;
- Increase women's access to ICTs and their ability to use them for their own daily needs and thereby improve their capacity for development-related decision-making;
- Increase the opportunities for communities to update their information on governance;
- And increase the opportunities for communities to use ICTs to upgrade their traditional information systems and networks.

Box 3.9: (Continued)

Central Isukha: Ongoing activities in this locality include those of women's groups, mainly supported by the Ministry of Culture and Social Services (MCSS), bilateral or multilateral donors, and non-governmental agencies. These activities include civic training conducted by community-based civic educators and coordinated by the Catholic Justice for Peace Commission. The Family Planning Association of Kenya (FPAK) provides education for women's groups, using folk media and drama. FPAK also uses puppet shows to train women in family planning and AIDS awareness and prevention. MCSS supports women's activities in the areas of farming methods (to increase yields), estate management (house building and renting), a handicrafts industry, revolving loan funds, social welfare, and adult literacy. In addition, line ministries, NGOs, and community members implement sectoral activities. But the donor and NGO presence is more limited in Central Isukha than in other parts of Kenya.

Nguumo has access to electricity through the government-funded Rural Electrification Program. Water is available through the Integrated Rural Water System of the Ministry of Water Development, the efforts of NGOs, and bilateral programs. Nguumo has a community-based resource center, established by the African Medical Research Foundation (AMREF) with funding from the International Development Research Centre (IDRC)and the Swedish Agency for Research Cooperation with Developing Countries. The resource center, which serves 12 villages and focuses on community-based health information systems (HIS), was the output of an applied research project on health information and primary health care. It used a geographic information system to develop an intersectoral database for sub district-level planning and management. Various HIS components were tested by the Integrated District Diagnosis project, which was implemented in the former greater Kibwezi division between 1989 and 1992.The communities run the project with the help of AMREF and in close collaboration with the government. The project trains local community members, who generate survey and qualitative information and prepare and produce manuals on the use and development of community-based health information in rural areas and on health-care management.

The government has stepped up efforts to raise the status of women through general awareness, civic education, and the participation of women's groups in promoting equal rights and women at all levels. Until recently, women's civic participation was mainly restricted to electoral politics. Even within the electoral process, women are seriously manipulated through bribery, violence, and intimidation, owing to their illiteracy, civic ignorance, poverty, and cultural marginalization. The introduction of multiparty politics has provided the opportunity to enhance women's civic knowledge and increase their participation in governance (broadly defined to include electoral politics and development conditions of ordinary life).

Source: Shanyisa Anota Khasiani (1999).

vanced to foster political inclusion and address the problem of ethnic fragmentation. Each African country will have to determine which political system best suits its circumstances. In South Africa's constitutional negotiations in the early 1990s, for example, it was agreed that the legislature should be elected by proportional representation.

No matter what form of political system is adopted, some basic principles must be adhered to and these include constitutional government, rule of law and respect for human rights. Reform, where it is undertaken, must enhance the capacity of the citizen to participate in governance, organize an active civil society and hold governments accountable and responsible. In addition, the power of government to respond to the needs of citizens and deliver socio-economic development must be enhanced without jeopardizing any of the basic principles.

Conclusion

Notwithstanding the progress made by many African countries towards democracy, much remains to be done to improve the conduct of governance. For one thing, there are still many parts of Africa where progress would need to be made towards greater adherence to the axioms of good governance including basic political order, political legitimacy, rule of law, and popular participation (Box 3.10). Moreover, there are still cases where democracy is of merely a token and superficial nature, or else is based on ethnic elections that do not reflect the judgement of the people on the performance of government. This may explain why the practice of electoral democracy is yet to be translated into tangible benefits, in terms of improvements in the livelihoods of the African peoples.

Box 3.10: Political Governance for Development

Basic Political Order: where internal conflicts and war have undermined public authority in almost all sphere of life. In the Great Lakes Region, the Horn of Africa, the Mano River Basin, and the Niger Basin countries have been rocked by internal conflicts and civil strife that make it difficult for people to engage in any productive activities to improve their lives. In these war-torn countries, the settlement of conflicts, the establishment of peace and the creation of basic political order are necessary conditions for good governance as a prelude to fighting poverty.

Political Legitimacy: through periodic free and fair elections during which results are acceptable to both winners and losers. As Africa enters the new millennium, there seems to be renewed hope that, with improved governance, economic growth can once more be rekindled and poverty reduced. The wave of multi-party elections that have been held across the continent are given as indicators of growing democracy and good governance. The smooth changes of government through democratic elections in Senegal, Ghana and Benin are cited as testimonies to maturing democracies and institutionalizing good governance. When constitutional, legislative and electoral rules make it hard to change laws and procedures arbitrarily, then governmental legitimacy becomes more institutionalized to ensure that legal and bureaucratic systems function effectively, efficiently and relatively honestly. Such institutionalized legitimacy is good for business, job creation, income generation and hence the fight against poverty.

The Rule of Law: as an aspect of government without privileged regard to any individual on the basis of tribe, region of origin, race, sex, income or any other ground for discrimination. A legitimate and democratic system of government needs to be based on the rule of law. This means that, on the basis of rules and regulations laid down by the legislature, imple-

Box 3.10: (Continued)

mented by the executive arm of government and adjudicated by the judiciary (in the event of a dispute), individuals will seek to maximize their interests as citizens endowed with rights and obligations by the state. While accepting basic human rights as inalienable, the rule of law assumes every citizen will assimilate the principles and ideals of citizenship as the basis of exercising his or her rights and claiming the same from the state.

Popular Participation: in policymaking and decisions on resources allocation from the grassroots to the national level. Democracy is premised on the fact that the ruled (the people) participate in a process of freely electing their rulers (the governors). Participation, however, goes much further beyond elections. It must also embrace daily acts of decision making, policy formulation and resource allocation from local level institutions of government to the national level. Democratic participation, or popular participation, also assumes that formal institutions of government make policies and allocate resources on the basis of interests, preferences, ideas and biases from multiple sources in *civil society*.

Source: Peter Anyang' Nyong'o (2000).

The existence of societal peace and the promotion of an environment that respects human rights are insufficient, as evidenced by the number of African countries struggling amidst instability and conflict. The relationship between societal conflicts and poverty appears to be one of both cause and effect. By destroying economic and social infrastructures, hampering productive activities and diverting resources from essential programs, conflicts retard growth and increase

poverty. Conversely, poverty increases the risk of societal conflicts. Where poverty is widespread and the chances for more secure livelihood not evident, conditions tend to be ripe for civil conflicts and their horrendous consequences.

Corrupt practices in Africa are partly responsible for the high incidence of poverty in the continent because it exacts heavy economic costs by distorting the operation of free markets, hampering economic development and destroying the ability of institutions and bureaucracies to deliver services to the public. In some cases, it distorts decision-making processes to the extent that decisions are made solely on the motivation of receiving private benefits. In addition to creating an environment that is not conducive to corruption, African countries must also develop specific policies and programs to prevent corruption, enforce laws against it and mobilize public support. The fight against corruption should go hand in hand with efforts to improve Africa's image in the world, for there is an inherent tendency on the part of foreign investors to overstate risk perceptions in Africa.

Improved political governance is an imperative for avoiding conflicts, reducing corruption and promoting social cohesion and socio-economic development. African countries must endeavor to move away from authoritarianism and a history of misrule with a focus on building effective participatory forms of governance. African countries must aim to empower their citizens through effective participation and decentralization, to enable their governments to fulfil their functions by building both institutional and human capacity, to enforce compliance with the rule of law and to ensure greater transparency. These issues and their importance to economic governance and economic development are discussed in the next Chapter.

CHAPTER 4
Promoting Economic and Corporate Governance

Introduction

Chapter 3 discussed issues relating to good political governance, such as accountability of those in government to the governed, popular participation in decision-making and the rule of law and due processes. Good political governance is not only a worthy goal in itself but is also essential for providing the foundation for good economic governance which is central to the process of economic growth and development.

Economic outcomes such as economic growth, employment generation and poverty reduction all hinge crucially on economic governance. The importance of good economic governance, in this regard, relates not only to creating the right macroeconomic environment or addressing market failures but also to creating the extra-economic conditions that are necessary for sustained economic growth (Kifle, 1993). In this context, the concept of economic governance contains a range of issues that have many overlapping elements. Using a broad sweep, these overlapping elements might be grouped into five dimensions:

- *Defining the Development Vision of the State.* The first dimension in addressing issues pertaining to economic governance is the development vision of the state—the map that guides the government on the road to achieving its socio-economic objectives. The vision contains the main strategic choices of the state and defines the economic paradigm that the

government would adopt. At the heart of such an economic paradigm is the balance between the government and the private sector and the extent of discretionary powers over the conduct of the economy that the government would want to assume.

- *Creating an Enabling Environment.* for business to thrive through government policies and actions. Within its overall development vision, the government initiates, designs, formulates, implements and monitors policies to realize shared objectives and national goals. This process must be credible and sustainable and should inspire the confidence of both domestic and foreign entrepreneurs who risk their capital and managerial skills by investing in the country.

- *Fostering Accountable and Transparent Economic Management.* The third dimension of good economic governance relates to the extent to which the government adheres to the axioms of good governance, such as accountability, transparency and good economic and financial management in those areas under its direct control. These include public enterprise management, the provision of social services—particularly education and health—and the provision of hard infrastructure such as roads and telecommunications.

- *Building the Institutional Foundations for Development.* The fourth dimension comprises the role of the government as a facilitator and regulator of economic activity. This dimension covers issues such as the availability of a functioning legal system with clear and simple procedures for enforcing contracts and for defining and defending property rights and for providing a level playing field and a strong and impartial judicial system. It also covers the regulatory framework and the availability of a central banking system that can regulate credit provision and effectively enforce banking rules and regulations.

- *Promoting Responsible Corporate Citizenship.* The fifth dimension covers the creation of the conditions for good corporate governance. Such conditions include the rules and regulations already mentioned, as well as company law that provides the rules protecting the interests of the shareholders. It covers the institutions that can be entrusted to provide a level and competitive playing field and to discipline the behavior of insiders, whether managers or shareholders. It also includes the policy and regulatory frameworks that minimize the divergence between social and private returns.

Against the background of these five dimensions, this Chapter reviews the record and prospects of economic governance in Africa. It be-

gins by examining past economic paradigms and the subsequent reorientation in the development vision of African countries. The Chapter then investigates issues pertaining to economic governance in the domains of domestic policy management, covering monetary and fiscal policies, debt management and regulatory mechanisms. It outlines the policies needed for institutional capacity building including public sector management, civil service reforms and pay policy, delivery of social services, decentralization and strengthening supporting institutions.

Changing Perception of the Development Vision in Africa

The starting point in addressing issues pertaining to economic management is to define the development vision of the state, which delineates such strategic choices as the balance between the state and market and the adoption of an inward-looking or outward-looking development approach. The vision should contain clear short- and long-term policy targets and the policy instruments to pursue them. It should also contain criteria for choosing between policy instruments in accordance with their probability of effect, whether they act directly on the problem or not, and their resource cost and flexibility (Killick 1989). The development vision provides the framework in which medium-term plans could operate and ensures that the long-term impacts of short-term decisions are considered (Caiquo and Adesida, 1994). Using shared development visions as the basis for development management will require revitalizing long-range planning, which is now seen as a cornerstone for good governance and economic policy reform in Africa (Wohlmuth, 1999).

A state's development vision has to take account of the likely public reaction to the policies of the state (the gainers and losers), and the width and the depth of their impact on societal groups. Consistency in the system of the instruments used, and the appropriate sequencing of both objectives and policies, are also important components of the development vision of the state. Within the framework of the vision, policy-making would have to involve prior consultation with those likely to be affected by the policies. There must be an extensive dialogue with private interests and the government should have adequate knowledge of the interests of particular societal groups. The process involves three stages: agenda setting, policy formulation, and policy implementation.

Africa's post-independence development experience can be divided into three phases, each with a distinct pattern of policy design and growth outcomes. The first phase, falling roughly between 1960-79, could be classified as government-led and inward-looking. The second, and shorter period, covering 1980-85, was a period when the development vision of most of African countries was in a state of transition, characterized by crisis management. The third, from 1986 to the present, marks the shift in many African countries towards a vision of private sector-led growth and outward orientation.

In the first era, 1960-79, many African governments took on the role of entrepreneurs, which was reflected in the dominance of large-scale production by public enterprises (mainly of an import substitution nature). The primary rationale for public sector involvement in the ownership of industries was to address the perceived pervasive market failures in African economies (ADR, 1997). Local entrepreneurs were thought to be few in number, with limited technical skills and

little capital to undertake major investments. The capital markets were underdeveloped. In short, for most African countries it was concluded that if the aspirations for rapid growth and development were to be realized the government would have to participate substantially in industrial expansion.

The objective set by most governments was to achieve a target growth rate of 6 percent per annum, which was seen as necessary for political and socio-economic stability and development. Food security at national level was rarely an explicit target before the late 1970s because it was not perceived as a secular problem. In general terms, most development plans in Africa postulated domestic food production to rise slightly faster than population with any gaps to be met by commercial imports. Although poverty reduction was an implicit objective, policies and projects were not subjected to poverty impact assessment, proportions of absolutely poor households were not set and outcomes were not monitored (ADR, 1996).

Instruments used to influence economic outcomes were determined by bureaucratic commands of the state more than by market signals. To this effect, governments exercised control over bank activities through the setting of interest rates and the allocation of credit. Real lending rates were kept low and often negative (reflecting the ceiling imposed by central bank on nominal interest rates) which meant that governments could finance their expenditure cheaply, but it also caused low productivity of investments. Credit rationing by the banking system was used to divert credit to the government, which became the major borrower from the banking system, thereby crowding out the private sector.

In the era immediately following independence until the oil crisis of 1973, African countries managed to make some progress with socio-economic development. GDP growth averaged close to the set targets at 5.7 percent per annum while per capita incomes increased at 1.5 percent annually. During this period, all macroeconomic indicators were positive. Investment in low-income African countries grew at a rate of close to 10 percent a year, the savings rate increased at 12 percent and exports at 8.2 percent. There was also some evidence of structural transformation in the African economy with manufacturing growing at 7.3 percent a year. The period also witnessed relative macroeconomic stability and gains in social indicators such as increases in literacy and life expectancy and reductions in infant and maternal mortality. The food security objective was realized in many countries with the exception of those in West Africa, which were afflicted by an apparent climatic cycle change (ADR 1995, 1996).

The oil price crisis of 1973, and the series of external shocks that followed it, not only reversed these gains, but also exposed and exacerbated the weaknesses of the development paradigm and the apparatus of economic governance. The combined effects of massive external shocks, along with domestic production difficulties in many public enterprises, caused large external deficits for many countries. Faced with large import bills emanating from the oil crisis and consequent inflation in the prices of industrial goods, many African countries chose to finance their current account deficits rather than to take the necessary adjustment measures. As a result, GDP growth decelerated to less than 2 percent per annum, with per capita income declining by one percent per annum. The average rate of inflation soared from 6 percent in the first period to 22 percent in the second period, and the rate of capital accumulation of about 10 percent per annum in the first period turned into capital de-accumulation of one percent per annum in the second period.

The region, thus, entered a period of serious economic crisis in the late 1970s. The symptoms of the profound economic situation were evident in sluggish growth rates, widening fiscal imbalances, increasing external trade deficits, and heavy external debt burden. The relationship between institutions of economic governance and the economic crisis was one of both cause and effect. On the one hand, the inherent weakness of many institutions proved to be particularly damaging to the corrective intervention role of governments. On the other hand, the economic crisis further depleted their ability to manage the economy as government financial capacity deteriorated, real wages for civil servants declined and the quality of public administration diminished.

By the mid-1980s, it was becoming clear to a growing number of countries that the African crisis required drastic action, if the deterioration in economic and social indicators were to be checked and reversed. This perception led a number of countries to pursue reform programs, with support from bilateral and multilateral development agencies. The implementation of the reforms which characterized the second period (1980-1986) were aimed at improving the policy environment by putting more emphasis on maintaining macroeconomic stability, and reducing the state's role in production and in regulating the private sector. The rationale, effectiveness and shortcomings of these policy reforms were examined in previous *African Development Reports* (e.g. ADR 1995 and 1996). It can be remarked, here, that the reform programs, which occasioned public debate, have, nonetheless, been credited with bringing about marked reorientation in Africa's approaches to the development challenge which took hold over the subsequent period (1986 to present).

An increasing number of African countries now recognize that the road to effective development lies not only in the pursuit of short-term economic reforms, but also in the adoption of a long-term vision based on clear strategic choices aimed at attaining substantive goals such as the reduction of absolute poverty. Indeed, efforts led by countries such as South Africa, Nigeria, Senegal and Tanzania – which launched the "Millennium Africa Renaissance Program"—show a firm commitment to the sustainable development of the continent (see Box 4.1). While the specific contours of a long-term visionary plan may differ according to country circumstances, the lessons drawn from past experience and from the implementation of economic reforms have been evident in the adherence of African policy-makers to four important development guidelines:

- *Poverty reduction as an overarching objective.* The importance of placing poverty reduction at the center of all development efforts is widely recognized. It would be difficult today to defend patterns of economic growth that do not result in substantial poverty reduction and in such key indicators of social welfare as adequate nutrition and access to safe water, minimum schooling, primary health care, and gainful employment opportunities. The Libreville declaration adopted by African leaders in 2000, in which they pledged to reduce poverty by half by 2015, is a clear affirmation of their commitment to poverty reduction (see Box 4.2). Progress in poverty reduction will come through sustained and

Box 4.1: Millennium Africa Renaissance Program

Progress in developing the Millennium Africa Renaissance Program (MARP) was revealed by the President of South Africa at the World Economic Forum meeting in Davos, Switzerland, on 28 January 2001.

The MARP is a declaration of a firm commitment by African leaders to take ownership and responsibility for the sustainable economic development of the continent. The program contains a vision, a perspective and the outlines of a plan for the redevelopment of Africa. It clarifies Africa's objectives and approach to development projects that are going to be appraised, further developed and negotiated with Africa's partners in Africa and the rest of the world. The starting point is a critical examination of Africa's post-independence experience and an acceptance that things have to be done differently to achieve meaningful socio-economic progress.

Among MARP's objectives, priority areas are the creation of peace, security and stability, and democratic governance, without which it would be impossible to engage in meaningful economic activity. The program aims at investing in Africa's people through a comprehensive human resource strategy and harnessing and developing Africa's strategic and comparative advantages in the resource-based sectors to lead the development of an industrial strategy. MARP also aims at: increasing investments in the information and communications technology (ICT) sector, without which Africa will not be able to bridge the digital divide; and development of infrastructure, including transport and energy, and of financing mechanisms.

The ultimate objective of the implementation of the Millennium Africa Renaissance Program is to achieve accelerated and sustained growth, so as to eradicate poverty on the continent, and to significantly increase new investments by mobilizing both domestic and especially foreign savings. The plan envisages both Africa-wide and regional initiatives. Conflict prevention and eradication of infectious diseases

Box 4.1: (continued)

are examples of the programs that will be continental in scope.

Economic development initiatives like the development of agriculture and agro-industries, economic infrastructure, promotion of competitiveness and economic integration will be managed at regional or sub-regional levels. Another continental initiative would be the development of regulatory frameworks for key sectors like telecommunications and energy. The Africa Connection (the telecommunication strategy for Africa already agreed to) is a case in point.

An important prerequisite is a partnership with the rest of the world, especially the developed countries, multilateral institutions and (global and national) private sector players. The focus of the program is not on increased aid but on increased investment. However, some targeted aid and technical support to address capacity constraints and urgent human development priorities will also be required.

The African leaders pioneering the program have expressed their awareness that in a world where perceptions are important, Africa will have to give significant attention to counter the erroneous legacy of "Afro-pessimism". They have also affirmed that the implementation of the program requires strong states, taking into account the fact that African countries, with a few notable exceptions, have weak states – for a range of complex reasons. There is thus a need to create a continent-wide program to develop state capacity with the support of developed countries, the private sector and multilateral institutions. Participation will be open to all African countries prepared and ready to commit themselves to the underlying principles guiding the initiative.

Source: President's Office, Government of South Africa (2001).

broad-based economic growth, complemented by efficient provision of infrastructure and social services, such as education and health care. The government would have to deepen its economic and institutional reforms, so as to promote the development of the private sector and strengthen the sustainability of private investment. To reduce poverty, the government would also need to be active in areas such as food security, education, health and rural development.

- *The private sector as the main engine of economic growth.* Many African countries now recognize that the market serve as an effective instrument of production and resource allocation. It has, thus, been realized that the private sector would have to play a central role, if African countries are to accelerate their rates of economic growth. The public sector has begun to yield its economic dominance through the process of privatization, in favor of greater reliance on market forces and private sector initiatives. In tandem with the shift to market economy, greater importance is now attached to foreign private investment as a crucial ingredient in the processes of economic growth and development. This derives from the increased recognition that private investment yields many financial, technological and efficiency gains. Africa's strategic choice of the private sector as the main engine of growth has also transcended the long held belief that the development of infrastructure should be carried out in the public sector. Disil-

Box 4.2: Poverty Reduction and the Libreville Declaration (2000)

Africa enters the 21st century with a large segment of its population still living in abject poverty. Depending on the poverty line used, between 45-70 percent of the region's population is classified as being extremely poor. Women are particularly vulnerable, as nearly three-quarters of African women are believed to be living in a state of poverty. Non-income measures of poverty also show that Africa lags far behind other regions. Infant and maternal mortality rates are among the highest in the world and life expectancy and school enrolment the lowest.

Confronted with such realities, in January 2000 African leaders held a summit meeting in Libreville together with the African Development Bank, the IMF and the World Bank. At the conclusion of the summit, the leaders adopted the Libreville Declaration in which they solemnly pledged to reduce poverty by half by 2015.

As a follow-up to the Libreville Summit, two workshops (in Addis Ababa and Abidjan, March 2000) were held in order to determining how best resources could be mobilized. It was also agreed that the elaboration of Poverty Reduction Strategy Papers (PRSPs), which were endorsed at the Libreville Summit, would constitute the plan of action that must be implemented in order to address the poverty problem.

PRSPs have three important features. First, governments will have the primary responsibility for preparing them, in line with recent efforts to encourage the formulation of home-grown socio-economic policies so that the impact of these policies on growth and poverty reduction is maximized. Secondly, the proposal calls for the preparation of PRSPs in a participatory manner with the involvement of various groups in civil society. The main rationale behind this proposal is to ensure that policies and interventions do respond to the needs and demands of potential beneficiaries. Extensive consultations with the donor community are also envisaged. Thirdly, the strategies adopted in the framework of PRSPs are expected to be outcome-oriented with achievements to be monitored at periodic intervals.

The new strategy for poverty reduction thus emphasizes country ownership. Governments will have the primary responsibility for formulating effective poverty reduction strategies that take into account the specific economic, social, and institutional conditions of their countries. They will also have the responsibility of co-ordinating the financial and technical support that their international development partners will provide.

Source: ADB (2000).

lusionment with public sector performance, combined with the fiscal crises, induced governments to encourage more private sector participation in the provision of infrastructure.

- *The state as an effective regulator and facilitator.* While it is readily acknowledged that sustained economic develop-

ment and social progress depend importantly on the strength and the vitality of the private sector, the government still has an important role to play—as a regulator, as a facilitator and as a provider. Recent experiences in parts of Africa, and in other countries in transition, have shown that weak states cannot support market economies and that the failure of the government to play its essential role could result in political and economic failure. The government would need to establish the regulatory institutions which set the platform for private competition and the rules protecting consumers. And it is the government that should design plans and programs in order to solicit concessional assistance for infrastructure development and for the social sector, especially in low-income and war-affected countries.

- ▪ *The imperative of meeting the challenge of globalization.* African countries are increasingly becoming aware of the risks and opportunities presented by globalization. It is, thus, essential that countries draw up plans to take advantage of the immense possibilities offered by globalization while at the same time seeking to minimize its adverse effects. This challenge would also imply rethinking regional co-operation and integration arrangements so that these become vehicles and not obstacles for enhancing competitiveness and integration into the global economy. Regional integration groupings would thus need to adopt a policy of "open regionalism" that promotes the joint production of goods and infrastructure services. The pursuit of open regionalism accentuates Africa's needs for strong institutional capacity. The public sector must understand and reconcile regional trade arrangements with the new global trade regime, negotiate within the new global trade framework, and support local enterprises to take ad-

vantage of opportunities. African countries must adapt to global standards in areas such as trade, environment and labor, which were traditionally within the purview of national governments.

The scope and urgency of pursuing this development agenda is highlighted by the fact that a large proportion of Africans continues to live in abject poverty. The recent improvements in socio-political environment and in economic performance do support some optimism that Africa has indeed embarked on the right development path. Between 1995 and 2000, real output growth averaged about 4 percent per annum compared with an average of 1.5 percent during the first half of the decade. Growth was widespread with over 40 countries, out of 53 in the region, recording positive growth rates, compared to only 20 countries at the beginning of the decade. The improving level of economic growth has been associated with positive developments in macro-economic fundamentals and economic freedom. The improvement in the policy environment and the challenges that lie ahead in this domain can be gathered from the Index of Economic Freedom as measured by the report produced jointly by Heritage Foundation and Wall Street Journal (see Box 4.3). Sustaining and improving the current positive momentum is, however, indispensable for poverty reduction and for sustained economic growth.

In addition to defining the agenda, the realization of the objectives stipulated in the development vision requires effective policy formulation and implementation. These issues have been discussed extensively in previous *African Development Reports*. In the following sections emphasis will be placed on issues pertaining to state capac-

Box 4.3: Economic Freedom and Growth

The 2001 Index of Economic Freedom of the Heritage Foundation and The Wall Street Journal indicates that economic restrictions are finally easing in most parts of Sub-Saharan Africa. The index measures 50 economic variables in eight broad categories: corruption in the judiciary and civil service; non-tariff barriers to trade; the government's fiscal burden; the rule of law, i.e. ability to enforce contracts; regulatory burdens on business; restrictions on banks; labor market regulations; and the incidence of smuggling and piracy of intellectual property rights.

This finding is significant, given that in the previous six annual indices economic freedom was reported as having declined in Sub-Saharan Africa. Despite the significant improvement, no African country is ranked as economically "free". Seven countries are deemed "mostly free", 29 are ranked as "mostly unfree" while two – Guinea-Bissau and Zimbabwe – are ranked as repressed. The countries that were seen to have made advances in economic freedom included Mozambique, Senegal, Burkina Faso, Botswana, Mali, Madagascar, and Rwanda. The list of poor performers (those countries where economic restrictions are increasing) includes Mauritius. An examination of rankings show little correlation between economic freedom and economic growth, as the fastest-growth countries, such as Uganda or Lesotho, are deemed mostly unfree, while the more liberal states did not grow rapidly in the 1990s. Nevertheless, it will be wrong to conclude that economic freedom does not matter. The direction of change in economic freedom is important, and also there is bound to be a time-lag between the improvement in economic freedom and the achievement of rapid economic growth. Therefore, the region's overall improvement in economic freedom should translate into more rapid expansion in the next decade. However, it is disturbing to see Uganda, South Africa, Zambia, Malawi, Namibia, and Mauritius in the group whose economic freedom has declined since the mid-1990s.

Source: Heritage Foundation/Wall Street Journal, 2001 Index of Economic Freedom. EIU (2000).

Table B.4.3.1: Economic Freedom in Africa

Country	Rank in Africa	Rank in the World	2001 Index(a)	% Change 1995/96
Mostly free				
Morocco	1	48	2.7	8.5
Tunisia	2	63	2.9	-
Benin	3	63	2.9	9.5
Botswana	4	68	2.95	10.6
Mali	5	68	2.95	10.6
Mauritius	6	68	2.95	-11.3
Namibia	7	68.7	2.95	-1.7
Average	**4**	**64**	**2.9**	**4.4**
Mostly unfree				
Côte d'Ivoire	8	75	3	6.25
Swaziland	9	75	3	-
Uganda	10	81	3	-7.9
Senegal	11	81	3.05	16.6
South Africa	12	81	3.05	-1.7
Ghana	13	84	3.1	6.1
Guinea	14	84	3.1	1.6
Madagascar	15	84	3.1	10.1
Kenya	16	87	3.15	4.5
Zambia	17	87	3.15	-1.6
Algeria	18	90	3.2	8.6
Cameroon	19	90	3.2	3
Gabon	20	93	3.25	-8.3
Burkina Faso	21	95	3.3	13.2
Cape Verde	22	97	3.35	1.5
Djibouti	23	97	3.35	-3.1
Gambia	24	97	3.35	1.5
Mozambique	25	97	3.35	20.2
Nigeria	26	97	3.35	-3
Lesotho	27	104	3.4	2.9
Niger	28	110	3.5	12.5
Tanzania	29	110	3.5	2.8
Malawi	30	114	3.55	-1.4
Chad	31	120	3.6	10
Rwanda	32	120	3.6	16.3
Ethiopia	33	124	3.65	2.7
Congo	34	127	3.7	9.8
Mauritania	35	127	3.7	1.3
Togo	36	130	3.75	3.8
Equa. Guinea	37	137	3.9	1.3
Average	**22.5**	**99.8**	**3.3**	**4.5**
Repressed				
Guinea-Bissau	38	141	4	4.8
Zimbabwe	39	146	4.25	-11.8
Average	**38.5**	**143.5**	**4.1**	**-3.5**
Africa; average	**20.0**	**95.6**	**3.3**	**4.0**

Notes: (a) Where 1 = most conducive to economic freedom and 5 = least conducive.

ity which measures government's ability to implement its policies and its goals. State capacity has four dimensions: regulatory, extractive, administrative and technical. These necessitate addressing issues such as creating effective public management and public administration, a functioning legal framework, efficient regulatory and tax regimes, and transparent and accountable financial systems. They also necessitate creating the platform for private competition and the conditions that foster social responsibility in the corporate sector.

Regulatory Capacity

African countries are faced with major challenges in their reorientation towards private sector-led growth and the development of private sector participation in the provision of services. To harness the full potential of private sector initiatives, the state would need to address the challenges of establishing effective regulatory rules and ensuring their enforcement. The state also needs to create proper incentive regimes to encourage and sustain private sector participation. The regulatory functions of the state can be grouped into those pertaining to the participation of the private sector in the provision of services and those related to the functioning of the financial system.

Regulatory Framework for Private Participation

Regulation is a difficult and costly business, and wherever possible, competition should be used instead. However, where necessary, the proper design of the regulatory rules and institutions is critical to the objective of increasing private participation in the provision of infrastructure services. The regulatory process consists of three

closely interrelated components —setting the rules or standards; monitoring for compliance; and enforcement (Otobo, 1996; ADR, 1999). The regulatory framework would need to be simple and yet be sophisticated enough to address the fundamental objective of regulation, which is to correct for market failure. The regulatory framework typically includes rules governing entry, exit, scope of participation, and cost recovery. The framework should also provide performance criteria against which the operation of the franchise can be assessed. Hence, to be effective, it should be one that strikes the right balance between removing restrictions on private participation, protecting consumers and safeguarding the country's socio-economic objectives.

The quality of regulatory rules is closely related to the state of political governance, as the latter provides the institutional framework within which regulatory agencies operate. A sound legal framework requires enforcement to be credible. Without effective enforcement, the legal framework and government lose credibility. From the perspective of the private operators, failure to comply with the rules and regulations leads to negative impressions and may damage a country's reputation. As a result, both government and the private sector must have a mutual interest in the transparent and consistent application of enforcement procedures. In some countries, to avoid abuse due to over-concentration of power, efforts are made to separate the roles of adjudication and enforcement. The regulatory agency monitors the performance of private operators to ensure compliance with rules and investigates complaints. However, disputes and conflicts are referred to the judiciary or arbitration panels for resolution. The regulatory body is entrusted with the task of implementing the rulings of the court or arbitration panel. Judgements can range from imposing public apologies to ordering the payment of fines. The success of regulatory and enforcement systems is largely dependent on the clarity of rules and the consistency with which they are applied. Country differences, diversity of experience and the complexities of enforcement indicate the need for African countries to adopt a prudent, commonsense approach that best suit their situations.

As a result of new challenges emanating from globalization, African countries must devote as much effort to creating and updating the information on global and regional conventions as to national rules. African countries will have to comply with laws or norms set at the global level to guide corporate governance while also participating in enacting these regulations. The very approach used in formulating some of these international rules or norms poses a challenge to Africa and other developing countries. In many cases, rules are harmonized or standardized without Africa's participation. In cases when they are present, African countries are not adequately represented. African countries will have to address these problems by becoming more active and getting involved in developing international regulations.

An effective regulatory framework cannot be built on a foundation of discipline without appropriate incentives. A sound framework will normally provide proper incentives for the board and management of private firms to pursue objectives that are in the interests of the company and shareholders. As infrastructure often involves sunk investments, an incentive framework that supports cost recovery is a prerequisite for promoting private participation at a level that is mutually beneficial to investor, government and consumer.

It is mainly for cost-recovery reasons that investors in an uncertain regulatory environment prefer the pricing system to be determined and authorized by regulatory statute. Price cap regulations provide incentives to reduce costs through efficiency gains and promote efficient use of resources. However, they have the drawback of increasing regulatory risk, with the possible capping of investment as a consequence, because of the pressure to keep profits within reasonable limits. But the limitations of price cap regulation can largely be overcome by a carefully-designed system of regulatory review.

An important issue concerns the nature of the institutions responsible for implementing regulatory rules. In general, regulatory institutions are single-industry and/or multi-industry. The choice between multi-industry and a single-industry regulatory institutions has been posed as an issue for African countries for reasons varying from effective regulatory decisions to the absence of the required technical skills, the often small size of the industry, and the cost of regulation.

The single-industry approach to regulation certainly provides for specialist experience and expertise in a particular industry, which translates into more effective regulatory decisions. But these are the attributes of a regulatory institution that can afford full-time regulators and specialist staff who are expected to address issues of investment, tariffs rates, licensing abuses, access, performance standards, and customer services on a daily basis. In the case of African countries, it could be argued that it might not be desirable to have as many regulatory agencies as there are utility sectors. Indeed, where the primary function of the regulatory institution in Africa is to address issues of income distribution, empowerment, quality of service and cost recovery, the need for consistency and universality in regulatory approaches and decisions is paramount. Moreover, the regulatory decisions from a single source provide investors with a better reading on the government's position on issues of concern to the private investor at a time when sending the "right signals" is an important determinant of private capital flows.

Central Bank and Financial Systems

Among its several functions, the Central Bank has an important supervisory and regulatory role to play to ensure that the banking system operates prudently and efficiently to avoid financial distress. This requires laying down rules for the establishment of new banks, and monitoring procedures to ensure proper accounting and auditing. The Central Bank has also a crucial role to perform in the stabilization of an economy, to regulate the level of aggregate demand in the economy.

Central banks in Africa are state-owned and have a powerful role in economic policy-making. They help to determine the structure of interest rates and, through their control over other banks, they also influence the volume and allocation of credit. In spite of the powers entrusted by legislation establishing central banks in African countries, it has proved difficult in many countries for them to carry out their regulatory duties adequately. Inadequate personnel, both in terms of quantity and quality, can limit the ability to supervise the banking system. In some cases the actual enforcement of regulations is lax, because of corruption or for political reasons. Politics sometimes enters into the licensing process itself through the rent-seeking activities of politicians and bureaucrats. In some countries, licenses have been granted by political entities that were not subsequently responsible for the supervision of the institutions after

the licenses were issued. In other countries, government interference in banking operations in favor of public sector enterprises, or state-supported projects, has made it difficult for the central bank to conduct strict banking supervision and monetary control.

Making the central bank an independent agency is important both for the development of the financial system and for the effectiveness of monetary policy. The basic argument in favor of independent central banks is the separation of the power to create money from the power to spend money and the prevention of the use of monetary institutions and instruments for political and material gains. Central bank independence means, first, that it has broad latitude to decide what to do in pursuit of its basic goals of macroeconomic stability and employment creation. Secondly, it means that once the monetary policy decisions are made, no governmental organ can reverse them, except under extreme circumstances stipulated by the legislature. A third condition for central bank autonomy is to have independence of personnel; this includes the selection and appointment of board members with a high professional competence and without an obligation to yield to political and other pressures. Finally, it must have instrumental independence, which means control over the instruments that affect the inflation process, including in particular the prevention of any direct financing of government deficits.

Empirical studies have clearly established that there is strong correlation between central bank independence and low inflation. They have also found that countries with independent central banks tend to have smaller budget deficits than those with government-controlled central banks (Blider, 1995; Alesina and Gatti, 1995; Bruno, 1995; Fischer, 1996). In recognition of the many benefits ensuing from independent central banking several African countries such as South Africa have introduced legislation that grant statutory autonomy to the central banks in the management of monetary policies and other related activities (see Box 4.4).

The central bank should also encourage and facilitate the establishment of other financial institutions, especially institutions to provide long-term loan finance for development, and to provide a market for government securities. The development of the financial sector is among the first priorities of a development strategy. The financial sector is an integral component of private sector development. If no functioning financial system exists, it is difficult to promote a strong private sector. Many African countries have undertaken financial reform programs to reduce financial repression by limiting the monetization of fiscal deficits, liberalizing interest rates, eliminating credit controls, and reducing directed credit programs (ADR, 1997). These measures constitute the first steps towards making the financial systems responsive to the needs of the private sector. There is, however, a need to deepen these reforms particularly in the areas of addressing the problems of distressed banks, supporting microfinance, and developing non-bank financial instruments.

The problems of distressed banks would need to be addressed through recapitalization, restructuring, privatization or liquidation. However, recapitalization and restructuring without changes in the incentive environment have been accompanied by recurring banking crises in countries such as Kenya, Nigeria and Zimbabwe. Privatization of public sector banks is one way of improving their performance and efficiency. But without an improved competitive framework, privatization

Box 4.4: Central Bank Independence: The Case of South Africa

As banker to the government, the Reserve Bank of South Africa administers exchange control regulations, monitors the prudential soundness in the banking system and handles the weekly tenders for Treasury bills and government securities. The Reserve Bank also takes care of various aspects of South Africa's dealings and relations with institutions such as the IMF and the World Bank on behalf of the government. In performing these activities, the Bank only acts as an agent of government and the final responsibility and decision making rest with the Minister of Finance. This kind of activity can undermine the functional independence of the Reserve Bank.

The personnel independence of the Reserve Bank is determined in section 4 of the Reserve Bank Act, indicating the conditions of appointment of the Governor, three deputy governors and other board members of the Reserve Bank. This section clearly precludes any person who is actively involved in politics, non-residents or officials of private banks from becoming a member of the board of the Bank. Seven of the directors, including the Governor and three deputy governors, are appointed by the President of the Republic, and the other seven are elected by the shareholders. By means of these appointments the government does, as some would argue, have an effective say in the policies of the Bank. The governors, however, after their appointment, normally operate independently without fear or favor.

Certain conditions are given in the regulations under the Reserve Bank Act, which will disqualify a person for remaining a board member, such as conviction for theft, fraud, forgery or perjury. However, mechanisms for the dismissal of governors are not entrenched in the Act. Grounds for dismissal and the actual procedure could perhaps be more explicitly stated in legislation to improve the functioning of the Reserve Bank. Consideration could also be given to lengthening the tenure of office of the Governor and deputy governors, say to seven

Box 4.4: (Continued)

years, to improve the autonomy of the Bank further by separating the five-yearly political cycle from the appointments of governors.

The instrumental independence of the Reserve Bank is clearly spelled out in the Act and the Reserve Bank is precluded in section 13(f) from making excessive direct purchases of government stock. This section states that the Bank may not "hold in stocks of the Government of the Republic which have been acquired directly from the Treasury by subscription to new issues, the conversion of existing issues or otherwise, a sum exceeding its paid-up capital and reserve fund plus one-third of its liabilities to the public in the Republic." This section therefore restricts the direct financing of government deficits.

At the same time, the Act also allows the Reserve Bank to provide unsecured loans and advances to government and companies in which it has acquired shares. Although there are limits on government borrowing, serious consideration in the revision of the Reserve Bank Act should be given to removing this potentially dangerous provision. The Reserve Bank is also financially independent from the government because of its adequate financial resources and full control over its own budget.

Source: Adapted from the Address by Mr. T. T. Mboweni (2000).

of public banks may simply result in ownership transfer without improved financial intermediation. Privatization of banks would need to be implemented only after obtaining adequate information about portfolio quality, personnel, and buyers to avoid fraud and concentration of economic power. Liquidation, as part of an overall competitive program that allows for entry of new banks, should be contemplated where attempts to restructure or privatize state-owned banks fail.

The private sector in Africa is dominated by microenterprises (MEs) and small- and medium-sized enterprises (SMEs). These enterprises usually operate in the informal sector where they face a variety of constraints and, particularly, a lack of finance. Efforts should concentrate on upgrading informal financial arrangements, strengthening their links with formal institutions, and improving the legal framework. Efforts should also be made to upgrade informal financial arrangements such as savings clubs and, credit associations and cooperative banks. Co-operative finance is one way of increasing access of MEs and SMEs to financial resources. On the other hand, where co-operatives tend to be donor-driven, there is a proportional reduction in the incentives for members to provide their own resources. Linkages between formal and informal institutions can be forged and promoted by providing fiscal incentives, such as tax relief on the profits of formal financial institutions with informal linkages. There is also a need to improve the legal environment through better definition and enforcement of the property rights of MEs and SMEs.

Non-bank financial instruments, such as venture capital schemes and bond and equity markets, need to be developed to promote competition and diversification of financial markets and attract foreign portfolio investment. However, stock markets in Africa remain quite limited in both quantity and quality and, with the exception of the South African market, the stock exchanges are insignificant in terms of the number of listed companies, market capitalization and turnover as well as in terms of their contribution to economic growth. In addition to deepening macroeconomic reforms, the development of stock markets can benefit from pooling resources through regional integration. The regionalization of these exchanges could assist them in enhancing their capacity to mobilize both domestic and global financial resources which would, in turn, enable them inject more liquidity into the markets by funding regional companies. The acceleration of the process of privatization can also promote the development of stock markets, as evident in the experience of countries such as Egypt and Morocco.

While bond markets in Africa are generally underdeveloped, a few are strongly emerging in such countries as Egypt, Nigeria and South Africa. To promote and deepen such markets government needs to undertake, in consultation with the private sector, a review of regulations to ensure that the current regulations do not favor other asset classes over bonds. Also, pension system reforms would not only invigorate the bond markets but would also ensure that the citizens can meet their financial needs during retirement. Issuers of bonds would need to be more transparent in the disclosure of information. The existence of mature market for government bonds also facilitates macroeconomic management, as it provides central banks with an effective instrument for monetary policy. Government bonds can be used to regulate the economy through open market operations by selling government bonds when the target is to reduce money supply and inflation and buying them when the target is to increase money supply and stimulate the economy.

Extractive Capacity

Traditionally, the extractive capacity of the state is confined to the domain of fiscal policy and addresses the extent to which the government is able to extract resources and use them efficiently in the delivery of public goods and services. However, in developing countries where there is heavy reliance on official capital flows, the extractive capacity might be viewed to go beyond the domain of traditional fiscal policy to encompass the manner in which foreign resources are obtained and utilized. Fiscal policy plays a significant role in the development of an economy, affecting its competitiveness, resource allocation and social equity. Fiscal adjustment and macroeconomic performance are closely related and causally linked. The capacity of the State to obtain foreign resources and manage its debt repayments is also an important determinant of the economic prospects of African economies

Fiscal Policy Management

In the new democratic dispensation, the power to tax and approve all public expenditure is vested in the legislature, acting in the interest of taxpayers and voters. Their role in sanctioning annual budgets and expenditures must not be merely ceremonial. They must undertake critical reviews, as dictated by the constitution and by their responsibility to taxpayers. Greater parliamentary awareness of the wider economic and political consequences of tax policies and expenditure issues will be required. The legislature will have to use its legislative oversight and rely on independent auditors who report directly to parliament. This will require strengthening the human resource capability of national audit bureaus and judiciaries. The legislature must be willing and able to act under the law to prosecute errant government functionaries on both the revenue and expenditure sides.

Fiscal policy management, which comprises tax administration and expenditure management, is crucial to economic outcomes. Tax policies have significant implications for investment decisions and could be used to enhance national competitiveness and economic performance. Similarly, expenditure management has important ramifications for the performance of government functions and for the economy. As a result of external shocks and inability to increase their tax base many African countries were faced with fiscal imbalances. The situation was worsened because of expansionary fiscal policies. After independence, the need for development led many African governments to make significant investments in providing education, health care, and infrastructure. In addition, many countries made a major foray into industrial development through the creation of public enterprises. The consequent over-extension of African governments' commitments led to both internal and external borrowings to finance their deficit spending.

African economic reform programs have embarked on improving fiscal performance and the introduction of new tax regimes. In principle, the reform of the tax regime should be guided by three axioms. First, the tax system must promote economic efficiency by limiting its interference in labor, investment and consumption decisions. It should consider the extent to which the tax code alters economic decision-making and the impact of the tax structure on economic outcomes. Secondly, the tax system should involve a strong notion of fairness and strive to ensure that the overall tax burden is fairly distributed among members of society. Fair distribution of burdens

is frequently called tax equity, which has two directions: horizontal equity and vertical equity. Horizontal equity involves imposing similar burdens on people in similar circumstance, i.e. ensuring that individuals with equivalent incomes pay equivalent tax. Vertical equity involves creating an appropriate differential in burdens for people in unlike circumstances. The desire to instill vertical equity is the rationale for a "progressive" tax system, which imposes higher tax rates for individuals with higher incomes. Thirdly, the administrability of the tax regime should be ensured. What may appear as an ideal tax policy on paper may fail to achieve its objectives on the ground due to the difficulty of enforcing it or a lack of adequate information and education among taxpayers.

A key priority in developing a capable fiscal administration regime is to build a revenue department made up of competent and committed professionals, and a fair integrated tax assessment and collection mechanism. In addition to the right infrastructure for assessing and collecting revenues, it is important to design and formulate appropriate tax policies. This will help to overcome the problem of compliance. Tax evasion, in which both the taxpayer and tax collector can escape legal censure, is all too common in African countries as a result of corruption and ineffective state institutions. Private gain from tax evasion, in Africa, is quite high, while the risk of punishment is low because of corruption and the lack of enforcement. As part of the fiscal reform process, it will be important to find ways to encourage citizens to pay their taxes, to introduce strong checks and balances to minimize corruption, and to put in place strong enforcement systems to increase the risks associated with tax evasion. On the expenditure side, African governments must begin to keep fiscal expansion within limits that are compatible with domestic stabilization and long-term growth. The practice of true democracy in the interests of peace and social cohesion would serve to divert funds from military expenditure to the most vitally-needed services of education and health care.

Delivery of Social Services

A key developmental function of government is to provide social services or public goods. Despite the emerging consensus on the need to rely more on the private sector, there is certainly a case for the government to continue to participate in the provision of certain services. The questions of what the government should provide in terms of services will necessarily depend on a country's circumstances and its stage of development. However, the general consensus is that from the point of view of citizens' rights, governments ought to be active in such basic services as education and health. Also, from the point of view of market failure, they ought to be active in the provision of infrastructure in areas where the private sector initiatives are not forthcoming.

In the period immediately following independence from the late 1950s to the 1980s, most African countries invested significantly in the provision of education, health and infrastructure and there was remarkable progress in these areas. In education, the proportion of children in primary school doubled between 1960 and 1980, while the proportion in secondary school increased by a factor of four (ADR, 1998). Life expectancy increased significantly while mortality declined by more than a quarter. In infrastructure, the average main telephone lines per 100 inhabitants in 1980 was 0.74 – a 64 percent increase compared to 0.45 main telephone lines per 100 inhabitants in

1965, and by 1986 that figure had increased again by 43 percent to 1.06 mainlines. In the same way electricity production increased from a per capita of 43 kilowatts in 1965 to 87 kilowatts in 1986, a 100 percent increase, only to remain virtually stagnant since then.

The economic crisis of the 1980s slowed down these gains. In education, primary enrolment ratios stagnated while secondary enrolment ratios increased, but at a much slower rate (ADR, 1998). Higher education, which experienced a notable expansion in the earlier two decades, encountered difficult problems, particularly with regard to finance, the quality of education, and its relevance to employment opportunities. In health, HIV and its associated diseases emerged as one of the greatest threats to the health of African peoples. Malaria remained one of the most important causes of mortality and morbidity in Africa. In infrastructure, the explosion of urban populations and subsequent shrinking of resources in the wake of economic crisis after the mid-1980s have rendered public provision incapable of meeting the needs of economy and society. This is evidenced in the combination of poor management, inadequate capital structures, bad investment decisions and the bureaucratization of the decision-making, which characterized public providers.

In response to these growing challenges, African countries have endeavored to find alternative modalities of delivery, taking into account resource constraints as well as the limitations of the public sector model. In the education sector, more efforts would need to be made to redirect public resources toward primary education, while relying more on private funding at secondary and higher levels in order to promote efficient and equitable public spending on education. Information technology is another delivery mechanism which can be employed by government to provide services cheaply and more efficiently. Of particular importance is the use of information technology to provide education and health care to many more people while keeping the cost down (See Box 4.5 on IT and education). In the health sector, African countries are presently encountering serious hazards. Information technology can help control and sometimes eradicate some of the health problems plaguing the continent. It has brought about the powerful innovations of "virtual medicine" and "telemedicine". With the applications of these innovations, patients located in rural areas could have access to medical experts located thousands of miles away. Information technology can facilitate the development of computer-aided diagnosis of diseases for the rural areas where highly specialized physicians are not available. Isolated medical institutions and practitioners can treat people better by communicating with colleagues and researchers worldwide.

In education, the systems of primary and secondary education in many African countries suffer from serious shortcomings—including low teacher-student ratios, limited availability of instructional materials and poor quality of education. In higher education there are few libraries, most of them lacking access to international journals and being generally deprived of educational materials, while research facilities are limited. Most of these educational problems are related to inadequate funding and inefficient use of available resources. Here too, information technology offers a wide range of low-cost solutions. One of the most important applications of information technology in this area is distance education in Africa, which could be extensively used to pursue

---

Box 4.5: IT and Education Delivery

Education is crucial, to entrench democracy and improve governance, increase productivity, diversify the product base, raise exports, reduce population growth, improve the health status of the population and reduce poverty. Development will probably remain sluggish unless Africa is able invest in its people. After four decades of development experience, it is quite clear that education is essential for socio-economic and industrial development. Without using information and communication technologies (ICTs), how can Africa educate its citizens and facilitate life-long learning, with declining resources?

ICTs offer African countries effective tools to educate its citizens, build the capacity of its labor force and improve the quality of life. The use of ICTs can help reduce the cost of education and make education accessible to a much wider audience. ICTs, especially the Internet and web, can facilitate distance education, provide new methods of learning while also improving educational productivity. The new technologies are increasing the opportunities for life-long learning for those wanting to update their knowledge or skill in order to remain competitive.

From the African Virtual University – initiated by the World Bank – to much smaller programs, efforts are being made in the continent to employ ICTs to educate the people and build capacity for socioeconomic development. The African Virtual University was set up to remedy the shortfall in education and particularly in science and technical education. A new Satellite University in Uganda has been launched under the auspices of Makerere University in Kampala. Twenty sites will be established when it is fully operational and students in the sites can participate in courses and programs offered by Makerere University. The effect of this will be the expansion of educational opportunities in Uganda and a lowering of the cost of education.

Box 4.5: (Continued)

The United Nations Educational, Scientific and Cultural Organization (UNESCO) launched in 1997 the Learning Networks for African Teachers (LNAT) to help teachers "become better learners and teachers." Pilot projects are being implemented in Zimbabwe, Senegal, and Namibia with proposals for other pilot projects.

Another ICT project to promote education within the continent is Global Education Network for Africa (GENA). GENA is a regional project to share national programming for distance education. The project will allow broadcasters to share the cost of accessing educational programming. The initial participating countries in GENA are Kenya, Namibia, Swaziland, Uganda and Tanzania. Ghana has recently developed special programs to network schools to provide distance learning and telemedicine applications.

Adapted from Dzidonu et al (1998); World Bank (2000); ADB (1998); Opoku-Mensah (1999).

entirely conventional educational ends. The main advantages of distance education are economy, flexibility, and suitability for widely scattered student bodies.

Information technology could not only help Africa to attain universal primary education, but it could also turn some of its disadvantages in this field into advantages. It is well known that Africa's population has the youngest age structure where children below the age of 15 years constitute about 45 percent of population, compared with 30 percent for the rest of the world. It is also well known that children take quickly to computer knowledge the way they do to languages. Hence, introducing properly instructed computer education, could turn Africa's high dependency ratio, which has always been viewed as a retarding load, into a powerful source of growth and socio-economic development. In addition, information technology has the potential to connect African educational institutions continent-wide, and link them with international universities, hence, facilitating research and the exchange of ideas. Access to data and educational materials would also be simplified (Oshikoya and Hussain, 1998).

Governments in Africa are increasingly turning to the private sector to provide infrastructure services and health care. Private participation in infrastructure has been pursued through various approaches, including divestiture, leases, management contracts, and concessional arrangements, such as build-operate-transfer (BOT) and build-own-operate (BOO). Although the private sector invested in virtually all infrastructure sectors, its early beginnings were in telecommunications, which provided learning experiences for engagement in other sectors. In telecommunications, private sector participation has been predominantly in the form of concessions and demonopolization followed by divestiture and management contracts.

Three main drivers may be expected to push the African infrastructure market forward. An important factor is the renewed interest within Africa in revitalizing regional groupings, which is expected to expand markets and increase regional infrastructure projects which would attract more private investment. A second factor that should enhance private sector participation is the increased realization, on the part of private investors, that risk perceptions in Africa are often overstated and that building relationships in the region is necessary to take advantage of the emerging investment opportunities. This is particularly true in view of the potential market growth in the continent and its rich but underutilized resources. A third positive element is the catalytic role played by regional and international financial institutions and financiers such as the African Development Bank.

The private sector is now an important partner in the health care sector of many countries. While the contribution of the private sector to health care is significant, there are concerns that their services are usually priced beyond the accessibility of average-income citizens. Governments may need to work closely with private providers to address such concerns. There should be more collaboration on training, improved co-ordination on price setting, and potential for contracting arrangements. All governments need considerable capacity to plan and co-ordinate diverging interests and to ensure that private sector providers are accountable. These goals require fundamental changes in health policy to achieve institutional, organizational, managerial and financial reforms. They also place some burden on the administrative or political capacities of the administration. For the contribution of the private sector to be fully harnessed, there is a need for clear legal frameworks for national policy and for strengthening supervisory capacity of the public sector. Regulatory issues concerning private sector participation are discussed below.

Debt Management and Practice

The accumulation of foreign indebtedness in the case of many African countries is related, partly, to the structure of their economies and, partly, to the manner in which the borrowed funds are contracted and utilized. The production structure and pattern of trade in many African countries is such that these countries consistently import more than they export (invest more than they save), and hence borrow from abroad to bridge the gap. The persistence of this pattern led to accumulation of debt and to the debt repayment problems. Such an outcome indicates that the borrowed funds to bridge the external financing gap were either embezzled through corrupt deals, used to finance consumption, or invested in activities that did not alter the pattern of trade to generate sufficient foreign exchange earnings for debt repayment (Hussain, 2000). While it is difficult to ascertain the magnitude of each of these contributory factors, the result is evidenced in the heavy debt burden shouldered by African countries. The essence of good debt management practice is to ensure that borrowed funds are fully and efficiently utilized.

For many African countries, the debt overhang places severe constraints on economic recovery and achievement of sustained growth (see Chapters 1 and 2). It further threatens to undermine the recent improvements in economic performance as the gains in income and output are absorbed by unsustainable debt service payments. Recent empirical research has shown that a significant accumulation of external debt could stifle investment, slow down economic growth and induce macroeconomic instability through a complex series of price and disincentive effects. Indeed, as a result of the debt overhang, investment has continued to decline, hindering economic recovery and growth in many countries. For Africa as a whole, the investment rate in the 1990s averaged about 16.8 percent of GDP compared to 23.2 percent in the 1970s. The decline was even more severe in the lower-income African countries.

Since the onset of the debt crisis, a number of international initiatives and debt relief mechanisms have been implemented to assist the indebted developing countries cope with external financial obligations. These include actions undertaken under the Baker Plan (1985), the Toronto Terms (October 1988), the Brady Plan (1989), the London Terms (December 1991), the Naples Terms (January 1995) and the Lyons terms (1996). In 1996 the World Bank, IMF, the ADB and other multilateral creditors launched the Heavily Indebted Poor Countries Initiative (HIPC). The basic rationale for debt reduction initiatives is that debt reduction is not an end in itself, but a means to prevent the recurrence of the debt problem. Thus, international efforts to reduce foreign debt must be accompanied by the promotion of internal debt management policies, which aim at optimizing the contribution of foreign borrowing to economic growth and avoiding the emergence of an indebtedness crisis. This necessitates making external borrowings consistent with a country's macroeconomic objectives.

The process of borrowing and utilization of funds must be guided by a clear productivity criterion. When foreign exchange is the binding constraint, which is the case of most African countries, the yield of utilizing foreign resources ought to be measured in terms of foreign exchange earnings (or savings, in the case of import substitutes). This does not mean that all borrowed funds must necessarily be used in the tradeable goods sector. It rather means that, on the aggregate, the utilization of borrowed funds must generate more foreign exchange than what is needed for debt repayment (Hussain, 2000).

In the same vein, debt management functions must be linked to the government's development and economic management program, particularly to the budgetary process and the balance of payments. Effective debt management system involves many coordinated, interrelated and interdependent functions performed by a number of government agencies. While the organizational arrangements can vary greatly between countries, it needs to be co-ordinated by a central policy unit with authority on all debt matters, with the involvement of top officials responsible for the financial management of the country.

Debt management has two broad classes of integrated functions: Executive Debt Management and Operational Debt Management functions. Effective debt management would require situating the Executive Debt Management (EDM) functions at the appropriate level of government, commitment, endorsement and access to the highest level of government (see Box 4.6). The representations should be, preferably, at the ministerial level. At the operational level, there should be a clear allocation of responsibilities and tasks among government agencies, with a clear definition of their relationships in the process. It would be most appropriate for an autonomous and separate debt office to co-ordinate a country's debt management functions, reporting to the ministry or government agency that has the statutory responsibility for the government domestic and external debts. To be effective, the debt management unit should possess the necessary administrative and political clout to decide on its budget and staffing needs.

The main functions of a debt management unit involve the regulation of activities of units of government involved in raising and administering external debt and monitoring sources of funds and approaching them with appropriate borrowing techniques. These techniques include capacity for skilful loan negotiation and operating

Box 4.6: Executive and Operational Debt Management

Executive Debt Management (EDM) consists of actions at the highest levels of government that give direction and organization to the system. These functions are closely related to governance and need the commitment and endorsement at the highest level of government. They include policy, regulatory, and resourcing functions.

- The policy function involves formulation of national debt policies and strategies that apply to all agencies responsible for the economic management of a country. An important element of the policy is to set sustainable levels of external debt as part of an overall economic strategy.

- The regulatory function makes the legal, institutional and administrative arrangements for debt management and sets the rules for the operating units in debt management, co-ordinating their roles and supervising their work.

- The resourcing function ensures the availability of the necessary resources for debt management through representations at international, regional and national fora.

  Operational Debt Management (ODM) actions refer to accounting, resource mobilization and analysis, disbursements and debt servicing, and other supporting functions.

- The accounting function breaks down each loan contract into debt servicing obligations, records them, and sets up effective payments mechanisms.

- The resource mobilization and analysis function develops and adopts strategies for sourcing funds and handling of the debt portfolio. This includes watching currency and interest rate movements, following the development of new financial instruments, analyzing options for borrowing, managing the debt portfolio and negotiating loan agreements.

- The disbursements and debt servicing function involves recording and monitoring of actual debt inflows, while the debt servicing function involves the day-to-day management of debt repayments in accordance with executive direction and organization and is concerned largely with debt payments, recording, analysis and control.

- Other supporting functions involve auditing, statistics and information services, and providing politicians, the media and the public at large with relevant information about the country's debt situation.

Source: E.c Anusionwu (2000).

schemes for withdrawing loan funds and paying debt service. The debt management unit must also create and co-ordinate statistical and analytical capacity on debt to underpin management decisions. The purpose of these activities is to assure smooth flow of relevant information to and among debt managers, and from them to decision-makers, creditors and the public. The debt management unit must have adequate staff resources, office space and equipment, and communications systems.

Administrative Capacity

Good economic governance requires strong administrative capacity comprising efficient, open, accountable and transparent public service that is competent to help design and implement appropriate policies and manage the public sector. Without an effective public sector and civil service, it would be difficult for government to formulate or implement sound economic strategies and policies, create an enabling legal and regulatory framework, and to efficiently provide social services such as education and health. Effective implementation of development policies requires strong administrative capacity not only in central government but also at national, provincial and local levels. While the central administration can concentrate on strategies and policies, the local and provincial administrations can assist with implementation and monitoring. Local and provincial governments could enhance the administrative process by helping to monitor expenditures, generate taxes, spread information and assist with rolling investment plans.

Public Sector Management

Public sector management must play a supportive role to allow private sector operators to assume the new role that has been assigned it. It has to create a sound economic and social environment that is conducive to investment and to enhancing the capacity of a nation's private sector to be internationally competitive. As public administration is a rare source of national competitive advantage, a crucial factor that differentiates the winners and losers in the race to realize economic development is sound public management. This is so because the relative competitiveness of nations depends on the efficiency and effectiveness of their public administrations as the cost of public administration corresponds to the indirect cost of production by firms (Bienayme and Courtier, 1993).

Too often, public agencies and institutions in Africa are synonymous with poor service, corruption and inefficiency (see Box 4.7). Lack of openness, transparency and accountability results in public dissatisfaction and lack of confidence in public institutions and undermines the legitimacy of governments. At the roots of the malaise affecting the public services in Africa was, at first, the failure to adapt the inherited colonial public administration to African culture and society and, subsequently, the changing perception of the development vision. While the culture of the inherited public institutions was suitable to the needs of the colonial period, it often distanced the rulers from the people. In many countries, the military foray into governance and politics caused public sector management and administration to be further centralized, while local and provincial systems were impoverished. In most countries, local governance has remained too weak to make a meaningful impact in the provision of social services.

The evolution of the development vision since the 1960s has also contributed to the weakness of the public sector in Africa. On the one hand, the development paradigm of the 1960s and 1970s advocated a prominent role for the government as an entrepreneur with the public sector as a large employer and serving as a means for creating and distributing wealth. The supposed corrective intervention role of the government led to a bloated bureaucracy providing a platform for rent seeking and graft, incompetence and corruption to thrive. On the other hand, the ensuing

Box 4.7: Indicators of Government Capacity and Institutional Structures in Sub-Saharan Africa

Ali (2001) provided a measure of Africa's public sector capacity with reference to three elements including "law and order", "bureaucratic quality" and "corruption". He combines the three into a composite indicator with equal weights 0.375 for the "rule of law" and "corruption" and a weight of 0.25 for the "bureaucratic quality". The composite indicator are scaled on a zero to one ranking order with a score of less than 50 percent indicating low quality institutional capacity while a score more than 8 indicating high quality institutional capacity. His results, which exclude the Northern Africa Region, are shown below.

Table B.4.7.1: Institutional Structure in Sub-Saharan Africa: 1984-2000

Region Period	1984-1989	1990-1999	2000
Central Africa	4.33	4.41	3.74
Eastern Africa	3.98	3.83	3.76
Southern Africa	4.38	5.13	4.74
West Africa	4.24	4.18	3.81
SS Africa	4.23	4.39	4.01

The table reveals that all regions suffer from low quality institutions and that over the period since 1984 and up to 2000 the quality of institutions deteriorated for all the four sub-regions. However, the period 1990-99 register a marginal improvement over that of 1984-89, with the southern region having a slightly better institutional structure. While progress made in improving institutional capacity in recent years is encouraging, both the magnitude and speed of institutional improvements were minute. During the last decade or so, the improvement in the quality of Africa's institutions in Sub-Saharan Africa is estimated at 0.37 percent per annum. With such a low rate of improvement, it would take the continent more than a century to reach the lower limit of high quality institutions (Ali 2001). This last observation calls for urgent and concerted actions on the part of African countries as well as their development partners to speed up and deepen institutional reforms.

Ali (2001) also provided another measure of the quality if institutions based on the work of Kaufmann, Kraay and Zoido-Lobaton (1999). The measure includes "voice and accountability" and "political instability and violence", to reflect the process; "government effectiveness" and "regulatory burden", measures the capacity

of the government; "rule of law" and "graft", to measure the respect of institutions. The quality of institutions are measured as the distance from the average quality in terms of standard deviations, with a range of −2.5 to 2.5 and with higher values corresponding to better governance outcomes. Assuming equal weights for the sub-indicators, their average is reported as a composite indicator of institutional quality. Table B.4.7.2 summarizes the results.

The table shows that for all indicators all regions have institutional structures of below average quality. The ranking of the regions, in terms of the overall composite measure, is such that the best performing region is Southern Africa, while the worst region is central Africa. The author's results for individual countries show that Botswana enjoys the best quality institutions in terms of government effectiveness and regulatory capacity, while Congo Democratic Republic has the lowest quality institutions in these two areas. Mauritius ranks as the country with the highest quality institutions in terms of the rule of law, with Congo Democratic Republic being the country with the lowest quality institutions. In terms of graft Botswana is the country with high quality institution and Niger is the country with the lowest quality institutions. On an indicative overall index of quality of institutions, Mauritius ranks as the country with high quality institutions and Congo Democratic Republic as the country with the lowest quality institutions.

Table B.4.7.2: Governance Indicators of Institutional Structure in Sub-Saharan Africa: 1998

Region	Gov't Effective- ness (36)	Regulatory Burden (41)	Rule of Law (41)	Graft (35)	Ave- rage
Central	-0.763	-0.716	-1.019	-0.826	-0.831
Eastern	-0.905	-0.680	-0.813	-0.821	-0.805
Southern	-0.435	-0.014	-0.062	-0.141	-0.163
Western	-0.342	-0.504	-0.593	-0.508	-0.487
SSA	-0.611	-0.479	-0.622	-0.574	-0.572
Maximum	0.221	0.570	1.279	0.535	0.501
Minimum	-1.769	-2.340	-2.153	-1.567	-1.955

Figures between brackets are the number of countries for which the indicator is reported.

Source: Ali (2001).

economic crisis of the 1980s reduced the ability of the state to manage the economy as government financial capacity deteriorated, real wages for civil servants declined and the quality of public administration diminished. This eroded the competence of the public sector to formulate and implement policies as well as deliver social public services. On policy-making, for instance, most African countries relied increasingly on foreign experts to design and supervise the implementation of reforms. These side-effects of economic reforms undermined the internal administrative capacity of the state.

Public sector management in Africa needs to adapt to the changing economic and political contexts and requires a new approach and orientation. It requires putting in place mechanisms that will enhance and guarantee the quality of public services. Greater accountability must be promoted. Systems must be put in place to strengthen mechanisms for expenditure control, exposure of and sanctions against misspending and corruption. It will also be necessary to develop and build democratic institutions and strengthen the independence of government agencies. Independent institutions to promote public and private sector accountability —such as the Auditor General's Office, the Ombudsman and the Public Accounts Committee of Parliament—need to be established and given the power to undertake their duties without fear of reprisals. Competent governing boards for public enterprises must be established and promoted. Professionalism and meritocracy must be brought to civil service to ensure effective and efficient delivery of public services and to combat bureaucratic corruption (ADB et al., 2000).

Efforts at reforming the public service in Africa have been aimed at improving public sector management by introducing new approaches.

A common strategy is to replicate the efficiencies of the private sector in public sector management and create quasi-market conditions in public service delivery. Examples of policies normally introduced include: introduction of user fees or cost recovery in social services; exposure of public sector enterprises to market competition; introduction of performance measurement; reward for public service employment; and strengthening managerial autonomy. Ghana is an important case study given its early adoption of structural adjustment programs and its implementation of several reforms (see Box 4.8). Three key reform areas—civil service reform, pay policy and decentralization—are discussed below.

Civil Service Reform

Developing countries that have made socio-economic progress have invariably achieved such progress through the creation of a relatively autonomous, coherent, capable, technocratic, and committed civil service. They have also built a development-oriented and politically insulated technocratic elite that formulates economic policies. At the heart of reform efforts to ensure good governance in Africa is the need to make the civil service more effective, accountable and transparent. For most African countries there is need to streamline the public services, improve systems, reform wage structure, and reallocate redundant employees and workers. To fulfill the changing role of the state, African societies must build a civil service that is based on meritocracy, foster quality recruitment and promotion systems, increase salaries and reduce wage differentials between the public and private sectors, and develop programs to build the capacity of the civil service.

Box 4.8: Public Sector Reform Programs in Ghana

Ghana embraced reform in 1983 by introducing the Economic Recovery Program (ERP). In 1992, Ghana adopted a multiparty democratic constitution, which embraced the core characteristics of good governance. Since then, Ghana has introduced and implemented several programs to reform the public sector in order to enhance its administrative capacity for good governance.

In September 1994, Ghana launched the National Institutional Renewal Program (NIRP) with the purpose of encouraging institutions under the executive, legislative and judicial arms of government to discharge their duties in a transparent, competent, accountable and cost effective fashion. To achieve these objectives, a Public Sector Management Reform Program (PSMRP) was launched to assist in redefining the role and functions of the state, design appropriate institutions and systems to implement this role and rationalize the existing structure and systems to respond to the new design. Efforts were made to adjust central government structures and organizations to make the public sector consumer-friendly, more effective and efficient, and to allow the private sector and social partners to fully participate in the development process by strengthening the capacity of the government as a facilitator.

A follow-up program, Civil Service Performance Improvement Program (CSPIP), was launched in 1995 to make the civil service more efficient and effective. In 1996, a National Gover-

nance Program (NGP) was launched to enhance the capacity of autonomous institutions and civil society to effectively perform their roles as "watch dogs". Under this program, several institutions including the parliament, judiciary, electoral commission, human rights commission, civic education commission and several civil society organizations such as International Federation of Women Lawyers (FIDA) and Center for Democracy and Development were supported.

In 1997, the national parliament approved a strategy document, Public Sector Reinvention and Modernization Strategy (PUSERMOS), that provided the framework for undertaking further public sector reforms. Other programs which have been developed include the Public Financial Management Reform Program (PUFMARP) to improve financial management and Medium Term Expenditure Framework (MTEF) launched in 1996 as a component of PUFMARP to strengthen budgetary procedures and system.

Laudable as these efforts are, a lot remains to be done as improvements in the quality, timeliness, and efficiency in delivery of government services, while co-ordination among various governance institutions is still inadequate. Major improvements can still be made to enhance the collaboration between government, the private sector and civil society organizations.

Source: Adapted from ADB (2000).

Civil service reform efforts in Africa have been mostly in the context of adjustment programs under the guidance, support and finance of the multilateral financial institutions. The focus of these structural adjustment inspired reform efforts have been directed, in the main, to reducing the wage bill rather than improving quality and building

capacity across the board. Progress has been made however in building capacity in certain key economic management institutions such as central banks and ministries of finance. Capacity building efforts should now be broadened beyond economic management to focus on revitalizing the public sector, reversing the decline in public service and improving service delivery and quality. Efforts to revitalize the public service by African governments and their development partners should aim to build transparent, merit-based recruitment systems. They should also aim at building promotion systems based on performance, sound management, and in-service training and career development. The functioning of civil service must contain a system of checks and balances to deter corruption and promote professional ethics. Rules within the public service would have to be applied consistently and impartially.

Reform efforts must not be piecemeal and should be consistently implemented if chances of success are to be enhanced. For reform efforts to succeed, they must be guided by a holistic vision, which is shared by the key stakeholders. The ends must be identified first, followed by drawing an overarching strategy that will spell out the things to be done, how they should be done and the sequencing of the actions to be taken. Specific programs or projects to be implemented must also be designed. In addition, civil service reforms require champions and political commitment from the highest levels of government and society.

Pay Policy in the Public Sector

Public sector reform in African countries will neither be complete nor succeed without also addressing the pay policy for civil service. In an increasingly open, integrated, and highly competitive global economy, policy makers are more and more confronted with new challenges of economic management. Policy makers must not only master the new realities of the new economy, they must also command the respect and maintain confidence of markets. The end result is that civil servants must be highly skilled and have the capacity to design, monitor and implement a consistent set of macroeconomic and sector policies. In addition, governments will need high quality civil service to operate more effectively the public sector. Essential to this is the upgrading of the quality of civil service and the productivity of civil servants.

The need for an efficient and effective civil service will require reform efforts that go beyond cost containment and retrenchment to address the crisis of public incentives that plague African countries. Pay and promotion systems are too often not related to performance. Opportunities for training and skills building is almost non-existent except in macroeconomic issues. Earnings are far below local market levels, and real wages have fallen severely for most public sectors in Africa. The compression in real wages is as tight as a factor of two to one in Tanzania (ADB et al., 2000). The public sector is very often unable to attract and retain highly-skilled officials. Public service cannot be improved until professional and technical staff is given the necessary incentives to perform.

Recommendations to attract and retain highly-skilled civil servants include creating a cadre of senior civil service in which entry will be competitive and based only on merit. The senior cadre should be given better professional opportunities and rewarded with higher pay that is close to or even higher than the levels in the private sector. This will require African governments to accept widening differentials between low- and high-skill civil servants. This, it is hoped, will reduce the brain drain from the civil service. The promotion of E-Government (see below) may be one way to help retain a small but highly paid civil service.

Decentralization

In an era of continuing economic problems and adjustments, many national governments in Africa have been forced by circumstances to withdraw from certain activities and reduce the services they provide. Justification for government withdrawal from providing certain goods include resource constraints, the need for adjustment, and the fact that development experience has shown that highly centralized and top-down approach to service delivery is expensive, cumbersome, inflexible, and prone to abuse (Wunsch, 1999). Although the private sector can and should provide some of these services, the problem is that some services are non-profitable public goods. In these cases, the most logical step is for the services to be provided by sub-national or local governments.

Beyond delivering public services, building effective and efficient local governance is increasingly seen as a crucial component of the democratic project in Africa and as way to establish a well-functioning economic and political system. The relevance of local governance for socio-economic progress stems from the need for local economic development, improved service delivery, increased popular participation in governance, and the desire to bring governments closer to the people. Good governance must be rooted in the effective participation of the people in decision-making, and functioning local self-governance institutions. Box 4.9 outlines the experiences of selected African countries with urban development at the local government.

Effective local economic management means that development functions should be taken over by local governments. This requires that local authorities should be able to mobilize resources (financial, human and technological), initiate, plan and implement development projects, and obtain adequate support from national governments. Despite efforts by many governments to decentralize or devolve power, the local government system has not been very effective (Wohlmuth, 1999). The problems vary and are numerous. Local governments are very dependent on regional and national governance systems. Political intentions notwithstanding, the creation of local governments has not necessarily led to real allocation of power and funds. Underdeveloped local civil society and turbulent economic and policy environments undercut local institutions. Studies of Kenya, Tanzania, Ghana and Tanzania reported by Wohlmuth (1999) shows local governance in Africa to be highly inadequate with regard to development planning, financing, and administration. In many cases, there are uncertainties in the way the local authorities and national governments interact whether in project initiation and implementation or in other areas of responsibilities. Manpower and financial resources are mostly inadequate as most local governments fully depend on financially strapped central governments. As a result, in many countries, local authorities have neither political autonomy, real power and function, nor the capacity to raise revenue.

Sustained long-term development in Africa will require viable local governance. The consolidation of local governance is necessary to create the democratic developmental state. This will require not just decentralization but also devolution of authority to local governments and building a viable local political process that can mobilize people and demand accountability from local officials. Effective local governance, which will facilitate long-term growth and development, will require real decentralization. Decentralization must not be used by the central governments as a way

Box 4.9: Better Urban Governance for Poverty Reduction

Africa has the highest rate of urban growth – a startling 4 percent per annum compared to 2 percent for the rest of the world. However, given the general state of poverty on the continent urbanization in Africa is associated with an unprecedented process of "poverty urbanization". Among many different measures, better urban governance could be instrumental in reducing urban poverty. The examples sited below, show that bringing government closer to those being governed could make a difference to the livelihood of the people.

Abidjan

Participatory democracy and transparent local government structures have already improved the lives of millions of people around the world. In the early 1990s, the mayor of Adjame, in Abidjan, has opted to focus on unemployment, poverty and environmental degradation. Neighborhood committees (CDQs) were established to engage the energies and resources of local communities and channel efforts towards improving their living conditions and economic situation. The CDQs are involved in many different activities including street cleaning and garbage collection, security services and operating commercial enterprises. They also undertake some infrastructure improvements such as road maintenance, cleaning of drains and street lighting. In 1994, the *commune* launched two new CDQ initiatives. The first aims to create a health center in each of the 19 *quartiers* managed by a health CDQ. The first center opened in April 1995. The second initiative combines micro-incubators and training programs to encourage young Ivorians to start commercial enterprises. The first stores operated by the trainees were opened in May 1995.

Dar es Salaam

The Community Infrastructure Program (CIP) of the city of Dar es Salaam in Tanzania was established in 1995 to address infrastructure problems in deficient communities by working with them. The program involves the government, parastatals and other stakeholders in the development process by adopting a partnership and participatory approach. It also creates a sense of responsibility to the communities and at the same time building their capacities in the management of the constructed infrastructure. Since the introduction of the initiative there have been remarkable achievements including: capacity building of the communities, such as the preparation of community development plans; institutional strengthening (establishment of offices in each community); neighborhood infrastructure upgrading, such as the establishment of community-owned and locally-managed water systems.

Cairo

The rehabilitation and upgrading of the Manshiet Nasser Informal Settlement, located in the heart of Cairo, is a unique initiative to improve the living environment of more than half a million inhabitants by relocating a percentage of them to a close by planned settlement equipped with all services and amenities (water and sanitation, roads, open space, vocational training and heath centers, libraries, schools, phone network, and environment friendly crafts workshops). The project then carries out a phased land development and renewal on the site of the existing slum. With nine phases, it is the biggest project of its kind in Egypt, aiming to build 70,000 housing units. By end of 2000, the urgent phase of the project, which represents a part of its first phase (760 units), had been completed. The process of relocating residents to the project is ongoing.

The project is based on participatory socio-economic surveys and mechanisms of transparent dialogue with local inhabitants in both the planning and management phases. Major achievements of the project include affordable housing options to the poorest of the poor; empowered civic engagement at early stages of decision making; institutionalized participatory urban management; maintained and enhanced livelihood systems of inhabitants by location proximity; preserved social capital and ties of original dwellers; and socio-economic sustained development. All these have the effective participation of residents in defining priorities and objectives of the project. Be-

---

Box 4.9: (Continued)

fore the initiative began, residents had no legal tenure of their shelter or lands, no basic infrastructure services or amenities, and paid exorbitant prices for informal vendors of services (e.g. water). They also suffered all manner of social decay and were exposed to a plethora of environmental and health hazards.

For sustained poverty alleviation, the project makes available serviced lands to non-polluting crafts to create jobs in the area linking it with the old quarter of Cairo located near by. Soft credits were extended to all residents and vocational training centers developed to equip youth and women with necessary skills for income generating activities. A micro-credit for small and micro-enterprises program has been developed and being implemented by the Social Fund for Development, targeting women and youth in the area.

The innovative approach adopted in planning, implementing and managing Manchiet Nasser provides a wealth of lessons to be learned and replicated to informal settlements elsewhere.

Source: UNCHS: www.bestpractices.org

to reduce their responsibilities. It must be part of a national strategy to create more responsible and equitable governance. Effective communication must be maintained between central and local governments. Resources should be equitably shared among the levels of government in addition to putting in measures to promote accountability and reduce corruption. Local institutions will have to be strengthened and capacity of local authorities

built to manage the development process. Uganda is one of a few countries that are attempting to decentralize governance and enhance popular participation through improving government at the local level (see Box 4.10).

Technical Capacity

If African countries are to realize sustained economic development, there is a need to build and strengthen the institutions that design and implement economic management. African countries also need to build their capacities in many other areas that support the functioning of political and economic governance as well as the activities of the private sector and civil society. There is, thus, a need to promote the institutions that enhance the capability of the state to govern and the capacity of the private sector to produce. An important component of government capacity is E-Government, which aims to harness the power of information technology in order to increase a government's capacities to provide services and manage the development process.

Building Supporting Institutions

In the area of political governance, there is an acute need for building electoral assistance support services for the conduct and preparations for the elections. These include the design of electoral and legal frameworks, computerization of electoral roles and the training of election supervisors. Support for local municipal elections and the organization of political referendums are also areas where Africa needs to build capacity. Another related domain is parliamentary support for building legislative capacity in shaping priorities related to the complex issues of accountability, decen-

Box 4.10: Improving Local Governance Capacity

In a few African countries, attempts have been made to decentralize political power and enhance popular participation within local authorities and local governments. A good example is Uganda. In 1986, the government of Uganda initiated a comprehensive program of democratic governance to establish transparency, accountability and good governance for decentralized governance in Uganda. Reforms of local governance have featured most prominently in government policies and programs. The ongoing radical restructuring of government aims at redefining the role of the state, restoring the quality of public services, decentralizing power to the lowest feasible levels of government and introducing mechanisms for democratic accountability at all levels.

Decentralization, one of the major reforms under democratic governance, involves the devolution of functions and powers to the people at appropriate levels where they can best manage and direct their own affairs. The process was initiated with the introduction of the Resistance Council system in 1986, which is currently known as the Local Council System. The Local Government Statute (1997) augments the principles of the Local Council System. The thrust of decentralization is to empower local governments so as to increase local people's participation in planning, managing and controlling the affairs that concern them, increasing accountability, and building management and institutional capacities at local level. This process enhances democratic legitimacy and accountability. The local councils and their chairpersons are directly elected through a competitive system with a provision for women, youth and disabled representatives. Democratic control of affairs at local levels is further enhanced through the committee structure, which ensures the joint participation of elected councilors and civil servants in service delivery and decision making.

Similarly in South Africa, the system of local government allows for active election by the people of their representatives to local authorities where substantial decisions are made regarding allocation of local financial resources and provision of services. The central government continues to raise the lion's share of the revenue since provinces generate only 5 percent of their revenue needs. The central government sets the policy frameworks and disburses funds to lower levels in accord with the responsibilities devolved to them for supplying basic education and health care. As in other case of decentralization, lower levels of government have increased responsibilities but not increased control over funds.

In Kenya, on the other hand, local authorities have remained weak, both in terms of raising their own revenues as well as being in charge of services at the local level. Since 1974, the central government has assumed financing and running health and education nationally, reducing county councils to peripheral services like running markets, and providing municipal water and sanitation. But even in the latter regard municipal governments have performed inefficiently, leading to the mushrooming of neighborhood organizations to provide security, sanitation, garbage collection, water and even to collect rates for electricity. Thus weak governance at the local level has given "political space" to the emergence of autonomous people's organizations in the form of "neighborhood associations" that are perhaps more legitimate and more representative of the people's interests.

In Ghana, the restructuring of local governments has given more scope of redressing local concerns without prior clearance from the regional governments within the national framework for poverty reduction. Of the national budget known as the common fund, 5 percent is distributed to districts, which are further instructed to use 20 percent of this for poverty reduction activities. Districts also raise revenues through local taxes and have the authority to negotiate directly with donors for district level projects.

In the final analysis, the litmus test for the fight against poverty in Africa is rapid economic growth in national economies. However, the competence of national governments to induce and manage economic growth needs to be looked into.

Source: Adapted from Peter Ayang' Nyong'o (2000).

tralization and constitutional reforms.

Promoting access to justice, legal reforms, and legal aid to the poor, civic education and human rights are all areas where many African countries need to build capacity. Equally important are supporting services for consensus building, conflict prevention and information exchange among government and civil society. These supporting functions are best pursued through establishing or strengthening institutions such as parliamentary studies and legislative information centers, Ombudsman offices and human rights institutions and organizations.

There is also a need for national centers to help generate information and knowledge on particular issues and undertake policy dialogue. For a long time, such policy think-tanks were non-existent in African countries. More and more new centers are being created with the support of donors and multilateral development organizations. The African Capacity Building Initiative, established in 1992, has assisted in financing many economic policy units in African countries. Despite their donor dependency, they are beginning to make some contributions on macroeconomic policy issues in Africa. The next step is to strengthen the centers that already exist, broaden their scope beyond macroeconomics and begin to seek ways to make them endogenous, financially sustainable, and relevant to issues facing African countries. They should begin to undertake policy studies relevant to crucial policy issues, which can be relied upon by parliament and the executive branch of government. They can also help undertake policy studies on implication of global trade regimes and agreements to strengthen the negotiating position of African countries. African universities can also participate in this process. It is increasingly becoming crucial for policy-makers to have access to information, research and knowledge of issues before making policies. It will be important for government, private sector, and civil society to support the creation such policy centers. Models exist, such as the Nigerian Institute for Social and Economic Research (NISER), and the Al-Ahram Center for Political and Strategic Studies established by the government of Egypt in 1968 (see Box 4.11). To address regional issues, policy centers can be established on a regional basis, such as the Southern Africa Regional Institute for Policy Studies (SARIPS) based in Harare, Zimbabwe.

Institutions that promote technology development in Africa are either non-existent or neglected. There is a view that technology development is irrelevant at this stage of Africa's development. However, technology development refers to the ability of enterprises to use modern technologies efficiently, to master imported knowledge and equipment, to adapt them to local needs, to use local inputs and to offer an efficient supply base for foreign investors. It needs to cover both large-scale enterprises and smaller ones, as both show striking weaknesses in their technological capabilities in Africa (ADR, 1996).

African countries would need to establish and promote the institutions that can provide extensive extension services delivering comprehensive packages of assistance comprising technical know-how, finance, management skills, training and sales information. In South East Asia which has been very successful in this respect, such institutions go by different names including Productivity Councils (Hong Kong); Productivity Centers (China); and, Medium and Small Business Administration (Taiwan). Such institutions are entrusted with the tasks of going into private enterprises to identify their problems and devise appropriate remedies and training packages. They

Box 4.11: Al Ahram Center for Political and Strategic Studies in Egypt

The Al-Ahram Center for Political and Strategic Studies (ACPSS) was established in 1968 as an independent research unit functioning within the framework of Al-Ahram Foundation. ACPSS undertakes multidisciplinary research dealing with regional and international developments, as well as Egyptian strategic, political, economic, and social affairs. This includes: major changes of the international system, international conflict and conflict resolution, political, economic, and social aspects of Arab society in general and Egyptian society in particular. The work of the ACPSS is carried out through a number of units including political systems, international relations, Arab research, economic research, sociological research, military research, historical research, mass communications and the Egyptian revolution.

The ACPSS co-operates with organizations and research institutions all over the world through the exchange of publications and information on topics of mutual interests. In addition, the Center receives a number of visitors from abroad, including academic staff, prominent scholars, representatives of press and publishing agencies and the media, as well as members of diplomatic missions in Cairo. The target audience for the research includes political leaders, policy makers, legislators, political organizations, political parties, national government, international community, military, policy analysts and researchers, academia, media and journalists, and the general public.

The Arab Strategic Report is an annual report issued by the ACPSS since 1985. The Report analyzes the main strategic issues annually from a strategic, military, political, and economic perspective. Another important report of ACPSS is the "State of Religion", which, presents a comprehensive view of religions in Egypt, examining their various institutional structures, codes of beliefs, interactions, and the role of religion as a behavioral determinant. This Report derives its importance from the fact that it is aimed at removing the misconceptions that have dominated the religious sphere in Egypt since the 1970s. The problem, of misconceptions, has led to a certain degree of sectarian tension, and even violence, and thus jeopardized the foundations of national integration.

Source: adapted from: www.acpss.org

provide information on international standards and quality and give training, consultancy and demonstration services on productivity and quality to small firms at subsidized rates. They also act as technology transfer and technology development agents and provide specialized technical services for new industries. Furthermore, they import relevant technologies for local industries and adapt and disseminate them to private sector operators and provide credit, technology, management, accounting, and marketing assistance (Lall, 1996; Hussain 1997).

Promoting E-Government

E-Government refers to the use of information technology application to perform government functions with maximum efficiency and at minimum cost. Most African countries need to enhance their capacity in this regard. Information systems which can help governments design, implement, and assess the effectiveness of economic measures are now powerful instruments of public policy. Such information systems could increase the speed, volume, quality, transparency, and accountability of government transactions, yielding large productivity increases in government services.

In fiscal monitoring, governments can use information systems to design and follow-up the process of tax collection and validate its revenue collections against its expenditure. In budgetary planning, information technology provides simulation techniques to simultaneously maximize revenue and minimize the tax burden on selected income groups and economic actors. In public procurement, the adoption of information technology can help simplify purchasing procedures through electronic advertising, qualification, tendering, selection and payment. In debt management, information systems can be used to co-ordinate the processes of borrowing and debt repayment transactions with the various bilateral and multilateral creditors in order to improve the efficiency and transparency in the use of foreign capital and avoid the problems of corruption and excessive debt burdens. Such applications are also labor-saving and can also help governments to keep a small, efficient and well-paid civil service (Oshikoya and Hussain 1998).

There is almost an infinite number of information technology applications that will provide powerful catalysts to confront Africa's complex mix of development challenges. It must be underscored, however, that information technology is not a panacea in itself. It is rather a powerful tool that can bear results only if it is put into effective use. And to do this, African countries would have to overcome, as a matter of priority, numerous obstacles including the inadequate state of telecommunications services and the high cost of computers and software.

Corporate Governance

The use of the term governance has become almost synonymous with civil or political governance. But in recent years, the importance of both economic and corporate governance has come to the fore. The relationship among political governance, economic governance and corporate governance is analogous to a series of concentric circles in which the political governance forms the outside circle, followed by economic governance circle, with corporate governance at the center (Otobo, 2000).

Political governance sets the orientation of the economy and it supplies the institutional infrastructure for economic governance. In turn, economic governance provides the context in which corporate governance is practised. In particular, it provides the laws under which corporations are established and the regulatory framework for the conduct of corporate affairs, and sets the macro-economic framework. Corporate governance, thus, stands at the intersection of law, public policy, and business practice.

The various dimensions of governance, political, economic and corporate, seek mainly to use incentives and discipline to foster transparency and accountability. Sound corporate governance is crucial for socio-economic development. Without transparency and accountability within the private sector, growth and development will be stymied as investors shy away and seek to invest where there is better corporate governance. Robust corporate governance in Africa should be responsive to the needs of internal and external stakeholders and must be based on political and legal traditions of the country. The key challenge facing African countries will be to devise the corporate governance institutions that can help nurture and regulate the private sector in order for it to fulfil its developmental role.

Why Corporate Governance Matters for Africa

Increasingly for developing and transition economies, a healthy and competitive corporate sector is fundamental for sustained and broad-based growth. The increased emphasis on private sector development in Africa is based on the recognition that it is private initiatives that create wealth and jobs with which poverty can be reduced. The privatization process in Africa has deepened the influence which private firms have on the lives of people. Moreover, privatization is taking African governments from the familiar terrain of governance of public enterprises to the unfamiliar territory of creating the legal and regulatory framework for governance of private sector firms. As the reform process deepens in Africa and increased emphasis is placed on developing the private sector, the regulatory capacity of the state will have to be strengthened to meet the challenges of this new economic context.

Corporations must be able to tap both domestic and international capital markets in today's world. Increasingly, individual investors, funds, banks, and other financial institutions base their decisions not only on a company's outlook, but also on its reputation and its governance. It is this growing need to access financial resources, domestic and foreign, and to harness the power of the private sector for economic and social progress that has brought corporate governance into prominence.

It is for these reasons that countries are now beginning to realize that just as public governance is important in the public sector so also is corporate governance in the private sector. Public governance can have a major impact on private corporate behavior. Sound governance of corporations is potentially a source of competitive advantage and critical for economic performance and social progress.

The East Asian financial crises that began in 1997 is a crucial example of why there is a need for sound corporate governance. Observers have attributed the financial crises partly to a wide range of poor corporate governance practices in such areas as the securities market regulation, accounting and auditing standards in financial institutions, and bankruptcy laws. As African countries make the transition from state-led to private sector-led development, corporate governance issues are assuming greater importance.

Perspectives on Corporate Governance

There are several perspectives on corporate governance; its purpose, its definitions, and how to bring it about. But two perspectives—public and private —provide a framework for corporate governance that reflect an interplay between internal incentives (which define the relationships among the key players in the corporation) and external forces (notably policy, legal, regulatory, and market) that together govern the behavior and performance of the firm.

From a corporation's perspective, the emerging consensus is that corporate governance is about maximizing value, subject to meeting the corporation's financial and other legal and contractual obligations. This definition stresses the need for boards of directors to balance the interests of shareholders with those of other stakeholders—employees, customers, suppliers, investors, communities—in order to achieve long-term sustained value for the corporation. In a narrow sense, corporate governance can be viewed as a set of arrangements internal to the corporation that defines the relationships between managers and shareholders. The shareholders may be public or private, concentrated or dispersed. These arrangements may be embedded in company law, securities law, listing requirements, and the like or negotiated among the key players in governing documents of the corporation, such as the corporate charter, by-laws, and shareholder agreements.

The main issues that dominate the internal operating environment of corporate governance are fairly clear and straightforward (see Box 4.12). These include disclosure rules; directors' duty of care and diligence; rights and obligations of shareholders; role and responsibilities of the board; equal treatment of shareholders; and managerial discretion. Other issues include methods of appointment to the board; communication from the board to the shareholders; accountability to shareholders; board performance assessment; review of financial performance; and business ethics for the board and management. Many of the codes or guidelines on corporate governance, or reforms of corporate governance, developed at the national or international levels focus on these issues (OECD, 1999; CACG, 1999).

Corporate governance, from the public policy perspective, is about nurturing enterprises while ensuring that they are accountable in their exercise of power and patronage. Public policy aims to provide firms with the incentives and discipline to minimize the divergence between private and social returns in addition to protecting the interests of stakeholders. Another dimension of the public nature of the corporation is to view private companies as serving not only the interest of, or responsible to, the shareholders alone, but the larger society as well. This raises the issue of the accountability of the corporation.

Traditionally, corporations are expected to be accountable only to their owners (shareholders) through the management. In this view, the role of company law is to provide the rules that protect the interests of the shareholders and enable a company to make maximum profits for them. Accordingly, public purpose is best served through the profit-maximizing behavior of the corporation, because this leads to more wealth creation for the society. If the corporation is required to incorporate social consideration or accommodate any other public interest in its operations, this should be explicitly set out in law.

Set against this view is the notion that corporations, especially large corporations, must be seen as social enterprises because their activities affect not just the shareholders but also the larger society. In particular, the decisions of the big corporations can affect unemployment, trade, the physical environment and other aspects of society. As such, the corporation should act as a socially responsible citizen, and should incorporate social considerations into its operations (Box 4.13). This is the idea of corporate social responsibility, which entails incurring costs for socially desirable but not legally mandated action (Parkinson, 1994). It involves a corporation making positive contributions to the development of the communities in which it operates in the hope that the company will do better as a result of accrued goodwill. In Africa, there is evidence that a correlation exists between an entrepreneur's fund of social capital and the health and survival prospects of his enterprise (Box 4.14).

Box 4.12: Principles of Corporate Governance

To assist its members states in their efforts to evaluate and improve the legal, institutional and regulatory framework for corporate governance in their countries and to provide guidance suggestions for all parties that have a role to play in achieving good corporate governance, the Organization for Economic Co-operation and Development (OECD) in 1998 developed a set of principles that build on national experiences. The principles focus on governance problems that result from the separation of ownership and control. Among the elements recommended in the principles are:

Rights of Shareholders: Shareholders have the right to receive relevant information about the company in a timely manner, to have the opportunity to participate in decisions concerning fundamental corporate changes, and to share in the profits of the corporation, among others. Markets for corporate control should be efficient and transparent, and shareholders should consider the costs and benefits of exercising their voting rights.

Equitable Treatment: All shareholders of the same class, especially minority and foreign shareholders, should be treated equally with full disclosure of material information and prohibition of abusive self-dealing and insider trading. Members of the board and managers should be required to disclose any material interests in transactions.

Role of Stakeholders: The role of stakeholders in corporate governance as established by law is must be recognized. Corporate governance framework should encourage active co-operation between corporations and stakeholders in creating wealth, jobs, and financially sound enterprise.

Role of the Board: The board is responsible for the strategic guidance of the company, the effective monitoring of management, and it is accountable to the company and shareholders.

Transparency: Timely and accurate disclosure and transparency should be required on all matters material to company performance, ownership, and governance relating to other issues such as employees and stakeholders. Financial information should be independently audited and prepared to high standards of quality.

These principles for corporate governance are based on the recognition that a key element in improving economic efficiency is corporate governance, which involves a set of relationships between a company's management, its board, its shareholders, and other stakeholders. Corporate governance also provides the structure through which the objectives of the company are set, and the means to attaining those objectives and monitoring performance are determined.

Good corporate governance should provide incentives for the board and management to pursue objectives that are in the interests of the company and shareholders and should facilitate effective monitoring, thereby encouraging firms to use resources more efficiently. Additionally, the degree to which corporations observe good corporate governance is an increasingly important factor for investment decisions, as international flows of capital allows companies to source funds around the world.

Source: Adapted from: OECD (1999).

Corporate governance requires institutions that can be entrusted to provide a level and competitive playing field and discipline the behavior of insiders, whether managers or shareholders. These institutions and policies, which are more developed in the advanced market economies, minimize the divergence between social and private returns. They also reduce costly agency problems,

Box 4.13: Ownership Structure of Firms and Corporate Governance

Reliable data on the ownership structure of companies, and on mergers and acquisitions, in Africa are generally scanty or not available. In the few cases in which data are available, many of the listed firms belong to both local and multinational investors, the ultimate owners of which are unreported. La Porta et al., (1998) constructed an ownership concentration measure in which they cumulate the ownership stake of the three largest shareholders among the top ten publicly-traded firms worldwide. They found the mean concentration ratio to be 46 percent, leading them to conclude that "dispersed ownership in large public companies is simply a myth". They also found that even in the US, the average for the ten "most valuable" companies is 20 percent. In South Africa, where wealth is highly concentrated, Anglo-American alone controlled 60.1 percent of the listed firms on the Johannesburg Stock Exchange in 1987. In 1991, the top five shareholders controlled 84.9 percent, and in 1997, approximately 66.4 percent (Goldstein, 2000).

Some of the largest industrial concerns in developing countries are owned by families or a small clique of large shareholders acting in concert. The owners rarely sell their stakes because they are unwilling to dilute their control. If they sell, they do so mostly to other large shareholders.

The most basic information on the condition and prospects of the enterprise tends to be considered proprietary by controlling parties. As such, closely held firms seldom meet the transparency and financial disclosure requirements of public companies. Additionally, company insiders often use corporate assets for their own personal benefit. However, closely held family-controlled companies are not bad in themselves since the main shareholders have a vested interest in paying close attention to the health of the business. This type of ownership structure may be better suited for developing countries where external monitoring and regulatory capacity are weak. In fact, oversight may not be necessary if there are no outside shareholders. While agency costs may not be a problem, society should still have an interest in the governance of these enterprises and the efficient use of their assets, because when they fail, society ultimately bears social and reputational costs. In addition, society can also bear direct financial costs if failed firms obtained their financing through the banking system.

Examples of firms having easy access to bank loans as a result of close relationships abound. This tends to lead to over-investment in non-productive assets that do not meet benchmark rates of return. Reducing controlling ownership of banks by commercial entities and restricting bank lending to related parties are some of the ways to minimize this problem. Improved banking supervision and strict adherence to prudential regulation will force banks and other financial institutions to lend on the basis of credit analysis and exposure limits rather than by means of their relationships.

Source: Melvin Ayogu (2000).

primarily through greater transparency, compliance mechanisms, and monitoring by regulatory and self-regulatory bodies. Key among the institutions and instruments are the legal framework for competition policy, the legal machinery for enforcing shareholders' rights, systems for accounting and auditing, a well-regulated financial system, the bankruptcy system, and the market for corporate control.

The need to improve corporate governance standards has highlighted the importance of transparency, and proper accounting and reporting. In today's global economy, this will require the adoption of international accounting and auditing stan-

---

Box 4.14: Good Governance in the Private Sector: The Case of Ecobank

Banks have a role to play in promoting good corporate governance and ethics in the private sector. As financiers of the private sector, banks should not only be motivated by profit but should also seek to make a difference.

Barely three years ago, Ecobank, established as a tool for the integration of West Africa through the private sector, was at the brink of extinction. Its capital had to be written down by 50 percent, its shareholders had received no dividend, its subsidiaries were drifting apart. The parent company was not functioning.

Ecobank's shareholders demanded reforms. A new board was elected and a new management identified. Over the past three years, a code of ethics and good governance to govern the conduct of its operations was put in place by benchmarking, reviewing and adapting existing international standards and practice. Training sessions were organized at each subsidiary to reinforce these policies. Compliance units to monitor and review the bank's governance and compliance have been established.

The key reform measures taken include:

(i) separating the role of chairman from that of chief executive to reduce the risk of concentrating too much power in one person;
(ii) introducing a "code of conduct for directors" and "rules of procedures" to reduce the risk

of loans to director-controlled entities and the perpetuation of directorships. The code enjoins directors to avoid conflict of interest situations, such as soliciting contracts from group companies.
(iii) introducing a code of business ethics and an anti-money-laundering policy. Management and staff are required to sign and abide by these policies, which include a requirement that no bank personnel may give or receive a bribe.

Over the three years that the new policies have been in place, Ecobank has increased: employment in the group from 450 to 1,287 persons; the number of branches from 16 to 40; the number of countries with an Ecobank presence from five to 11; profits from $14.9 million to $18.2 million (1999 budgeted figures); the balance sheet from $516 million to $833 million (1999 budgeted figures); the share capital from $16 million to $51 million. The share price rose from about $0.50 to $2.60. The bank has been able to attract reputable international investors such as the IFC, Kingdom Holdings and WAGF. There has also been a significant improvement in the bank's relationships with its shareholders, the regulatory and government authorities, its customers and the general public.

Source: Gervais Djondo (1999).

---

dards. Compliance with standards on consolidation of accounts, for example, gives a much clearer picture of a corporation's financial state by shedding light on intragroup transactions, balances, investments, and unrealized profits. Group accounts are particularly important for conglomerates with substantial cross-shareholdings. The best

disclosure policies will be ineffective unless the corporate sector adopts clear international standards. Nonetheless, adopting standards will have to be accompanied with rigorous enforcement. Corporate governance should enable firms to act like responsible citizens, to act within the law, to be ethical, and to be socially-conscious. In the interconnected world of today, corporations do not wish to be seen as irresponsible or non-responsive to the needs of communities and environmental concerns in areas where they operate.

The ownership structure of private operators also had an important bearing on the issue of responsible corporate citizenship. For instance, closely held family-controlled companies, which characterize private ownership in many African countries are, arguably, more inclined to behave as politically-correct citizens (see Box 4.15). Oversight may not be necessary where there are no outside shareholders in family-controlled companies, but regulations governing private sector operations are still needed. Private sector operations in an open economy are not confined to endogenously-owned firms and they usually involve foreign firms with different ownership structures. Additionally, the society still has an interest in the governance of all private enterprises operating in the country, because when they fail, the society ultimately bears social and reputational costs.

Conclusion

In the aftermath of their weak economic performance of the 1980s and the first half of the 1990s, most African countries have now embarked on a new development path comprising a set of strategic choices that place poverty reduction at the center of the development process. These strategic choices recognize the pivotal role of the private sector in economic growth, the importance of strong public institutions to facilitate and regulate private activities, and the importance of an outward orientation and open regionalism to enable countries to compete in the new global economy. Recent improvements in the policy environment and in economic performance provide some optimism that Africa has embarked

Box 4.15: Reconciling Corporate and Societal Culture for Entrepreneurial Success

The ability to reconcile cultural and corporate leadership and create trust and harmony in companies is an important factor explaining the ability of small businesses in Africa to grow and flourish. Such attributes are important because they help the entrepreneur to play the role of a benevolent yet strict parent, establish effective communication, and offer culturally sensitive motivation all in an integrated and mutually reinforcing manner while at the same time preserving hierarchical distance. The degree to which endogenous entrepreneurs display the nurturing values on which traditional societies thrive yet do not abdicate authority or decisiveness, seems to be the recipe for equilibrium and enhanced productivity. Both owner and staff perceive the work place as an extension of the home. Also family connections are found to be an essential element of their management approach. While empirical evidence is scanty, there is good reason to believe that social capital (the cumulative legacy of all of an entrepreneur's gestures of social benevolence) translates into public loyalty and as well as goodwill from government. It is therefore a worthwhile leadership attribute to accumulate. The following two success stories may help to illustrate these points.

Kanazoe (born 1927), a Burkinabe residing in Yako outside Ouagadougou started out as a weaver with thread given to him by his mother and weaving and dyeing skills gained from his late father. He sold woven cotton fabrics in Burkina Faso and neighboring Côte d'Ivoire, Ghana and Mali using his earnings to buy other goods for trading back home and with the profits was later able to diversify. In 1948 he started a shop in Yako and in 1955 used his savings to purchase a truck to work the routes between countries. By 1957 Kanazoe had built a fleet of seven such vehicles with which he carried building materials for individuals and construction and public works companies as a subcontractor until 1973 when he started his own construction and public works company. A

Box 4.15: (Continued)

high point in Kanazoe's career came in 1976 when he competed with multinational companies for a public works contract. The Burkina Faso government through an agreement with the World Bank subcontracted to him the construction of 50 kilometers of a 187-kilometer stretch of road contracted to a consortium of four European companies. Kanazoe's company did the job within the specified time and financial limits while the main companies ran one year late and exceeding costs by about two thirds. The company has become a technical leader in the field and sets benchmarks for both quality and timeliness. Kanazoe is now a multimillionaire and has been expanding his business into neighboring Benin, Mali and Niger.

In a similar story Pokou born in 1916 near Kumasi in Ghana of a businessman started his petty trading business with a gift of $4.00 from his mother. A short stint working with a pharmacist attracted him to the retail drug industry, and he started hawking medicines from village to village. In 1941 he opened a large drug store while contact with large firms enabled him to diversify his stock to include a wide range of products. Growing revenues led to the purchase of a Bedford truck, launching Pokou in the transport business, while he also won a number of lucrative government contracts, including the delivery of mail and parcels. His fleet of vehicles continued to grow until 1952 and along the way he diversified into the sawmill sector. In 1979 he extended his operations to Abidjan where he set up a transport and trading company. He then identified Cote d'Ivoire's acute housing problem as a window of opportunity to invest in real estate. He has since contributed enormously to relieving the housing difficulties of institutions, schools and universities as well as private individuals.

Source: Mamadou Dia (1996).

on the right development path. To sustain and improve the current positive momentum, African countries still have to deepen their economic and structural reforms, particularly, in the area of economic governance. The desired improvement in economic governance needs to be reflected in effective and transparent systems for financial supervision and legal accountability, effective public administration systems, a functioning legal framework, and predictable regulatory structures.

In the area of monetary management, distressed banks need to be restored not only through privatization but also through changes in the incentive environment. If the competitive framework is not changed, privatization of public banks may simply result in ownership transfer with little impact on the process of financial intermediation. Privatization of banks needs to be pursued in a manner that avoids fraud and concentration of economic power. Central Bank independence, which prevents the use of monetary instruments for political or material gain, is important for the development of the financial system and for effective monetary policy. The creation of effective debt management units that control the process of borrowing and repayment and conducts periodic analysis of the foreign exchange productivity of borrowed funds is also important to avoid debt repayment problems and debt crises.

Fiscal management, which comprises tax administration and expenditure management, is an important policy instrument that determines as we have stressed, socio-economic outcomes. To improve tax regimes increased adherence must be made to the three principles of efficiency, fairness and administrability of tax regimes. An efficient tax system must consider the impact of the tax structure on economic outcomes, it should maintain horizontal equity and vertical equity in the distribution of the tax burden and it should be easy to enforce. An important component of the fiscal reforms is to introduce strong checks and balances to minimize corruption and tax evasion. Tax compliance could at the same time be better motivated by improvements in the state's ability to deliver basic services in the areas of education, health care and infrastructure. The promotion of local and provincial governments could be instrumental in attaining these goals—they can help monitor expenditures, generate taxes, spread information and assist with rolling investment plans in infrastructure, education and health care.

To perform the state's role more effectively, African governments need to build an efficient, open, accountable and transparent civil service capable of understanding the challenges of development, analyzing development policy proposals and designing and implementing effective policies in a changing domestic and global environment. An efficient and effective civil service requires not only cost containment and retrenchment of employment in the public sector but also incentives to attract and retain top administrative officials. A sound public sector must respond to the demands of development management of the 21st century. Also the promotion of E-Government can provide not only technology applications that will improve government performance, but also a viable means of establishing a small and highly paid civil administration.

In addition to strengthening the institutions that design and implement economic policies, African countries also need to build capacities in areas that support the functioning of political and economic governance and the activities of the private sector and civil society. The conduct and preparations of elections at the central and local levels need to be supported by promoting electoral assistance support services. Research centers that help generate information and knowledge on particular political-economy issues would need to be supported by government as well as the private sector, and civil society. Particular attention would need to be given to the institutions that promote technology development and increase the ability of local enterprises to use modern technologies efficiently.

Effective regulatory institutions are also crucial for fostering private sector participation and good corporate governance. Key among the institutions and instruments are the legal framework for competition policy, the legal machinery for enforcing shareholders' rights, systems for accounting and auditing, the bankruptcy system, and the market for corporate control. Strengthening the regulatory capacity of the state is vital to ensuring not only sound corporate governance but also the larger issue of good governance. Effective regulatory institutions for corporate governance and for private sector participation cannot be built on a foundation of discipline without appropriate incentives. A sound framework must create the platform for private competition and the conditions that foster social responsibility in the corporate sector.

CHAPTER 5
Global Dimensions of Governance

Introduction

The evolution of governance over the last four decades has derived impetus from both national and international factors. While the major underlying national factors relating to governance in Africa were considered in Chapter 4, this chapter examines the global dimensions of governance.

The trend toward democratic governance has been a global phenomenon. This century has often been described as the democratic century. According to Freedom House, the number of sovereign states increased from 55 in 1900 to 192 in 2000 while the number of democracies increased from zero to 120 respectively (Table 5.1). According to UNDP, in 1999 alone, 90 countries conducted local elections and created 1,621 jurisdictions at the intermediate level and a staggering 478,000 jurisdictions at the local government level.

Globalization is altering the world economic landscape in fundamental ways. It is driven by a widespread push towards the liberalization of trade and capital markets, increasing internationalization of corporate production and distribution strategies, and technological change, which is rapidly dismantling barriers to the international tradability of goods and services and the mobility of capital. Globalization is also observed in the power of inter-governmental institutions and in the spread of transnational corporations. In an increasingly globalized world, states are bound together by a web of multilateral and bilateral agreements that create mutually binding obligations and place governments under greater scrutiny.

Globalization has profound implications for governance, including the erosion of state sovereignty as transnational bodies increasingly mediate national concerns and press for universal laws. Another dimension is the increased globalization of political, social, economic and environmental problems. Thus good governance cannot be considered a closed system. The role of the state is to find a balance between taking advantage of globalization and providing a secure and stable social and economic domestic environment.

The global dimensions of governance considered in this chapter include: the impact of foreign aid on governance in Africa; the global trading system; global financial architecture; global responses to corruption; preventing and controlling conflicts; and information and communications technologies.

Development Aid and Governance

At the global level, governance in Africa is shaped predominantly in the context of foreign aid. Donors loom large in Africa's small, aid-dependent countries, shaping development policies and identifying, designing, implementing, and evaluating projects. Donor dominance has several implications for governance in Africa (see Box 5.1). African countries have been among the world's largest recipients of aid. Many receive net official development assistance equivalent to 10 percent of their GNP (at market exchange rates).

Table 5.1: The Democratic Century

1900	1950	2000
55 sovereign states	80 sovereign states	192 sovereign states
0 democracies	22 democracies	120 democracies
37% of world population lived in Absolute Monarchies	34% of world population lived in Totalitarian States	63% of world population lives in Democratic States

Source: Freedom House.

Aid successes in Africa include controlling river blindness, polio vaccinations, oral rehydration and family planning. Other areas where aid has made significant impact on development include building of infrastructure such as roads, communication facilities, ports, and the expansion of education and health facilities. Aid has supported institutional capacity-building efforts and played a pivotal role in the adjustment programs embarked on by African countries since the 1980s.

After four decades of political independence, African countries are more aid-dependent than ever and relatively more so than any other region. For countries such as Uganda, aid represents over 50 percent of the national budget. Yet, political support for aid is waning. The expectations in the 1980s were that official development assistance to Africa would increase as a result of peace dividends which were to accrue to developed countries following the end of the Cold War. The reality today is the opposite. Aid to Africa is on the

decline. Net transfers per capita to Africa have fallen from $32 in 1990 to $19 in 1998, a 40 percent decline in eight years, at a time when aid is becoming a major share of African countries' budgets.

Despite the decline in development aid in the last decade, substantial resources have been spent by donors on official development assistance. After more than four decades of aid, the incidence of poverty in Africa has not been significantly reduced. In some cases, poverty is actually deepening and it is expected to increase. Such factors are sometimes cited as justification for the declining aid flows and as an explanation of so-called "donor fatigue". Although the stated goal of aid is development, it is only one of numerous objectives. In the past, donors used aid to advance their values, commercial interests, political and diplomatic agenda, and cultural and national aspirations. During the Cold War, aid for the most part was used for political aims and, in

Box 5.1: The Impact of Aid Delivery Mechanisms on Governance

Aid has had a significant impact on development in Africa. Despite the success in certain areas, aid delivery mechanisms have been shown by various studies (undertaken by both donors and the recipient countries) to have some unintended negative impacts on governance. This is especially important given the fact that donors loom large in Africa and play a crucial role in determining what is done and how things are done in various aid-dependent and vulnerable African countries. Some of the implications of aid delivery mechanisms on governance are:

Weakened ownership of development policies and programs: Aid tends to come with conditions. The aid programs are rarely negotiated with broad local consultation and so are widely seen by Africans as being an external imposition. The result is a lack of ownership and commitment. Furthermore, aid programs are highly fragmented with multiple donors pursuing different priorities with different procedures. Compounding the problem is the fact that there are no efforts to coordinate different aid programs. In addition, the habit of creating special implementing units weakens the civil service as the best civil servants are siphoned away to work on aid programs as project managers. This fragmented approach to aid delivery prevents integrated management of public spending.

Less accountability to recipients: With 50 percent or more of some countries' budgets funded by donors, there is less incentive to strengthen domestic accountability and economic governance for the use of resources. With the tendency for donors to micromanage aid in some highly aid-dependent African countries, development activities are geared primarily towards satisfying their demands. Aid is not the cause of weak institutions in Africa but, in an environment where institutions are already weak, aid can make recipient governments less accountable to their people.

Capacity-building and destruction: Despite massive spending on provision of technical assistance to African countries, aid programs have probably weakened capacity in Africa. Yet, capacity-building (human and institutional) is a crucial factor in addressing many aspects of development, including governance. Technical assistance has displaced local expertise and drawn civil servants to administer aid-funded programs. This is precisely the opposite of what aid is intended to do—build capacity. With tied technical assistance, most of the benefits flow back to the donor country. The end result is less impact on recipients' economies and a negative impact on human and institutional capacity-building in some extreme situations.

Reduced sustainability and transparency: Aid and its reforms have not been well understood in Africa, partly because people are not involved in the design. As a result, recipient countries tend to have a limited understanding of what aid and its reforms are intended to achieve and how they can be achieved. This is especially so where complicated reforms or technical assistance programs have been urged on governments. In most cases, parliaments are not involved in the discussion despite sizeable budget impacts. Additionally, many donor initiatives are not integrated within national budgets and national development plans. Donors have supported capital investments without adequate attention to the need for counterpart funding and additional domestic resources to operate and maintain facilities. As such, many funded capital programs do not get the additional funding and support that is needed to ensure sustainability and effective utilization.

Excessive debt: High debt crowds out the effect of new aid because in stagnant economies rising debt service drains fiscal resources needed for development, and a large stock of debt raises questions about policy credibility and sustainability of reforms. The large volumes of unserviceable debt may pressure donors to continue to fund countries despite weak development policies and may reduce a recipient's sense of accountability for outcomes. In such an environment, the impact of new aid may not offset the negative effects of the debt stock.

Source: Adapted from ADB et al. (2000).

many cases, to shore up anti-developmental, despotic and corrupt regimes in Africa. This left a legacy of ineffective aid and huge indebtedness. As a result, criticism of the failure of aid as practised by the donors, recipients and the technical co-operation agencies became widespread. In one review, the UNDP (1993) concluded that technical assistance is not only ineffective in many aspects but it has also weakened human and institutional capacity in Africa.

Development assistance can no longer be a matter of "business as usual" and the approach to aid must change. There is appreciation on both sides (among donors and recipients alike) of the need for a revamp to make development aid more effective. Many of the factors that have undermined the effectiveness of aid can clearly be reformed. They include the multiplicity of aid processes and instruments, intrusive micro-management of aid by a host of unco-ordinated donors, support for trusted political allies even when they pursue poor policies that are inimical to development, and aid delivery that ignores the real needs of local communities. An identification of the factors undermining aid effectiveness in Africa has led to calls for robust solutions and has highlighted the need for a new partnership to make development aid effective in addressing the challenges of development in Africa (see Box 5.2).

First, there is now a consensus on the need for aid to focus on poverty reduction, with the international community's endorsement of the International Development Goals for 2015. As such, key multilateral development finance institutions including the African Development Bank Group, the World Bank and the International Monetary Fund (IMF) have found common ground, anchored on poverty reduction. In its new Vision statement, the African Development Bank

Box 5.2: Forging a New Strategic Partnership

A crucial question facing Africa and its donor partners today is how to ensure that aid fosters development. In light of the development experience of the last four decades, this question is a challenge that requires dialogue and consensus on what the purpose of aid should be, how to deliver aid and the role of the recipients and the donors. Serious rethinking is underway and consensus is emerging on two key issues: the approach and the principles that should guide development aid.

There is consensus that the new approach must:

- Clarify the purpose of aid in the post-Cold War era;
- Deconcentrate aid flows to bring delivery closer to recipients;
- Broaden aid beyond national boundaries to fund and encourage cross-border public goods; and
- Take decisive action on the lingering debt burden.

There also seems to be consensus that four key principles should underpin this approach, as follows:

- Being more selective in choosing aid recipients;
- Designing aid programs with the participation of potential beneficiaries and implementing them in partnership with other development organizations;
- Strengthening the capacity of the recipients – whether central or local governments, private enterprises or NGOs – responsible for implementing programs; and
- Restructuring aid delivery mechanisms to make recipients responsible for development – while recognizing the interest of donors that resources be used effectively.

Source: Adapted from ADB et al. (2000).

Group has decided to focus its efforts on poverty reduction. Similarly the World Bank, through its Comprehensive Development Framework (CDF), and the IMF, through the Enhanced Structural Adjustment Facility (ESAF), have restated poverty reduction as their central mission.

Secondly, there is agreement on the need for African countries and their donor partners to work together for a more effective aid regime – one that ensures that Africans take the leadership and responsibility for setting development objectives and goals, and one that deconcentrates aid delivery mechanisms. In this regard, the underlying principles for aid must take a new direction to ensure a comprehensive approach, strong local ownership, selectivity, participation and decentralization. In short, aid must be integrated into the socio-economic development processes of the recipient countries to support their changing needs. This will require donors to adjust their procedures and to allow the shared national vision and national priorities of recipient countries to guide their development assistance.

Thirdly, given the realization that rapid and sustained development in Africa requires regional co-operation and integration, there is a need to develop mechanisms for aid delivery at the regional level. Africa is a highly fragmented continent with too many small countries. Without regional co-operation, Africa will fall farther behind the rest of the world. As such, aid should support regional integration, build regional infrastructure for transportation, communication and research, and encourage policy co-ordination.

Fourthly, a comprehensive strategy will have to be developed to ensure that Africa outgrows its aid dependence. This requires a strategic partnership between Africa and its partners to use aid to raise domestic and foreign investment, build productive capacity and enhance global competitiveness. This is the only way aid will succeed in reducing poverty, by putting Africa on a path towards economic independence.

Governance of the Global Trading System

Over the last three decades, Africa has lost trade equal to about 20 percent of GDP – far more than it has received in aid (ADB et al., 2000). This loss reflects partly inappropriate policies, lack of diversification of products and markets, declining terms of trade, and protectionist policies in industrial countries.

At the bilateral level, the governance of the trading structure is such that many impediments to open market access affect African exporters in processed and temperate agricultural products and textiles and clothing. African exporters need full, tariff-free access to OECD markets for a wide range of exports, with exemptions from antidumping measures, countervailing duties, and other safeguards that create uncertainty about market access. Such arrangements can be made compatible with World Trade Organization (WTO) requirements by embedding them in a framework of reciprocity, where African countries and their industrial trading partners gradually move toward free trade arrangements, with a longer transition in Africa. This principle is included in the successor agreement to the Lomé Convention, which was concluded between the European Union (EU) and the African, Caribbean and Pacific (ACP) nations in 2000, and it also underlies the United States' Africa Growth and Opportunity Act.

At the multilateral level, the WTO has emerged as a key organ in the governance and management of the globalizing world economy. Effective participation in the WTO process can generate several beneficial outcomes. The first and, perhaps, most obvious benefit is the gain in market access. Negotiation can bring about substantial reduction in the external barriers facing a country's exports. Secondly, reciprocally bargained multilateral agreements can provide a basis for resisting undesirable protectionist measures and thus help to maintain a more rational trade regime. In this context, the WTO's program of trade policy reviews has the potential of playing a significant role in making trade policies more transparent in Africa and making more explicit the true costs and benefits of specific trade policy initiatives. The WTO offers a multilateral forum for Africa to take advantage of a rules-based system for trade and development. Africa can also use the opportunity to lock in its reforms and so increase investor confidence.

While new structures of global trading governance can increase Africa's market access and clarify its rights in the international trading framework, they also bring obligations, including giving up a degree of sovereignty over trade and investment. In particular, the establishment of the WTO as a forum for continuous negotiations on an expanding range of trade and trade-related issues is imposing new and challenging demands on African countries with respect to various dimensions of participation.

Full-fledged integration of African countries into the global trading system will require the building up of the requisite capacity to enable them to contribute to shaping and designing the rules and regulations for the management of the system. Countries will need to maintain a continuous presence at trade negotiations in Geneva and to enhance the capacity of policy-makers based in home capitals to support and guide their negotiators, and to ensure systematic preparation in advance of WTO meetings and negotiations.

There are several dimensions to participation in the WTO process. Active involvement in designing the rules of multilateral trade-related interactions constitutes one dimension of this participation. Another critically important dimension relates to the give-and-take involved in the process of multilateral trade negotiations in which countries seek favorable terms and secure access for their exports in exchange for granting similar "concessions" in their own markets to their trading partners. But after having designed the underlying trade rules and after capping the negotiations with specific agreements, a third dimension of participation comes into play. This involves effectively using the established rules and institutional mechanisms to ensure that each country's rights are enforced and its obligations met.

Several factors have limited the effectiveness of African participation in previous multilateral trade negotiations, up to and including the Uruguay Round. There is, first, a perception that the processes and mechanisms associated with these negotiations were "unbalanced" and weighted against developing and least-developed countries. The developed countries are seen to have packed the negotiating agenda with issues of interest to them and to have kept introducing new issues before the developing and least-developed countries have managed to acquire sufficient information and knowledge on the emerging "new issues" as a basis for engaging in meaningful negotiation. In addition, the decision-making mechanisms associated with these negotiations have typically been less than fully transparent; the developed and larger countries invariably settle the most crucial issues in "closed" meetings and in consultations among themselves.

Over and beyond these in-built biases of the WTO process are the inherent inadequacies of the African participants. Studies suggest that many African countries have generally been overwhelmed by the complexity of the negotiations and by the technical nature of many issues being discussed and/or negotiated. This could be attributed to the lack of technical expertise and negotiating experience on the part of many African negotiators. The lack of expertise was further aggravated by the dearth of in-depth analysis of the implications of various proposals from the perspective of specific national interests and by the absence of appropriate and timely support and guidance from the negotiators' home-based principals.

A few African countries are now more actively involved in various aspects of the WTO process. In addition, a more active African Group has emerged which has been trying to develop a set of common African negotiating positions. However, the extent to which the on-going attempts by African countries to act in a co-ordinated fashion will be fully operationalized, prove effective and yield desirable results, remains unclear

There is a need for regional co-ordination of African trade policy, particularly in the WTO process. The smallness and low income of many African countries adversely affect their ability to harness the human, material and institutional capacity required for effective participation in the WTO process on an individual basis. The larger and richer countries can generally find the resources to build such capacity, both in the public and private sector. But for the small and poorer countries,

Michalopoulos (1998) argues that it may not necessarily be an optimal use of their scarce resources to seek individual representation in the context of the WTO process. These countries should, instead establish a process of consultation with "like-minded" countries in the context of which their interests can be reflected in the WTO. Similarly, many analysts point to the growing recognition of the role of open regional economic integration in promoting multilateral liberalization and suggest that regional organizations could play an important role in enhancing African capacity to participate effectively in the WTO process. In particular, these organizations can, through the pooling of resources, provide services to their member states in a more cost-effective way than when the member states act on their own.

Global Financial Architecture

International financial market integration —fostered by the development of new financial techniques, by the globalization of investments, and by the introduction of new technologies – has accentuated the rapid flow of capital across borders while simultaneously magnifying the contagion effect of financial crises. This has had far-reaching implications for financial policies both in domestic economies and internationally. The financial crisis which originated in East and South East Asia in the late 1990s is a case in point. The widening of spreads in fixed interest markets and the decline in stock prices following the financial crisis made it difficult for emerging market issuers to tap international markets to finance current account deficits. In addition, several countries were forced to raise their interest rates to curtail capital outflows. These trends slowed the flow of direct and portfolio investment to Africa's emerging markets while reducing their ability to borrow abroad. African countries such as Egypt, Morocco, South Africa, Tunisia, and Zimbabwe were not immune from the global financial market contagion. In Morocco, Tranche 'A' loans suffered along with other hard currency debt in the emerging market universe. This occurred despite the fact that the country's economic fundamentals did not indicate the usual combination that would justify selling pressure. The country has a comfortable cushion of foreign reserves, the fiscal and current account deficits are modest, and inflation is low.

For the majority of African countries where the inflow of private capital is small and where public debt is dominant, traditional risk management policies —adopting competitive exchange rates, reducing government deficits and maintaining low inflation rates—should be their primary concern. But as the role of private capital increases—as is already the case in South Africa, Egypt, Morocco, Nigeria and Zimbabwe—economic policymakers need to learn from the Asian experience.

Adapting regulatory and supervisory frameworks to rapidly-changing financial markets will remain a daunting challenge and will require further co-operation between supervisors, markets, and individual market participants. Financial regulators will need to focus on increasing transparency and on strengthening prudential regulation and supervision in a manner that facilitates market discipline and supervision by allowing both the public and bank supervisors to better assess the risk profiles of financial institutions. It will be important to ensure that incentives exist to encourage individual countries to reform their domestic financial sector, increase prudential supervision, transparency and accountability while utilizing appropriate surveillance information to act quickly to prevent a crisis from developing.

In the meantime, there seems to be a case for African countries to weigh carefully the benefits of capital account liberalization against the costs associated with increased vulnerability to financial crisis. Here, the evidence points towards the need to encourage the flow of foreign direct investment (FDI), because its benefits clearly exceed its costs, and to restrict more volatile short-term capital because of the opposite reasoning (World Bank, 1998).

International agencies and groups such as the ADB, IMF, the World Bank, the Bank for International Settlements and the Basel Committee have supported and complemented the work of national agencies in addressing the challenges that globalization poses for the stability of financial sectors. To enhance transparency, these international agencies and groups have begun developing guidelines to consolidate financial statements and achieve greater cross-country harmonization in accounting and auditing standards and in disclosing information. They are also working to identify and close gaps in regulatory and supervisory regulations in order to avoid problems such as regulatory arbitrage—that is, taking advantage of looser regulations in particular jurisdictions. Adopting and monitoring compliance with standards are part of these efforts.

At the international level, recent phenomena such as the consolidation of institutions, globalization of operations, development of new technologies, and universalization of banking, have led to proposals for global surveillance as a method of preventing a financial crisis in one country or region from spreading contagion effects across the world economy. There is, as yet, no consensus on how the world's financial architecture should be reformed, other than perhaps broad agreement that existing institutions should be restructured to perform necessary and different tasks than in the past, rather than be replaced or supplemented by additional institutions.

Global Responses to Corruption

Corruption is a cancer which is robbing Africa and especially Africa's poor. The corrosive influence of corruption on investment, economic growth, political stability and development of market-based and democratic institutions is widely recognized. Corruption affects the realization of good governance and it festers in any environment that is characterized by bad governance. Although corruption is first and foremost a national problem, its international dimension is increasing as the world becomes more and more globalized. Bribery by foreign firms—whether to secure a procurement contract, obtain monopoly rights and privatized firms or to circumvent regulations—can play a significant role in the persistence of corruption. International responsibility for corruption in Africa is quite significant.

The fight against corruption must be a global one and there is a strong case for international co-operation in fighting corruption, on the following grounds:

- international co-operation can reinforce national efforts to combat corruption;
- countries embarking on an anti-corruption strategy can learn from the experience of other nations;
- cross-border transactions are increasing but are often difficult to monitor by national authorities acting alone;
- international transactions can provide a conducive environment for corrupt practices, especially when actors are willing to engage in dubious practices in foreign countries that would be unacceptable at home; and

- international financial transactions provide opportunities for the laundering of financial gains from corrupt practices.

Given its global nature, there is a need for an international effort to fight corruption (see Box 5.3 and 5.4). All countries participating in global commerce, especially OECD members, should enforce anti-bribery laws abroad. In addition, international institutions must also make curbing corruption a priority when providing assistance to their member countries (Gray and Kaufman, 1998). However, the fight will only succeed if there are no double standards and actions are targeted at both the demand and supply sides. As such, anti-corruption measures should apply equally to rich and poor countries, and should target all those who are directly guilty of corrupt behavior, as well as those who facilitate corruption (e.g. by providing money laundering opportunities). Those who offer or accept bribes should be penalized equally, as should those institutions that knowingly facilitate embezzlement.

Corruption is bad for governance and development, especially in Africa. It distorts decisions and contributes to the sluggishness of Africa's economic performance. African countries must combine their efforts at the regional level and also join the international community to develop an international consensus on anti-corruption norms. These norms may include:

- Promoting a global response and regional approaches to address corruption;
- Establishing open and accountable economic governance practices, including vigorous enforcement of anti-bribery laws and transparent economic decision-making;
- Promoting openness and accountability in the private sector;

Box 5.3: Selected Global Initiatives on Corruption

Corruption is recognized worldwide as a major problem in society, one capable of endangering the stability and security of societies, undermining the values of democracy and morality, threatening social, economic and political development. The global dimension of corruption has gained in significance with the growing globalization of markets of services, goods and people, accompanied by the internationalization of illegal activities. Selected global initiatives against corruption are outlined below:

United Nations: Concerned about the seriousness of the problems posed by bribery in international transactions, the UN General Assembly adopted in 1996 a Declaration against Corruption and Bribery in International Commercial Transactions, which called for criminalizing foreign bribery and denying tax deductibility of bribes. In 1998, the General Assembly adopted a resolution that urges Member States to criminalize, in an effective and co-ordinated manner, the bribery of public office holders of other states in international commercial transactions, and encourages them to engage in programmatic activities to deter, prevent and combat bribery and corruption.

United Nations Centre for International Crime Prevention: The UN Centre for International Crime Prevention (CICP), the Office for Drug Control and Crime Prevention (ODCCP), Vienna, jointly with the United Nations Interregional Crime and Justice Research Institute (UNICRI), Rome, have elaborated a Global Program against Corruption. The purpose of this program is to provide reliable and timely information on trends in corruption as well as on policy strategies to reduce and control corruption and provide technical co-operation to developing countries and countries in transition, to prevent, detect, and fight corruption.

European Union: The European Commission adopted in May 1997 a Communication to the Council and the European Parliament on a Union Policy Against Corruption. This communication sets out the EC's comprehensive policy on cor-

ruption inside the European Union as well as in its relations with non-member countries. The communication deals with a number of actions, including the ratification of conventions criminalising the active and passive corruption of EC officials and officials of member countries, eliminating the tax deductibility of bribes, reforming public procurement and auditing systems. For non-member countries, the European Union's policy aims at establishing anti-corruption programs with countries that have concluded co-operation or assistance agreements with the EC.

International Chamber of Commerce: The International Chamber of Commerce (ICC) has been participating in the national and international efforts to curb corruption for several years. In 1996 the ICC issued revised Rules of Conduct to Combat Extortion and Bribery in International Business Transactions. To promote the rules – which are not binding on ICC members, but companies may endorse them voluntarily – the ICC has set up a standing committee on extortion and bribery and several sub-committees dealing with issues of interest to the private sector such as "private to private" bribery.

Trade Union Advisory Committee: Worldwide, workers and their trade unions have a major stake in the fight against corruption. With few exceptions those countries and companies that engage in corrupt practices also violate basic workers' and trade union rights. Contracts won through corrupt practices often result in the loss of jobs at companies with good employment practices. In addition, bribery and corruption undermine democracy itself. Corruption is a global problem requiring a global solution, involving partnerships between governments and the social partners. This partnership approach extends to the international trade union movement. The Trade Union Advisory Committee to the OECD (TUAC) and the International Confederation of Free Trade Unions (ICFTU), working closely together, have a trade union network of unions from 143 developed and developing countries and territories.

Box 5.3: (continued)

Transparency International: Non-governmental organizations (NGOs) around the world are participating in the efforts of national governments and international organizations to combat and curb corruption. Civil society programs include increased citizen participation and civic monitoring. Among the international NGOs, Transparency International (TI), based in Berlin, Germany, aims to fight corruption and bribery in international business transactions through international and national coalitions encouraging governments to establish and implement effective laws, policies and anti-corruption programs; building public support for anti-corruption programs; and developing "islands of integrity". TI has more than 70 national chapters at the national level and is co-operating with international organizations, including the OECD.

Source: OECD Anti-Corruption Unit.

- Strengthening institutions that ensure public and private accountability, including strong and impartial judiciaries as well as a free press;
- Safeguarding integrity among justice, security and financial regulatory officials;
- Encouraging the setting of global standards in key areas; and
- Promoting equal treatment of those that give and receive bribes.

The current OECD convention on Combating Bribery of Foreign Public Officials in International Business Transactions should be ratified and fully implemented. The convention is a good start,

but it should be extended to all countries participating in international trade and should include bribery of all other officials not currently covered. The global convention on corruption should be extended to take into account African interests. For example, the convention should be strengthened to address those who offer bribes and the institutions who assist corrupt leaders to launder and keep illegally-obtained wealth in foreign banks. In addition, OECD countries must stop offering tax deductions on bribes.

Global NGOs such as Transparency International should also get involved in publicizing corrupt practices of government officials and corporations. As part of the global efforts to fight corruption, the international community should support activities by NGOs to report corrupt practices. The current corruption index published by Transparency International should be supported and enhanced to include bribery in the private sector. Other indexes on those that give bribes should also be developed. A global information act should be enacted to ensure that banks are obliged to release information on the financial dealings of public officials involved in corruption cases.

Preventing and Controlling Conflict

Since 1960, about 20 African countries have experienced at least one period of civil strife, excluding wars of independence. The reasons for violent conflict in Africa are varied but the contributory factors often include low incomes and a lack of democratic rights. Systematic analysis suggests that Africa's civil wars conform to a global pattern and can be explained by political and economic factors as well as by ethnic, cultural and religious diversity. Ethnic diversity may play a role

Box 5.4: Prevention of Money-Laundering in Global Banking System

Banks and other financial institutions may be used as intermediaries for the transfer or deposit of funds derived from criminal activity. Money-launders use the global financial system to make payments and transfers of funds from one account to another; to hide the source and beneficial ownership of money; and to provide storage for bank-notes through a safe-deposit facility. In particular, offshore banks have played prominent roles in capital flight from Africa. For example, The Swiss Federal Banking Commission (SFBC) has found that six Swiss banks did not fulfill their business obligations in the case of the offshore accounts of the Nigerian ex-President, suspected to run into almost $4 billion. The investigation by SFBC was requested for by the Nigerian Government.

The Basle Committee on Banking and Regulations and Supervisory Practices consider that banking supervisors have a general role to encourage ethical standards of professional conduct among banks and other financial institutions. The Committee believes that one way to promote this objective, consistent with differences in national supervisory practice, is to obtain international agreement to a Statement of Principles to which financial institutions should be expected to adhere. This Statement of Principles is intended to outline some basic policies and procedures that banks' managements should ensure are in place within their institutions with a view to assisting in the suppression of money-laundering through the banking system, national and international. The Statement thus sets out to reinforce existing best practices among banks and, specifically, to encourage vigilance against criminal use of the payments system, implementation by banks of effective preventive safeguards, and cooperation with law enforcement agencies.

The Statement consists of ethical principles which encourage banks' management to put in place effective procedures to ensure that all persons conducting business with their institutions are properly identified; that transactions that do not appear legitimate are discouraged; and that cooperation with law enforcement agencies is achieved. The Statement is not a legal document and its implementation will depend on national practice and law. In particular, it should be noted that in some countries banks may be subject to additional more stringent legal regulations in this field and the Statement is not intended to replace or diminish those requirements. Whatever the legal position in different countries, the Committee considers that the first and most important safeguard against money-laundering is the integrity of banks' own managements and their vigilant determination to prevent their institutions becoming associated with criminals or being used as a channel for money-laundering. The Statement is intended to reinforce those standards of conduct.

Also in response to mounting concern over money laundering, the Financial Action Task Force on Money Laundering (FATF) was established by the G-7 Summit that was held in Paris in 1989. Recognizing the threat posed to the banking system and to financial institutions, the G-7 Heads of State or Government and President of the European Commission convened the Task Force from the G-7 member States, the European Commission, and eight other countries.

The Task Force was given the responsibility of examining money laundering techniques and trends, reviewing the action which had already been taken at a national or international level, and setting out the measures that still needed to be taken to combat money laundering. In April 1990, less than one year after its creation, the FATF issued a report containing a set of Forty Recommendations, which provide a comprehensive blueprint of the action needed to fight against money laundering. The Forty Recommendations set out the framework for anti-money laundering efforts and are designed for universal application. They provide a complete set of counter-measures against money laundering covering the criminal justice system and law enforcement, the financial system and its regulation, and international co-operation.

The Eastern and Southern Africa Anti-Money Laundering Group, an FATF-style body for fourteen countries of the region, was launched at a meeting of Ministers and high-level representatives in Arusha, Tanzania, on 26-27 August 1999. A Memorandum of Understanding (MoU), based on the experience of the FATF was agreed at the meeting.

Sources: Basle Committee on Banking and Regulation; OECD Financial Action Task Force on Money Laundering.

but is not —as is commonly believed—the main reason for civil conflicts in Africa. In fact, allowing for other factors, Africa's ethnic diversity is a deterrent rather than a cause of civil war (ADB et al., 2000). The crucial issues are poverty, lack of education and political repression.

Armed conflicts in Africa have been destructive not only in terms of human cost but also in the loss of development opportunities. A key casualty is trust between warring factions, as conflict polarizes society. Civil conflict imposes severe economic and social costs. It leads to substantial destruction of economic and social capital and a decline in the economy. In many cases conflict has hampered development for decades.

By weakening national institutions, wars effectively reduce the capacity of the state to govern. In all cases, governments become preoccupied with fighting for survival rather than with development. The damaging impacts of war are felt beyond the borders of the country where it occurs. Neighboring countries are especially affected by the destruction of the environment caused by movements of large numbers of people and refugee problems. The economic costs are enormous as foreign investors tend to avoid conflict-ridden regions. War-ravaged countries and their neighbors also suffer increased insecurity, violence and crime.

Once conflict begins, it takes on a life of its own so that resolving it becomes a complex challenge. Conflict resolution, peacebuilding and reconstruction require committed assistance from neighboring countries and the international community. The United Nations used to be the primary institution in peacekeeping and peacebuilding but lately the Organization of African Unity, the Economic Community of West African States (ECOWAS) and the Southern African Development Community (SADC) have taken up responsibilities for dealing with conflicts in Africa.

Collaboration between the international development community and regional and sub-regional organizations in Africa is vital, not only to establish peace but also in rebuilding efforts. This requires strategies and approaches on how to address the special problems of post-conflict countries. Reconstruction requires a comprehensive approach, an ongoing dialogue between the stakeholders, shared goals and objectives to guide assistance, considerable resources, and a long-term commitment.

If at all possible, the prevention of civil conflicts should be the preferred option. Early warning mechanisms should be developed to alert the international community to impending crises. This should be augmented by rapid and effective action to follow up early warnings.

Most importantly the international community needs to support African countries to build their economies and to ensure good governance. Better political rights, higher standards of living, more diversified economies and sustained high economic growth are the best forms of prevention of conflict. Achieving these goals should be the priority for African countries and the international community (Box 5.5).

Global Information Technologies

The information and knowledge age is upon us due to rapid advances in information and communication technologies (ICTs). These new technologies are changing the way we live and work, and they are transforming many aspects of social and economic organization in ways we could have hardly imagined less than two decades ago. ICTs offer developing countries formidable and cost-

Box 5.5: A Strategy for Post-Conflict Countries

Societal conflict in Africa has its roots in a wide range of historical legacies, recent geopolitical developments and economic motives. These factors have combined to create a climate of enduring poverty, corruption and bad governance in most African countries. This has made it possible for factions and individuals to stake exclusive claim to the returns from the countries' natural resources. Conflict usually erupts when this perceived exclusivity is challenged. Pervasive poverty contributes to the enduring and entrenched nature of these conflicts, as the large pool of unemployed and disaffected youth see conflicts as an alternative source of livelihood.

The complexities of conflict in Africa – coupled with the mutually reinforcing nature of conflict, poverty and bad governance – demand a co-ordinated and multifaceted response that involves the pugilists, respective governments, regional organizations and the international community. It is for this reason that the Bank Group is collaborating with bilateral and multilateral organizations to develop a framework of assistance that entails the development of a mechanism for a more effective and targeted response. This approach should establish a sustainable constituency for socio-economic reform in post-conflict countries.

Poverty in Africa has been exacerbated by widespread societal conflicts in parts of the continent, which has resulted in massive displacements of people. At national level, human capital development has been seriously hampered as over 2 million lives have been lost in the last decade and well over 12 million people (40 percent of the world total) have been displaced. Furthermore, the severe disruptions to economic activity have stifled growth, heightened fiscal pressures, and occasioned an accumulation of arrears. At the international level, conflicts have prompted a shift in the composition of official flows, from long-term development finance to short-term emergency relief operations – which at present account for as much as 12 percent of total development assistance.

If any lasting impact is to be made on poverty in Africa, stakeholders in Africa's development process must address the problem of securing

and sustaining durable peace expeditiously. Particular attention must be paid to the reconstruction of infrastructure and resumption of basic social services, as well as the provision of adequate incentives for all parties to have a stake in maintaining the peace. In this regard, Bank Group operations will continue to emphasize sustainable and equitable growth and good governance. These priorities are encapsulated in the Bank Group's Vision Statement as well as in its policy and operational guidelines for the promotion of good governance.

Providing Concessional Resources

Multilateral development banks (MDBs), like the Bank Group, are traditionally precluded from providing assistance to post-conflict countries, primarily on account of their high level of arrears. This has made it impossible for these countries, some of which are fledging democracies, to avail themselves of either concessional resources or technical assistance grants. Consequently, countries in dire need of concessional resources for budgetary support, reconstruction and the restoration of basic social services, have not been able to benefit from such assistance.

Cognizant of this fact, the Bank Group is working with other international institutions to develop a new framework for providing assistance to post-conflict countries, which aims to regularize the relationship between these countries and the international community. This general assistance framework will be applied on a case-by-case basis to provide: (a) rapid mobilization of resources in co-ordinated support from all donors; (b) substantial short-term debt relief during the crucial reconstruction phases; and (c) access to HIPC assistance if longer-term debt relief is required. The new framework is based on a three-phased approach: namely (i) the pre-arrears clearance stage, (ii) the arrears clearance stage, and (iii) the HIPC follow-up stage.

During the first stage, all MDBs will work with the government, in a co-ordinated fashion, to develop a strategy to regularize the country's arrears

---

Box 5.5: (continued)

position and chart a course for reconstruction and the resumption of economic growth. Once agreement is reached in principle, arrangements for an arrears clearance plan will be finalized. This should allow a temporary deferment of debt service payments, as well as the disbursement of emergency financial support for reconstruction. In addition, post-conflict countries will be in a position to benefit from policy and technical support from MDBs. In the second stage, the country would adopt a monitorable economic recovery program and operationalize its clearance plan. Particular emphasis will be placed on structural and institutional reforms. Progress made during this period will qualify as part of the HIPC eligibility track record. After a track record is established, a debt sustainability analysis will be used to determine eligibility for HIPC assistance. At this stage – the HIPC follow-up stage – efforts will be expended to secure most-favorable terms on the country's external debt from bilateral and multilateral creditors.

It is anticipated that this framework will provide much-needed assistance to Africa's growing number of post-conflict countries, while also providing a positive incentive to countries currently experiencing societal conflict. Furthermore, as the assistance is linked to country performance, the framework emphasizes demonstrable commitment to reform and minimizes moral hazard problems. It also ensures co-ordinated and equitable participation of all donors, thereby preserving their financial integrity and preferred creditor status.

effective tools for accelerated development. Not only do ICTs facilitate information exchange, they are deepening the process, creating new modes of sharing ideas, and reducing the costs of collecting and analyzing information. ICTs present an opportunity for accelerated development and offer a serious chance for developing countries to catch up with the rest of the world.

ICTs as Tools for Good Governance

As Hans d'Orville (2000) pointed out, ICTs if properly used can reduce poverty, empower people, build capacities, skills and networks, inspire new governance mechanisms and reinforce popular participation at all levels. The range of applications covers electronic commerce, the empowerment of communities, the promotion of good governance and decentralization, the observance of human rights, long-distance education, telehealth and environmental monitoring. The opportunities to apply ICTs for development purposes are almost limitless.

Throughout the world, there are efforts at various levels to bring ICTs to bear in the way society is governed and managed. It is expected that after the e-commerce revolution the next is e-government, where there are opportunities to improve the quality of service, increase effectiveness and reduce costs. The key benefits come from the way in which ICTs can reduce purchasing and fulfillment cycles and reduce administrative costs. Some of the big multinationals that have embraced e-commerce intensely by putting their supply chains online are saving upwards of 20 percent, reducing inventories by about 50 percent and in some cases lowering their administrative costs by up to 75 percent (The Economist, 2000).

ICTs are potentially capable of transforming the way in which most public services are delivered and also the relationship between government and the citizen. Richard Heeks (1999) identified three basic change potentials for ICTs within the context of governance:

Support: ICTs can be used to facilitate existing tasks and processes;

Supplant: ICTs are particularly useful for automating repetitive and tedious tasks, especially when it comes to storing, processing and transmitting information; and

Innovate: ICTs can be used effectively to undertake new tasks and processes that did not exist before.

In the African context, governments can deploy ICTs to meet developmental challenges and facilitate good governance. Governance is a highly information-intensive and expensive activity, and ICTs offer an efficient way of cutting costs associated with generating and disseminating this information (Mansell and Wehn, 1999). ICTs can be used to enhance the democratic process, ensure effective participation and bring government closer to the people.

A key characteristic of well-functioning states all over the world is democracy. Strong elements of democracy are people's participation in governance through regular elections and a vibrant civil society (see Box 5.6). If the new efforts at re-democratization in Africa are to lead to genuine democracy there is a need to create a democratic culture, a culture that is receptive to political competition through popular participation not just in elections but also in decision making. In a democratic culture, the spirit of open and public dialogue is critical.

Box 5.6: Enhancing Women's Participation in Governance

Kenya: Kenya's Family Support Institute (FASI), a non-governmental organization, is currently implementing a women and governance project. FASI has established two community resource centers equipped with ICTs in the Eastern and Western provinces.

The project aims to strengthen the participation of women in the democratic process and governance in Kenya. More specifically, FASI aims through the project to inform Kenyans, especially women, of critical issues, to enhance women's interaction, to enable women to make informed decisions and participate effectively in the electoral process. The project will use ICTs to facilitate co-operation among women, gain peer support, campaign effectively, and further the interests of women.

At the community resource centers women are provided civic education, trained, and consultative meetings are organized. The results are increased women participation in the political process by attending political meetings and actually voting. Significantly, more women voted in 1997 elections compared to 1992 and more women are presenting their candidacy in elections both at the civic and parliamentary levels.

Uganda: In Uganda – a no-party democratic state in which women's participation in politics is encouraged through the establishment of quotas – a non-governmental organization has been set-up to enhance the capacity of women parliamentarians. The Forum for Women in Democracy (FOWODE) accesses critical and relevant information on the Internet for women parliamentarians, information which makes a difference to their contributions in parliament. FOWODE has trained most members in basic computer skills. In addition, FOWODE program officers use the Internet to gather information on important issues for parliamentarians. The program officers serve as information brokers and undertake research on issues at the request of parliamentarians.

Source: Adapted from: Khasiani (1999); Opoku-Mensah (1999).

Democratic governance requires an open government and easy access by citizens to the government. In Africa, especially, poor infrastructure networks exacerbate the difficulties of communications between citizens and government. For almost 70 percent of the African population in rural areas, access to government is like accessing the distant galaxies. ICTs, especially the Internet and Web, can be used to develop a democratic culture in Africa through revitalizing open and public debate, establishing open government, enhancing interactions between the "governors" and those being "governed", promoting equity, and strengthening the capacity of public officials.

As Joe Coates (1994) and Sam Pitroda (1993) have pointed out, ICTs are among the most potent democratizing tools that can be used to enhance participation in the democratic process. ICTs can be used to open the government to the public and can also provide the citizens with an ability to enhance their interaction with each other and with the government. Parliaments and government agencies can provide information on programs and pending legislation online. Citizens can be invited to send in comments and their views to government officials or parliamentarians. By so doing, their views can be taken into account before laws are passed and policies made. This can have the effect of making government more transparent, accessible, accountable to its constituents and can reduce public cynicism about the political process.

In addition to expanding the democratic space, ICTs are powerful tools that can be used to facilitate macroeconomic and public sector management. Efforts to stabilize the macroeconomic environment, and strengthen the efficiency, accountability, and transparency of government can benefit a great deal from the introduction of information technology applications (Oshikoya and Hussain, 1998). Information systems which can help government design, implement, and assess policy reforms are now powerful instruments of public policy. Such information systems could increase the speed, volume, quality, transparency, and accountability of government transactions, yielding large productivity increases in government services (see Box 5.7).

Africa is a predominantly agrarian society with the majority of the population dependent on subsistence agriculture. If productivity in this sector and access to information can be increased, significant progress can be made in the continent's war against poverty. In addition, wise use of environmental resources will facilitate sustainability. ICTs hold considerable promise in both of these areas. The application of ICTs in agriculture and environmental management include multimedia public information kiosks, air and water quality monitoring, warning systems, market information, harvest management and disease monitoring. ICTs can be used to capture and share information on advances in agricultural research and new techniques. ICTs can also facilitate agricultural extension. In the agricultural sector, ICT applications are being promoted to facilitate wide access to information and intensive sharing of knowledge.

ICTs can also be used to build the capacities of farmers through distance education and lifelong learning programs. Access to information and training will allow farmers to learn new techniques in order to raise their productivity. In addition, geographic information systems (GIS) can combine information on soils, hydro-geology and rainfall with socio-economic data, allowing for early warning. An example of this is the US Agency for International Development (USAID) funded project (Image Display and Analysis) which uses

Box 5.7: Egypt: Providing Information Decision Support

To improve its decision-making process, the Government of Egypt created the Information Decision Support Center (IDSC) in the 1980s. The center was created to provide advisory services to the cabinet of Egypt. To show the importance of IDSC, the director was given cabinet rank. With the support of the government, IDSC was able to place its own staff in all government ministries and all the 27 governorates of Egypt. A key role of these IDSC employees is to collect information.

One of the first tasks embarked upon by IDSC was to build and implement a debt management system for the Egyptian government. At the time, Egypt's external debt stood at about US$33 billion, covering about 5,000 loans. The debt management system developed by IDSC helped the government in the rationalization of debt utilization and was used to facilitate debt rescheduling and reduction. The debt management system made a major impact and led to the debt rescheduling with over 14 countries. The system is now used to manage Egypt's external debts and has allowed loans to be looked at as part of a comprehensive, integrated and dynamic portfolio.

Since its success with the debt management system, IDSC has started many other projects, including TradeNet, a trade information system.

Source: Adapted from: Sherif Kamel (1998).

data from satellites to forecast crop yields and provide early warning on food security. Other projects in which ICTs are being used to facilitate sustainability and food security in Africa include the UNDP's Sustainable Development Networking Project (SDNP), the Ghana Agricultural Information Network System (GAINS), Business Intelligent Trade Point in Burkina Faso, and UNEPnet of the United Nations Environmental Program.

ICTs provide African countries with new opportunities and tools to strengthen democratic governance, empower the people and increase government's effectiveness and efficiencies in service delivery and public sector management. The challenge which must be addressed is the "digital divide" between and within nations. Compared to other continents, Africa today is at the bottom of the ladder in the information society. Within African countries, there is major divide between the "information-rich" and the "information-poor". Only a very few can afford ICTs, there is a widespread lack of education and the necessary infrastructure—especially telephones and electricity —is often unavailable.

First, in order for people to take advantage of the opportunities created by ICTs, alternative solutions have to be sought by governments to provide access through community centers. Secondly, governments will need to employ ICTs in service delivery, management and decision-making processes. Thirdly, infrastructure issues need to be addressed from a regional perspective. African countries can join together to build their telecommunications infrastructure and build the necessary capacity to take advantage of ICTs. Lastly, the international community, especially the multilateral finance institutions such as the Bank Group, can play several important roles in supporting

African countries to employ ICTs for improved governance and socio-economic development. These roles might include providing finance to build insfrastructure, funding innovative programs to democratize access to ICTs, developing and implementing capacity building programs, supporting countries to develop ICT strategies and policies, and funding innovative experiments in the use of ICTs to improve governance and sharing of experiences.

Conclusion

In this chapter, the implications of the global dimension of governance for African countries and what can be done at the international level to address the challenges of governance have been reviewed. The chapter specifically explores key areas such as development aid, the global trading system, global financial architecture, international responses to corruption, conflict prevention and the potential uses of ICTs for improved governance by African countries. The review indicates that we live in a new world, a world that is more global and interconnected and one that poses some challenges for governance and development in Africa. Critical among the challenges uncovered is the lack of expertise and institutional capacity to participate effectively in the globalization process.

To improve governance in Africa and to mitigate against the threats posed by globalization while capturing the opportunities, African countries will need to develop effective institutions and technical expertise to participate actively in the process of globalization. For example, the realm of influence and power of the nation state is declining while that of multinational firms is increasing. Moreover, the system of global standards that is evolving in many areas is also limiting the purview of nation states. Declining national sovereignty is coupled with a demand for enhanced state capacity to participate in setting and implementing global standards. This is a major problem for African countries, especially with regards to trade. The new rules-based trading system under the WTO is a major challenge for African countries, as most African countries do not have representation at trade negotiations and discussions. Yet, African countries must abide by the rules and standards. Many countries are not adequately represented and their negotiators may not have the required expertise or the government support that is necessary.

The global challenges of making aid more effective, building capacity to participate effectively in the globalization process and adopting new technologies are some of the areas where the role of international finance institutions such as the World Bank, IMF and the Bank Group will be crucial. International finance institutions in collaboration with bilateral donors can work with African countries to ensure that Africa benefits from the new global order to improve governance and facilitate development. The next chapter focuses on these issues from the perspective of what the Bank Group can do to foster good governance in Africa.

CHAPTER 6

Bank Group Policy on Governance

Introduction

The mandate of the Bank is to contribute to the economic development and social progress of its regional member countries (RMCs). In this context, the Bank's development priorities are the acceleration of economic growth and the reduction of poverty in RMCs. In furtherance of these intertwined objectives, the Bank engages in lending operations, provision of technical assistance, policy dialogue and exchange of best practices. These activities are designed to increase productive capacity, to enhance efficiency in national economic management, and to promote the development of the private sector.

The Bank's operations also aim to address critical cross-sectoral issues, particularly those relating to: gender mainstreaming; population; regional cooperation and economic integration; participation and environmental management. The Bank is well aware that for these activities to thrive, it is necessary to adhere to the axioms of good governance within the development agency itself particularly as it relates to the recipient countries. It is for this reason that the Bank has embarked since 1995 on an evolving process of internal reform with the aim of maximizing its development effectiveness (see Box 6.1). The Bank has also sharpened its focus on issues pertaining to good governance in RMCs. Figure 6.1 outlines issues of governance that are of concern to the Bank. These include:

- Ensuring accountability of public agencies and officials through formal transparent processes for monitoring and reporting;

- Fostering transparency at all levels of government and public administration, including budgetary transparency;
- Combating corruption;
- Fostering greater participation, and freedom of speech and association, to enable the beneficiaries of government programs to participate effectively in determining and meeting their needs;
- Nurturing an objective and efficient judiciary; and,
- Enhancing efficiency within public and private institutions by building technical and management capacities.

Operationalizing Good Governance in Bank Group Activities

In operationalizing its agenda for good governance, the Bank will be guided by the following:

- The country's institutional capacity, social and political situation. The objective in each case is to help in the development of an enabling environment, taking on board all the necessary economic and non-economic factors;

- The need to take into consideration the effects of bad governance on development performance;

- The ownership of development programs and policies by RMCs; and

Box 6.1: The Bank Group: Internal Governance and Institutional Reforms

By mid-1995, the Bank Group was experiencing serious issues of governance pertaining to relations among major shareholders as well as to the internal management of the institution. The governance crisis put into doubt the ability of the institution to continue to meet its development mission. In September 1995, the governing bodies of the Bank mandated a new management to institute a wide-ranging reform program.

The reform program had four main goals: first, to improve the quality of Bank operations; second, to strengthen its financial management; third, to overhaul the organizational and management structure of the Bank and to enhance its efficiency; and fourth, to improve its institutional governance.

Enhancing Operational Effectiveness: In respect to operations, the reform measures have focused on improving project quality and the development effectiveness of the Bank's lending program. Sector policies that guide Bank operations have been updated and new policies have been formulated. An important milestone in this regard was the adoption of the Bank's Vision statement in 1999. The Vision identifies priority areas for the Bank's interventions in regional member countries. The Bank Group has enhanced its Country Strategy Papers, which are now its main programming tool for lending and technical assistance. These are prepared in a participatory manner involving borrowing countries, our development partners, and other major stakeholders. For ongoing projects, the consolidated Annual Portfolio Performance Review process has enhanced the quality of the Bank's loan portfolio by reducing the proportion of problem-projects. As part of a medium-term plan to gradually strengthen its presence in regional member countries, the Bank opened six country offices in 2000. This will enable the Bank Group to monitor more closely its portfolio and to coordinate better its operations with clients and other development partners.

Strengthening Financial Management: The Bank has implemented a comprehensive financial reform program aimed at strengthening its policies relating to loan recovery, balance sheet risk management, borrowing, and liquidity management and to ensure that the risks inherent in the Bank's activities are adequately covered. In line with best practices, the Bank has established an Asset Liability Management Committee to provide oversight for the implementation of its financial activities. As part of its financial reform program, the Bank has also introduced new financial products that more adequately respond to client needs as well as improve their debt-servicing capacity. The Bank is, for example, among the first multilateral financial institutions to introduce Rand-denominated loans for its borrowers in Southern Africa.

Enhancing the Bank's Organizational and Management System: Following the major re-organization of the Bank in early 1996, the Bank's human resource management system has been rationalized through a series of measures including the introduction of new staff performance evaluation and job classification systems, and an improved staff remuneration and benefits package, revision of the staff rules and regulations, and strengthening the staff appeals process, and a comprehensive staff training program, including a Management Development Program. The Bank has also put in place an Information Technology and Telecommunications Modernization Program. This aims at improving and strengthening the quality and efficiency of Bank Group operations, as well as facilitating the adaptation of the Bank to its changing business environment.

Resource Mobilization and Institutional Governance: The final area of reform that the Bank has been engaged in during the last five years has involved strengthening its fundamental governance structures. These reforms have had as their goal enhancing the Bank's operational effi-

Box 6.1: (continued)

ciency, strengthening its financial standing, and preserving the rights and interests of its member states. Accordingly, in May 1998, the Board of Governors authorized a fifth general capital increase of 35 percent, and a restructuring of the Bank's capital base. It also approved the establishment of the Governors' Consultative Committee (GCC).

The reforms in all these four areas have been substantially completed and are beginning to yield fruits. One immediate outcome of the enhancement of the operational effectiveness is that our lending operations have doubled over the last five years and have averaged US$1.7 billion in the last two years. The Bank's high financial credit rating, which ensures that we are able to minimize the cost of funds to clients, is backed by prudent financial policies, membership support and a solid capital structure. As a consequence, the Bank Group has now regained its place among the MDBs, and stands as the premier development finance institution for the continent. It has also made great strides to fulfil its mission of mobilizing resources from its development partners, and to contributing to Africa's social and economic development. The continued success of the Bank Group in the coming years will depend on continued support from its governing bodies and on building stronger partnerships with its regional members and development partners.

Source: Omar Kabbaj (2000).

- The concern for effective partnership among government, private sector, civil society and the international development community in the implementation of governance initiatives/activities.

The Bank Policy Paper on Governance, from which this Chapter draws, acknowledges the complexity of the governance concept and the interrelated nature of its different components. Against this background, the Bank also recognizes the need for a more differentiated approach between countries. Therefore, the Bank's interventions in the area of governance will be chosen selectively from the range of activities summarized in Figure 6.2, taking into account the interrelations between the different axioms of good governance, country circumstances, the state of dialogue with the country and budgetary and staff constraints. These activities are outlined below:

Accountability

Public Sector Management

Operationalizing accountability involves putting in place mechanisms that will enhance and guarantee the quality of public services. Therefore, Bank Group interventions to promote accountability in public sector management will focus on strengthening mechanisms for expenditure control, exposure of and sanctions against misspending and corruption. This will also extend to the monitoring and evaluation of public expenditure programs for effectiveness and performance.

For enhanced accountability in public sector management, internal controls or the supply side of accountability must be underpinned by the demand and political side of accountability. Thus, Bank Group activities will also focus on public

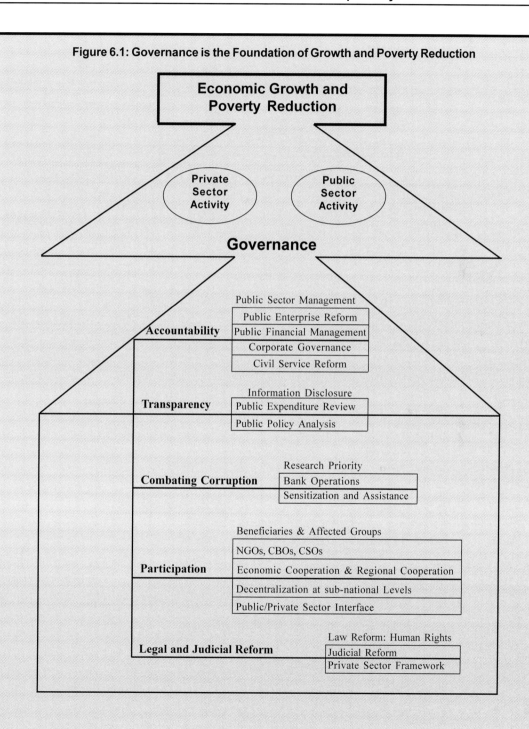

Figure 6.1: Governance is the Foundation of Growth and Poverty Reduction

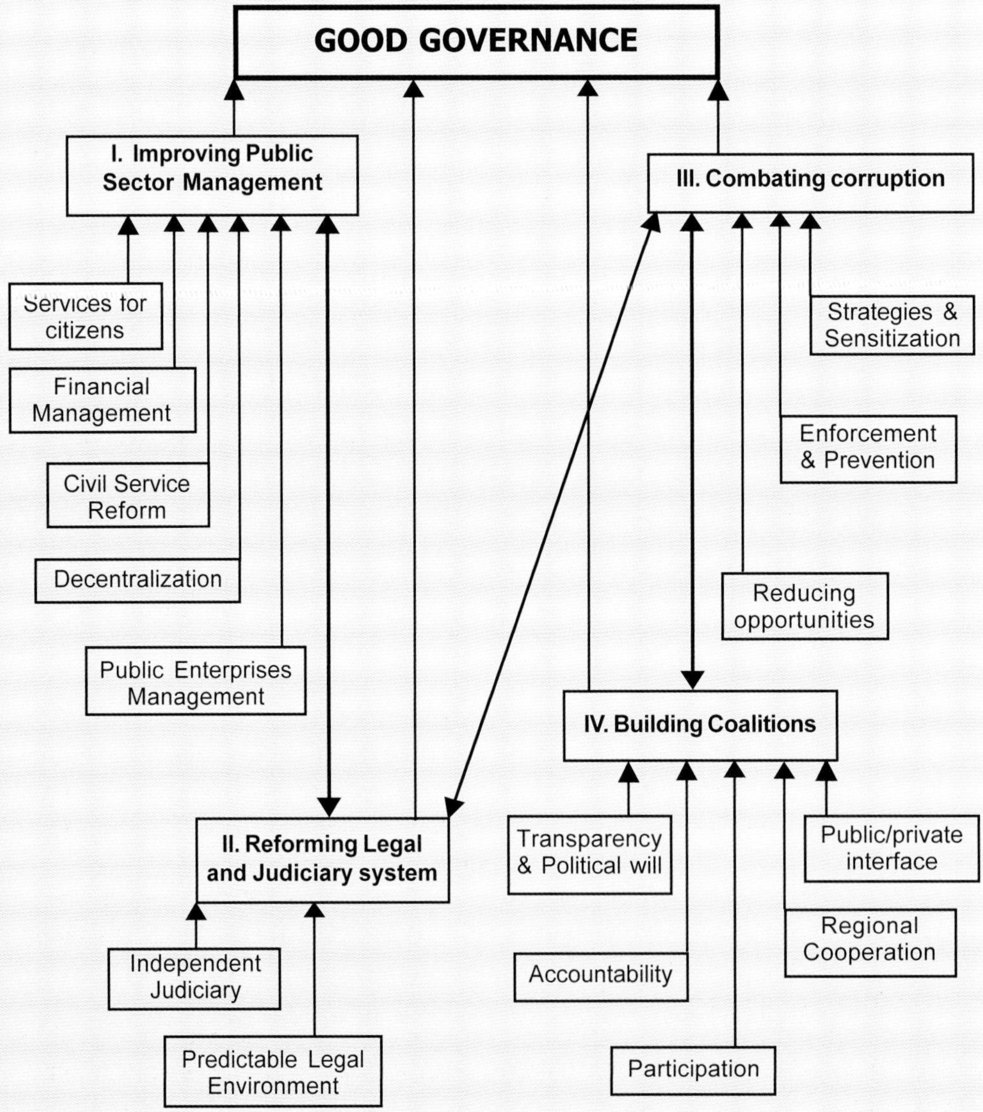

Figure 6.2: Interrelation between the Different Axioms of Good Governance

management reforms that will engender better service delivery of public institutions to their clients, and empower citizens to demand better services from public institutions.

The Bank Group activities will take advantage of the new espousal of democratic institutions in RMCs, and help establish or strengthen the legal and financial independence of the formal agencies of promoting public sector accountability, such as the Audit Service/Auditor General's Office, Public Accounts Committee of Parliament and Ombudsman.

Public Enterprise Management and Reform

Insufficient transparency and accountability have been key among the factors impeding public enterprise reform in general, and privatization in particular in most RMCs. In addition to the economic inefficiencies they entail, inadequate transparency and accountability are key factors that fuel public suspicion about rent-seeking, corruption and resistance to reforms. The Bank Group is, therefore committed to improving accountability in public enterprise management and institutional reform.

Bank Group activities to enhance accountability will aim at encouraging RMC governments to increase the use of transparent modes of privatization and outsourcing of privatization management to private sector firms and the stock exchange, in addition to publicizing divestiture bids, sales and payments. For both publicly and privately-owned enterprises, the Bank will support efforts to develop and enforce rules of corporate governance, to reduce conflicts of interest, and to promote the establishment of credible and competent governing boards.

Public Financial Management

A key dimension of accountability of particular interest to the Bank Group is that of financial and budgetary accountability. It involves establishing the requisite infrastructure for sound financial management, for both public and private sector institutions. The Bank Group activities will center on the modernization of government accounting procedures, training of accountants and auditors, the development and strengthening of a professional code of ethics and disciplinary procedures.

Improving public expenditure management and enhancing budgetary discipline are an important aspect of effective and accountable public financial management. To this end, the Bank Group will work closely with RMCs and the donor community to provide training in project development, analysis and budgeting, and to improve information systems in RMCs. Projects of this nature have been undertaken by the Bank in Eritrea, Gambia, Rwanda and Uganda (see Box 6.2).

Corporate Governance

Internal discipline and respect for corporate codes of conduct directly influence efficiency and consequently economic growth. With the increasing efforts to privatize and to use the private sector as a fulcrum for economic development, the need for greater accountability and transparency in the way corporations are governed becomes even more imperative. Corporate governance affects the stakeholders, the corporation's potential to access global markets and its societal relationships. Proper corporate governance can have the effect of furthering commercial activities on a regional level, curtailing of corruption, reduction of pov-

Box 6.2: Improving Expenditure, Management and Enhancing Budgetary Discipline

Eritrea
Institutional Support for Economic and Financial *Management Program* (1998)

The program supports the efforts of the government of Eritrea to build institutional capacity at the newly-created Eritrean Development and Investment Bank (EDIB) for delivering development credit. The program will be implemented over a period of two years, and financed by the TAF and the Government of Eritrea. The grant represents 92 percent of the total program costs.

Gambia
Institutional Support Project (1998)

Project objectives are to strengthen the ability of Department of State for Finance and Economic Affairs, and other related departments to manage national debt, monitor the evaluation and implementation of development projects and programs, and to help increase the numbers of qualified female teachers in the basic education cycle. The project will be implemented over a period of three years and financed by the TAF and the Government of Gambia. The grant represents 66 percent of total project costs.

Rwanda
Institutional Support to the Ministry of Finance and Economic Planning and the *National Bank of Rwanda* (1997)

The objective of the project is to strengthen national economic and financial management capacity by supporting the principal institutions responsible for macroeconomic management and

monetary and financial policies. The components are: provision of technical assistance to the Ministry of Finance and Economic Planning; training of national managerial staff through seminars, short training courses and training abroad; procurement of the necessary equipment for the services involved in the project; and funding the operating costs of the implementation unit and other elements of the project. The project will contribute to re-building the institutional capacity that was seriously affected by the civil war of 1994. It will improve the skills of the present civil servants. The project will give special attention to women's integration into the development process in the country. The loan was approved by the Board on 5 November 1997 and the ADF/TAF grant will finance 90 percent of the project cost and the Government of Rwanda will contribute the remaining 10 percent. The project will be implemented over a period of three years.

Uganda
Institutional Support for External *Aid Management Project* (1998)

The objective of the project is to develop sustainable capacity in government to effectively manage external aid and to help create an integrated network of all external aid management agencies and improve Bank Group portfolio management. The project will be implemented over two years and financed by TAF, the UNDP, and the Government of Uganda. The TAF grant represents 60 percent of the total project cost and the government contribution approximately 6 percent.

Source: ADB (1997-98).

erty, and environmental protection. Bank Group activities will support efforts to introduce improved rules and standards applied among shareholders, directors, and management, with a view to strengthening corporate contributions to economic development.

Civil Service Reform

The reform of the state institutions to render them more effective, accountable and transparent is a cornerstone of good governance. Bank Group activities aim at helping RMCs refine and adopt models being developed by international and specialized agencies, for fostering civil service accountability and for strengthening the local capacity to design and implement development programs.

The Bank Group will continue to collaborate with the World Bank and other donors to streamline African public services, improve systems, reform wage structures, and reallocate redundant employees. Bank Group activities will support efforts to foster meritocracy and quality recruitment systems in the African public services, and work towards the reduction of salary differentials between the private and public sectors. Bank Group activities to support civil service reforms will include updating of service regulations (e.g. the civil service manual/code), as well as helping to develop realistic and enforceable codes of ethics for public servants that incorporate elements of transparency, accountability and democratic governance. In addition, the Bank Group will encourage RMCs to promote professionalism and to free public services from stifling and corrosive political control.

Transparency

Information Disclosure

The Bank Group subscribes to and enforces the principle of transparency and information disclosure both in its relations with RMCs and in the execution of its internal activities. It employs open international competitive bidding procedures for the procurement of most works, goods and services that it finances. Similarly, the Bank Group adheres to strict requirements of transparency in all transactions relating to the proceeds of its financing. Board approval and execution of the Bank Group Information Disclosure Policy, the maintenance of a constantly updated Website, and the establishment of a Public Information Center (PIC) at its headquarters are ways in which the Bank Group manifests its own corporate transparency.

The Bank Group recognizes that the political and institutional pluralism and the expansion of media freedoms in RMCs have improved general information availability. However, official transparency continues to be severely constrained by the existence and application of laws restricting public access to information. Therefore, Bank Group activities to help improve transparency at all levels of government and public administration in RMCs will be geared towards reducing the prevailing legal and systemic factors promoting official secrecy and inhibiting public access to information.

The Bank Group will support RMCs' efforts to promote the free flow of information to enhance good governance, including the development of suitable legislation that would promote freedom of information, information disclosure, and public access to information. A skilled core of investigative journalists is indispensable for promoting accountability and transparency. Therefore the Bank Group will collaborate with relevant international, regional and national organizations to build the local capacity in basic journalism and to improve the management of relevant institutions.

Public Expenditure Reviews (PERs)

The Bank Group is fully committed to budgetary transparency. In collaboration with the World Bank, IMF and relevant bilateral institutions, it will intensify public expenditure reviews with a view to making the budgeting system in RMCs more transparent. These reviews have led to the prioritization of public sector expenditures, and keeping budgetary issues, including the general problem of expenditure efficiency, at the forefront of economic reforms. Through policy dialogue with RMCs, the Bank Group will address concerns for effective public resource management, with special attention given to issues such as the level of military expenditures and the need for increased priority for social sector programs.

A key element of Bank Group intervention in support of budgetary transparency is the building of local capacity in public expenditure reviews. Therefore, the Bank Group will support programs to provide and/or upgrade economic management and enhance competence among public and private agencies involved in the review of public expenditures. In this regard, the Bank Group will initiate or collaborate with other donor agencies to build capacity in expenditure review among local think-tanks and economic research institutions, and for specialized economic and financial oversight (e.g. Auditor, Inspector and Accountant General Departments).

Capacity in Public Policy Analysis and Dissemination

The Bank Group activities to foster transparency in policy making will focus on expanding participation in policy analysis and dissemination by state and non-state actors, and other stakeholders. In this regard, the Bank Group will initiate, or collaborate with bilateral partners and other donors to host policy "forums" in RMCs to promote and facilitate the discussion of key national economic and social policies. In some RMCs these fora have been used to expand the participation of key stakeholders in macroeconomic policy-making and review, and to generate consensus on its key elements.

To help build local capacity in policy analysis, the Bank will provide support for national and regional policy research institutes and think-tanks to undertake independent data collection and analysis, and to monitor and evaluate policy. It will also help in the dissemination of the results of such work, to ensure wider participation and ownership of development programs and initiatives.

Combating Corruption

The Bank Group is keenly aware of the impact of corruption on the economic development of RMCs. Corruption hinders proper resource management, undermines efforts to enhance growth and reduce poverty and obstructs sound and sustainable private sector development. Moreover, the Agreement establishing the Bank entrusts it with a responsibility to install effective control mechanisms to ensure probity in its business transactions and calls for the elimination of all forms of fraud and corruption from its lending operations and financial assistance. The Bank Group is therefore committed to working with its international partners, RMC governments, relevant non-governmental and civil society organizations to combat corruption.

The Bank Group anti-corruption efforts will focus on the following areas: support for research on the nature, origin, development and impact of corruption on African societies; reduction of opportunities for rent-seeking and corrupt practices; strengthening civil society capacity in investigating corruption matters; sensitization of, and assistance to, RMCs for combating corruption; and prevention and control of corruption relating to Bank-financed projects and programs.

The Bank considers combating corruption as pivotal to the promotion of good governance in RMCs. This factor is being taken into account in the country performance assessment and allocation of the concessional ADF resources. The Bank and its development partners will also encourage RMCs to introduce anti-corruption measures aimed at the detection and deterrence of fraud and corruption in their own procurements. In this regard, it is worth noting that some African countries have already embarked on piloting the new integrated strategy to fighting corruption sponsored by the World Bank.

Support for Research on Corruption

Corruption is a complex phenomenon. It has both international and domestic dimensions and the process of eradicating it is bound to be long and difficult. Identifying the root causes is an important first step to the selection of appropriate strategies for its deterrence. It is therefore vital to gain an awareness and understanding of its complex-

ity, its evolution and repercussions. Supporting research by national and regional research centers to review the various causes of corruption in RMCs will be one of the Bank's priorities in the years to come.

Prevention and Control of Corruption in Bank-financed Operations

As noted above, the Agreement establishing the African Development Bank requires it to ensure that the proceeds of any loan made or guaranteed by it are used only for the purposes for which the loan was granted, with due attention to considerations of economy and efficiency. The spirit of this requirement broadly guided the rules of procedure for the procurement of goods and services laid down by the Bank in 1980. These rules and procedures were significantly revised in 1996 and 1999. It is now possible for the Bank to cancel part or all of a loan or grant if the procurement procedure is tainted by acts of fraud or corruption. Similarly, the Bank may sanction a firm found guilty of fraud or corruption following a special audit or judiciary decision.

At the internal level, the Bank has earmarked resources, prepared documentation and perfected procedures to ensure that the procurement process is as transparent as possible, and enables a close monitoring of the manner in which contracts financed with Bank loan and grant resources are awarded (see Box 6.3). The Bank will remain alert to changes in international procurement practices and adapt its own rules accordingly. It will maintain permanent dialogue with other international financial institutions and all governmental and non-governmental organizations working towards greater transparency in procurement. It will also strengthen its role in monitoring and ensur-

Box 6.3: Bank-Financed Operations: Prevention and Control of Corruption

The Bank is well aware that the development effectiveness of its loans will be greatly enhanced if sound procurement procedures are put in place. To this end, the Bank has defined new rules of procedure for the procurement of goods and services applicable to all ADB Group-financed operations. It has also organized its services to ensure that these rules are effectively applied not only by its staff but also by the executing agencies of the projects and programs financed with its loans. Also, since 1996, an independent unit endowed with the power to control the procurement process has been created, documentation for use by Bank staff and borrowers prepared, and a mechanism for the review of complaints lodged by bidders established. This important mechanism has enabled the Bank to enhance its proficiency in procurement standards to better meet the requirements of its borrowers and consolidate the confidence of the business community. Through the establishment of the Procurement Review Committee, the Bank can at all times receive and examine complaints by bidders who are not satisfied with the way in which their bids were processed by borrowers or executing agencies. This Committee is independent and its decisions, which can even lead to the cancellation of the procurement process or of the financing, are final.

Source: ADB Procurement.

ing effective use of the resources provided to member countries, while remaining open to complaints from bidders, and organizing reviews of current contract award procedures.

Sensitization and Provision of Assistance to RMCs

The Bank will continue to organize meetings with its regional member countries on public procurement reform in Africa. These conferences provide an opportunity to sensitize participants to the high incidence of corruption during public procurement, define the key elements of a strategy to combat the phenomenon, and to specify the type of assistance the Bank could provide to RMCs. The Bank will encourage and assist RMCs to equip themselves with procedures that give priority to open competition in the award of official contracts, establish transparent and well-balanced relations with the business community and invest in the training and professionalization of their civil servants. In this regard the Bank will support regional initiatives aimed at promoting modernization and harmonization of the national public procurement systems in regional blocs.

Participation

The Bank recognizes that the development challenge facing most RMCs can no longer be met with past practices of autocratic governance, and that good governance requires the participation of all citizens. Participation promotes equality, especially in gender terms and for disadvantaged communities, and ensures sustainability through ownership.

Accordingly, Bank Group interventions to enhance participation in RMCs will center on the following areas: (i) increased stakeholder participation in policy and project cycle activities; (ii) expanded co-operation with civil society and in particular with NGOs/CBOs; (iii) support for economic co-operation and regional integration;

(iv) support for decentralization through capacity-building at the various sub-national levels; and (v) discussion of public/private sector interface in policy dialogue with RMCs.

Participation of Beneficiaries and Affected Groups

The Bank Group is concerned about the failure of many development programs to be delivered successfully to the intended beneficiaries. To enhance the responsiveness of and support of RMCs and the Bank Group to the needs of society, and particularly of its most vulnerable groups, the Bank will help to create a favorable environment to enable citizens to take responsibility for and share authority in decision-making and to generate legitimate public demands. To enhance the overall sustainability of projects it funds in RMCs, the Bank Group will ensure that decisions about social and economic priorities and investment strategies enjoy broad consensus and hence legitimacy. Particular attention will be given to expanding participation in project design, implementation and evaluation to include women particularly through groups that represent them credibly.

The Bank Group recognizes that local communities are likely to be more sensitive to and informed about their environment, and that participation induces positive behavior, especially in the long term. It can also provide a good incentive for social and economic mobilization and, when necessary, it ensures the development of an acceptance of shared hardships. Hence, empowerment of local communities will be a major issue that will be addressed in project design. The Bank Group will also promote such broad participation either directly or indirectly through organizations that best represent their interests, dur-

ing the process of preparing Country Strategy Papers (CSPs). It will expand its practice of holding consultative meetings with representatives of private sector, civil society, government and other development partners as a means to mobilize stakeholder input into the preparation of CSPs.

Co-operation with NGOs, CBOs, and CSOs

The Bank fully appreciates the developmental value of non-governmental organizations (NGOs), community-based organizations (CBOs), and civil society organizations (CSOs). In fact, these organizations act as channels of communication between the local stakeholders and the Bank, providing it with useful information and local knowledge and at the same time helping to convey a project's benefits to beneficiaries. They can help to build confidence and enhance the ability of local people to manage and negotiate development projects. To help achieve its key objective of poverty reduction, the Bank will strengthen its collaboration with NGOs and CBOs, through effective partnership building with all civil society organizations.

The Bank is also conscious of the fact that the participation of NGOs, CBOs, and CSOs can constitute a destabilizing force in project planning and design, and upset established socio-political relationships. It will, therefore, ensure that participating NGOs, CBOs, and CSOs have the necessary credibility and are adequately trained and equipped to contribute to the improvement of projects. In that connection, the Bank will increase its assistance to NGOs, CBOs, and CSOs to improve their credibility, strengthen their internal management and capacities to undertake training, monitoring and evaluation activities. The ADF

Micro Finance Initiative for Africa (AMINA) pilot program for assistance to micro-finance agencies is a good example of such collaboration and partnership.

Economic Co-operation and Regional Integration

Economic co-operation and regional integration offer tremendous opportunities for economic growth, enabling RMCs to overcome the constraints of small national markets, increasing intra-African trade and providing opportunities for integrating African economies into the global economy. The effective implementation of economic co-operation and regional integration are founded on enabling environments that promote accountability and transparency. Also a strong institutional framework at the regional and national levels is fundamental to streamline regional agreements into national policy. At the same time the harmonization of national policies and the establishment of effective transnational implementation tools offer opportunities to push reforms that are conducive to good governance at regional level. For example, the adoption of a regional legal framework and the establishment of a related judicial institution (OHADA) is proving to be an effective instrument for improving the regional environment for private sector promotion. The Bank will therefore, provide support for such regional initiatives in the context of its efforts to advance economic co-operation and regional integration in Africa.

Support for Decentralization At Various Sub-National Levels

Decentralization can be one of the prime strategies for advancing good governance. It is a key means of obtaining greater transparency and accountability, and it can be used effectively to combat corruption by placing resource management in closer proximity to citizens. Legislative reform for enhancing the role of local governments via decentralization and devolution is often the precursor to wider reforms shifting the balance away from central bureaucracies and towards multi-level governance and the strengthening of a pluralistic civil society. Experience in Africa and elsewhere indicates that, to be effective, the vesting of duty, responsibility and accountability in local government units should also be accompanied with provision for adequate resources to discharge their powers and to effectively carry out their functions.

Bank Group experience suggests that central governments are only part of the solution to the problems of poverty, inequality and environmental degradation affecting most RMCs. The Bank is aware that centralized systems of service delivery have often proved to be inadequate especially with respect to satisfying demands for basic services generated by rapid growth and urbanization. It recognizes that while most of these problems are acutely felt at the local level, local governments and other institutions that are expected to tackle them lack the necessary financial, technical and human resources.

The Bank will, therefore, actively support the involvement of local governments in the provision and management of services, as well as enhance their capacity for resource mobilization and investment planning. Experience has shown that,

CBOs and users contribute significantly to efficient service delivery and cost savings when they are involved in project design and implementation. The Bank Group will, therefore, encourage the creation of mechanisms that support co-ownership and co-responsibility for the provision of essential services.

Public Sector/Private Sector Interface

The Bank Group regards both the private and public sectors as key players in the drive towards sustainable development. Civil society, governments and the private sector are all considered as participants in a joint effort to combat poverty. The private sector can become a key partner with the government and civil society in addressing development challenges through its adherence to and promotion of good governance.

The Bank will, therefore, promote public-private sector dialogue as well as reforms conducive to private sector development. It will encourage the private sector to mobilize financial, technological and management resources to facilitate the creation of efficient production systems. However, the Bank will also work towards ensuring that the most vulnerable segments of the society, including women and disadvantaged groups, are protected. In this framework, greater attention will be paid to issues that relate to corporate governance, and to the Core Labor Standards (CLS), which are gaining increasing acceptance as a basis for establishing criteria to which countries, all over the world, are held accountable. The main elements of the CLS as developed by the ILO include freedom of association and collective bargaining, elimination of forced or compulsory labor, abolition of child labor and the elimination of discrimination in employment.

Legal and Judicial Reform

Law Reform

The Bank Group regards the creation and sustenance of a predictable legal environment, with an objective, reliable, and independent judiciary as an essential component of good governance. The Bank Group will provide technical assistance to RMCs to review existing laws, with a view to achieving modifications to update and address deficiencies, especially those that infringe on human rights of women, minorities and other groups of people.

Consistent with its commitment to mainstream gender issues in its good governance interventions, the Bank Group will collaborate with RMCs, other donors, and relevant NGOs to introduce measures that strengthen actions by the legal system in this area. It will also provide support for reforms that affirm gender equality under the law, including property and land rights, family law and working conditions (see Box 6.4).

Judicial Reform

An independent and well-equipped judiciary, whose decisions are consistently enforced, and court administration that ensures cases are dealt with expeditiously and at reasonable cost to the parties, are essential factors in the promotion of the rule of law. Similarly, the creation of honest law enforcement agencies that effectively carry out court decisions, the effective and timely implementation of sanctions against corrupt political officials, as well as better access by poor people to judicial services are prerequisites for good governance.

Box 6.4: Bank Group Law for Development Program

In December 1999, the Boards of Directors of the African Development Bank and of the African Development Fund adopted a Policy on Good Governance. The Bank Group's good governance policy highlights legal and judicial reform as indispensable components of good governance in its initiative to reduce poverty and promote regional economic integration among regional member countries (RMCs). The Bank implements this aspect of its good governance policy through its Law for Development Program, in which the law is used as a tool to help promote economic development in Africa. The Bank Group believes that efforts and achievements in legal and judicial reform must be measurable over time, and most importantly, must be sustainable.

The level of funding for judicial and law-related functions and services in most RMCs is inadequate. The mechanisms used to fund judiciaries in RMCs affect the independence of judicial actions and the delivery of legal services. The Bank works closely with governments to get policy support, particularly economic policy support which is key to any successful reform program. It's objective is to facilitate greater responsiveness and effectiveness of the judiciary as an independent organ.

The Bank will seek to develop a consensus that is tailored to addressing the peculiar challenges of each RMC. This approach requires the involvement of various groups within society, including the judiciary, law societies, legal aid groups, academia and poverty reduction specialists.

The Law for Development Program supports efforts to ensure access to justice for the poor as a means of redressing injustices, ensuring stability, marshalling resources, and of promoting informal transactions. Consistent with the Bank's Vision, the program emphasizes regional economic co-operation and integration, including regional harmonization of approaches to legal and judicial matters. The Bank Group co-operates with other international and bilateral institutions and NGOs in promoting legal and judicial reform.

Projects under the Law for Development Program are not, exclusively, stand-alone projects, but include projects within the mainstream of other Bank and Fund capacity building projects. The Legal Department collaborates closely with the Operations Complex in this respect. A Unit on Good Governance, headed by a chief counsel, is being established in the Office of the General Counsel specifically for the Program. The establishment of this unit enables the Legal Department to: (i) effectively participate in facilitative research on legal and judicial reform for economic development; and (ii) manage related technical assistance projects.

The Legal Department will assist in preparing key types of model legislation that would be made available for adoption by RMCs. These will include a model anti-corruption legislation (preventative and curative measures) and a uniform banking law. These could be used by regional organizations to bring greater harmony and facilitate cross-border banking transactions. The Bank will also prepare model codes of conduct.

The Law for Development Program seeks to further promote economic co-operation and regional integration by supporting the development of regional registries both for movable collateral used in secured transactions and for companies. There is an urgent need to establish registries, at both the national and regional levels, to facilitate financings and cross-border secured transactions.

To promote the twin purposes of legal and judicial reform, the Bank is considering spearheading the establishment of a facility exclusively for these purposes. The facility would provide or arrange technical assistance to RMCs to improve selected areas of legislation, enhance judicial capacity-building, fund law-related studies, and furnish legal assistance for technical projects. This latter assistance could take the form of the Project Preparation Facility recently made available to RMCs by the Bank Group.

Box 6.4: (continued)

Issues pertaining to securitization, insolvency, security interests in movable properties, and other laws that affect the economic environment are critical to the development of RMCs. The Bank Group's policy promotes the adoption of modernized laws. The Bank assists in building the requisite legal and judicial infrastructure for the implementation of these laws and is working to establish electronic databases and websites on laws and other relevant information that would facilitate cross-border transactions in African countries.

In the short term, priority is placed on: (i) strengthening of the Legal Department to execute the Law for Development Program; (ii) preparation of a comprehensive strategy paper for legal and judicial reform; and (iii) organizing and convening an All-Africa Conference on legal and judicial reform in Africa during 2001.

In the medium term, the Bank will: (i) establish the electronic and other information databases; (ii) work with OHADA and other regional organizations interested in establishing commercial and corporate registries; (iii) arrange a feasibility study on the African Legal Support Facility; and (iv) commence law-related training programs.

It is anticipated that in the long run, the program will ensure the adoption of legislation in the various RMCs and equip their legal systems with the tools and infrastructure needed for effective delivery of legal and judicial services.

The Law for Development Program is fashioned within the context of the prevailing legal regimes in the relevant RMCs. Particular emphasis in promoting the Bank's strategy for legal and judicial reforms depends on the active participation of various stakeholders in the member countries of the Bank Group.

The Bank Group will collaborate with RMCs and other donor agencies to undertake projects that would simplify filing procedures, including the automation of systems for judges' chambers, court rooms, and court registry as well as to improve law reporting. The Bank Group will also assist in the training of judicial officers and provision of continuing legal education, especially for judges who operate commercial courts. In addition, it will support programs aimed at improving remuneration for judges.

Instruments for Enhanced Governance in RMCs

In operationalizing its agenda in the area of good governance, the Bank will focus on accountability, transparency, promotion of human and civil rights, combating corruption, stakeholder participation, and legal and judicial reforms. These interventions will be pursued in collaboration with the Bretton Woods Institutions, regional and specialized organizations, and bilateral agencies through economic and sector work, policy dialogue, and lending and non-lending activities.

Economic and Sector Work

The Bank Group is well placed to raise and discuss the issues of good governance with its RMCs. Through policy dialogue, and in the context of economic and sector work (ESW) and preparation of the Country Strategy Papers (CSPs), the Bank will continue to impress upon member governments the importance of good governance for sustained development. And through such dialogue and interactions, effective programs and projects that seek to improve governance could be jointly identified, designed and implemented.

Advocacy Role

The activities identified to promote good governance will be pursued through a combination of advocacy, policy dialogue and consultation with RMCs. Therefore, the Bank will continue to participate in, and to organize senior level seminars, conferences and workshops.

While the Bank may find it difficult to tackle directly political aspects of good governance, it will nonetheless make it clear to RMCs that these issues are explicitly taken into account in assessing country performance and determining resource allocation. Thus, the new Country Performance Assessment (CPA) methodology includes issues such as political stability, anti-corruption policies and practices, property rights and rule-based governance, and accountability and transparency of the public service.

Lending Activities

The Bank has for some time now been supporting activities and programs that seek to improve governance. A list of selected Bank operations with a governance component during the period 1996-1999 is shown in Table 6.1. As it is clear from the table, such activities have, however, been largely designed as components of larger structural adjustment or sector adjustment operations. Recent examples of such interventions include the Public Resource Management Program for Mauritania (Box 6.5); the Health Services Development Project for Gambia (Box 6.6); and, Education Development Project for Cape Verde (Box 6.7). More recently, policy-based lending has started to address issues of governance more directly. However, projects that give matters of governance their due priority and importance are still

rare. There is, thus, a need to tackle the issues of governance in a much more proactive, direct and integrated manner. In this regard, the issues of civil service restructuring, reform of legal and judicial systems, strengthening financial management capacity, and instituting participatory approaches, will be targeted for sustained support. In the design of projects and programs of governance in RMCs, attention will also be given to the creation of transparent systems of administration and accountable public authorities and institutional decentralization.

Capacity-building activities and assistance for legal and judiciary reforms are the central focus of the Bank's efforts in improving governance in its RMCs. Building capable institutions at the local and national levels, as well as in civil society and the private sector, is essential to secure the effectiveness and sustainability of Bank Group intervention in governance. The Bank activities will aim at enhancing the effectiveness of public administration and development management. They will promote institutional support for capacity building in policy analysis, oversight and audit functions, civil society organization and decentralization efforts in RMCs.

Non-Lending Activities

The emphasis of Bank Group non-lending activities will be on the expansion of co-operation and collaboration with civil society organizations and other development partners by lending support and credibility to their advocacy role. The Bank will also provide technical assistance in support of the reforms of legal and judicial systems, privatization initiatives of RMCs, public sector reform programs, and work towards strength-

Table 6.1: Bank Group Operations having Governance Components (1996-1999)

Loans Title	UA Million			Date	
	ADB	ADF	Total	Approved	Sector
ALGERIA					
Second Line of Credit to the Banque de l'Agriculture et du Développement Rural (BADR)	157.5	0.0	157.5	1999	Agriculture
BENIN					
Promotion of Women's Activities in Oueme Province	0.0	2.0	2.0	1996	Social Sectors
BURKINA FASO					
Health Services Strengthening Project	0.0	10.0	10.0	1999	Social Sectors
Reduction Poverty at the	0.0	14.0	14.0	1998	Multi-sector
Municipal Level	0.0	(Grant 1.5)	1.5	1998	Multi-sector
CAMEROON					
Education II	0.0	7.5	7.5	1999	Social Sectors
CHAD					
Poverty Reduction and actions in Favor of Women	0.0	5.3	5.3	1997	Multi-sector
CONGO					
Emergency Reconstruction Support Program	13.4	0.0	13.4	1998	Social Sectors
DJIBOUTI					
Social Fund for Development	0.0	6.5	6.5	1998	Multi-sector
EGYPT					
Social Fund for Development Phase II	0.0	15.0	15.0	1997	Multi-sector
Support to Women's Economic	0.0	6.0	6.0	1997	Multi-sector
Empowerment in the New Lands	0.0	(Grant 0.2)	0.2	1997	Multi-sector
ERITREA					
Institutional Support for Economic and Financial Management Program	0.0	1.1	1.1	1998	Multi-sector
GABON					
Public Enterprise Restructuring Privatization Program	11.0	0.0	11.0	1998	Multi-sector
Pilot Public Works Project for Employment Promotion	6.1	0.0	6.1	1998	Multi-sector
GAMBIA					
Institutional Support Project	0.0	0.8	0.8	1998	Multi-sector
GHANA					
Institutional Support Program	0.0	2.0	2.0	1998	Multisector
GUINEA					
Support to Women's	0.0	3.0	3.0	1997	Multi-sector

Table 6.1: (continued)

Loans Title	UA Million			Date Approved	Sector
	ADB	ADF	Total		
MALAWI					
Support to the National AIDS Control Program	0.0	(Grant 1.0)	1.0	1999	Social Sectors
MALI					
Poverty Alleviation Project	0.0	10.0	10.0	1999	Multi-sector
	0.0	(Grant 2.5)	2.5	1999	Multi-sector
MAURITANIA					
Health and Social Welfare Development Plan Support Program	0.0	10.1	10.1	1999	Social Sectors
The Education Development Support Project	0.0	5.9	5.9	1999	Social Sectors
Public Resource Management and Capacity Building Program	0.0	7.8	7.8	1996	Multi-sector
MOROCCO					
Economic and Social Reform Program	148.2	0.0	148.2	1998	Public Utilities
Institutional Savings Development Program	130.9	0.0	130.9	1997	Multi-sector
MOZAMBIQUE					
Capacity Building for Poverty Reduction	0.0	2.3	2.3	1998	Multi-sector
NIGER					
Public Finance Reform	0.0	11.0	11.0	1998	Multi-sector
RWANDA					
Institutional Support to the Ministry of Finance and Economic Planning and the National Bank of Rwanda	0.0	1.5	1.5	1997	Multi-sector
SENEGAL					
Basic, Mid-Level and Sectors	0.0	11.5	11.5	1999	Social Sectors
Secondary Education Development Support Project	0.0	(Grant 1.5)	1.5	1999	Social Sectors
Poverty Alleviation Project	0.0	10.0	10.0	1999	Multi-sector
	0.0	(Grant 1.75)	1.75	1999	Multi-sector
	0.0	(Grant 1.75)	1.8	1999	Multi-sector
UGANDA					
Institutional Support for External Aid Management	0.0	1.5	1.5	1998	Multi-sector
ZAMBIA					
Education III Project	0.0	8.5	8.5	1999	Social Sectors
Health Sector Support Project	0.0	8.9	8.9	1999	Social Sectors

Source: ADB (1996-1999), Annual Report.

Box 6.5: Mauritania: Public Resource Management and Capacity Building Program

The program falls within the context of economic reforms undertaken with the support of the Bretton Woods Institutions. It aims at increasing domestic savings through internal resource mobilization and improved allocation and management of public expenditure. In that regard, a series of institutional reforms were to be implemented starting in 1997 and ending in the year 2000. These include the extension of the fiscal base, improvement of the fiscal administration quality, and review of direct and indirect taxation. These reforms were to be accompanied by the preparation of a three-year rolling public expenditure program and the reallocation of public expenditures to basic infrastructure and programs. The program was expected to achieve an increase in the budgetary balance excluding grants, from -0.8 percent of GDP in 1995 to 2.5 percent in 1998; an increase in domestic savings from 11.2 percent of GDP in 1995 to 17.1 percent in 1998; and an increase in budgetary receipts from 24 percent of GDP in 1995 to 26 percent in 1998.

Other components of the program included: a decrease in total public expenditure from 24.8 percent of GDP in 1995 to 3.5 percent in 1998; a public expenditure program (PEP) in keeping with the macroeconomic framework elaborated and implemented each year from 1997; core public investment three-year rolling program (CPIP) in line with the macroeconomic framework elaborated and implemented from 1997; and financing of public poverty reduction programs from 300 million Mauritanian Ouguiya (MU) in 1995 to 600 MU in 1998. Other actions included: creation of a central filing system assigning to each taxpayer an individual identification number; cross-checking between customs and tax; implementation of the tax exemption reform on contracts and public projects; adoption of new regulations on corporate income tax; and adoption of new regulations on the income tax of physical entities. The program is supported by the IBRD (UA 13.90 million) and the European Union (UA 11.6 million). The ADF loan will be used to finance 3 percent of the total project cost.

ening financial management capacity, and compilation of best practice, in the region and elsewhere, that are relevant to governance activities.

The effectiveness of the Bank's activities in good governance will be ensured through policy harmonization and program co-ordination with partner institutions at the national, regional and continent-wide levels. Programming in this area will leverage the efforts of regional and international partners through existing co-ordination mechanisms, including Donor Round Tables and Country Consultative Meetings. The Bank Group will collaborate with the Bretton Woods Institutions and with specialized partner institutions (OAU, ECA, WB, IMF, OECD- DAC, UNDP and others) in developing regionally relevant benchmarks, codes of conduct, and indicators of good governance to assist RMCs improve priority setting and activities in governance.

Conclusion

Good governance is an essential requisite for sustainable development. The absence of good governance has proved to be particularly damaging to the "corrective intervention" role of government. Programs for poverty alleviation, for example, have been undermined by a lack of public accountability, by corruption, and by the lack of participation of the beneficiaries. Pervasive corruption is damaging to development. It weakens the ability of governments to carry out their functions efficiently, including by diluting equity from the provision of government services. It squanders government revenues and distorts and deters investment flows, thus undermining growth. Other causes of poor development management are the high degree of concentration of decision-making power, and the absence of consultation and accountability.

Box 6.6: Gambia: Health Services Development Project

The objective of the project is to create enabling conditions for delivery of adequate primary and secondary health care services. The project will support health care services in six health centers as well as ensure effective planning and management of health services and resources through cost effectiveness and technical efficiency in providing health services. It will also seek to improve essential laboratory and support services by providing one Central Medical Store and one clinical reference laboratory. At full implementation, the project is expected to result in a 10 percent increase in the catchment population covered by the health centers by the year 2000. Out-patient services would increase by 10 percent while in-patient services would expand by 25 percent. The increased availability of maternity beds and trained health workers will improve health services for expectant mothers, since maternal health care services represent about 73 percent of clinic visits and hospital admissions. The project is therefore expected to contribute to a reduction in the maternal mortality rate.

In recent years, the issue of governance has been given new impetus by five important factors. First, the development failures of the African continent in the 1980s, in particular, the difficult experience with and mixed record of structural adjustment reforms. Second, the recognition of the failure of command economies and the emergence of a consensus on the relative efficacy of neo-liberal development strategies. Third, the rise of pro-democracy movements in Africa and other parts of the developing world, with the demand for good governance and more responsive forms of government as a rallying point. Fourth, the growing concern that widespread corruption is siphoning away both domestic and external resources. And fifth, the phenomenal increase in globalization and its even stronger imperatives for sound domestic policy environment and economic management.

There is consensus that good governance should build on: (i) effective states; (ii) mobilized civil societies; and (iii) efficient private sectors. All three factors are necessary for sustained development. Effective states create an enabling political and legal environment for equitable economic growth. Active and vibrant civil societies mobilize individuals, groups and communities, facilitate political and social interaction, help to generate social capital, and foster societal cohesion and stability. Productive private sectors generate jobs and income. There is also a wide consensus that the key elements of good governance include accountability, transparency, combating corruption, participatory governance and an enabling legal/judicial framework.

Globalization has profound implications for governance, including the erosion of state sovereignty as transnational bodies increasingly mediate national concerns and press for universal laws. Another dimension is the increased globalization of political, social, economic and environmental problems. Thus good governance cannot be considered a closed system. The role of the state is to find a balance between taking advantage of globalization and providing a secure and stable social and economic domestic environment. Against this background, governance can more appropriately be defined as: "the manner in which power

Box 6.7: Cape Verde: Education Development Project

The objectives of the project are: to increase the intake capacity and improve the quality of education at the secondary level; to strengthen the planning and management capacity of the Ministry of Education, Science and Culture, and, to develop non-formal education. The project involves the construction of 29 classrooms, 8 laboratories, 3 technology rooms and 3 art education rooms. A total of 250 teachers and five inspectors will be trained under the project while training of trainers will be strengthened with specialization training in various fields for five teachers of the College of Education. Specialists in the Ministry of Education, Science and Culture will be trained in educational planning. Furthermore, a post-literacy program will be implemented in favor of 11,304 persons, of which 9,045 will be women.

The project will contribute to improvement of the quality of education through a reduction in the repeat ratio from 19 percent to 7 percent, and the dropout rate from 4 percent to one percent; improvement the institutional capacity of the Ministry of Education, Science and Culture; reduction of the country's illiteracy rate and permitting acquisition of vocational skills by more women. The design of the project components has ensured that no teaching aid and other products with negative impact on the environment will be used. In addition, the staff and social training manual to be prepared under the project will lay special emphasis the environment and ecology. The loan was approved the Board on 5 May 1997 and the ADF will finance 90 percent of the project cost and the Government of Cape Verde will contribute the remaining 10 percent. The project will be implemented over a period of four years.

is exercised in the management of the affairs of a nation, and its relations with other nations". It follows, therefore, that solutions to some governance problems, such as a reduction in corruption and excessive military expenditure, can be facilitated by actions at the global level. However, though recognizing the important dimension and implications of globalization, this policy focuses more on the national elements of good governance.

The Bank Group's interest in governance arises from its mandate to ensure the effectiveness of the development efforts it supports. It is also in line with the Bank's Vision for sustained African development in the 21st Century. For the Bank Group the key elements of good governance include accountability, transparency, combating corruption, participatory governance and an enabling legal/judicial framework.

The Bank acknowledges the complex nature of governance issues, and is aware that, the work in this area is likely to prove difficult and may not yield quick results. It recognizes the need for a long-term engagement and differentiated approaches between regions, countries and project types. The activities to be undertaken to effectively operationalize the Bank policy on good governance will reinforce linkages both within the Bank and with the Bank's partners, including RMC governments, multilateral lending institutions, bilateral donor agencies, and CSOs/NGOs. These activities will be implemented in stages, within a specified time frame and at different levels: (i) within the Bank itself; (ii) with regional member countries (RMCs); and (iii) in collaboration with other partners and stakeholders.

BIBLIOGRAPHICAL NOTE

Introduction

The background papers prepared specially for the Report are listed below, along with the selected bibliography used in the Report. These papers synthesize relevant literature. The Report has drawn on a wide range of Africa Development Bank reports, including ongoing research as well as countries' economic, sector and project work. It has also drawn on outside sources, including published and the unpublished works of institutions such as the IMF, the World Bank, IFC, the United Nations and its agencies such as the ECA, FAO, ILO, UNCTAD, UNIDO, UNDP, WTO and OECD. Other sources include publications from various national economic and statistic agencies, Africa Economic Digest, Africa Financing Review, Africa Research Bulletin; Business Africa , The Economist, Economist Intelligence Unit, Financial Times; International Capital Markets; Middle East Economic Digest; Southern Africa Monitor; WEFA Group's economic Profiles for Africa Countries.

Background papers

(i) Adesida Olugbenga (2000a), "Governance in Africa: the Role for Information and Communication Technologies".

(ii)   (2000b), "Governance for Development in Africa".

(iii) Anyang' Nyong'o Peter (2000), "Governance and Poverty Reduction in Africa".

(iv) Gogué Aimé Tchabouré (2000), "Gouvernance en Afrique: Etat des lieux".

(v) Ayogu Melvin Damian (2000), "The Record of Corporate Governance in Africa".

(vi) Otobo Ejeviome Eloho (2000), "Contemporary External Influences on Corporate Governance: Coping With Challenges in Africa".

Sources for Boxes

1.1   EC (European Commission) (2000).

1.2   African Development Bank Group (2000).

1.3   Mlambo and Oshikoya (2001); Devarajan, Easterly and Pack (2001); Hussain (2000).

1.4   ECA (2000).

2.1   FAO (2000).

2.2   Buabeng C.S. (2000).

3.1   Goldsmith Arthur (2000).

3.2   IPEP (International Panel of Eminent Personalities) (2000).

3.3   Daniel Edevbaro (1998), "The Political Economy of Corruption and Underdevelopment in Nigeria" and S.O. Osoba "Corruption in Nigeria: Historial Perspectives" Review of African Political Economy No. 69 (September 1996).

3.4   Johnston Michael (1997) and Commonwealth (2000).

3.5   Commonwealth (2000), and Ofosu-Amaah et al., (1999).

3.6 Commonwealth (2000) and Ofosu-Amaah et al. (1999).

3.7 International Federation of Journalists (1999) Clement D. Ebri (2000); Dana Ott (1998).

3.8 Ofosu-Amaah Paati W., Raj Soopramanien, and Kishor Uprety (1999).

3.9 Shanyisa Anota Khasiani (1999).

3.10 Anyang' Nyong'o Peter (2000), "Governance and Poverty Reduction in Africa", Background Paper for the African Development Report 2001.

4.1 President's Office, Government of South Africa (2001).

4.2 ADB (2000), Poverty Reduction Strategies in Africa and Follow up Documentation.

4.3 EIU (2000).

4.4 Mboweni T. T. (2000).

4.5 Dzidonu et. al (1998); World Bank (1999); ADB (1998); Opoku-Mensah (1999).

4.6 Anusionwu Chukwuma (2000).

4.7 Ali Abdel Gadir Ali (2001).

4.8 ADB (2000), "Ghana Country Strategy Paper 1999-2001." Memorandum, ADF/BD/WP/2000/48.

4.9 UNCHS Database Search, www.bestpractices.org .

4.10 Anyang' Nyong'o Peter (2000), as cited in Box 3.10.

4.11 Al Ahram Center. http://www.acpss.org.

412 OECD (1999), OECD Principles of Corporate Governance. http:www.oecd.org/daf/governance/principles.htm.

4.13 Melvin Damian Ayogu (2000), "The Record of Corporate Governance in Africa", Background Paper for the *African Development Report 2001*.

4.14 Gervais Djondo (1999).

4.15 Mamadou Dia (1996), "Africa's Management in the 1990s and Beyond-Reconciling Indigenous and Transplanted Institutions."

5.1 ABD/AERC/GCA/UNECA/World Bank (2000).

5.2 ABD/AERC/GCA/UNECA/World Bank (2000).

5.3 OECD Anti-Corruption Unit.

5.4 Basle Committee on Banking and Regulating, OECD Financial Action Task Force on Money Laundering (FATF).

5.5 ADB (1999).

5.6 Shanyisa Anota Khasiani (1999); Opoku-Mensah (1999).

5.7 Sherif Kamel (1998).

6.1 Omar Kabbaj (2000).

6.2 ADB (1997-98), *Annual Report*.

6.3 ADB, Procurement.

6.4   ADB, Legal Department.

6.5   ADB (1996), *Annual Report*

6.6   ADB (1997), *Annual Report*

6.7   ADB (1997), *Annual Report*

Selected bibliography

Adamolekun Ladipo (1986), "Politics and *Public Administration in Nigeria*", Ibadan: Spectrum Books, 1986.

Abdelghani Abouhane (1999), "La Transition démocratique au Maroc", Dans Diop et Diouf, *Les Figures du politique en Afrique : Des pouvoirs hérités aux pouvoirs élus*. Codesria-Karthala. pp. 359-383.

Ademolekun L., G. de Lusignan et A. Atomate (éds.) (1997), *Réforme de la fonction publique en Afrique francophone : Actes d'un atelier*, EDI Banque mondiale. Abidjan, 23-26 janvier 1996.

African Capacity Building Foundation (2000), "*Etudes sur les besoins de renforcecement des capacités en gestion économique au Cameroun*", ACBF, Harare, Zimbawe.

African Development Bank (1995-99), *African Development Report*. Abidjan, Côte d'Ivoire.

(1999), "Business Opportunities under Operations Financed by the African Development Bank Group", Abidjan, Côte d'Ivoire.

(1996-99), *Annual Report*. Abidjan, Côte d'Ivoire.

(2000), "African Development Bank Group Policy on Good Governance", Abidjan, Côte d'Ivoire.

AERC/GCA/UNECA/World Bank (2000), "Can Africa Claim the 21st Century", Washington, D.C.: The World Bank, 2000.

Aida Opoku-Mensah (1999), "Democratizing Access to the Information Society", *African Development Forum 1999*. Addis Ababa, United Nations. Economic Com-mission for Africa, 1999.

Ake Claude (1996), "Democracy and Development in Africa", Washington, D.C.: The Brookings Institution, 1996.

Alesina Alberto and Robert Gatti (1995), "Independence Central banks: Low Inflation at no Cost?", Paper and Proceedings of the Hundredth and Seventh Annual meeting of the American Economic Association. *American Economic Review*. May 1995, Vol. 85, No.2.

Ali Abdel Gadir Ali (2001), "Africa's Children and Africa's Development: A Duration of Development Framework", A Study prepared for UNICEF.

Anusionwu E.C. (2000), "Debt Crisis and Management Pratices in Africa", Paper presented at a Regional Conference on Sovereign Debt Management. Johannesburg, 5-6 December 2000.

Anyang' Nyong'o P. (2000), "The Context of Privatization in Kenya", Nairobi: Academy Science Publishers.

Asian Development Bank (1998), *Annual Report 1998, Governance in Asia: From Crisis to Opportunity*. Manila, Philippines.

Assogba Yao (1996), "Problématique de la gouvernance en Afrique au sud du sahara : Tendance générale en Afrique francophone", *Revue canadienne d'études du développement*. Numéro spécial, pp. 57-73.

Ayogu M. (2000), "Africa in Comparative Corporate Governance", Hassan Toorawa Trust Occasional Paper #6. Du Bois Institute, Harvard University, and Hassan Toorawa Trust, Mauritius.

Ben Achour Rafâa (1999), "La Succession de Bourguiba", Dans Diop et Diouf, *Les figures du politique en Afrique: Des Pouvoirs hérités aux pouvoirs élus*, Codesria Karthala pp. 217-241.

Bienayme Alain and Henry Courtier (1993), "Recentrage des missions et des mo-yens de l'état", In Cannac, Yves. *Pour Un Etat Moderne*. Paris: Commentaire/Plon. 1993.

Biggs T. and M. Ratauri (1997), "Productivity and Competitiveness in African Manufacturing", RPED Discussion Paper no. 80, World Bank.

Blinder Alan S. (1995), "How to Run a Central Bank", *The International Economy*. Sept-Oct 1995, Vol. 9, No 5.

Bratton M. et Nicolas Van de Walle (1992), " Vers la gouvernance en Afrique : Exigences populaires et réactions gouvernementales", In Hyden, G. et Bratton, M. (eds.), *Gouverner l'Afrique : Vers un partage des rôles*, Nouveaux horizons, pp. 39-82.

Brautigam Deborah (1996), "State Capacity and Effective Governance", In Ndulu, Benno, Nicholas van de Walle et. al (eds.); *Agenda for African Economic Renewal* New Brunswick: Transaction Publishers, 1996.

Bruno Michael (1995), "Does Inflation Really Lower Growth?", *Finance and Development*. September 1995; Vol. 32, No 3.

Buabeng C.S. (2000), "Ecowas Second Monetary Zone", Business News.

CACG (Commonwealth Association for Corporate Governance) (1999), "Principle of Corporate Governance in the Commonwealth: Towards global Competitiveness and Economic Accountability", CACG Guidelines, August 1999. Malborough New Zealand, CACG.

Caiquo Ben and Olugbenga Adesida (1994), "Integrating Futures Studies into Development Planning", *Futures*. Volume 26, Number 9. November 1994.

Chege Michael (1999), "Politics of Development: Institutions and Governance", Paper for Presentation at the Second Research Workshop. African Development Bank, Abidjan-Côte d'Ivoire. July 6–11.

Clement Dzidonu, Tony Rodrigues and Rogers Okot-Uma (1998), "The Emerging Messaging and Networking Technologies: An analysis of their Potential Development Impact in Africa", *Africa Development Review*, Volume 10, Number 1 (Abidjan, African Development Bank).

Collier P. (1999), "On the Economic Consequences of Civil War", *Oxford Economic Papers*. 51: 168-8.

Collier Paul and Jan Gunning (1999), "Explaining African Performance", *Journal of Economic Literature*.

Commonwealth (2000), "Commonwealth Principles on Promoting Good Governance and Combating Corruption", Commonwealth Heads of Government Meeting Durban, South Africa 12-15 November.

Decalo, Samuel (1994), "The Future of Participatory Democracy in Africa", *Futures,* Volume 26, Number 9 London, Butterworth-Heinemann, 1994.

Devarajan S. , W. R. Easterly and H. Pack (2001), "Is Investment in Africa Too Low or Too High? Macro and Micro Evidence", *Journal of African Economics,* Forthcoming.

Diop Moumar-Couba et Diouf Mamadou, (éds.) (1999), "Les Figures du politique en Afrique . Des pouvoirs hérités aux pouvoirs élus", Codesria-Karthala.

Djondo Gervais (1999), "The Role of the Private Sector in the Promotion of Good Governance in Africa with particular reference to The Role of Banks", Conference on Good Governance and Sustainable Development in Africa.

Economic Intelligence Unit (EIU) (2000), "Free to Grow", *Africa Business*, November 1-15, 2000.

Economist (2000), "A Survey of Government and the Internet", London, *The Economist*, June 24, 2000.

EC (European Commission) (2000), ACP–EU Partnership Agreement, Brussels.

Eizenstat E. Stuart (1999), "An Anti-Corruption and Good Governance Strategy for the 21st Century", Global Forum on Fighting Corruption: Safeguarding Integrity Among Justice and Security. Officials, Washington, D.C., February 24, 1999.

Elbadawi I. and N. Sambanis (2000), "Why are there so many Civil Wars in Africa? Understanding and Preventing Violent Conflict", *Journal of African Economies*, 9 (3): 244-69.

Elkrief Esther (1999), "La Justice: Axe majeur de la gouvernance", Communication présentée à la conférence Internationale sur la bonne gouvernance ET le développement durable en Afrique au sud du sahara, Abidjan, 22-24 novembre 2000.

FAO (2000), "Food Supply Situation and Crop Prospects in Sub-Sahara Africa", Global information and early warning systems on food and agriculture, FAO, Rome. No. 3 December 2000. ND CROP PROSPECTS IN

Fisher Stanley (1996), "Maintaining Price Stability", *Finance and Development*. December 1996; Vol. 32, No 3.

Freedom House (2000), "The Democratic Century", UNDP (United Nations Development Programme). Governance for Human Development.

Gibbons R. (1998), "Incentives in Organizations", *Journal of Economic Perspectives* 12(4): 115-132.

Gogué A.T. (1991), "Bilan et perspectives économiques africains dans INED", Congrès et colloques, n°13, pp. 47-59.

        (1999), "Responsabilité des débiteurs et des créanciers dans la dette de l'Afrique au sud du sahara", Communication présentée à la conférence de la banque mondiale sur le développement économique; Paris.

Goldsmith Arthur (2000), "Risk, Rule, and Reason: Leadership in Africa", Africa Forum. June 2000.

Goldstein A. (2000), "Big Business and the Wealth

of South Africa: Policy Issues in the Transition from Apartheid", Mimeo, OECD.

Gray Cheryl W. and Daniel Kaufman (1998), "Corruption and Development", *Finance and Development*, March 1998.

Hans d'Orville (2000), "Knowledge and Information: New Levels for Development and Prosperity", *Choices-The Human Development magazine*. New York, United Nations Development Program. June 2000.

Healey John and Mark Robinson (eds.) (2000), *Democracy Governance and Economy Policy: Sub-Sahara Africa in Comparative Perspective*. Overseas Development Institute.

Heilbrum John and Philip Keefer (1999), "Assessing Political Commitment to Fighting Corruption", *PREMnotes Newsletter series*, Note No. 29, Washington, D.C.: World Bank, September 1999.

Heritage Foundation/Wall Street Journal, 2001 Index of Economic Freedom. EIU (2000).

Hewitt de Alcantara, Cynthia (1998), "Du bon usage du concept de gouvernance", *Revue internationale des sciences sociales,* No 155, mars, pp. 109-117.

Hussain Nureldin M. (1992), "Food Security and Adjustment Programmes: The Conflict", In Simon Maxwell (ed.), *To Cure all Hunger: Food Policy and Food Security in Sudan*. Intermediate Technology Publications 1991.

(1997), "Africa's External Sector and Economic Growth: Possible Areas for Development Cooperation", In Henock Kifle, Adebayo O. Olukoshi and Lennart Wohlgemuth (eds.), *A New Partnership for African Development: Issues and Parameters.* Nordiska Afrikainstitutet, Uppsala, 1997.

(2000), "Exorcism of the Ghost: An Alternative Growth Model for Measuring the Financing Gap", Economic Research Papers No. 57. Abidjan, African Development Bank, 2000.

Hyden Gorand (1983), "No Shortcuts to Progress: The African Development Management in Perspective", London: Heinemann.

(1992), "Governance and the Study of Politics", In Hyden Gorand and Bratton Michael (eds.); *Governance and Politics in Africa*. Boulder & London: Lynne Rienner Publishers.

IIF (2001), "Capital Flows to Emerging Market Economies", January, 2001

IMF (International Monetary Fund) (2000), *World Economic Outlook*. Washington, D.C.

IPEP (International Panel of Eminent Personalities) (2000), "International Panel of Eminent Personalities to Investigate the 1994 Genocide in Rwanda and the Surrounding Events", Background of the Eminent Personalities and the Secretariat. 7 July 2000.

Iskander Magdi and Nadereh Chamlou (2000), "Corporate Governance: A Framework for Implementation", Washington, D.C.: World Bank, 2000.

Jessop Bob (1998), "L'essor de la gouvernance et ses risques d'échec : le cas du développement", *Revue internationale des sciences sociales*, No 155, mars, pp.31-49.

Joe Coates (1994), "The Deadening Power of Dilemmas", *Futures,* Volume 26, Number 10. London, Butterworth-Heinemann, 1994.

John K. and W. Senbet (1998), "Corporate Governance and Board Effectiveness", *Journal of Bank-*

ing and Finance. 22: 371-403.

Johnston Michael (1997), "What Can Be Done About Entrenched Corruption", Washington, D.C.: World Bank, 1997.

Kane O. (1999), "Marchés publics & corruption", Communication présentée à la conférence internationale sur la bonne gouvernance et le développement durable en Afrique au sud du sahara, Abidjan, 22-24 novembre, 1999.

Kapstein Ethan (1996), "Governing the Global Economy: International Finance and the State", Cambridge, Mass: Harvard University Press.

Kaufman Daniel, Sanjay Pradham and Randi Ryterman (1998), "New Frontiers in Diagnosing and Combating Corruption", *PREMnotes newsletter series.* Note No. 7 Washington, D.C.: World Bank, October 1998.

A. Kraay, and P. Zoido-Lobaton (1999), "Aggregating Governance Indicators", World Bank Working Paper #2195.

Kester G. et O. O. Sidibé (éds.) (1997), *Syndicats africains : A vous maintenant ! Pour une démocratie durable.* L'Harmattan.

Kifle Henock (1993), "Government and Development in Africa: Issues and the Role of the African Development Bank and Other Multilateral Institutions", African Development Bank.

Killick T. (1989), "Principle of Policy for the Adaptive Economy", Working Paper No. 32. London: Overseas Development Institute.

Ki Zerbo, J. (1978), "Histoire de l'Afrique Noire", Hatier.

Kouassi B. (1996), "Evaluation des besoins en renforcement des capacités nationales en Afrique : Exemple de la Côte d'Ivoire", Banque mondiale, Abidjan.

La Porta R., F. Lopez-de-Silanes, and A. Shleifer (1998), "Corporate Ownership Around the World", NBER. Working Paper #6625.

Lall S. (1996), "Industrialization: Towards Policies for Long-Term Development", Background Paper Prepared for the *African Development Report, 1996.*

Landes David (1998), "The Wealth and Poverty of Nations: Why some are Rich", New York Norton and Company.

MacGaffey J. (1992), "Initiatives de la base: L'autre cheminement social du Zaïre et la restructuration économique", In Hyden, G. et Bratton, M. (éds.), *Gouverner l'Afrique : Vers un partage des rôles,* Nouveaux Horizons, pp. 345-372.

Mbembe Achille (1992), "Transitions de l'autoritarisme et problèmes de gouvernement en Afrique sub-saharienne", *Afrique et développement,* Vol. XVII, No.1, pp. 37-64.

Mekamcha Ghaouti (1999), "Pouvoirs et recompositions en Algérie", In Diop et Diouf, *Les figures du politique en Afrique : Des pouvoirs hérités aux pouvoirs élus,* Codesria-Karthala, pp. 385-412.

Meredith Martin (1985), "The First Dance of Freedom: Black Africa in the Post War Era", London, Abacus.

Mkandawire Thandika and Soludo Charles C. (1999), "Our Continent, Our Future Future: African Perspectives on Structural Adjustment", Trenton, New Jersey: African World Press Inc.

Mlambo K. and A. B. Elhiraika (1997), "Macroeconomic Policies and Private Savings and Investment in SADC Countries", African Development Bank, Economic Research Paper. Series No. 33.

            and T.W. Oshikoya (1999), "Macroeconomic Factors and Investment in Africa", Paper Presented at the May 1999 Plenary on Business Environment and Investment Organised by the African Economic Research Consortium, (AERC), Accra, Ghana.

Mule Harris (2000), "Challenges to African Governance and Civil Society", *Africa Notes,* May 2000, page 8.

Michalopoulos C. (1998), "WTO Accession for Countries in Transition", The World Bank, Development Research Group. Working Paper 1934.

Modisi M. (1997), "Réforme de la fonction publique au Botswana depuis les années 80 : Leçons d'expériences", In Ademolekun et al., 1997, pp. 67-83.

Monks Robert and Nell Minow (1996), "Watching the Watchers: Corporate Governance for the 21st Century", Cambridge, Mass: Blackwell Publishers Inc., 1996.

North Douglass (1990), "Institutions, Institutional Change and Economic Performance", New York: Cambridge University Press.

Nyerere Julius (1998), "Good Governance for Africa", *Southern African Political and Economic Monthly* (SAPEM), April 1998.

Ofosu-Amaah Paati W., Raj Soopramanien, and Kishor Uprety (1999), "Combating Corruption: A comparative Review of Selected Legal; Aspects of State Practice and Major International Initiatives", Washington, D.C.: The World Bank.

Oshikoya Temitope W. (1994), "Macroeconomic Determinants of Domestic Private in Africa: An Empirical Analysis", *Economic Development and Cultural Change.* Vol. 42, pp 573 – 596.

            and M. Nureldin Hussain (1998), "Information Technology and the Challenge of Economic Development in Africa", *African Development Review*, Volume 10, Number 1. Abidjan, African Development Bank, 1998.

Osterkamp R. (1998), "Strengthening of the Economic Political Competence of Governments of African Developing Countries in the Interest of Long-Term Political, Social and Ecological Goals", Munich: FES.

Otobo Ejeviome Eloho (1996), "Regulatory Reform: An Imperative for Successful Privatization", Paper Presented at the Annual Conference on African Privatization Network Accra, Ghana. Nov. 4-6 1996.

            (1999), "Regulatory Reform: An Imperative for Successful Privatization", Paper Presented at the Annual Conference of African Privatization. Network, Accra, Ghana. Nov. 4 – 6, 1996.

            (2000), "Contemporary External Influences on Corporate Governance: Coping With Challenges in Africa", Paper Prepared for Presentation at the ACDESS Millennium Symposium on Making Africa Face the Challenges on the 21st at Ijebu-Ode, Ogun State, Nigeria.

OAU (1998), "Inventory of African Conflicts Since the Establishment of the Organization of African Unity-1963", (Draft), Addis Ababa, November.

Padgen Anthony (1998), "La Genèse de la "Gouvernance" et l'ordre mondial 'Cosmopolitique' selon les lumières", *Revue internationale des sciences sociales,* No. 155, mars, pp. 9-17.

Parkinson J. E. (1994), "Corporate Power and Responsibility: Issues in the Theory of Company Law", Oxford: Clarendon Press, 1994.

Pleskovic Boris and Joseph E. Stiglitz (eds.) (1997), "Annual World Bank Conference on Development Economics", The World Bank, Washington D. C.

République de Côte d'Ivoire (1998), "Réunion du groupe consultatif : Renforcement des capacités nationales", Document de stratégie.

République du Cameroun, Ministère de l'Economie et des Finances (2000), *Rapport du programme national de gouvernance.*

Richard Heeks (1999) (ed.), *Reinventing Government in the Information Age.* London, Routledge Press, 1999.

Robin Mansell and Uta When (eds.) (1999), *Knowledge Societies: Information Technology for Sustainable Development.* London, Oxford University Press, 1998, page 77.

Rose-Ackerman Susan (1997), "Corruption and Development", Washington, D.C.: World Bank, 1997.

Sam Pitroda (1993), "Democracy and the Village Telephone", *Harvard Business Review*, December 1993.

Sambanis N. (2000), "Ethnic War: A Theoretical and Empirical Inquiry Into its Causes", World Bank, Washington D.C.

Short H. (1998), "Corporate Governance: Cadbury, Greenbury and Hampel–A Review", *Journal of Financial Regulation and Compliance* 7(1): 57-67.

Stoker Gerry (1998), "Cinq propositions pour une théorie de la gouvernance", *Revue Internationale des sciences sociales*, No 155, mars, pp. 19-30.

Rodrik Dani (2000), "Development Strategies for the Next Century", Paper Presented at the Conference on 'Developing Economies in the 21ˢᵗ Century' Institute for Developing Economies. Japan External Trade Organisation. January 26-27 in Chiba Japan.

Touraine A. (1994), "Qu'est-ce-que la démocratie?", Editions Fayard : Paris.

Tripp A.M. (1992), "Organisations locales et participation face à l'état, dans les villes de Tanzanie", In Hyden, G. et Bratton, M. (eds.), *Gouverner l'Afrique : Vers un partage des rôles*, Nouveaux horizons, pp. 311-343.

UNDP (United Nations Development Programme) (1993), "UNDP Rethinking Technical Cooperation: Reforms for Capacity Building in Africa", New York: UNDP, 1993.

＿＿＿ (2000), "Governance for Human Development", UNDP Sustainable Human Development. October 2000.

UNECA (United Nations Economic Commission for Africa) (2000a), *Economic Report on Africa 2000.* Addis Ababa.

＿＿＿ (2000b), "Financing African Development: An Issues Paper", Conference of African Finance Ministers, November, Addis Ababa

UNCTAD (United Nations Conference on Trade and Development)(2000), *World Investment Report*. UNCTAD, Geneva.

UNIDO (United Nations Industrial Development Organization) (2000), "African Industry 2000: The Challenge of Going Global", Austria, January 2000.

Wohlmuth Karl (1999), "Governance and Economic Development in Africa: An Introduction", In Wohlmuth, Karl, Bass, Hans H., and Messner, Frank (eds.), *Good Governance and Economic Development*. African Development Perspectives. Yearbook, Hamburg, Lit Verlag Munster.

World Bank (1981), "Accelerated Development in Sub-Saharan Africa: An Agenda for Action", Washington: World Bank.

            (1990), *World Bank Development Report*, Oxford University Press, Oxford.

            (1992), "Governance and Development", Washington, DC. The World Bank.

            (1997), *World Development Report 1997: The State in a Changing World* Ox ford University Press, Oxford.

            (1998), *World Development Report 1998/ 1999: Knowledge for Development*. Washington, D.C., The World Bank.

            (2000), *Global Economic Prospects*. Washington, D.C., The World Bank.

WTO (World Trade Organization) (1998), *Electronic Commerce and The Role of the WTO*, Geneva: WTO Publications, 1998.

Wunsch James S. (1999), "Decentralization, Local Governance and the Democratic Transition in Southern Africa: A Comparative Analysis"

Yonaba Salif (1997), "Indépendance de la justice et droits de l'homme : Le cas du Burkina Faso", Centre for the Independence of Judges and Lawyers, Genève.

Electronic Sources

Al Ahram Center for Political and Strategic Studies in Egypt, http://www.acpss.org.

Basle Committee on Banking and Regulating, http://www.bis.org/publ/bcbs33.pdf.

Ero Confort (1995) "ECOWAS and Subregional Peacekeeping in Liberia", *The Journal of Humanitarian Assistance*, September 1995, http://www.jha.ac/articles/a005.htm).

FAO (Food and Agriculture Organization) (2000), http://www.fao.org/reliefoperations/media/download/moz00.pdf.

Ghana's new national information plan at, http://www.nici.org.gh.

International Federation of Journalists (IFJ): The Role of Media in Promotion of Human Rights and Development in Africa. Brussels: IFJ, December 1999, http://www.ijnet.org/Archive/2000/6/29-7163.html.

Mbeki Thabo (2000); President's Office, Government of South Africa, http://www.polity.org.za/govdocs/speeches/2001/sp0128a.html

Mboweni T. T. (2000), "Central Bank Independence: The Case of South Africa", Reuters Forum Lecture, Johannesburg, 11 October 2000, http://www.bis.org/review/r001018b.pdf.

OECD (1999a), OECD Principles of Corporate Governance, http:www.oecd.org/daf/governance/principles.htm.

(1999b), OECD Anti-Corruption Unit, http://www.oecd.org/daf/nocorruption/.

(2000), OECD Financial Action Task Force on Money Laundering (FATF), http://www.oecd.org/fatf/.

Omar Kabbaj (2000), Acceptance Speech on the occasion of His Election to a Second Term as President of ADB Group, http://www.afdb.org/news/speeches/pdt-closing-am2000.html.

Ott Dana (1998), "Power to the People: The Role of Electronic Media in Promoting Democracy in Africa", *First Monday: Peer Reviewed Journal on the Internet*, http://www.firstmonday.dk/issues/issue3_4/ott/index.html.

Prevention of Criminal use of the Banking System for the Purpose of Money-Laundering (1988), www.bis.org/publ/bcbsc137.pdf.

Sherif Kamel (1998), "Decision Support Systems and Strategic Public Sector Decision. Making in Egypt", http://www.infozone.telluride.co.us/InfoZone.html.

Shanyisa Anota Khasiani (1999), "Enhancing Women's Participation in Governance: The Case of Kakamega and Mukueni Districts, Kenya", Chapter 8 in IDRC, *Gender and the Information Revolution in Africa*. Ottawa, International Development Research Center, http://www.idrc.ca/books/focus/903/11-chp08.htm.

Transparency International (2000), http:www.transparency.de.

UNCHS Database Search, www.bestpractices.org.

UNDP (United Nations Development Programme) (1999), "UNDP and Good Governance: Experiences and Lessons Learned." New York, United Nations Development Programme, http://magnet.undp.org/docs/gov/Lessons1.htm.

PART THREE

ECONOMIC AND SOCIAL
STATISTICS ON AFRICA

Contents

Preface

The main purpose of this part of the Report is to present basic data that enable the monitoring of economic and social progress in regional member countries of the African Development Bank (ADB), and provide benchmark data for analysts of African development. The data cover the Bank's 53 regional member countries, with statistics on Basic Indicators, National Accounts, External Sector, Money Supply and Exchange Rates, Government Finance, External Debt and Financial Flows, Labor Force, and Social Indicators.

Throughout this part of the Report, statistical tables are arranged in sections and according to indicators. The tables contain historical data from 1980 to 2000. Period averages are provided for 1980-90, and 1991-00.

The data are obtained from various international sources and supplemented, to the extent possible, with data directly obtained from ADB regional member countries, and estimates by the ADB Statistics Division. Statistical practices vary from one regional member country to another with regard to data coverage, concepts, definitions, and classifications used. Although considerable efforts have been made to standardize the data, full comparability cannot be assured. Care should be exercised in their interpretation. They provide only indications on trend or structure that allow for the identification of significant differences between countries.

Technical information on these data is provided in the explanatory notes to facilitate appropriate interpretation. However, users are advised to refer to technical notes of the specialized publications of the main sources for more details.

The designations employed and the presentation of data therein do not imply any opinions whatsoever on the part of the African Development Bank concerning the legal status of any country or of its authorities. They were adopted solely for convenience of statistical presentation.

Symbols used

...	not available
0	zero or insignificant value
|	break in the comparability of Data

TABLE 1.1
BASIC INDICATORS

COUNTRY	AREA ('000 Sq. Km)	POPULATION (Millions) 2000	GNP PER CAPITA (US $) 1999	CONSUMER PRICE INFLATION (%) 2000	LIFE EXPECTANCY AT BIRTH (Years) 1999	INFANT MORTALITY RATE (per 1000) 1999	ADULT ILLITERACY RATE (%) 1999
ALGERIA	2,382	31,471	1,520	5.5	70	38	33
ANGOLA	1,247	12,878	220	120.0	48	115	…
BENIN	113	6,097	380	1.7	54	82	61
BOTSWANA	600	1,622	3,240	8.2	43	59	24
BURKINA FASO	274	11,937	240	-0.6	46	93	77
BURUNDI	28	6,695	120	27.4	44	112	53
CAMEROON	475	15,085	580	2.8	54	68	25
CAPE VERDE	4	428	1,330	4.0	70	51	27
CENT. AFR. REP.	623	3,615	290	3.0	45	93	55
CHAD	1,284	7,651	210	0.9	48	105	59
COMOROS	2	694	350	5.0	60	69	41
CONGO	342	2,943	670	3.5	50	86	21
CONGO DEM. REP.	2,345	51,654	…	540.0	52	79	40
COTE D'IVOIRE	322	14,786	710	2.0	47	81	54
DJIBOUTI	23	638	790	2.5	52	99	37
EGYPT	1,001	68,470	1,400	2.9	68	42	45
EQUAT. GUINEA	28	453	1,170	1.6	52	101	18
ERITREA	118	3,850	200	…	52	84	45
ETHIOPIA	1,104	62,565	100	3.7	44	106	63
GABON	268	1,226	3,350	1.1	52	82	…
GAMBIA	11	1,305	340	1.5	49	114	65
GHANA	239	20,212	390	16.9	62	60	30
GUINEA	246	7,430	510	4.9	48	116	…
GUINEA BISSAU	36	1,213	160	3.6	45	124	62
KENYA	580	30,080	350	5.4	49	64	19
LESOTHO	30	2,153	550	6.0	53	89	17
LIBERIA	111	3,154	…	…	53	83	47
LIBYA	1,760	5,605	…	12.0	71	26	21
MADAGASCAR	587	15,942	250	9.5	59	75	34
MALAWI	118	10,925	190	27.0	40	129	41
MALI	1,240	11,234	240	-1.2	55	111	60
MAURITANIA	1,026	2,670	380	2.7	55	86	58
MAURITIUS	2	1,158	3,590	4.0	72	14	16
MOROCCO	447	28,351	1,200	1.9	68	43	52
MOZAMBIQUE	802	19,680	230	12.0	40	115	57
NAMIBIA	824	1,726	1,890	8.7	43	72	19
NIGER	1,267	10,730	190	1.5	50	107	85
NIGERIA	924	111,506	310	9.5	50	77	38
RWANDA	26	7,733	250	2.5	41	117	35
SAO T. & PRINC	1	147	270	5.0	…	…	…
SENEGAL	197	9,481	510	0.9	54	59	64
SEYCHELLES	0.5	77	6,540	6.8	…	…	…
SIERRA LEONE	72	4,854	130	-2.6	40	150	…
SOMALIA	638	10,097	…	11.5	49	114	…
SOUTH AFRICA	1,221	40,377	3,160	4.0	48	62	15
SUDAN	2,506	29,490	330	14.4	57	66	43
SWAZILAND	17	1,008	1,360	0.2	62	58	21
TANZANIA	945	33,517	240	6.1	48	76	25
TOGO	57	4,629	320	5.4	50	78	44
TUNISIA	164	9,586	2,100	3.1	71	26	30
UGANDA	241	21,778	320	2.9	44	97	34
ZAMBIA	753	9,169	320	24.5	42	76	23
ZIMBABWE	391	11,669	520	56.3	42	67	12
AFRICA	**30,061**	**783,446**	**684**	**12.7**	**53**	**76**	**39**

TABLE 2.1
GROSS DOMESTIC PRODUCT, REAL
(MILLIONS US DOLLARS, CONSTANT 1995 PRICES)

COUNTRY	1980	1990	1995	1999	2000	Av. Ann. Real Growth Rate (%) 1980-1990	1991-2000
ALGERIA	31,561	40,937	41,248	46,950	48,734	2.5	1.4
ANGOLA	5,116	6,561	5,187	6,300	6,501	1.5	-0.3
BENIN	1,253	1,632	2,009	2,458	2,581	3.1	4.6
BOTSWANA	1,366	3,580	4,420	5,686	6,027	10.5	5.5
BURKINA FASO	1,445	2,002	2,355	2,937	3,098	3.1	4.2
BURUNDI	728	1,126	1,000	955	955	4.2	-1.8
CAMEROON	6,319	8,765	7,965	9,640	10,044	3.1	0.7
CAPE VERDE	171	381	491	625	656	11.3	5.4
CENT. AFR. REP.	964	1,069	1,122	1,228	1,263	0.6	1.4
CHAD	787	1,308	1,438	1,631	1,647	4.5	3.2
COMOROS	167	223	215	211	212	3.6	-0.4
CONGO	1,536	2,456	2,510	2,402	2,493	6.4	0.2
CONGO DEM. REP.	8,458	9,234	6,338	4,785	4,474	1.1	-6.0
COTE D'IVOIRE	8,556	9,187	9,992	12,244	11,999	-0.4	3.3
DJIBOUTI	505	540	491	499	510	1.1	-1.1
EGYPT	29,896	50,915	00,150	74,583	78,312	5.9	4.1
EQUAT. GUINEA	106	117	164	509	617	0.2	19.7
ERITREA	...	...	574	692	626	...	6.2
ETHIOPIA	4,002	5,134	5,779	7,042	7,366	3.2	3.4
GABON	3,565	4,263	4,958	5,159	5,009	2.1	3.3
GAMBIA	243	347	382	461	486	2.4	2.9
GHANA	4,231	5,236	6,457	7,693	8,001	2.1	4.4
GUINEA	2,608	3,106	3,729	4,406	4,582	2.2	4.1
GUINEA BISSAU	134	217	254	217	233	2.9	-0.3
KENYA	5,612	8,360	9,047	9,910	9,881	4.2	2.0
LESOTHO	490	764	933	1,032	1,055	4.0	3.8
LIBERIA	1,523	482	135	...	...	-8.6	...
LIBYA	37,811	32,265	29,717	30,678	31,752	-1.1	-0.8
MADAGASCAR	3,048	3,212	3,160	3,641	3,815	0.6	1.0
MALAWI	992	1,234	1,429	1,688	1,742	2.0	3.8
MALI	2,013	2,136	2,466	2,964	3,098	0.2	3.5
MAURITANIA	753	887	1,068	1,252	1,315	1.9	3.9
MAURITIUS	1,743	3,127	3,973	4,863	5,223	4.6	5.3
MOROCCO	21,590	31,507	32,986	38,387	38,695	4.4	2.8
MOZAMBIQUE	2,006	2,036	2,392	3,417	3,547	-1.8	5.9
NAMIBIA	2,446	2,752	3,503	4,058	4,200	0.8	4.5
NIGER	1,833	1,813	1,881	2,194	2,259	0.6	2.6
NIGERIA	22,357	24,864	28,109	30,988	31,918	1.6	2.7
RWANDA	1,660	2,029	1,286	1,952	2,059	2.7	2.2
SAO T. & PRINC.	48	42	45	49	50	0.8	1.7
SENEGAL	3,057	4,150	4,476	5,487	5,789	2.7	2.9
SEYCHELLES	314	441	508	562	569	2.9	3.5
SIERRA LEONE	934	1,118	866	683	709	2.2	-4.7
SOMALIA	1,401	1,610	1,564	...	...	1.1	...
SOUTH AFRICA	127,410	144,763	151,113	165,467	170,431	1.9	1.5
SUDAN	5,040	5,621	7,194	9,236	9,864	1.2	5.7
SWAZILAND	591	1,113	1,267	1,446	1,485	6.2	2.9
TANZANIA	3,475	4,808	5,255	6,151	6,471	3.4	2.6
TOGO	1,175	1,304	1,309	1,493	1,538	2.4	1.8
TUNISIA	10,509	14,915	18,029	22,672	23,816	4.0	4.6
UGANDA	2,796	4,102	5,756	7,458	7,839	3.3	6.8
ZAMBIA	3,351	3,716	3,471	3,832	3,985	1.3	0.2
ZIMBABWE	4,347	6,689	7,120	8,345	7,886	5.4	3.0
AFRICA	**384,041**	**470,197**	**499,297**	**572,025**	**590,570**	**2.5**	**2.3**

TABLE 2.2
GROSS DOMESTIC PRODUCT, NOMINAL
(MILLIONS OF US DOLLARS AT CURRENT MARKET PRICES)

COUNTRY	1980	1990	1995	1999	2000	Av. Ann. Nominal Change (%) 1980-1990	1991-2000
ALGERIA	42,345	61,902	41,248	47,857	52,609	6.2	-1.0
ANGOLA	5,423	10,260	5,187	8,545	8,617	6.8	2.7
BENIN	1,405	1,845	2,009	2,414	2,219	4.9	3.4
BOTSWANA	1,130	3,489	4,420	6,024	6,471	14.4	6.7
BURKINA FASO	1,709	2,765	2,355	2,580	2,392	6.1	-0.5
BURUNDI	920	1,132	1,000	714	735	3.7	-3.8
CAMEROON	6,741	11,152	7,965	9,187	8,346	6.6	-1.9
CAPE VERDE	107	339	491	581	556	17.4	5.4
CENT. AFR. REP.	797	1,488	1,122	1,053	973	8.1	-2.9
CHAD	1,033	1,739	1,438	1,530	1,387	5.7	-1.3
COMOROS	124	250	215	193	173	8.3	-2.9
CONGO	1,706	2,799	2,510	2,217	2,679	9.0	1.6
CONGO DEM. REP.	14,924	9,348	6,338	5,334	4,503	-2.8	-6.3
COTE D'IVOIRE	10,175	10,796	9,992	11,206	9,640	2.3	-0.1
DJIBOUTI	296	425	491	537	561	3.7	2.8
EGYPT	22,912	43,130	60,159	88,781	94,716	8.6	8.5
EQUAT. GUINEA	108	132	164	696	1,064	3.1	27.6
ERITREA	...	...	574	645	654	...	5.6
ETHIOPIA	4,106	6,842	5,779	6,439	6,603	5.8	0.5
GABON	4,279	5,952	4,958	4,594	4,676	7.7	-1.7
GAMBIA	241	317	382	393	398	5.0	2.4
GHANA	4,445	5,886	6,457	7,774	4,819	4.0	-0.7
GUINEA	2,638	2,818	3,729	3,733	3,789	1.3	3.1
GUINEA BISSAU	111	244	254	218	224	8.2	-0.4
KENYA	7,265	8,533	9,047	10,638	10,240	3.2	4.0
LESOTHO	432	622	933	923	846	6.8	3.6
LIBERIA	1,117	384	135	...	...	-7.0	...
LIBYA	35,721	28,587	29,717	...	...	1.6	...
MADAGASCAR	4,042	3,081	3,160	3,721	3,857	-0.2	3.0
MALAWI	1,238	1,803	1,429	1,810	1,950	5.3	5.2
MALI	1,787	2,421	2,466	2,608	2,390	4.6	1.5
MAURITANIA	709	1,020	1,068	958	940	4.5	-0.4
MAURITIUS	1,132	2,642	3,973	4,228	4,495	8.2	5.6
MOROCCO	18,821	25,821	32,986	34,998	33,143	5.4	2.8
MOZAMBIQUE	3,526	2,512	2,392	3,981	3,874	-0.1	5.1
NAMIBIA	2,169	2,340	3,503	3,458	3,467	1.6	4.2
NIGER	2,509	2,481	1,881	2,018	1,873	2.6	-1.8
NIGERIA	64,202	28,472	28,109	35,045	38,588	-2.5	4.6
RWANDA	1,163	2,584	1,286	1,956	1,811	8.7	2.6
SAO T. & PRINC.	43	50	45	47	47	6.9	-0.2
SENEGAL	2,987	5,698	4,476	4,801	4,439	8.1	-1.4
SEYCHELLES	147	369	508	545	599	10.5	5.1
SIERRA LEONE	1,166	897	866	669	639	1.1	-2.6
SOMALIA	603	917	1,564	...	...	4.5	...
SOUTH AFRICA	80,544	112,014	151,113	130,220	125,892	8.1	1.4
SUDAN	7,617	13,167	7,194	...	...	6.0	1.6
SWAZILAND	582	860	1,267	1,223	1,195	8.7	3.6
TANZANIA	4,918	4,259	5,255	8,636	8,921	-0.3	8.2
TOGO	1,136	1,628	1,309	1,405	1,276	6.9	-1.1
TUNISIA	8,743	12,291	18,029	20,888	19,811	5.3	5.2
UGANDA	1,245	4,304	5,756	6,411	6,140	16.9	5.1
ZAMBIA	3,884	3,288	3,471	3,150	3,156	2.7	-0.0
ZIMBABWE	6,679	8,784	7,120	5,608	7,327	5.8	-0.5
AFRICA	**393,799**	**466,877**	**499,297**	**545,008**	**552,149**	**1.9**	**1.8**

TABLE 2.3
GROSS NATIONAL SAVINGS
(PERCENTAGE OF GDP)

COUNTRY	1980	1990	1995	1999	2000	Annual Average 1980-1990	Annual Average 1991-2000
ALGERIA	30.4	31.5	25.9	28.6	34.4	26.7	29.3
ANGOLA	20.8	4.5	8.3	10.0	12.8	12.4	10.7
BENIN	29.3	12.0	13.0	11.8	11.5	9.9	11.7
BOTSWANA	31.0	41.2	36.5	32.7	32.6	34.6	38.6
BURKINA FASO	13.3	16.9	18.2	15.2	19.2	16.7	16.9
BURUNDI	4.8	3.5	8.8	4.4	-1.0	7.0	5.6
CAMEROON	20.4	16.2	13.6	15.2	17.0	20.0	14.0
CAPE VERDE	...	19.0	32.0	28.3	24.3	25.1	31.7
CENT. AFR. REP.	-2.8	5.7	7.2	8.1	8.0	4.9	7.5
CHAD	11.3	0.4	1.1	-2.4	3.9	2.6	2.0
COMOROS	14.7	10.1	5.4	11.2	13.7	12.7	11.0
CONGO	59.3	69.2	20.9	18.6	23.7	59.4	12.9
CONGO DEM. REP.	6.4	4.1	3.1	2.2	-0.5	6.1	-1.6
COTE D'IVOIRE	22.1	-2.1	9.2	11.8	13.1	8.3	7.9
DJIBOUTI	27.4	14.7	2.0	3.0	3.6	8.9	2.1
EGYPT	16.5	22.4	22.6	20.6	16.9	16.3	20.3
EQUAT. GUINEA	...	...	...	...	...	...	...
ERITREA	...	...	...	...		...	...
ETHIOPIA	7.3	8.6	12.3	7.1	5.6	9.5	7.3
GABON	41.9	24.2	27.2	26.0	26.0	34.7	26.0
GAMBIA	-1.2	17.8	11.7	15.1	15.7	16.4	15.2
GHANA	4.9	10.7	15.6	19.5	19.0	8.1	13.7
GUINEA	9.0	8.9	17.7	15.7	16.6	7.7	17.7
GUINEA BISSAU	9.5	14.2	4.7	2.7	1.6	9.3	6.1
KENYA	7.5	19.9	18.1	13.4	11.6	18.1	16.5
LESOTHO	43.1	46.4	25.5	7.2	6.2	31.9	19.2
LIBERIA	31.8	12.0	11.3	8.1	...	17.9	10.9
LIBYA	...	...	...	...	...	...	...
MADAGASCAR	1.2	4.1	1.2	7.3	6.4	3.2	4.2
MALAWI	8.1	12.1	-4.0	1.6	1.8	11.2	1.3
MALI	7.0	18.3	18.5	16.1	15.8	11.2	18.5
MAURITANIA	14.2	6.4	10.6	20.8	23.9	11.4	15.8
MAURITIUS	15.6	25.9	25.4	34.7	35.0	20.8	28.3
MOROCCO	16.5	22.9	17.3	23.3	22.8	19.3	20.7
MOZAMBIQUE	-8.4	2.3	11.2	16.0	20.1	-4.6	7.2
NAMIBIA	20.6	34.8	27.3	24.2	27.4	19.5	24.4
NIGER	17.1	7.4	2.6	6.2	5.4	10.0	6.2
NIGERIA	23.3	28.0	14.9	13.4	18.6	15.2	18.2
RWANDA	8.8	3.6	19.2	12.1	11.6	8.8	7.1
SAO T. & PRINC.	-10.4	-9.3	27.6	13.8	11.2	-6.2	10.9
SENEGAL	-1.8	10.4	16.1	15.4	15.7	4.4	14.6
SEYCHELLES	11.5	25.9	21.6	29.4	28.6	11.8	26.2
SIERRA LEONE	3.6	-1.5	-11.7	-2.8	-2.8	3.2	-3.8
SOMALIA	10.5	6.8	4.8	4.4	...	19.4	3.2
SOUTH AFRICA	33.9	19.1	16.5	14.8	14.7	23.8	15.9
SUDAN	...	9.3	...	...	...	22.5	...
SWAZILAND	7.4	20.4	28.7	8.4	6.0	9.7	16.9
TANZANIA	20.7	20.9	1.9	0.2	0.3	16.7	8.6
TOGO	18.8	18.2	11.3	8.9	5.4	13.3	8.2
TUNISIA	24.6	20.0	20.5	25.3	24.8	22.5	22.9
UGANDA	44.9	6.2	15.6	14.4	13.5	17.6	13.9
ZAMBIA	11.8	14.8	8.9	8.2	9.5	8.9	9.8
ZIMBABWE	14.5	15.6	14.5	15.0	10.7	14.7	14.3
AFRICA	21.5	18.9	16.8	16.9	18.7	18.3	16.9

TABLE 2.4
GROSS DOMESTIC INVESTMENT
(PERCENTAGE OF GDP)

COUNTRY	1980	1990	1995	1999	2000	Annual Average 1980-1990	Annual Average 1991-2000
ALGERIA	39.1	29.3	32.1	27.4	27.6	33.5	28.6
ANGOLA	10.6	11.7	4.1	32.3	33.0	14.9	15.7
BENIN	15.2	14.2	19.6	17.8	18.8	15.0	16.8
BOTSWANA	36.8	38.0	28.6	35.1	21.3	29.7	28.7
BURKINA FASO	17.0	20.6	23.9	27.8	30.9	19.8	24.9
BURUNDI	13.9	14.5	9.6	9.1	6.8	16.4	11.1
CAMEROON	21.0	17.8	14.5	19.5	18.0	23.3	16.5
CAPE VERDE	51.6	22.9	42.4	37.6	35.8	41.6	37.2
CENT. AFR. REP.	7.0	12.3	13.5	14.3	16.2	11.0	11.7
CHAD	3.2	15.9	10.3	10.3	15.0	6.6	12.2
COMOROS	33.2	19.7	17.6	14.6	24.0	27.9	18.6
CONGO	35.8	15.9	30.8	22.3	24.9	31.0	31.3
CONGO DEM. REP.	10.0	9.1	9.4	4.1	7.6	11.5	6.6
COTE D'IVOIRE	26.5	6.7	13.5	16.3	17.6	15.6	13.0
DJIBOUTI	16.6	20.6	8.6	10.1	13.9	20.4	12.3
EGYPT	27.5	28.8	17.2	22.8	19.8	28.7	18.7
EQUAT. GUINEA	55.4	17.4	76.3	41.4	20.5	30.7	58.0
ERITREA	...	...	19.3	47.3	...	...	27.8
ETHIOPIA	10.0	11.8	16.4	18.1	14.6	13.7	14.9
GABON	27.5	21.7	23.7	26.6	22.2	33.4	25.6
GAMBIA	26.7	22.3	20.2	17.8	19.7	20.0	19.8
GHANA	5.6	14.4	20.0	23.2	24.2	8.4	21.3
GUINEA	14.6	17.5	16.4	17.0	20.3	15.8	17.4
GUINEA BISSAU	28.2	29.9	22.3	16.3	26.8	31.8	25.4
KENYA	24.5	19.7	17.5	13.5	16.0	20.2	16.0
LESOTHO	37.0	53.2	60.5	46.0	30.4	41.2	53.9
LIBERIA	27.3	11.4	9.6	7.1	...	15.6	9.2
LIBYA	24.3	18.8	12.6	14.0	...	22.4	14.3
MADAGASCAR	15.0	17.0	10.9	12.9	15.1	11.2	11.7
MALAWI	24.7	19.7	17.0	14.8	16.4	18.7	17.0
MALI	15.5	23.0	22.9	21.2	22.6	17.8	22.5
MAURITANIA	26.3	20.0	19.3	17.8	22.6	26.8	19.3
MAURITIUS	20.7	30.9	25.8	26.4	26.0	24.3	27.9
MOROCCO	24.2	25.3	20.7	24.2	25.3	24.4	22.3
MOZAMBIQUE	5.9	15.6	22.8	32.6	37.7	8.7	22.0
NAMIBIA	30.5	33.8	21.7	23.5	24.1	19.8	21.8
NIGER	28.1	8.1	7.3	10.2	10.7	14.7	9.1
NIGERIA	21.3	14.7	16.3	31.9	21.5	16.3	21.8
RWANDA	16.1	14.6	15.0	14.3	17.9	15.3	14.8
SAO T. & PRINC.	34.2	36.0	38.1	40.0	50.5	36.1	41.0
SENEGAL	11.7	13.8	16.7	18.8	19.6	12.3	17.1
SEYCHELLES	38.3	24.6	30.3	37.5	28.0	26.2	31.9
SIERRA LEONE	17.7	9.4	5.6	0.3	12.8	11.7	7.2
SOMALIA	9.1	15.5	13.1	11.3	n.a.	15.0	12.8
SOUTH AFRICA	23.4	17.2	18.0	15.1	15.6	18.7	16.1
SUDAN	14.7	13.6	10.0	7.8	17.4	14.3	11.9
SWAZILAND	30.3	19.6	34.1	12.9	33.8	25.9	26.3
TANZANIA	32.5	26.1	19.8	15.5	16.1	22.1	20.3
TOGO	28.4	26.6	16.1	13.4	16.4	20.1	14.6
TUNISIA	29.4	27.1	24.7	26.4	29.5	28.6	26.8
UGANDA	7.0	12.7	16.4	16.4	18.2	8.6	15.9
ZAMBIA	23.3	17.3	15.9	14.4	16.2	16.2	13.7
ZIMBABWE	16.9	17.4	23.6	14.5	13.4	17.3	19.6
AFRICA	**23.6**	**20.3**	**19.0**	**20.4**	**19.9**	**21.6**	**19.0**

TABLE 2.5
TERMS OF TRADE
(1995 = 100)

COUNTRY	1980	1990	1996	1999	2000	Average Annual Growth (%) 1980-1990	1991-2000
ALGERIA	163.9	124.4	111.4	98.2	158.4	-1.1	4.7
ANGOLA	278.6	140.6	123.5	129.6	188.4	-3.7	5.4
BENIN	61.2	105.9	91.0	75.2	72.9	6.6	-2.7
BOTSWANA	28.1	80.5	119.3	146.5	144.9	14.8	6.5
BURKINA FASO	63.4	91.0	93.2	85.2	75.8	4.0	-1.6
BURUNDI	141.1	78.6	72.8	71.7	61.7	-3.2	-0.2
CAMEROON	160.8	98.9	91.4	77.7	103.5	-3.3	1.3
CAPE VERDE	277.4	186.4	94.4	96.7	96.7	2.9	-5.2
CENT. AFR. REP.	105.5	99.4	85.5	73.7	70.8	-0.4	-3.1
CHAD	60.8	73.5	110.5	122.3	117.7	3.1	5.2
COMOROS	62.3	170.4	92.9	73.4	66.4	18.3	-8.7
CONGO	254.7	122.5	140.7	126.4	172.5	-6.9	5.5
CONGO DEM. REP.	85.8	80.8	96.4	92.9	98.1	-0.2	2.1
COTE D'IVOIRE	100.5	77.7	82.5	78.6	71.1	-1.5	-0.4
DJIDOUTI	154.2	103.4	100.4	101.7	102.2	-3.4	-0.1
EGYPT	169.9	111.9	89.5	90.0	97.6	-3.1	0.6
EQUAT. GUINEA	81.8	73.7	100.7	125.7	186.5	-0.0	12.2
ERITREA							
ETHIOPIA	68.8	84.6	77.9	78.7	68.4	4.3	-0.6
GABON	120.2	128.8	121.2	115.2	152.6	1.0	3.6
GAMBIA	79.0	90.3	105.9	90.5	90.3	9.8	0.4
GHANA	144.0	95.0	96.4	118.5	100.6	-2.2	1.3
GUINEA	67.0	113.3	100.4	97.8	105.3	6.4	-0.0
GUINEA BISSAU	153.6	118.3	99.9	111.5	112.2	-1.4	-0.2
KENYA	141.0	82.0	102.6	98.0	94.8	-4.6	1.6
LESOTHO	100.1	100.0	100.0	100.0	100.0	-0.0	-0.0
LIBERIA	127.3	117.8	102.0	...	...	-0.5	...
LIBYA	...	...	...	...	...	...	...
MADAGASCAR	112.5	79.4	83.2	83.6	72.9	-2.6	-0.4
MALAWI	130.6	86.3	68.3	66.6	55.5	-3.8	-2.8
MALI	129.7	129.6	98.7	91.5	83.4	0.4	-4.1
MAURITANIA	73.8	115.2	101.4	91.1	89.6	5.7	-1.2
MAURITIUS	64.0	95.7	100.6	120.2	120.5	4.3	2.4
MOROCCO	165.5	112.3	110.9	123.1	116.6	-3.4	0.7
MOZAMBIQUE	76.0	99.4	99.6	103.0	105.3	3.8	0.7
NAMIBIA	143.3	115.2	102.7	98.7	105.8	0.2	-0.5
NIGER	209.0	115.9	91.3	83.4	80.1	-4.4	-3.5
NIGERIA	324.8	145.5	126.3	112.2	171.8	-2.9	4.3
RWANDA	222.8	83.9	85.3	88.4	84.1	-6.7	3.5
SAO T. & PRINC.	240.7	85.8	108.6	71.3	68.6	-7.5	0.3
SENEGAL	95.3	111.9	98.2	105.2	100.2	1.9	-1.0
SEYCHELLES	13.5	71.5	96.3	92.7	93.5	27.0	4.0
SIERRA LEONE	41.4	40.5	40.5	40.5	40.5	0.5	7.4
SOMALIA	112.8	100.8	99.9	...	...	-1.0	...
SOUTH AFRICA	65.0	100.0	101.4	98.5	96.4	5.3	-0.4
SUDAN	71.8	93.8	97.7	108.4	119.6	3.2	2.7
SWAZILAND	87.2	106.2	102.1	106.3	102.9	2.7	-0.2
TANZANIA	193.9	89.8	90.2	91.0	89.9	-7.2	0.2
TOGO	188.5	117.2	104.8	122.6	123.3	-4.3	0.8
TUNISIA	124.4	100.8	101.6	104.3	104.4	-1.9	0.4
UGANDA	95.3	86.5	70.7	66.6	60.4	4.3	0.2
ZAMBIA	141.1	95.1	77.0	79.4	82.8	-1.6	0.0
ZIMBABWE	61.9	93.8	109.6	103.0	110.0	4.7	1.8
AFRICA	141.3	107.9	104.8	101.6	117.5	-2.4	1.1

TABLE 2.6
CURRENT ACCOUNT
(AS PERCENTAGE OF GDP)

COUNTRY	1980	1990	1995	1999	2000	Annual Average 1980-1990	Annual Average 1991-2000
ALGERIA	0.6	3.0	-5.4	0.0	12.6	-0.5	2.0
ANGOLA	1.3	-2.2	-19.7	-32.2	0.4	-4.0	-14.5
BENIN	2.1	-2.2	-6.6	-5.8	-7.2	-1.7	-5.1
BOTSWANA	-15.6	-0.5	6.3	9.9	14.5	0.6	8.6
BURKINA FASO	-1.3	-3.6	-5.7	-12.6	-12.5	-3.0	-8.2
BURUNDI	-9.1	-11.1	-3.0	-4.3	-7.9	-9.5	-6.1
CAMEROON	-5.0	-4.4	-0.9	-4.3	-2.4	-1.6	-3.2
CAPE VERDE	...	-5.3	-6.7	-9.3	-12.8	-4.2	-5.9
CENT. AFR. REP.	-15.1	-6.0	-7.2	-6.3	-6.4	-7.6	-5.1
CHAD	...	-11.1	-7.7	-12.7	-11.7	-9.5	-10.2
COMOROS	-1.8	-9.5	-14.4	-15.0	-11.5	-10.2	-11.3
CONGO	18.0	-9.0	-15.7	-10.6	-2.1	7.9	-18.9
CONGO DEM. REP.	-1.6	-8.6	-6.4	-14.2	-16.0	-5.2	-10.0
COTE D'IVOIRE	-0.0	-12.2	-5.8	-4.0	-5.4	-4.3	-6.3
DJIBOUTI	10.8	-7.4	-3.7	-5.0	-3.6	-10.7	-6.3
EGYPT	-0.9	-7.3	0.7	-2.0	-1.8	-5.4	1.2
EQUAT. GUINEA	-62.8	-26.4	-61.0	2.7	17.2	-35.2	-42.3
ERITREA	...	...	...	...	...	...	...
ETHIOPIA	-3.4	-4.6	1.2	-10.7	-11.9	-3.6	-5.5
GABON	9.0	2.5	3.6	1.9	4.3	-2.2	0.9
GAMBIA	-32.5	-2.7	-4.3	-3.6	-1.2	-5.4	-3.8
GHANA	0.2	-3.5	-2.4	-10.6	-8.5	-1.6	-6.7
GUINEA	3.9	-8.7	-4.6	-4.1	0.8	-4.2	-3.2
GUINEA BISSAU	-43.9	-13.6	-17.6	-11.0	-27.7	-27.0	-19.2
KENYA	-15.3	-5.6	-5.6	-3.2	-4.0	-5.3	-2.3
LESOTHO	-9.5	-10.1	-34.3	-23.8	-20.8	-13.3	-29.8
LIBERIA	5.0	-1.2	0.3	0.3		1.9	0.4
LIBYA	...	...	...	...	...	...	...
MADAGASCAR	-13.8	-10.7	-9.7	-5.6	-7.8	-7.8	-7.6
MALAWI	-16.7	-3.7	-4.3	-5.4	-5.7	-6.0	-8.9
MALI	-7.7	-5.8	-8.8	-10.8	-14.9	-7.6	-8.2
MAURITANIA	-21.9	-9.1	-13.2	-11.7	-11.6	-16.3	-12.0
MAURITIUS	-13.5	-5.3	-5.1	6.5	7.0	-3.9	0.1
MOROCCO	-4.7	-2.8	-3.6	-0.8	-2.3	-5.9	-1.6
MOZAMBIQUE	-11.4	-16.7	-20.5	-24.0	-21.8	-13.7	-19.7
NAMIBIA	...	1.2	6.2	5.3	6.0	1.2	4.1
NIGER	-11.1	-4.4	-4.7	-3.5	-4.0	-5.0	-3.3
NIGERIA	6.7	7.4	-4.6	-11.0	2.4	-5.0	-3.0
RWANDA	-3.7	-8.1	-3.0	-5.8	-12.6	-6.4	-10.2
SAO T. & PRINC.	-34.8	-52.0	-60.1	-45.8	-48.8	-38.1	-50.3
SENEGAL	-14.5	-7.8	-5.3	-5.4	-6.2	-10.6	-6.3
SEYCHELLES	-11.0	1.3	-8.7	-0.1	0.9	-12.2	-4.9
SIERRA LEONE	-14.1	-10.9	-10.1	-3.1	-8.1	-8.5	-8.2
SOMALIA	-6.9	-8.7	-8.4	-5.2	0.0	-6.8	-7.9
SOUTH AFRICA	4.4	1.8	-1.5	-0.4	-0.7	0.9	-0.2
SUDAN	-8.8	-9.0	...	...	...	-13.1	...
SWAZILAND	-27.9	6.8	-2.3	1.1	-1.5	-11.2	-0.9
TANZANIA	-8.6	-4.9	-17.7	-14.8	-15.3	-4.7	-11.5
TOGO	-9.9	-6.1	-5.5	-8.8	-9.9	-7.0	-7.1
TUNISIA	-4.1	-5.5	-4.6	-2.0	-3.4	-6.4	-4.5
UGANDA	-3.3	0.0	-6.5	-7.4	-7.9	-0.8	-8.1
ZAMBIA	-15.2	-2.5	-4.2	-16.7	-13.4	-10.7	-5.7
ZIMBABWE	-5.6	-2.9	-5.2	0.5	0.7	-4.1	-4.9
AFRICA	1.9	-1.3	-2.9	-3.4	-0.3	-2.9	-2.1

TABLE 2.7
BROAD MONEY SUPPLY (M2)
(PERCENTAGE ANNUAL CHANGE)

COUNTRY	1980	1990	1995	1999	2000	Annual Average 1980-1990	1991-2000
ALGERIA	17.4	11.4	9.2	13.7	16.6	14.4	17.5
ANGOLA	...	...	...	...	...	...	...
BENIN	48.9	28.6	-1.8	34.8	3.0	12.7	12.4
BOTSWANA	19.0	-14.0	12.3	26.3	11.9	22.6	19.1
BURKINA FASO	15.1	-0.5	22.3	2.6	6.3	11.8	10.1
BURUNDI	1.4	9.6	-11.2	47.3	20.2	11.6	15.2
CAMEROON	21.4	-1.7	-6.2	13.3	15.6	11.1	3.6
CAPE VERDE	30.6	14.6	13.2	15.4	9.4	18.7	12.1
CENT. AFR. REP.	35.0	-3.7	4.3	11.1	7.7	8.4	8.8
CHAD	-15.3	-2.4	48.7	-2.3	5.9	8.4	6.8
COMOROS	...	3.9	-6.1	18.5	4.0	12.7	2.7
CONGO	36.6	18.5	-0.1	19.9	4.2	14.0	3.9
CONGO DEM. REP.	...	...	...	...	...	...	...
COTE D'IVOIRE	2.8	-2.6	18.1	-1.7	3.2	4.0	8.2
DJIBOUTI		3.6	5.3	-3.8	0.1	7.6	-1.1
EGYPT	51.4	28.7	9.9	5.7	0.0	25.7	12.0
EQUAT. GUINEA	...	...	48.9	68.7	14.6	-11.2	38.3
ERITREA	...	...	...	...	...	...	...
ETHIOPIA	4.2	18.5	9.0	...	11.4	11.9	12.2
GABON	24.6	3.3	10.1	-3.0	-0.5	8.6	5.4
GAMBIA	10.4	8.4	14.2	12.1	9.3	18.8	12.3
GHANA	33.8	13.3	40.4	16.2	12.1	42.2	32.4
GUINEA	...	...	11.3	...	15.0	...	12.9
GUINEA BISSAU	...	574.6	43.0	21.5	14.1	...	36.8
KENYA	0.8	20.1	24.8	6.0	7.4	12.7	20.3
LESOTHO	...	8.4	8.2	-5.1	7.9	18.0	11.8
LIBERIA	...	...	...	...	...	...	...
LIBYA	26.6	19.0	9.6	-5.2		7.2	4.5
MADAGASCAR	20.6	4.5	15.9	...	10.0	16.9	22.1
MALAWI	12.6	11.1	56.2	26.5	18.0	17.6	32.0
MALI	4.5	-4.9	7.3	1.0	3.8	8.1	11.3
MAURITANIA	12.5	11.5	-5.1	2.1	7.0	13.0	2.8
MAURITIUS	23.2	21.2	18.7	15.2	10.0	21.0	14.6
MOROCCO	10.8	21.5	7.0	10.2	7.4	14.1	9.8
MOZAMBIQUE	...	37.2	47.5	31.4	16.0	39.5	38.8
NAMIBIA	...	...	24.2	8.6	9.8	...	19.5
NIGER	20.8	-4.1	3.8	15.4	7.3	7.5	-2.3
NIGERIA	46.1	32.7	19.4	31.4	24.6	18.1	31.9
RWANDA	8.1	5.6	69.5	8.1	8.1	7.8	14.4
SAO T. & PRINC.	...	...	...	-2.2	8.5	...	42.0
SENEGAL	10.3	-4.8	7.4	13.1	7.3	7.6	8.7
SEYCHELLES	33.2	14.5	10.5	...	12.5	11.7	16.2
SIERRA LEONE	21.6	74.0	19.6	37.8	23.2	51.8	30.9
SOMALIA	...	...	...	...	...	...	...
SOUTH AFRICA	22.8	11.4	16.0	10.1	9.4	17.2	13.2
SUDAN	29.4	48.8	73.3	15.6	19.4	38.0	65.4
SWAZILAND	13.7	0.6	3.9	15.6	10.0	17.1	14.4
TANZANIA	26.9	41.9	33.0	18.6	11.1	25.7	24.0
TOGO	9.1	9.5	22.3	8.4	7.2	9.0	5.0
TUNISIA	18.5	7.6	6.6	18.8	6.8	14.9	9.6
UGANDA	34.6		15.0	...	15.9	83.6	22.8
ZAMBIA	9.0	47.9	55.5	...	16.5	38.6	44.9
ZIMBABWE	29.6	15.1	25.5	...	57.9	16.8	32.2
AFRICA	23.2	18.6	21.4	17.9	13.4	18.3	21.9

TABLE 2.8
REAL EXCHANGE RATES INDICES (PERIOD AVERAGE)
(NATIONAL CURRENCY PER US $, 1995 = 100)

COUNTRY	CURRENCY	1980	1990	1998	1999	2000*	Annual Average 1980-1990	Growth (%) 1991-2000
ALGERIA	DINAR	37.5	54.9	100.2	113.2	121.5	4.3	10.0
ANGOLA	NEW KWANZA	...	23,875.0	60.4	113.4	162.3	...	178.2
BENIN	CFA FRANC		78.2	110.2	117.0	133.0		6.9
BOTSWANA	PULA	75.0	104.2	127.6	133.2	137.6	3.6	3.0
BURKINA FASO	CFA FRANC	44.4	63.5	110.8	116.9	140.7	4.2	9.7
BURUNDI	FRANC	112.2	163.5	171.6	213.3	212.3	4.6	6.8
CAMEROON	CFA FRANC	74.4	69.7	119.5	121.4	141.4	0.8	8.5
CAPE VERDE	ESCUDO		104.7	113.8	116.3	125.2	-0.9	2.0
CENT. AFR. REP.	CFA FRANC	42.9	65.1	123.0	130.4	151.5	5.5	10.5
CHAD	CFA FRANC	...	67.2	103.2	117.0	135.9	1.6	8.0
COMOROS	FRANC		87.4	112.6	115.9	129.3	-0.9	4.7
CONGO	CFA FRANC	86.5	96.6	110.5	111.2	130.4	2.2	5.6
CONGO DEM. REP.	FRANC		...	...	...	...	...	
COTE D'IVOIRE	CFA FRANC	59.0	73.0	113.4	117.3	139.4	3.1	8.3
DJIBOUTI	FRANC	...	110.8	97.2	97.0	97.8	-0.8	-1.2
EGYPT	POUND	101.6	96.6	91.6	91.2	92.9	1.3	0.6
EQUAT. GUINEA	CFA FRANC		72.9	106.8	110.7	126.8	-7.5	7.7
ERITREA	NAKFA	...	...	...	...	...	...	
ETHIOPIA	BIRR	51.5	53.0	125.1	131.0	134.8	1.2	12.1
GABON	CFA FRANC	55.1	63.9	116.8	121.0	143.4	2.5	9.5
GAMBIA	DALASI	66.2	97.6	113.6	119.6	126.4	3.9	2.7
GHANA	CEDI	15.6	82.4	96.1	99.8	161.5	25.3	10.1
GUINEA	FRANC		93.7	120.8	128.1	58.6	...	-2.2
GUINEA BISSAU	CFA FRANC	...	310.0	52.1	55.9	61.7	...	-10.1
KENYA	SHILLING	70.3	112.5	97.4	112.9	118.5	4.5	1.4
LESOTHO	MALOTI	75.2	112.9	127.2	136.2	146.0	4.1	2.8
LIBERIA	DOLLAR	163.6	131.5	3,325.5	3,116.5	2,881.1	-1.9	...
LIBYA	DINAR	...	267.5	45.0	33.0	28.5	...	-19.2
MADAGASCAR	FRANC	38.5	85.1	102.7	110.2	112.6	8.0	3.6
MALAWI	KWACHA	51.7	61.9	111.7	111.6	100.4	2.1	7.2
MALI	CFA FRANC	...	62.2	114.3	120.6	146.0	1.8	10.6
MAURITANIA	OUGUIYA		75.2	131.5	143.4	160.5	2.3	8.2
MAURITIUS	RUPEE	74.2	103.2	121.5	121.8	124.4	3.2	2.0
MOROCCO	DIRHAM	67.4	110.9	112.7	116.5	126.6	5.7	1.5
MOZAMBIQUE	METICAL		61.2	89.7	96.5	103.0	10.1	5.9
NAMIBIA	DOLLAR	68.2	106.6	130.8	135.9	142.1	8.6	3.2
NIGER	CFA FRANC	37.0	61.2	111.8	119.2	140.5	5.6	9.8
NIGERIA	NAIRA	66.3	219.4	69.4	280.0	286.3	16.8	21.8
RWANDA	FRANC	85.8	79.2	99.8	111.6	127.4	-0.0	12.4
SAO T. & PRINC.	DOBRA	...	34.0	159.4	146.4	153.2	4.0	17.2
SENEGAL	CFA FRANC	56.2	65.1	119.6	123.7	147.0	2.7	9.6
SEYCHELLES	RUPEE	106.1	104.2	115.8	116.9	118.6	0.1	1.4
SIERRA LEONE	LEONE	80.4	110.3	115.5	101.5	128.1	5.5	2.2
SOMALIA	SHILLING	27.5	161.9	103.8	97.8	73.1	22.4	-0.0
SOUTH AFRICA	RAND	77.7	104.4	131.0	140.5	151.7	3.1	4.0
SUDAN	POUND	447.4	236.1	92.6	102.4	94.3	-2.3	44.9
SWAZILAND	EMALANGENI	75.3	112.5	131.2	141.0	159.9	3.6	3.8
TANZANIA	SHILLING	39.8	103.6	82.0	87.0	90.9	9.8	-0.9
TOGO	CFA FRANC	52.4	74.5	110.6	115.4	131.0	4.3	6.9
TUNISIA	DINAR	67.0	105.5	116.3	120.4	134.1	4.8	2.7
UGANDA	SHILLING	...	93.8	119.6	134.6	147.4	23.2	5.7
ZAMBIA	KWACHA	69.1	101.0	101.7	110.4	107.1	7.3	1.0
ZIMBABWE	DOLLAR	49.5	81.3	139.3	160.8	110.3	9.6	4.7

* estimates

TABLE 2.9
INTERNATIONAL RESERVES
(MILLIONS OF US DOLLARS)

COUNTRY	1980	1990	1995	1999	2000	Average Annual Growth (%) 1980-1990	1991-2000
ALGERIA	4,021.8	980.7	2,295.6	4,793.9	7,072.8	-4.3	30.7
ANGOLA	...	...	212.8	55.3	...	...	...
BENIN	8.6	69.1	202.2	402.9	467.7	116.0	29.2
BOTSWANA	344.2	3,389.6	4,768.6	5,768.9	...	28.8	6.2
BURKINA FASO	68.7	304.7	351.7	298.4	254.6	17.8	0.5
BURUNDI	104.7	111.6	216.1	53.0	48.0	8.4	-5.1
CAMEROON	206.5	37.0	15.3	3.4	...	12.7	-16.3
CAPE VERDE	42.4	77.0	57.3	40.4	...	6.8	-5.0
CENT. AFR. REP.	61.5	122.6	237.9	139.4	...	10.3	4.8
CHAD	11.6	131.8	142.5	148.2	...	33.5	9.5
COMOROS	6.4	29.9	44.7	40.9	...	34.5	4.8
CONGO	92.5	9.9	63.6	41.5	69.1	-0.4	...
CONGO DEM. REP.	357.2	261.3	157.4	...	...	1.2	-10.8
COTE D'IVOIRE	21.7	20.9	546.2	643.5	667.7	1.2	124.9
DJIDOUTI	...	93.6	72.2	66.3	...	14.8	-3.4
EGYPT	1,149.0	3,324.6	16,885.2	14,959.1	14,200.7	19.5	19.9
EQUAT. GUINEA	...	0.7	0.0	0.0	...	96.5	323.9
ERITREA	...	...	...	...	...	...	...
ETHIOPIA	104.6	29.6	782.9	458.8	...	6.6	54.5
GABON	115.1	278.4	153.0	20.4	138.6	107.4	338.0
GAMBIA	5.7	55.4	106.1	107.2	...	98.9	10.2
GHANA	199.4	282.1	774.9	532.7	430.2	6.0	21.9
GUINEA	...	...	86.8	...	...	...	11.0
GUINEA BISSAU	...	18.2	20.3	...	...	...	-3.6
KENYA	501.1	218.9	368.8	791.6	...	-4.9	62.8
LESOTHO	50.3	72.4	456.7	520.0	...	6.7	26.9
LIBERIA	5.5	...	28.1	...	...	194.6	171.0
LIBYA	13,220.4	5,991.2	...	7,474.2	9,423.3	5.9	8.0
MADAGASCAR	9.1	92.1	109.0	195.6	...	49.4	26.9
MALAWI	69.0	137.7	110.5	251.2	222.9	33.8	23.5
MALI	15.4	197.7	330.2	355.3	316.5	47.4	8.3
MAURITANIA	146.8	58.5	89.9	227.6	259.2	-2.3	21.0
MAURITIUS	95.3	742.6	867.4	743.3	692.2	62.4	0.6
MOROCCO	427.4	2,082.0	3,831.4	5,882.4	5,140.7	39.5	10.9
MOZAMBIQUE	...	231.7	195.3	667.7	...	32.1	15.5
NAMIBIA	...	...	221.0	305.5	...	...	38.2
NIGER	126.4	226.4	99.0	42.5	21.7	13.8	-19.0
NIGERIA	10,269.7	3,866.4	1,444.3	...	...	18.4	27.6
RWANDA	186.6	44.3	99.1	149.4	...	-7.5	25.7
SAO T. & PRINC.	...	...	5.1	9.0	...	...	28.9
SENEGAL	9.4	22.0	283.0	411.5	399.1	9.7	129.2
SEYCHELLES	9.4	22.0	283.0	462.1	...	9.7	145.1
SIERRA LEONE	30.6	5.4	34.6	15.5	...	-5.8	24.9
SOMALIA	...	...	...	...	...	...	...
SOUTH AFRICA	7,238.2	2,423.3	4,300.6	7,372.8	7,490.3	-1.2	21.4
SUDAN	48.7	11.4	163.4	153.1	...	17.2	56.0
SWAZILAND	158.7	216.5	298.2	368.8	...	8.9	9.2
TANZANIA	20.3	192.8	270.2	666.6	...	68.4	20.5
TOGO	78.1	357.9	135.2	125.8	134.3	20.4	-5.6
TUNISIA	598.3	800.0	1,610.1	2,265.0	6,169.6	8.2	29.8
UGANDA	3.0	44.0	458.9	740.2	...	103.5	40.4
ZAMBIA	88.6	193.1	222.7	66.9	...	32.0	-7.0
ZIMBABWE	326.4	218.8	735.2	373.4	257.8	-0.9	12.3
AFRICA	40,663.3	28,092.5	44,988.4	56,524.3	64,424.5	4.4	9.1

TABLE 2.10
CONSUMER PRICE INDICES (GENERAL)
(1995 = 100)

COUNTRY	1980	1990	1998	1999	2000*	Average Annual Change (%) 1980-1990	1991-2000
ALGERIA	11.6	29.3	131.7	134.9	142.3	9.7	17.6
ANGOLA	...	0.0	25,327.3	97,807.0	215,175.4	1.8	2,583.4
BENIN	...	59.8	114.8	115.2	118.8	1.7	7.3
BOTSWANA	20.2	55.2	127.6	136.6	147.8	10.9	10.3
BURKINA FASO	51.6	73.6	114.2	112.9	112.2	4.5	4.6
BURUNDI	29.0	60.0	186.6	192.8	245.6	7.2	15.5
CAMEROON	30.8	67.1	105.9	108.7	111.7	8.4	5.7
CAPE VERDE	...	74.6	120.2	125.6	130.6	10.2	5.8
CENT. AFR. REP.	53.3	71.9	102.9	101.2	104.2	3.3	4.2
CHAD	...	69.6	122.6	112.8	116.2	3.6	6.8
COMOROS	...	71.4	112.4	116.3	122.1	6.1	5.6
CONGO	26.5	48.4	114.6	118.7	121.1	6.5	10.6
CONGO, DEM. REP.	0.0	0.0	5,164.0	22,360.0	143,104.3	62.9	3,444.0
COTE D'IVOIRE	38.8	64.1	111.6	112.5	113.3	6.1	6.1
DJIBOUTI	...	77.4	110.2	112.7	115.5	5.3	4.1
EGYPT	11.0	52.4	116.8	120.4	123.9	17.3	9.1
EQUAT. GUINEA	...	64.1	118.5	119.2	124.5	17.0	7.9
ERITREA	...	...	118.6	128.4	...	...	8.0
ETHIOPIA	35.3	54.4	98.9	107.6	111.5	4.7	7.9
GABON	41.6	73.2	108.3	109.1	110.2	6.6	4.9
GAMBIA	14.7	72.6	105.1	109.1	110.7	17.0	4.4
GHANA	0.8	28.3	214.8	241.5	282.3	47.4	26.5
GUINEA	...	61.0	110.6	115.0	120.6	31.2	7.2
GUINEA BISSAU	...	15.1	242.7	236.2	255.8	45.8	33.5
KENYA	11.1	34.0	129.0	132.4	139.6	12.1	15.9
LESOTHO	15.4	54.2	128.3	135.2	143.3	13.6	10.3
LIBERIA	33.1	65.2	133.6	147.0	161.7	7.9	9.5
LIBYA	...	42.0	209.3	246.9	276.5	4.5	21.0
MADAGASCAR	7.0	35.3	133.0	146.1	160.0	18.0	17.1
MALAWI	5.6	24.7	194.9	282.4	358.7	16.3	32.1
MALI	...	75.2	110.7	109.4	108.1	3.4	4.0
MAURITANIA	...	70.8	118.3	123.1	126.5	8.1	6.0
MAURITIUS	32.2	71.0	121.7	130.0	135.1	11.4	6.7
MOROCCO	37.0	74.6	106.9	107.7	109.7	7.5	4.0
MOZAMBIQUE	...	14.4	157.1	160.3	179.5	52.3	30.6
NAMIBIA	17.0	57.4	124.8	135.5	147.3	17.5	9.9
NIGER	62.0	76.4	113.2	110.7	112.4	3.2	4.5
NIGERIA	2.0	14.3	154.3	164.6	180.2	21.6	30.9
RWANDA	22.3	34.1	127.8	124.7	127.9	4.7	16.3
SAO TOME & PRINC	...	25.4	325.7	374.3	393.0	17.4	32.5
SENEGAL	40.7	71.8	105.8	106.6	107.4	6.3	4.5
SEYCHELLES	68.5	92.3	102.1	104.9	112.0	4.0	1.9
SIERRA LEONE	0.1	15.6	191.9	257.2	250.4	67.4	34.6
SOMALIA	0.2	27.5	154.7	173.3	193.2	62.5	22.1
SOUTH AFRICA	14.9	58.6	124.6	131.0	138.0	14.6	8.9
SUDAN	0.1	2.8	399.8	463.8	530.5	38.5	75.2
SWAZILAND	15.4	54.3	123.3	130.6	130.9	13.9	9.9
TANZANIA	2.0	29.5	158.4	170.9	181.4	30.7	20.2
TOGO	43.7	62.8	114.4	114.3	120.5	4.7	7.1
TUNISIA	34.6	75.5	110.9	113.9	117.4	8.3	4.5
UGANDA	...	40.5	114.6	121.9	125.5	103.5	12.9
ZAMBIA	0.1	3.0	226.9	273.7	340.8	46.2	70.4
ZIMBABWE	8.1	29.8	190.1	300.7	481.8	13.2	31.6
AFRICA	5.9	26.4	160.7	180.1	203.5	15.7	23.0

* : estimates

TABLE 2.11
OVERALL GOVERNMENT DEFICIT(-) / SURPLUS(+) AS A PERCENTAGE OF GDP AT CURRENT PRICES
(PERCENTAGE)

						Annual Average	
COUNTRY	1980	1990	1995	1999	2000	1980-1990	1991-2000
ALGERIA	9.9	2.7	-1.1	-0.5	6.7	1.2	-0.6
ANGOLA	-9.9	-23.7	-27.4	-15.2	7.9	-10.2	-16.8
BENIN	-4.2	-4.1	-3.2	2.3	-0.4	-4.7	-1.1
BOTSWANA	-0.6	10.5	1.9	0.1	0.6	9.0	4.1
BURKINA FASO	-7.6	-4.6	-1.9	-3.4	-3.0	-4.9	-3.0
BURUNDI	-6.2	-2.7	-4.6	-6.6	-5.7	-7.6	-4.8
CAMEROON	0.3	-7.6	-3.1	-3.2	-0.2	-2.7	-3.9
CAPE VERDE	-8.0	-3.3	-12.9	-7.7	-5.4	-8.7	-9.0
CENT. AFR. REP.	-8.5	-6.8	-4.9	-0.7	-0.8	-3.0	-3.9
CHAD	6.4	-5.9	-4.5	-6.0	-5.6	-0.5	-5.5
COMOROS	-16.0	-0.5	-7.9	-1.2	-0.9	-8.3	-3.1
CONGO	-0.9	-6.6	-8.2	-8.1	4.5	1.3	-10.1
CONGO DEM. REP.	-0.4	-10.9	-9.3	-17.4	-16.7	-6.3	-15.0
COTE D'IVOIRE	-12.8	-12.0	-3.7	-2.9	-2.2	-9.1	-5.8
DJIBOUTI	6.8	-5.0	-8.1	1.1	-0.3	-4.5	-5.6
EGYPT	-9.6	-12.7	-1.3	-1.3	-1.3	-16.5	-3.7
EQUAT. GUINEA	-16.3	-5.3	-5.3	8.0	16.5	-10.5	-2.1
ERITREA	...	...	...	...	...	...	...
ETHIOPIA	-3.6	-9.7	-3.9	-4.9	-8.2	-6.0	-5.7
GABON	7.4	-4.1	3.2	1.2	8.5	-2.7	-1.2
GAMBIA	-10.7	-1.7	-3.3	-3.7	-1.1	-6.4	-2.2
GHANA	-11.7	-2.2	-6.4	-8.2	-7.2	-4.2	-7.9
GUINEA	-0.5	-5.2	-2.8	-3.0	-3.2	-2.8	-3.1
GUINEA BISSAU	12.2	-5.9	-1.4	-14.6	-14.3	-5.3	-13.3
KENYA	-7.8	-6.8	0.1	0.0	0.2	-5.7	-1.7
LESOTHO	-10.1	-0.9	3.5	-16.5	-1.6	-9.7	0.2
LIBERIA	-14.5	-18.5	-15.1	-9.6	...	-13.7	-14.6
LIBYA	...	...	...	...	...	...	...
MADAGASCAR	-14.2	-0.6	-6.2	-2.8	-4.1	-6.1	-5.4
MALAWI	-11.6	-2.8	-4.9	-4.1	-2.4	-7.1	-6.8
MALI	-14.3	-19.8	-3.3	-3.8	-4.6	-18.8	-9.0
MAURITANIA	-13.7	-5.4	1.1	5.3	1.3	-7.3	0.0
MAURITIUS	-10.6	-2.1	-3.7	-1.9	-0.8	-6.3	-3.2
MOROCCO	-11.2	-0.6	-5.9	-5.5	-6.6	-7.8	-3.9
MOZAMBIQUE	-2.0	-6.1	-3.1	-1.5	-4.5	-8.0	-3.2
NAMIBIA	...	0.5	-3.5	-4.9	-4.0	-0.1	-3.9
NIGER	-1.0	-7.0	-0.7	-1.9	0.6	-3.7	-1.7
NIGERIA	-3.4	3.1	3.5	-8.4	7.7	-5.2	-1.2
RWANDA	-3.3	-7.2	-2.4	-3.8	-5.8	-4.2	-5.9
SAO T. & PRINC.	-27.7	-42.2	-37.4	-25.8	-19.0	-26.7	-32.8
SENEGAL	-8.2	-0.5	-0.2	-1.4	-1.6	-4.2	-0.7
SEYCHELLES	-6.6	0.2	-11.4	-11.0	-12.0	-8.3	-9.9
SIERRA LEONE	-12.1	-8.8	-6.3	-10.3	-14.1	-9.1	-7.5
SOMALIA	-10.0	-1.1	-5.4	-4.3	...	-7.1	-4.6
SOUTH AFRICA	-1.0	-3.1	-5.2	-2.0	-2.6	-4.0	-4.9
SUDAN	-8.9	-12.7	...	...	1.0	-10.9	1.0
SWAZILAND	...	6.7	-1.7	-3.1	-4.1	-0.7	-1.3
TANZANIA	-5.7	-3.2	-3.3	-3.8	-0.4	-5.8	-1.9
TOGO	-5.7	-3.1	-6.4	-3.3	-1.6	-4.0	-6.2
TUNISIA	-2.8	-5.4	-4.2	-2.4	-2.3	-4.9	-3.5
UGANDA	-4.9	-4.3	-2.7	-1.3	-3.7	-6.1	-2.8
ZAMBIA	-18.5	-8.3	-3.8	-2.0	-3.6	-13.2	-3.3
ZIMBABWE	-9.6	-6.2	-10.1	-9.0	-11.4	-7.8	-7.4
AFRICA	-3.6	-4.4	-3.5	-3.4	-1.0	-6.4	-4.0

TABLE 2.12
TOTAL EXTERNAL DEBT
(MILLIONS OF US DOLLARS)

COUNTRY	1980	1990	1995	1998	1999	Average Annual Growth (%) 1980-1990	1991-1999
ALGERIA	18,685.9	27,877.0	32,810.0	30,450.0	28,315.0	4.5	0.4
ANGOLA	7,435.4	9,395.2	10,881.5	8,781.6	8,948.5	2.4	-0.1
BENIN	334.3	1,176.8	1,621.2	1,341.9	1,371.9	14.3	2.1
BOTSWANA	146.7	565.7	629.3	488.7	486.4	15.0	-1.3
BURKINA FASO	220.5	611.1	1,204.0	1,422.0	1,499.5	14.0	10.7
BURUNDI	158.3	885.0	1,183.4	1,168.5	1,142.9	19.4	3.0
CAMEROON	1,288.4	4,822.8	7,759.7	7,639.9	8,058.1	16.3	7.0
CAPE VERDE	0.0	131.0	190.8	228.9	261.4	11.4	8.4
CENT. AFR. REP.	171.6	647.8	869.3	905.4	806.7	15.6	2.7
CHAD	0.0	483.2	818.1	1,003.4	1,079.4	20.6	9.6
COMOROS	30.1	190.9	201.2	128.6	121.3	22.2	-3.7
CONGO	1,156.7	3,888.7	5,561.0	5,164.9	5,478.3	23.6	4.2
CONGO DEM. REP.	4,395.4	10,169.7	13,461.0	15,274.2	15,897.5	9.0	5.1
COTE D'IVOIRE	5,802.6	15,304.8	19,393.6	14,570.9	15,072.9	13.2	0.2
DJIBOUTI	33.0	210.4	265.3	290.8	309.0	27.4	4.6
EGYPT	29,638.2	44,900.0	31,794.0	28,076.5	28,223.7	4.3	-4.7
EQUAT. GUINEA	44.0	212.3	234.2	234.9	215.0	17.9	0.4
ERITREA							
ETHIOPIA	754.1	8,404.9	9,787.5	9,811.0	10,023.4	30.4	2.0
GABON	1,389.1	2,763.6	3,707.0	4,003.4	3,980.3	10.3	4.2
GAMBIA	212.8	259.1	402.3	432.2	440.7	3.9	6.3
GHANA	1,398.0	3,295.2	6,135.8	6,272.6	6,597.9	9.6	8.4
GUINEA	1,005.2	2,385.2	3,079.7	3,441.6	3,376.0	9.8	4.1
GUINEA BISSAU	401.6	708.4	856.1	779.6	788.7	5.9	1.4
KENYA	4,236.3	6,388.6	6,082.1	5,866.3	5,479.3	4.2	-1.7
LESOTHO	75.0	408.9	657.9	818.9	819.4	18.7	8.1
LIBERIA	652.8	2,087.5	2,170.6	2,085.2	2,036.4	13.0	-0.2
LIBYA	...	...	...	...	...	...	...
MADAGASCAR	1,041.0	3,462.7	4,380.0	3,836.0	4,030.8	13.6	1.9
MALAWI	799.4	1,674.6	2,080.8	2,438.3	2,494.8	8.1	4.7
MALI	708.0	1,977.6	2,731.2	3,237.4	3,345.7	10.9	6.0
MAURITANIA	838.6	1,889.6	2,350.0	1,939.8	1,837.2	9.2	0.2
MAURITIUS	335.1	808.6	1,157.6	1,192.0	1,217.5	9.7	4.9
MOROCCO	9,552.8	20,759.0	22,903.0	19,857.6	18,098.0	8.2	-1.4
MOZAMBIQUE	1,025.3	5,315.8	9,227.9	8,528.9	7,642.4	18.3	5.8
NAMIBIA	0.0	311.6	368.8	77.1	84.8	...	-5.1
NIGER	426.9	1,348.8	1,592.1	1,617.2	1,680.6	13.2	3.0
NIGERIA	6,478.0	33,764.0	31,929.6	29,851.0	33,526.5	19.6	0.2
RWANDA	189.8	675.3	1,066.8	1,222.1	1,201.0	14.6	6.8
SAO T. & PRINC.	22.3	173.9	253.6	294.6	305.1	24.9	6.5
SENEGAL	1,224.1	2,977.3	3,443.1	3,025.7	2,935.3	10.4	0.2
SEYCHELLES	21.7	123.5	196.6	181.3	163.3	20.6	3.6
SIERRA LEONE	482.0	1,257.0	1,081.0	1,176.3	1,218.1	11.6	-0.1
SOMALIA	791.0	2,048.3	2,712.8	3,032.6	3,155.0	10.1	4.9
SOUTH AFRICA	15,500.0	19,627.1	35,335.0	37,200.0	38,913.0	2.8	8.3
SUDAN	5,050.0	13,642.0	...	...	...	10.6	...
SWAZILAND	280.3	225.2	205.0	211.0	240.1	1.0	0.9
TANZANIA	2,675.9	6,059.1	7,323.0	8,076.9	7,751.7	8.6	2.8
TOGO	976.2	1,181.6	1,449.3	1,409.7	1,326.9	2.8	1.5
TUNISIA	3,586.0	5,983.3	10,720.8	11,184.9	11,534.7	5.6	8.2
UGANDA	657.4	1,570.0	3,387.0	3,631.1	3,479.5	9.5	10.7
ZAMBIA	3,772.1	7,303.8	7,040.5	6,224.5	6,236.2	7.7	-1.6
ZIMBABWE	1,269.8	3,239.8	5,322.7	5,206.8	5,084.3	9.9	5.5
AFRICA	140,469.5	140,469.5	140,469.5	140,469.5	140,469.5	7.6	1.7

TABLE 2.13
TOTAL DEBT SERVICE
(MILLIONS OF US DOLLARS)

COUNTRY	1980	1990	1995	1998	1999	Average Annual Growth (%) 1980-1990	1991-1999
ALGERIA	...	...	8,828.7	5,110.0	4,890.0	...	-8.9
ANGOLA	200.2	196.5	405.2	99.5	292.4	24.5	...
BENIN	12.6	30.1	50.6	53.1	69.8	160.1	13.4
BOTSWANA	...	109.9	101.2	70.3	87.4	...	-1.4
BURKINA FASO	16.0	69.0	63.5	60.5	68.0	48.6	13.8
BURUNDI	10.4	40.4	41.2	60.3	58.7	16.6	10.1
CAMEROON	...	151.4	307.3	767.4	401.5	-13.5	42.0
CAPE VERDE	...	12.6	24.7	31.7	34.6	18.5	19.9
CENT. AFR. REP.	5.2	10.7	7.8	16.4	9.2	-112.5	49.7
CHAD		13.8	45.7	31.2	28.5	41.9	27.5
COMOROS	1.6	1.1	0.8	0.3	2.3	14.3	218.4
CONGO	108.8	379.5	328.7	67.8	114.7	17.9	14.4
CONGO DEM. REP.	784.8	333.3	22.2	2.0	...	-4.3	...
COTE D'IVOIRE	1,094.1	1,029.3	1,601.6	1,314.4	1,004.7	3.8	4.0
DJIBOUTI	2.9	21.3	31.8	52.4	17.4	23.3	47.6
EGYPT	2,227.1	1,048.7	2,009.5	1,700.4	1,719.0	-0.1	25.8
EQUAT. GUINEA	5.3	8.6	53.8	53.8	60.0	14.4	61.4
ERITREA							
ETHIOPIA	30.4	229.7	178.5	202.5	189.4	25.4	11.9
GABON	1,139.6	798.7	1,105.1	738.1	820.1	1.5	5.8
GAMBIA	6.2	19.4	38.8	15.1	16.7	73.2	8.5
GHANA	...	248.2	501.0	576.8	516.5	-25.3	11.6
GUINEA	116.2	174.2	75.6	128.1	614.3	6.6	67.3
GUINEA BISSAU	2.9	22.9	187.6	-130.9	8.2	114.5	-7.5
KENYA	248.3	751.4	818.0	799.2	785.6	15.1	5.3
LESOTHO	12.0	49.5	33.5	65.3	76.5	50.0	14.4
LIBERIA	41.6	116.6	113.8	123.4	126.9	38.1	1.2
LIBYA	...	...	...	...	...	...	...
MADAGASCAR	157.0	207.1	408.3	182.2	108.4	8.1	-0.3
MALAWI	134.3	124.0	135.6	154.3	106.3	1.4	2.1
MALI	16.4	164.7	100.0	127.0	114.6	29.8	-0.7
MAURITANIA	93.1	0.8	117.0	78.9	133.1	-15.3	...
MAURITIUS	11.2	174.5	187.8	174.2	182.3	71.0	1.9
MOROCCO	1,309.9	2,088.1	3,382.8	2,984.5	2,952.7	6.8	4.3
MOZAMBIQUE	145.0	70.0	112.1	130.6	198.9	...	37.8
NAMIBIA	...	51.5	30.0	21.1	20.9	...	-7.1
NIGER	84.0	-101.3	104.8	73.4	74.8	-134.6	-25.1
NIGERIA	835.6	2,768.1	2,094.6	1,352.0	1,900.0	27.4	1.2
RWANDA	...	...	...	...	...	...	...
SAO T. & PRINC.	0.0	0.2	2.3	5.6	3.9	...	96.4
SENEGAL	166.1	462.4	338.7	229.2	184.8	11.6	-9.2
SEYCHELLES	0.2	27.6	13.1	33.5	31.9	80.2	9.1
SIERRA LEONE	39.3	55.7	294.7	8.9	39.7	...	67.9
SOMALIA	23.8	0.0	187.7	200.3	206.0	-21.8	...
SOUTH AFRICA	3,861.0	3,452.8	5,821.2	7,228.5	7,253.1	1.5	10.1
SUDAN	327.5	98.0	...	...	...	-1.9	...
SWAZILAND	16.9	58.8	40.2	70.5	49.1	15.9	1.2
TANZANIA	...	...	...	...	...	...	...
TOGO	-51.8	63.7	22.3	37.5	79.3	8.6	...
TUNISIA	470.1	1,279.3	1,565.8	1,530.7	1,652.5	17.9	3.1
UGANDA	88.3	363.7	143.8	142.5	110.6	16.8	-7.9
ZAMBIA	767.5	-961.0	1,640.8	591.8	147.4	...	12.4
ZIMBABWE	202.7	440.0	537.0	576.0	584.3	8.4	3.4
AFRICA	15,184.5	17,327.0	34,933.3	28,569.6	28,897.4	2.1	7.0

TABLE 3.1
LABOUR FORCE BY SECTOR
(PERCENT IN)

COUNTRY	AGRICULTURE				INDUSTRY				SERVICES			
	1980	1985	1990	1996	1980	1985	1990	1996	1980	1985	1990	1996
ALGERIA	31	25	19	14	27	29	32	35	42	46	49	51
ANGOLA	74	72	70	68	10	10	11	11	17	18	19	21
BENIN	70	65	59	54	7	7	8	10	23	28	32	36
BOTSWANA	70	61	52	42	13	19	28	41	17	20	20	17
BURKINA FASO	87	86	85	84	4	5	5	5	9	10	10	11
BURUNDI	93	92	92	91	2	3	3	3	5	5	5	6
CAMEROON	70	63	56	49	8	10	13	15	22	27	32	36
CAPE VERDE	52	46	40	35	23	27	31	36	26	27	29	29
CENT. AFR. REP.	72	67	61	56	6	8	10	12	21	25	29	32
CHAD	83	80	76	72	5	5	6	7	12	15	18	21
COMOROS	83	81	79	77	6	6	7	8	11	12	14	15
CONGO	62	61	60	58	12	12	12	13	26	27	28	29
CONGO DEM. REP.	71	68	64	60	13	14	16	17	16	18	20	23
COTE D'IVOIRE	65	60	54	49	8	10	12	14	27	30	34	37
DJIBOUTI	...	...	...	...	...	...	...	...	...	...	...	...
EGYPT	46	42	39	36	20	22	24	27	34	35	36	37
EQUAT. GUINEA	66	61	57	52	11	13	15	18	23	26	28	30
ERITREA	...	...	...	...	...	...	...	...	...	...	...	...
ETHIOPIA	80	77	74	72	8	9	10	12	12	14	15	16
GABON	75	73	71	69	11	12	12	13	14	15	16	18
GAMBIA	84	83	82	80	7	7	8	9	9	10	11	11
GHANA	56	54	53	52	18	18	19	19	26	27	28	29
GUINEA	81	78	76	74	9	10	11	13	10	11	12	13
GUINEA BISSAU	82	81	80	79	4	4	4	5	14	15	15	16
KENYA	81	79	77	75	7	7	8	9	12	13	14	16
LESOTHO	86	84	82	81	4	5	5	6	10	11	12	13
LIBERIA	74	73	71	70	9	9	9	9	16	18	20	21
LIBYA	18	14	11	8	29	30	32	34	53	55	57	58
MADAGASCAR	81	79	78	76	6	7	7	8	13	14	15	16
MALAWI	83	78	75	70	7	10	13	17	9	11	12	13
MALI	86	84	82	80	2	2	3	3	12	14	16	17
MAURITANIA	69	61	53	45	9	12	16	21	22	27	31	34
MAURITIUS	28	25	23	20	24	24	23	23	48	51	54	57
MOROCCO	46	40	35	30	25	29	35	40	29	31	31	30
MOZAMBIQUE	84	83	82	81	7	8	9	10	8	8	9	9
NAMIBIA	43	44	43	40	22	20	27	37	36	6	31	23
NIGER	91	89	88	86	2	2	2	2	7	9	10	12
NIGERIA	68	67	65	64	12	12	13	13	20	21	22	23
RWANDA	93	92	92	92	3	3	3	3	4	5	5	5
SAO T. & PRINC.	...	...	...	...	...	...	...	...	...	...	...	...
SENEGAL	81	79	78	77	6	7	7	7	13	14	15	16
SEYCHELLES	...	...	...	...	...	...	...	...	...	...	...	...
SIERRA LEONE	70	67	64	61	14	15	16	17	16	18	20	22
SOMALIA	76	74	72	70	8	9	10	11	16	17	18	19
SOUTH AFRICA	17	...	14	...	35	...	32	...	48	...	54	...
SUDAN	71	68	65	62	7	8	9	11	21	23	25	27
SWAZILAND	74	71	67	64	9	10	12	13	17	19	21	23
TANZANIA	86	84	81	79	5	5	6	7	10	11	12	14
TOGO	73	71	69	67	10	10	11	12	17	18	20	21
TUNISIA	35	31	28	25	36	43	49	56	29	26	23	19
UGANDA	86	84	82	81	4	5	6	6	10	11	12	13
ZAMBIA	73	71	70	68	10	11	11	12	17	18	19	20
ZIMBABWE	73	70	68	66	10	12	13	14	17	18	19	20
AFRICA	70	67	65	62	11	12	13	15	19	21	22	23

TABLE 3.2
LABOUR FORCE PARTICIPATION RATE
(Percentage of population of all ages in labour force)

COUNTRY	TOTAL			FEMALE			MALE		
	1980	1995	1999	1980	1995	1999	1980	1995	1999
ALGERIA	26.0	30.7	33.0	11.0	15.1	18.0	41.1	46.0	47.7
ANGOLA	49.5	46.3	45.9	45.7	42.4	42.0	53.3	50.3	49.9
BENIN	47.9	45.3	45.6	44.5	43.1	43.3	51.5	47.6	47.9
BOTSWANA	43.6	43.5	44.0	41.8	39.3	39.4	45.5	48.0	48.8
BURKINA FASO	54.6	50.4	49.4	51.6	46.9	45.9	57.7	54.0	52.9
BURUNDI	54.9	53.6	53.5	53.2	51.3	51.2	56.9	56.0	56.0
CAMEROON	41.9	40.5	40.7	30.4	30.2	30.7	53.6	51.0	50.8
CAPE VERDE	32.5	38.6	40.2	20.4	28.8	30.0	46.7	50.6	51.9
CENT. AFR. REP.	52.5	48.1	47.7	48.7	43.7	43.2	56.6	52.8	52.3
CHAD	49.9	46.6	46.5	42.7	40.9	41.1	57.3	52.4	52.0
COMOROS	45.2	46.2	47.3	39.5	39.9	40.9	50.9	52.5	53.8
CONGO	42.1	41.2	40.9	34.8	35.0	34.7	49.8	47.8	47.2
CONGO (DRC)	44.4	41.7	41.1	38.8	36.0	35.4	50.4	47.6	47.0
COTE D'IVOIRE	40.0	38.8	39.5	26.4	25.9	26.8	53.1	51.1	51.9
DJIBOUTI	...	...	...	...	...	...	...	...	...
EGYPT	35.0	36.4	37.7	18.9	21.3	23.1	50.7	51.1	52.0
EQUAT. GUINEA	44.7	42.1	41.7	30.7	29.6	29.5	58.3	55.4	54.6
ERITREA	...	50.0	49.8	...	47.1	46.9	...	52.9	52.7
ETHIOPIA	49.2	44.1	43.8	41.4	36.3	36.1	56.8	51.9	51.5
GABON	52.5	46.9	45.5	46.3	41.1	40.0	58.8	52.7	51.0
GAMBIA	51.5	51.0	51.2	45.6	45.2	45.6	57.6	56.8	57.0
GHANA	47.3	47.1	47.5	47.9	47.5	47.7	46.8	46.8	47.3
GUINEA	51.4	49.5	49.9	48.4	47.1	47.4	54.4	51.9	52.4
GUINEA BISSAU	50.1	46.8	46.3	39.3	37.1	37.0	61.2	56.8	56.0
KENYA	47.1	49.9	51.5	43.3	46.0	47.6	50.8	53.7	55.4
LESOTHO	42.0	41.6	41.8	30.9	30.1	30.5	53.8	53.6	53.6
LIBERIA	42.1	40.4	41.0	32.6	32.1	32.7	51.5	48.6	49.2
LIBYA	31.0	30.4	31.7	12.2	13.1	15.0	47.7	46.2	47.2
MADAGASCAR	49.9	49.3	48.3	44.8	44.1	43.1	55.1	54.5	53.6
MALAWI	50.3	48.3	47.6	49.3	46.7	46.0	51.4	49.8	49.3
MALI	51.5	49.6	49.1	47.0	45.2	44.6	56.2	54.1	53.8
MAURITANIA	48.1	44.9	44.8	42.8	39.0	38.9	53.5	50.7	50.8
MAURITIUS	35.5	42.4	43.6	18.0	26.5	28.1	53.5	58.1	59.1
MOROCCO	35.9	39.1	40.4	24.1	27.1	28.0	47.7	51.1	52.7
MOZAMBIQUE	55.3	52.3	51.8	53.3	50.0	49.5	57.3	54.7	54.1
NAMIBIA	43.3	41.4	41.3	34.4	33.4	33.5	52.7	49.4	49.0
NIGER	49.9	48.0	47.5	43.8	41.9	41.6	56.2	54.2	53.5
NIGERIA	40.7	40.3	40.7	29.1	28.6	29.3	52.5	52.1	52.3
RWANDA	51.1	52.8	53.4	49.6	51.0	51.5	52.6	54.7	55.4
SAO T.& PRINC.	...	...	...	...	...	...	...	...	...
SENEGAL	45.9	44.3	44.1	38.7	37.8	37.8	53.1	50.9	50.5
SEYCHELLES	...	...	...	...	...	...	...	...	...
SIERRA LEONE	38.6	37.2	37.2	26.9	26.4	26.8	50.7	48.4	48.0
SOMALIA	45.2	43.2	42.9	38.8	37.2	36.9	51.8	49.4	49.0
SOUTH AFRICA	38.3	40.4	40.9	26.8	30.1	30.7	50.0	51.0	51.5
SUDAN	36.6	38.3	39.3	19.7	21.7	23.2	53.4	54.8	55.4
SWAZILAND	35.7	34.8	35.7	23.5	24.9	25.8	48.0	45.4	46.2
TANZANIA	51.2	51.3	51.1	50.2	50.1	49.9	52.2	52.5	52.4
TOGO	43.6	41.5	41.2	33.8	32.8	32.7	53.8	50.3	49.9
TUNISIA	34.3	37.5	39.5	20.1	23.1	25.3	48.0	51.5	53.5
UGANDA	51.7	49.5	48.5	49.1	46.9	45.9	54.3	52.1	51.1
ZAMBIA	41.8	41.3	41.8	37.2	36.9	37.1	46.7	45.9	46.5
ZIMBABWE	44.9	47.2	47.8	39.5	41.5	42.2	50.4	52.9	53.6
AFRICA	42.9	42.9	43.3	34.2	34.4	35.0	51.7	51.4	51.6

TABLE 3.3
COMPONENTS OF POPULATION CHANGE

COUNTRY	TOTAL FERTILITY RATE (PER WOMAN)			CRUDE BIRTH RATE (PER 1000 POPULATION			CRUDE DEATH RATE (PER 1000 POPULATION)			RATE OF NATURAL INCREASE (PERCENT)		
	1980	1990	1999	1980	1990	1999	1980	1990	1999	1980	1990	1999
ALGERIA	6.4	4.3	3.4	40.6	30.8	27.2	10.4	6.4	5.2	3.0	2.4	2.2
ANGOLA	7.0	7.2	6.4	50.8	50.8	46.2	22.8	19.2	16.9	2.8	3.2	2.9
BENIN	7.1	6.3	5.4	51.4	44.2	39.9	17.7	14.4	12.5	3.4	3.0	2.7
BOTSWANA	6.0	4.8	4.0	44.1	36.8	32.2	9.5	8.0	18.9	3.5	2.9	1.3
BURKINA FASO	7.8	7.1	6.2	50.1	47.7	44.7	20.1	18.9	17.2	3.0	2.9	2.7
BURUNDI	6.8	6.8	5.8	46.2	46.2	40.2	17.9	21.5	18.6	2.8	2.5	2.2
CAMEROON	6.3	5.7	5.0	43.9	40.6	38.1	15.7	12.8	12.6	2.8	2.8	2.6
CAPE VERDE	6.3	3.9	3.3	38.3	33.9	29.8	10.6	7.7	5.7	2.8	2.6	2.4
CENT. AFR. REP.	5.7	5.3	4.6	42.4	39.6	36.6	18.5	17.4	18.4	2.4	2.2	1.8
CHAD	6.6	6.6	5.6	49.1	46.7	42.3	22.4	19.3	16.5	2.7	2.7	2.6
COMOROS	7.0	5.4	4.4	48.5	38.2	35.1	13.8	10.2	8.6	3.5	2.8	2.7
CONGO	6.3	6.3	5.7	43.9	44.7	41.7	15.7	16.1	14.6	2.8	2.9	2.7
CONGO DEM. REP.	6.7	6.7	6.0	48.3	48.2	43.6	16.4	14.7	13.3	3.2	3.3	3.0
COTE D'IVOIRE	7.4	5.7	4.7	50.1	38.9	36.2	16.0	14.9	15.5	3.4	2.4	2.1
DJIBOUTI	6.6	5.8	5.0	44.2	39.0	35.2	19.1	16.2	13.8	2.5	2.3	2.1
EGYPT	5.1	3.8	3.0	39.1	28.9	24.1	12.7	7.8	6.3	2.6	2.1	1.8
EQUAT. GUINEA	5.8	5.9	5.3	43.3	43.5	39.3	21.1	18.0	15.0	2.2	2.5	2.4
ERITREA	6.4	6.1	5.3	45.2	43.1	38.7	20.0	15.5	13.5	2.5	2.8	2.5
ETHIOPIA	6.8	6.6	6.0	48.0	46.5	43.4	22.1	19.2	19.0	2.6	2.7	2.4
GABON	4.5	5.2	5.0	33.1	36.6	35.3	18.1	16.1	15.6	1.5	2.0	2.0
GAMBIA	6.5	5.6	4.9	48.2	43.3	38.0	23.1	19.2	16.2	2.5	2.4	2.2
GHANA	6.5	5.7	4.8	45.0	40.1	35.8	13.1	10.6	8.7	3.2	3.0	2.7
GUINEA	7.0	6.0	5.1	51.3	44.1	40.7	23.8	19.4	16.3	2.7	2.5	2.4
GUINEA BISSAU	6.0	6.0	5.4	44.7	43.3	40.6	25.1	21.4	19.6	2.0	2.2	2.1
KENYA	7.5	5.4	3.9	48.7	37.5	32.4	13.2	10.6	13.7	3.5	2.7	1.9
LESOTHO	5.3	5.0	4.5	38.9	36.4	34.2	13.8	11.3	13.6	2.5	2.5	2.1
LIBERIA	6.8	6.8	5.9	47.0	41.7	47.0	15.9	23.6	12.8	3.1	1.8	3.4
LIBYA	7.2	4.1	3.4	45.6	28.6	28.1	10.9	4.6	4.6	3.5	2.4	2.4
MADAGASCAR	6.6	5.9	5.0	46.5	45.9	37.0	15.5	12.6	9.6	3.1	3.3	2.7
MALAWI	7.6	7.2	6.3	53.5	50.2	45.6	21.6	22.1	21.8	3.2	2.8	2.4
MALI	7.1	7.1	6.2	50.8	49.8	45.1	22.3	17.8	14.7	2.8	3.2	3.0
MAURITANIA	6.1	5.9	5.2	42.3	42.6	39.0	18.5	14.7	12.2	2.4	2.8	2.7
MAURITIUS	2.5	2.3	1.9	22.0	20.4	15.9	6.5	6.7	6.5	1.6	1.4	0.9
MOROCCO	5.1	3.3	2.7	35.1	25.3	23.4	11.2	7.4	6.3	2.4	1.8	1.7
MOZAMBIQUE	6.5	6.5	5.9	45.8	45.1	41.7	20.2	17.4	22.9	2.6	2.8	1.9
NAMIBIA	5.8	5.3	4.6	40.5	37.5	34.5	13.6	10.7	20.3	2.7	2.7	1.4
NIGER	8.1	7.4	6.4	59.4	52.5	46.2	22.1	18.9	15.5	3.7	3.4	3.1
NIGERIA	6.9	5.7	4.8	47.3	41.1	37.5	18.3	15.4	14.4	2.9	2.6	2.3
RWANDA	8.1	6.5	5.7	50.4	43.5	41.6	18.6	42.9	20.3	3.2	0.1	2.1
SAO T. & PRINC.	...	...	...	...	...	...	...	...	...	...	...	...
SENEGAL	6.7	6.1	5.2	47.2	42.2	38.3	19.4	14.8	11.9	2.8	2.7	2.6
SEYCHELLES	...	...	...	...	...	...	...	...	...	...	...	...
SIERRA LEONE	6.5	6.5	5.7	48.9	49.0	44.5	28.5	29.8	23.0	2.0	1.9	2.1
SOMALIA	7.3	7.3	7.0	51.8	52.0	50.4	22.0	25.1	17.1	3.0	2.7	3.3
SOUTH AFRICA	4.2	3.5	3.0	31.8	29.0	25.6	11.1	9.8	17.0	2.1	1.9	0.9
SUDAN	6.4	5.0	4.3	43.5	34.9	31.9	15.8	13.9	10.8	2.8	2.1	2.1
SWAZILAND	6.0	5.1	4.4	43.1	40.2	35.7	13.7	10.7	8.1	2.9	2.9	2.8
TANZANIA	6.7	5.9	5.1	46.5	43.0	39.4	15.0	14.9	15.1	3.1	2.8	2.4
TOGO	6.6	6.6	5.6	45.0	44.4	39.9	15.8	15.5	14.6	2.9	2.9	2.5
TUNISIA	4.9	3.1	2.4	33.7	24.1	19.9	8.4	6.4	6.4	2.5	1.8	1.3
UGANDA	7.0	7.1	6.8	49.9	50.8	49.6	18.5	24.6	18.1	3.1	2.6	3.1
ZAMBIA	6.9	6.0	5.1	48.4	43.9	41.0	14.8	17.9	18.3	3.4	2.6	2.3
ZIMBABWE	6.2	4.5	3.4	43.1	35.5	30.1	11.8	12.6	19.5	3.1	2.3	1.1
AFRICA	**6.4**	**5.5**	**4.8**	**43.2**	**39.8**	**36.3**	**16.9**	**14.5**	**13.7**	**2.8**	**2.5**	**2.3**

TABLE 3.4
MORTALITY INDICATORS

COUNTRY	INFANT MORTALITY RATE (PER 1000)			LIFE EXPECTANCY AT BIRTH (YEARS)					
	1980	1990	1999	1980 M	1980 F	1990 M	1990 F	1999 M	1999 F
ALGERIA	88	54	38	60	62	66	68	68	72
ANGOLA	149	125	115	40	44	45	48	47	50
BENIN	109	90	82	47	52	51	55	52	55
BOTSWANA	67	53	59	57	62	59	63	42	43
BURKINA FASO	120	104	93	43	46	44	46	45	47
BURUNDI	118	123	112	45	49	40	43	42	45
CAMEROON	103	82	68	49	53	53	56	53	55
CAPE VERDE	84	65	51	60	64	64	69	67	73
CENT. AFR. REP.	114	101	93	44	50	46	49	43	47
CHAD	143	122	105	41	44	44	48	47	50
COMOROS	106	84	69	51	55	55	59	59	62
CONGO	88	89	86	47	54	47	51	48	52
CONGO, DEM. REP.	109	93	79	48	52	50	53	51	54
COTE D'IVOIRE	105	93	81	48	52	48	50	47	48
DJIBOUTI	132	116	99	40	47	47	50	50	54
EGYPT	115	63	42	55	58	62	66	66	69
EQUAT. GUINEA	138	117	101	42	46	46	50	50	53
ERITREA	133	101	84	42	45	48	51	50	53
ETHIOPIA	148	123	106	40	44	44	47	43	45
GABON	112	93	82	47	51	51	54	51	53
GAMBIA	154	132	114	39	43	43	47	47	50
GHANA	90	74	60	52	56	56	60	60	63
GUINEA	157	135	116	40	41	44	45	48	49
GUINEA BISSAU	164	141	124	38	41	42	45	43	46
KENYA	81	67	64	54	58	55	58	49	50
LESOTHO	117	98	89	53	56	57	60	52	54
LIBERIA	113	190	83	50	53	38	40	52	55
LIBYA	47	30	26	61	64	68	71	69	73
MADAGASCAR	112	92	75	50	53	54	57	58	61
MALAWI	164	147	129	44	46	41	43	40	40
MALI	159	123	111	46	48	50	53	54	56
MAURITANIA	117	101	86	46	49	50	53	54	57
MAURITIUS	28	18	14	64	70	66	74	69	76
MOROCCO	96	62	43	57	60	63	66	66	70
MOZAMBIQUE	135	116	115	43	46	46	50	39	40
NAMIBIA	84	61	72	52	55	57	60	43	43
NIGER	146	125	107	41	44	45	48	48	52
NIGERIA	101	86	77	45	48	48	51	49	52
RWANDA	124	135	117	45	48	23	24	40	42
SAO T. & PRINC.	...	...	...	...	...	...	...	...	...
SENEGAL	87	68	59	44	48	48	53	52	56
SEYCHELLES	...	...	...	...	...	...	...	...	...
SIERRA LEONE	190	195	150	34	37	33	36	39	41
SOMALIA	143	165	114	41	45	39	40	47	50
SOUTH AFRICA	67	57	62	53	60	55	64	46	51
SUDAN	92	85	66	48	51	50	52	55	58
SWAZILAND	94	75	58	50	55	55	60	60	65
TANZANIA	98	87	76	49	52	48	51	47	49
TOGO	105	90	78	49	52	48	51	48	51
TUNISIA	71	35	26	63	64	67	69	69	72
UGANDA	118	118	97	45	48	37	38	43	45
ZAMBIA	88	85	76	50	52	43	45	41	42
ZIMBABWE	76	67	67	54	58	51	53	42	42
AFRICA	112	95	76	48	51	50	53	51	53

Note : M and F refer to Male and Female respectively

TABLE 3.5
POPULATION WITH ACCESS TO SOCIAL INFRASTRUCTURES
(PERCENT OF POPULATION)

COUNTRY	SANITATION			SAFE WATER			HEALTH SERVICES		
	1985	1990-93	1994-98	1985	1990-93	1994-98	1985	1991	1992-96
ALGERIA	59	90	90	69	90	90	...	...	98
ANGOLA	18	31	32	28	31	32	70	24	...
BENIN	10	70	72	14	70	72	...	42	18
BOTSWANA	36	70	90	77	70	90	...	86	...
BURKINA FASO	9	42	42	35	42	42	70	...	90
BURUNDI	52	58	52	23	58	52	45	80	80
CAMEROON	36	41	54	36	41	54	20	15	80
CAPE VERDE	10	67	51	31	67	51	...	...	...
CENT. AFR. REP	19	18	23	24	18	23	..	13	52
CHAD	14	33	24	31	33	24	30	26	30
COMOROS	...	48	53	63	48	53	82	...	...
CONGO	40	27	68	20	27	68	...	...	83
CONGO DEM. REP	23	60	47	33	60	47	33	59	26
COTE D'IVOIRE	50	82	72	17	82	72	...	60	...
DJIBOUTI	37	24	80	43	24	80	...	...	...
EGYPT	80	64	84	75	64	84	99	99	99
EQUAT. GUINEA	...	95	95	...	95	95	...	...	...
ERITREA	...	68	68	...	68	68	...	...	...
ETHIOPIA	19	27	26	16	27	26	44	55	46
GABON	50	67	67	50	67	67	80	87	...
GAMBIA	...	76	69	45	76	69	90	...	93
GHANA	26	57	56	56	57	56	64	76	...
GUINEA	21	55	62	20	55	62	13	45	80
GUINEA BISSAU	25	27	53	31	27	53	64	...	40
KENYA	44	49	45	27	49	45	...	...	77
LESOTHO	22	62	62	36	62	62	50	80	80
LIBERIA	21	...	30	37	...	30	35	..	39
LIBYA	91	97	97	90	97	97	100	100	95
MADAGASCAR	3	16	29	31	16	29	65	65	38
MALAWI	60	77	60	32	77	60	54	80	35
MALI	21	49	48	17	49	48	35	...	40
MAURITANIA	...	72	64	37	72	64	30	...	63
MAURITIUS	97	100	98	99	100	98	100	99	100
MOROCCO	46	58	98	57	58	98	70	62	70
MOZAMBIQUE	20	24	46	15	24	46	40	30	39
NAMIBIA	14	60	83	52	60	83	72	...	59
NIGER	9	52	48	37	52	48	48	30	99
NIGERIA	35	40	49	36	40	49	66	67	51
RWANDA	58	79	79	49	79	79	80	...	80
SAO T. & PRINC	15	70	60	42	70	60	...	...	...
SENEGAL	55	50	81	44	50	81	40	40	90
SEYCHELLES	99	97	83	95	97	83	99	99	...
SIERRA LEONE	21	34	34	24	34	34	36	...	38
SOMALIA	15	37	...	31	37	...	20	...	...
SOUTH AFRICA	...	87	70	...	87	70	...	...	...
SUDAN	5	77	60	40	77	60	70	70	70
SWAZILAND	...	60	50	54	60	50	...	55	...
TANZANIA	64	49	66	52	49	66	73	93	42
TOGO	14	63	55	35	63	55	61	...	...
TUNISIA	52	99	90	89	99	90	91	100	...
UGANDA	13	42	34	16	42	34	42	71	49
ZAMBIA	47	59	53	48	59	53	70	75	...
ZIMBABWE	26	74	79	52	74	79	71	...	85
AFRICA	**35**	**55**	**58**	**42**	**55**	**58**	**60**	**64**	**64**

TABLE 3.6
SCHOOL ENROLMENT RATIO

	PRIMARY						SECONDARY					
	1975		1990		1996		1975		1990		1996	
		Ratio		Ratio		Ratio		Ratio		Ratio		Ratio
COUNTRY	Total	F/M	Total	F/M	Total	F/M	Total	F/M	Total	F/M	Tota l	F/M
ALGERIA	93	0.69	100	0.84	108	0.90	20	0.53	61	0.80	63	0.95
ANGOLA	130	0.60	92	0.92	68	0.89	9	0.40	12	0.66	12	0.66
BENIN	50	0.45	58	0.50	78	0.59	9	0.34	12	0.41	18	0.44
BOTSWANA	71	1.23	113	1.07	108	1.01	15	1.06	43	1.12	65	1.10
BURKINA FASO	14	0.56	33	0.63	40	0.67	2	0.46	7	0.53	9	0.55
BURUNDI	21	0.63	73	0.83	43	0.83	2	0.43	6	0.57	8	0.61
CAMEROON	95	0.80	101	0.86	85	0.87	13	0.50	28	0.70	25	0.68
CAPE VERDE	127	0.90	121	0.96	144	0.95	7	0.86	21	0.95	...	0.94
CENT. AFR. REP.	73	0.53	65	0.64	60	0.65	8	0.23	12	0.41	10	0.42
CHAD	35	0.35	54	0.45	58	0.52	3	0.20	8	0.23	10	0.25
COMOROS	64	0.43	75	0.73	73	0.86	13	0.39	18	0.68	24	0.81
CONGO	136	0.75	133	0.88	111	0.91	48	0.54	53	0.69	52	0.72
CONGO, DEM. REP.	93	0.67	70	0.62	70	0.69	17	0.36	22	0.48	30	0.62
COTE D'IVOIRE	61	0.57	67	0.71	71	0.74	12	0.39	22	0.47	24	0.48
DJIBOUTI	30	0.54	38	0.71	39	0.74	7	0.36	12	0.65	14	0.70
EGYPT	70	0.67	94	0.85	101	0.08	40	0.56	76	0.81	75	0.88
EQUAT. GUINEA	140	...	...	...	...	...	14	0.25	...	...	...	...
ERITREA	...	...	23	0.96	53	0.82	...	...	15	0.93	20	0.71
ETHIOPIA	21	0.49	33	0.67	43	0.55	6	0.38	14	0.77	12	0.79
GABON	178	1.65	163	...	...	...	30	0.55	...	...	...	...
GAMBIA	33	0.49	64	0.68	75	0.75	9	0.36	19	0.43	26	0.56
GHANA	72	0.77	75	0.83	75	0.85	36	0.61	36	0.64	31	0.63
GUINEA	31	0.52	37	0.47	53	0.58	14	0.35	10	0.34	13	0.35
GUINEA BISSAU	65	0.45	56	0.58	70	0.58	4	0.40	9	0.45	11	0.48
KENYA	104	0.86	95	0.96	84	0.99	13	0.55	24	0.73	24	0.85
LESOTHO	106	1.42	112	1.23	108	1.12	13	1.17	25	1.48	31	1.46
LIBERIA	40	0.52	30	0.69	33	0.69	17	0.32	14	0.40	14	0.40
LIBYA	137	0.82	105	0.94	112	1.00	55	0.54	86	1.03	100	0.94
MADAGASCAR	92	0.72	103	1.00	93	0.99	13	0.71	18	0.97	16	0.99
MALAWI	56	0.62	68	0.84	133	0.91	4	0.34	8	0.29	...	0.55
MALI	25	0.56	27	0.57	45	0.64	7	0.35	7	0.48	12	0.51
MAURITANIA	20	0.56	49	0.74	79	0.89	4	0.12	14	0.48	16	0.51
MAURITIUS	105	0.98	109	1.00	107	0.99	38	0.83	53	1.00	65	1.04
MOROCCO	62	0.58	67	0.69	86	0.76	17	0.57	35	0.74	39	0.76
MOZAMBIQUE	83	0.55	67	0.75	62	0.72	3	0.50	8	0.62	7	0.63
NAMIBIA	...	...	129	1.10	131	1.01	...	...	44	1.27	61	1.18
NIGER	19	0.54	29	0.56	29	0.62	2	0.37	7	0.43	7	0.54
NIGERIA	50	0.64	91	0.76	82	0.83	8	0.53	25	0.73	34	0.84
RWANDA	55	0.84	70	0.98	...	0.97	4	1.23	8	0.78	13	0.77
SAO T. & PRINC.	...	...	...	...	...	...	...	...	...	...	...	...
SENEGAL	40	0.73	59	0.74	68	0.81	11	0.40	16	0.52	16	0.60
SEYCHELLES	...	...	96	...	...	...	...	...	...	...	...	...
SIERRA LEONE	39	0.64	50	0.69	52	0.69	12	0.46	17	0.57	17	0.58
SOMALIA	42	0.71	10	0.52	8	0.52	4	0.30	6	0.53	5	0.53
SOUTH AFRICA	104	1.02	122	0.98	129	0.98	27	1.00	74	1.16	84	1.19
SUDAN	47	0.57	53	0.75	51	0.84	14	0.44	24	0.80	21	0.90
SWAZILAND	97	0.94	111	0.96	118	0.94	32	0.83	44	0.99	54	0.99
TANZANIA	53	0.71	70	0.98	66	0.97	3	0.55	5	0.71	5	0.88
TOGO	98	0.53	109	0.65	120	0.71	19	0.31	24	0.34	27	0.36
TUNISIA	97	0.67	113	0.89	116	0.94	21	0.55	45	0.80	65	0.97
UGANDA	44	0.66	71	0.80	76	0.85	4	0.33	13	0.54	14	0.59
ZAMBIA	97	0.84	99	0.93	88	0.94	15	0.52	24	0.61	29	0.63
ZIMBABWE	70	0.84	116	0.98	113	0.97	8	0.70	50	0.87	49	0.85
AFRICA	**71**	**0.68**	**78**	**0.85**	**80**	**0.85**	**14**	**0.54**	**25**	**0.77**	**29**	**0.81**

Explanatory Notes

The main objective of the notes below is to facilitate interpretation of the statistical data presented in Part III of the Report. Data shown for all African countries are annual totals or five year averages. Period average growth rates are calculated as the arithmetic average of annual growth rates over the period. These statistics are not shown in the tables when they are not significant or not comparable over years.

Section 1: Basic Indicators

This section contains one table (Table 1.1) which presents some basic indicators as background to the tables in this part of the Report. The table provides cross-country comparisons for area, population, GNP per capita, life expectancy, infant mortality and adult literacy rates. The main sources of data in this table are the United Nations Organizations, the World Bank and Regional Member Countries.

Area refers to the total surface area of a country, comprising land area and inland waters. The data is obtained from the Food and Agriculture Organization (FAO). The population figures are mid-year estimates obtained from the United Nations Population Division.

GNP per capita figures are obtained by dividing GNP in current US dollars by the corresponding mid-year population. GNP measures the total domestic and foreign value added claimed by residents. It comprises GDP plus net factor income from abroad, which is the income residents receive from abroad for factor services less similar payments made to nonresidents who contribute to the domestic economy. The data are obtained from the World Bank Atlas.

Life expectancy at birth is the number of years a new born infant would live, if patterns of mortality prevailing at the time of birth in the countries were to remain unchanged throughout his/her life. The infant mortality rate is the annual number of deaths of infants under one year of age per thousand live births. Adult literacy rate is the percentage of people aged 15 and above who can, with understanding, both read and write a short simple statement on their everyday life. The data are obtained from UNESCO.

Section 2: Macroeconomic Indicators

Table 2.1. Gross Domestic Product, real

National accounts estimates are obtained from regional member countries data, the World Bank, the IMF and the United Nations Statistical Division. In several instances, data are adjusted or supplemented with estimates made by the ADB Statistics Division. The concepts and definitions used for national accounts data are those of the United Nations System of National Accounts (SNA), Series F, no. 2, Revision 3.

Gross Domestic Product (GDP) measures the total final output of goods and services produced by a national economy, excluding provisions for depreciation. GDP figures are shown at constant 1995 market prices, and have been converted to US dollars using constant 1995 exchange rates provided by the IMF and the World Bank. For a few countries where the official exchange rate does not reflect effectively the rate applied to actual foreign exchange transactions, an alternative currency conversion factor has been used.

Aggregate growth rates for Africa are calculated as weighted averages of individual country growth rates using the share of the country's GDP in aggregate GDP based on the purchasing power parties (PPP) valuation of country GDPs.

Table 2.2. Gross Domestic Product, nominal

Data shown in this table are given at current market prices and are obtained by converting national currency series in current prices to US dollars at official exchange rates. Annual changes in GDP are presented in nominal terms.

Table 2.3. Gross National Savings

Gross National Savings (GNS) is calculated by deducting total consumption from GNP at current prices and adding net private transfers from abroad.

Table 2.4. Gross Domestic Investment

Gross Domestic Investment (GDI) consists of gross domestic fixed capital formation plus net changes in the level of inventories.

Table 2.5. Terms of Trade

Terms of trade estimates are obtained from the IMF and supplemented by ADB Statistics Division estimates. These are obtained by dividing unit value indices of exports by unit value indices of imports. The terms of trade indices

for the entire set of regional member countries are also ratios of the unit value of exports and the unit value of imports.

Table 2.6. Current Account Balance

Data in this table are obtained from the IMF, and based on the methodology of the fifth edition of the Balance of Payments Manual. The current account includes the trade balance valued f.o.b., net services and net factor income, and current transfer payments. The data is given as percentage of GDP.

Table 2.7 Broad Money Supply

Broad Money supply (M2) comprises currency outside banks, private sector demand deposits, (and, where applicable, post office and treasury checking deposits) and quasi-money.

Tables 2.8 Real Exchange Rate Index

The real exchange rate index is defined broadly as the nominal exchange rate index adjusted for relative movements in national price or cost indicators of the home country and the United States of America.

Table 2.9. International Reserves

International Reserves consist of country's holdings of monetary gold, Special Drawing Rights (SDRs) and foreign exchange, as well as its reserve position in the International Monetary Fund (IMF).

Table 2.10. Consumer Price Index

Consumer price index shows changes in the cost of acquisition of a basket of goods and services purchased by the average consumer. Weights for the computation of the index numbers are obtained from household budget surveys.

Table 2.11. Overall Fiscal Deficit or surplus

The overall surplus/deficit is defined as current and capital revenue and official grants received, less total expenditure and lending minus repayments. The data is given as a percentage of GDP.

Tables 2.12-.2.13 Total External Debt; Debt Service.

The main source of external debt data is the IMF. Total external debt covers outstanding and disbursed long-term debt, use of IMF credit, and short-term debt. Debt service is the sum of actual repayments of principal and actual payments of interest made in foreign exchange, goods, or services, on external public and publicly guaranteed debt.

Section 3: Labor Force and Social Indicators

This section presents data on labor force by sector (agriculture, industry and services) and also labor force participation rates, total and by sex.

Other tables in the section give data on components of population change (i.e. fertility, births, deaths and rate of natural increase), infant mortality rates, and life expectancy at birth, access to social infrastructure (sanitation, safe water and health services) and school enrolment ratios for primary and secondary levels.

Table 3.1. Labor Force by Sector

The labor force includes economically active persons aged 10 years and over. It includes the unemployed and the armed forces, but excludes housewives, students and other economically inactive groups. The agricultural sector consists of agriculture, forestry, hunting and fishing. Industry comprises mining and quarrying, manufacturing, construction, electricity, gas and water. Services include all other branches of economic activity and any statistical discrepancy in the origin of resources.

Table 3.2. Labor Force Participation Rates

The table shows the percentage of the population within each sex and age group that participates in economic activities (either employed or unemployed) from ILO data. Figures shown are ratios of the total economically-active population to the total population of all ages. Activity rates for females may be difficult to compare among countries because of the difference in the criteria adopted for determining the extent to which female workers are to be counted among the "economically active".

Table 3.3. Components of Population Change

Total fertility rate indicates the number of children that would be born per woman, if she were to live to the end of the child-bearing years; and bears children during those years in accordance with prevailing age-specific fertility rates. The crude birth rate represents the annual live births per thousand population. The crude death rate is the annual number of deaths per thousand population. Rate of Natural increase of the population is the difference between Crude Birth and Crude Death rates expressed as a percentage. The data in the table are obtained mainly from the United Nations Population Division, UNICEF and the World Bank.

Table 3.4. Mortality Indicators

The variables presented in this table - namely infant mortality rate and life expectancy at births - are as defined in Table 1.1. The sources of data are also the same.

Table 3.5. Population with Access to Social In-frastructures

The percentage of people with access to sanitation is defined separately for urban and rural areas. For urban areas, access to sanitation facilities is defined as urban population served by connections to public sewers or household systems, such as pit privies, pour-flush latrines, septic tanks, communal toilets, and other such facilities. In the case of the rural population, the definition refers to those with adequate disposal, such as pit privies and pour-flush latrines. Applications of these definitions may vary from one country to another, and comparisons can therefore be inappropriate.

The population with access to safe water refers to the percentage of the population with reasonable access to safe water supply (which includes treated surface water, or untreated but uncontaminated water such as that from springs, sanitary wells, and protected boreholes). The threshold for the distance to safe water in urban areas is about 200 meters, while in rural areas it is reasonable walking distance to and from sources where water can be fetched.

The population with access to health services refers to the percentage of the population that can reach appropriate local health services by local means of transport in no more than one hour. Data in this table are obtained from the World Bank.

Table 3.6. School Enrolment

The primary school enrolment ratio is the total number of pupils enrolled at primary level of education, regardless of age, expressed as a percentage of the population corresponding to the official school age of primary education. School enrolment ratios may be more than 100 per cent in countries where some pupils' ages are different from the legal enrolment age. Data in this table are obtained from UNESCO.

The secondary school enrolment ratio is the total number of pupils enrolled at secondary level of education, regardless of age, expressed as a percentage of the population corresponding to the official school age of secondary education.

Data Sources

1.	**Basic Indicators**	Food and Agriculture Organization: FAOSTAT Database, 2000. United Nations Population Division: Interpolated National Populations by Sex and Age, 1998 revision. World Bank: African Development Indicators, 1999.
2.	**Macroeconomic Indicators**	
2.1 - 2.4	National Accounts	United Nations: National Accounts Yearbook, various years. World Bank: Africa Live Database, February 2001. IMF: World Economic Outlook data files, October 2000. ADB Statistics Division. Regional Member Countries.
2.5 - 2.6	External Sector	World Economic Outlook, October 2000.
2.7 - 2.10	Money Supply, Exchange Rates and Prices	IMF: International Financial Statistics, February 2001, and International Financial Statistics, Yearbook, 2000. ILO: Yearbook of Labor Statistics, various years. ADB Statistics Division.
2.11	Government Finance	IMF: Government Finance Statistics CD-Rom, February 2001, and World Economic Outlook data files, October 2000.
2.12 - 2.13	External Debt	IMF: World Economic Outlook, October 2000.
3.	**Labor Force and Social Indicators**	
3.1 - 3.2	Labor Force	ILO: Labor Force Statistics, various years. World Bank: African Development Indicators 1999, ADB Statistics Division.
3.3 - 3.6	Social Indicators	UNICEF: The State of the World's Children, various years. World Bank: African Development Indicators, 1999. UN: Human Development Report, 1999. UN: Population Division, 1998 Revision. Regional Member Countries. ADB Statistics Division.

This publication was prepared by the Bank's Strategic Planning and Research Department (FSPR). Other publications of the Department are:

AFRICAN DEVELOPMENT REVIEW
A semi-annual professional journal devoted to the study and analysis of development issues in Africa.

ECONOMIC RESEARCH PAPERS
A working paper series presenting the research findings, mainly by the research staff, on topics related to African development policy issues.

COMPENDIUM OF STATISTICS
An annual publication providing statistical information on the operational activities of the Bank Group

GENDER, POVERTY AND ENVIRONMENTAL INDICATORS ON AFRICAN COUNTRIES
A Biennial publication providing information on the broad development trends relating to gender, poverty and environmental issues in the 53 African countries.

SELECTED STATISTICS ON AFRICAN COUNTRIES
An annual publication providing selected social and economic indicators for the 53 regional member countries of the Bank

Copies of these publications may be obtained from:

Strategic Planning and Research Department (FSPR)
African Development Bank

01 BP 1387 Abidjan 01
TELEFAX   (225) 20 20 49 48
TELEPHONE   (225) 20 20 44 44
TELEX   23717 / 23498 / 23263
WORLD WIDE WEB: http://www.afdb.org
EMAIL: @afdb.org
ABIDJAN - CÔTE D'IVOIRE